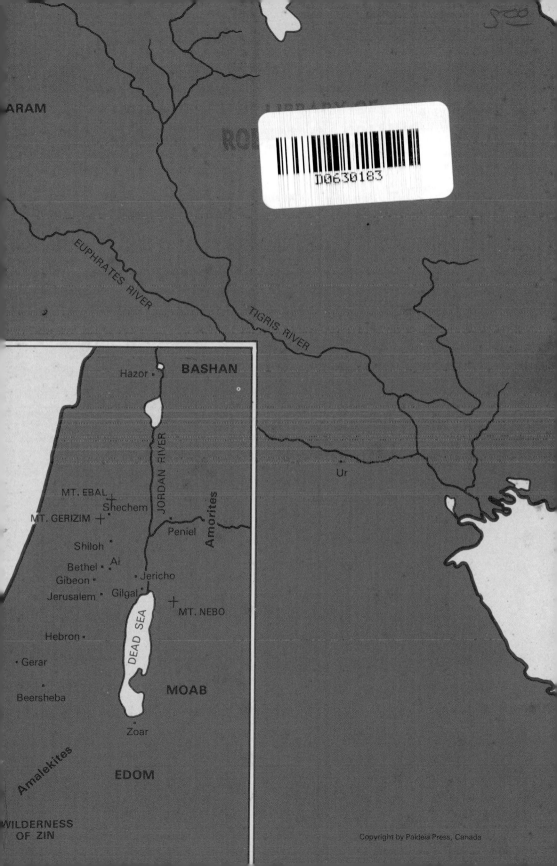

ARAM

EUPHRATES RIVER

TIGRIS RIVER

Ur

BASHAN

Hazor ·

MT. EBAL +
      +
    Shechem
MT. GERIZIM +

JORDAN RIVER

Peniel

Amorites

Shiloh ·

Bethel ·   · Ai

Gibeon ·   · Jericho

Jerusalem ·   · Gilgal

+
MT. NEBO

DEAD SEA

Hebron ·

· Gerar

Beersheba ·

MOAB

Zoar

Amalekites

EDOM

WILDERNESS
OF ZIN

PROMISE AND DELIVERANCE

S. G. DE GRAAF

PROMISE AND DELIVERANCE

VOLUME I

FROM CREATION TO THE CONQUEST

OF CANAAN

Translated by H. Evan Runner and
Elisabeth Wichers Runner

Presbyterian and Reformed Publishing Co.
1977

Table of Contents

JOB

ISAAC

JACOB

JOSEPH AND JUDAH

DELIVERANCE FROM EGYPT

AT MOUNT SINAI

IN THE WILDERNESS

Publisher's Note

Each chapter of *Promise and Deliverance* begins with a short discussion of points to bear in mind when studying the story or telling it to children. After this introductory section, the author formulates the story's main thought in a single sentence. For the sake of emphasis, this sentence is set off from the rest of the text and printed in italic type. Then comes the narrative itself, which makes up the bulk of the chapter. Since some readers will also want to use the narrative sections as a story Bible aimed at older children, the narrative is presented in slightly larger type than the background material at the beginning of each chapter, which is not intended for reading aloud.

Bible quotations are taken from the Revised Standard Version.

Translator's Introduction

Here, at last, is the first instalment of the English translation of S. G. De Graaf's well-known book *Verbondsgeschiedenis*. Many who know this work in its original Dutch form will be pleased to see it appear in English, for it is a unique treatment of God's revelation of Himself in the Bible.

This book has proven unusually helpful in bringing a couple of generations of Christians in the Netherlands to a clearer understanding of the particularity, comprehensive scope and fundamental unity of Scriptural revelation. Now Christians around the world will be able to read this book, study it, and reflect on it. Christians in all walks of life will benefit from it—young converts, believers of long standing, parents struggling to establish Christian homes, grandparents who tell Bible stories to their grandchildren, pastors, and even professors (including theologians).

What makes *Promise and Deliverance* a unique book? Why can this book be called *required* reading for all kinds and classes of people? (I speak of it as "required" because it is unique: there is no substitute available.) Why must this book, which is now being published in a language that makes it accessible to people everywhere in the world, become a familiar tool and resource not just in English-speaking countries but also in Latin America and the rising nations of Africa and Asia? Why is this book capable of speaking to those who call themselves social revolutionaries but are actually crying out in anguish of soul for righteousness, for social and economic peace? How can a book made up of outlines

10

or summaries of Bible stories, a book originally intended for Sunday school teachers, have such an impact and significance?

The answer to all these questions lies in the author's *perspective*. He tells us about that perspective in his brief but very important introduction, where he makes it clear what distinguishes his book from all other treatments of Biblical history. The pervasiveness of that perspective and its consistent application in chapter after chapter makes *Promise and Deliverance* much more than a collection of Bible stories.

The Rev. S. G. De Graaf (1889-1955) was a prominent Amsterdam preacher of the gospel. He spent a good part of his life thinking about Bible stories and teaching others how to tell them. His work had a profound impact on the presentation of Bible stories in Sunday schools, in Christian public schools, and in inner-city boys' and girls' clubs established for evangelistic purposes.

De Graaf's work was a continuation and refinement of the work that had been begun by J. C. Sikkel (1855-1920), who was also an Amsterdam preacher. Sikkel was a resolute and independent figure in the Dutch Reformed Church. In 1887 he joined the "Doleantie," a movement that called the churches in the Netherlands back to a greater faithfulness to the Word of God. Unfortunately, Sikkel remained too much in the shadow of Abraham Kuyper (1837-1920), the leader of the "Doleantie" movement. Although Sikkel differed with Kuyper on a number of theological issues, he shared with him and many of the other figures in the "Doleantie" an earnest and wholehearted commitment to the Word of God.

What uniquely characterized this evangelical awakening in the nineteenth century was its concern for what the Word of God has to say about man's life in society, about man as a complete being. The Christian community had been confronted with the stream of events that we speak of as the French revolution, events that shook Western society to its foundation. Turning to the Scriptures in these circumstances, the men of the "Doleantie" raised the question how human life and society are to be viewed in the light of divine revelation. The sermons of Sikkel and De Graaf, which steer clear of theological speculation and unfounded doctrine, brought believers in the Netherlands close to the Word of the living God. The light of that Word lit up the entire life of man in society.

What this return to Scripture brought to light surprised a Christian community that had grown used to accommodating itself to a secular society and had slipped further and further into a spiritualistic withdrawal to a life of private devotion, a life that left little room for genuine concern about God's world—the world which Christ rules as Lord. It gradually became clear to the Christian community that Biblical revelation is not just revelation about specific theological topics. The Word of God illumines and enlightens us; it sets our lives in the light of the truth. Scripture discloses the ultimate horizon of our personal and communal lives; it makes us aware that life *is* religion, that religion is not just one aspect or dimension of our lives. What the evangelical awakening behind the "Doleantie" made clear is that religion—as presented in the Scriptures—is life in its entirety, in its indivisible wholeness. It is not something we do, or some specific human activity. It is rather the situation in which we are created, the situation that underlies and undergirds all we do. We *live* before the face of God *(coram Deo)*. We were called into being by the life-giving Word of God and are sustained in life from moment to moment by that Word. We are dependent creatures—and not rational beings of autonomous freedom, as Rousseau, Kant, and modern Humanism right down to Sartre would have us believe. As servants of God, we are called to a task, namely, to work in the creation.

In Scripture, religion means *covenant*. By His Word, God called into being an order of creation culminating in man. By that Word He also gave man His favor and brought him into a life of conscious covenantal fellowship with Himself. As De Graaf himself puts it: "Without covenant, there is no religion, no conscious fellowship between man and God, no exchange of love and faithfulness. Without the covenant, man would be just an instrument in God's hand. When God created man, He had more than an instrument in mind: He made a creature that could respond to Him" (p. 36).

When we ponder what the Bible means when it speaks of God's covenant with man, we must not restrict our focus to the specific covenants made with Noah, Abraham, and the people of Israel at Sinai. "The friendship of the LORD is for those who fear him, and he makes known to them his covenant" (Ps. 25:14). Through the prophet Haggai, the Lord speaks of "the promise that I made you when you came out of Egypt" (Hag. 2:5). The scope of that promise goes far beyond the terms of any specific covenant recorded in Scripture.

It's true that the original covenant—let's call it the covenant of God's favor, or the covenant of creation—had to be replaced by the covenant of re-creation made with Christ, the second Adam. (This second covenant can also be called the covenant of God's grace, of the favor that forgives sin.) The point, however, is that the revelation of covenantal religion as the fundamental structure of our life sheds some much needed light on our situation and condition in this world. God's covenant is the underlying unity that embraces all human acts and all societal relationships.

This renewed insight into Biblical revelation is the perspective undergirding De Graaf's treatment of all the Bible stories. It makes his book a unique presentation of God's revelation of Himself in the covenant and keeps his interpretation of the stories from degenerating into mere moralizing. Religion is *not* morality.

De Graaf's theocentric preaching, which witnessed to God's sovereignty over the entire life of His people, gripped the hearts of his hearers in his day. The same emphasis, as it comes through in *Promise and Deliverance,* should be a matter of paramount interest and concern today to evangelicals who are manifesting a growing social awareness and seeking more and more points of contact between Christian beliefs and daily life. Much of the literature that circulates in evangelical circles is concerned with limited topics, such as angels, demonology, the return of the Jews to Palestine as a fulfillment of prophecy, or with the gifts of the Spirit, or with particular Bible books. Useful as such studies may be, in the final analysis they make little sense to minds that have not yet grasped the divinely established order of things and the basic covenant relationship to God in terms of which this order is to be understood. Moreover, almost all evangelical literature limits itself to a concern for the salvation of lost sinners—which concern is proper and necessary in its place—while failing to penetrate behind the drama of fall and redemption to the order of creation and the covenantal character of religion, which alone makes evangelism meaningful. It almost seems that we have forgotten the significance of the revelation that God is the Creator!

Much has been written and said about the renewed interest in

Christianity evident everywhere today, especially among young people. In many areas of the world, the issue comes down to choosing between Marx and Christ. Especially in Latin America, evangelicals who are frustrated by the failure of Christians to act out of faith toy with the idea of a compromise between Marx and Christ.

Wherever men long for righteousness and peace, wherever they hunger and thirst after Christ, it is absolutely imperative that they be directed to both the heart and the full range of the Good News of God's covenant with man and the earth. That covenant embraces all possible earthly relationships—family, marriage, education, economic life (work), politics, arts, communications, worship.

I am grateful to God that De Graaf's *Promise and Deliverance* is now being presented to a worldwide reading public. Indeed, I am thankful that there is such a book to offer, for Christianity is here presented as what it is, namely, a robust and earthy religion.

Of course the proof of all this is in the reading. So, as in the wonderful history of Augustine's conversion in the garden: *Tolle, lege,* that is, take up and read. Surely the book itself will justify all the effort that has gone into making it available in its new form.

Together with my wife, Elisabeth Wichers Runner, who has spent fully as many hours on this translation as I have, I would like to dedicate our joint endeavor to our children, with the prayer that it may enrich their lives for better service in the Kingdom of God.

H. Evan Runner

Preface

This book has come into being gradually. In my student days I attended a class given by the Rev. J.C. Sikkel of Amsterdam for his Sunday school teachers. Every Saturday he would go through the Bible story we were to tell the next day. At those sessions he would give us pointers to help us in relating the story. These we never forgot.

I took over that class years ago and have taught it ever since. For a number of years I have also written outlines for telling Bible stories at boys' and girls' "evangelism clubs." The same stories were dealt with in both the outlines and the class for Sunday school teachers.

Through this work I was repeatedly forced to face a certain question: How do we tell the Bible history? When I dealt with this question before an audience of Sunday school teachers, there would often be grade school teachers present as well. From time to time I would discuss this issue with the grade school teachers, for the stories are generally related in the same way in grade school* as in Sunday school. This is a practice I wish to defend in this book.

In these conversations the teachers repeatedly sought guidance on the practical implementation of the principles I was defending, especially for stories drawn from the Old Testament. In this book,

---

*Bear in mind that De Graaf is thinking of the *Christian public* schools as they have developed in the Netherlands.—TRANS.

15

therefore, I have devoted little space to the Introduction. The bulk of the book is instead made up of outlines for the actual telling of the stories.

This book is not for those who wish to learn an outline by heart and then "tell" it. Such a procedure can only lead to failure. The outlines given here are not even to be regarded as models for your own telling of the story. They are meant to serve simply as a traveler's guide with accompanying maps and comments, for they are intended to point out the various elements involved in the story. After you have studied the traveler's guide, you will have to *see for yourself*. These outlines are thus meant for people who are looking through the Scriptures for an understanding of the Word of God *before* they begin telling the story. Since I realize the difficulty of gaining that understanding, I am well aware of the many short-comings of these outlines.

Because the emphasis falls on the practical side of telling the stories, the Introduction does not detail all the principles that must govern the storytelling. The application of the general principles to relating a miracle or a parable, for example, must be gleaned from the outlines themselves.

Introduction

The form of our storytelling. There is no need to say a great deal about the question of form. This question is indeed very important, but telling the stories of the Bible history* is, to a great extent, the same as telling any other kind of story. Since enough has already been said by others on how to tell stories, a few special remarks will suffice.

You are to tell a story—and not give a lecture or deliver a sermon. To tell a story is to make it come alive, to make the children *see* it, to get them involved. To accomplish this goal, make use of whatever details the story offers. You should draw mental pictures and play on the imagination.

This method is limited, however, by the subject matter and the aim of our storytelling. Your primary purpose is not to keep the children amused but to bring them a message. Therefore, don't let the main point get lost in details or be buried by the imagination. You will have to guard particularly against the latter danger.

In telling a story that bears a message, there is always a main thought. Hence there will also be a climax. When the main thought is given its proper emphasis, there is no need to dramatize it.

---

*Because the God revealed in the Bible acts in history and in the lives of individual men and women, the Bible history is a series of incidents that can be told as stories. There is no opposition here between "story" and "history."—TRANS.

The aim of our storytelling. The aim is to encourage the children to believe, to "move them to faith." This is doubtless the aim of telling Bible stories at any evangelistic meeting. But are we also to regard it as the purpose of telling Bible stories in grade school?

Our aim in telling Bible history ought to be the same as God's purpose in recording it for us in His Word. God had the stories recorded "in order that we might believe." Accordingly, even in grade school,* this aim must be kept in mind when we are imparting knowledge. It makes no difference at all that the children in your classroom already believe. In their case, too, the story is told to evoke faith, to deepen and broaden it.

If our storytelling is to move the children to faith, each story must contain a single main thought. You must be clearly aware of the one message you are to bring. This awareness will enable you to tell the story without reading into it anything that is not there or giving it a biased slant. In each story God reveals Himself in a particular way. The important thing is to try to understand what God intends to reveal to us in the portion of history with which we are dealing.

The content of our storytelling. Thinking about the aim of telling Bible stories immediately leads us to a consideration of their content. We are to view the entire Holy Scripture as nothing more or less than the self-revelation of God. The history related in Scripture is part of God's self-revelation, then. This self-revelation is therefore the content of the stories we tell the children.

God reveals Himself in His grace only in the Mediator. As a result of the fall, there is no revelation of grace apart from the Mediator. Therefore, your stories should tell about Him, whether you tell the history of the Old Testament or of the New Testament. This is the second requirement for telling these Bible stories.

Not only is Christ the Mediator between God and man, He is also the Head of the covenant in which God lives with His people. Here we see another facet of Christ's relationship to us: He is the Head of His people, the second Adam. When you present the Christ of the Scriptures, you should also tell of the covenant. This,

---

*See the footnote to De Graaf's preface on p. 15.—Trans.

then, is the third requirement for telling the Bible stories. I will now elaborate on these three points.

God's revelation of Himself. Every time you tell one of these stories, you are telling about God. And you must tell not only what God did but also how He revealed Himself through His actions, for all these things have been written to instruct and enlighten us.

Don't think that such a procedure goes without saying. If we set aside no time for quiet reflection before telling the Bible story but simply follow the most natural course, we will find ourselves talking of men and their actions, of what they believed and how they sinned. God still enters the picture, of course; He intervenes now and then and offers rewards and punishments. Before we know it, we arrive at the "moral" of the story. We tell the children that God will deal with them according to their actions: if they are "good," He will reward them, but if they are "bad," He will punish them.

I venture to say that this is by far the most popular way of telling Bible stories to children. It is also the way many sermons are constructed. But while some people think that this procedure keeps the story simple and direct, they forget that they are not passing on what we are told in Scripture, the record of God's self-revelation.

Scripture is prophecy.* This is true even of its historical passages. In other words, every story in Scripture reveals something of the counsel of God for our redemption, even though every story tells it differently. And in every story God is the prime agent, revealing Himself through His acts as the Redeemer. The entire work of redemption can be seen in each story.

Consider the story of Joseph as an example. We could focus on the wicked brothers and on Joseph, who put his trust in God and was in turn saved by God. But when we do so, we are omitting an element that forms an actual part of the Scriptural record: it

---

*Prophecy is first of all speaking for or on behalf of God. Foretelling the future is just one element of prophecy.—TRANS.

was *God* who sovereignly brought all these things to pass in order to preserve the life of a great people. Now let's tell the story again from the latter point of view. From the very beginning, God and His people become our main concern. In a certain sense, Joseph becomes secondary—a mere instrument.

Now you can see why I object to the idea that the children will not remember anything unless some particular Bible personality is made the midpoint of the story being told. Little children, according to the usual line of argument, have to learn to identify with a particular person in the story. But that person, with *his* acts and *his* faith and *his* mistakes, then becomes the central figure. When we take this step, the story we tell is no longer the history of revelation.

I must admit that it is very difficult to tell the stories in the proper way. It is difficult enough to see things this way in our own minds. First we must subject ourselves to the Scriptures and their meaning. Learning to listen carefully to the Scripture passage we are studying will cost us a couple of hours of preparation (or perhaps more), but what else can we do? We have no choice, for we are dealing with Scripture! If we are not determined to tell of God first and last, of God as the Alpha and the Omega, we should not even bother telling the Bible story. But once we decide to proceed on the basis of the conviction that God must be first and last in our story, we should allow these guidelines to shape our telling of the story, making certain allowances, of course, for the age of the children we are addressing.

The typical sin of the child is putting himself first. The child has room in his life for God—as long as God comes second. Are we acting responsibly when we accommodate ourselves to this sinful inclination on the part of children? Or should we oppose it? Admittedly, grasping the Bible story from the proper point of view is very difficult for the child, not because his understanding is limited but because his heart says no. Little children have no more room for God in their lives than adults. If we make those children see God's centrality in human life, we will have reached our main goal.

In our stories we also tell about people, of course. We talk about what God did through and in them, and then about their responses to God's actions. The point to remember is that the work of God is mirrored in their responses. When Joseph receives the light of God's revelation in his dreams and becomes the bearer of that revelation and the preserver of his people, he suffers much tribulation (in part because of his sins). This shows us the greatness of God's self-revelation in Joseph's life. Such an emphasis teaches the children to fear the Lord* instead of looking to Joseph as a moral example.

If only we could rescue the children from their misguided spiritual egotism, which is at bottom thoroughly unspiritual! We are not in the business of persuading people to go to heaven! Therefore we must see to it that we do not encourage children and young people to worship their own salvation instead of worshiping God. From the very beginning, God must be made central to the Bible stories we tell the children. The children must learn to see Him in each story.

God's revelation of Himself in the Mediator. As a result of sin, there is no revelation of grace other than in the Mediator. This is made clear throughout the Scriptures—not only in the New Testament but also in the Old. Scripture is a unity. The Old Testament is the book of the Christ who is to come, while the New Testament tells us of the Christ who has come.

We do the content of the Old Testament an injustice when we repeatedly draw lines from its history to the Christ. We say, for example, that God saved Israel or sent Joseph to Egypt to save His people in order that the Christ might be born of that people. This is certainly a real aspect of revelation. It is a line we must follow because it is suggested by Scripture itself. But it is not enough.

The entire Scripture is God's revelation of Himself as the Redeemer. The redemption in the Mediator is revealed to us in every story. But this is not to say that the whole sweep of redemption is visible in every story. We believe in the progress of revelation. This progress is a development in which nothing new is added. In principle, the whole of redemption is revealed in the mother-promise (Gen. 3:15). Therefore, the seed of redemption is present in every story in the Old Testament. Our job is to use the light of the New Testament to uncover it. There is no veil covering our eyes when

---

*See the note on p. 54 on the Biblical meaning of the word *fear*.—TRANS.

we read the Old Testament (see II Cor. 3:14-16), for the testimony of Jesus is also the Spirit of Old Testament prophecy (Rev. 19:10).

The Mediator was operative throughout the Old Testament era. His work did not begin at the start of the New Testament. He already penetrated Old Testament history, moving among the people and shadows in order to reveal Himself. Everything is full of Him, and history has become one great miracle through His Spirit.

We will always have a great deal of trouble explaining the history in Scripture—particularly the Old Testament—if we do not proceed from the Mediator's eager efforts to reveal Himself. Even from a psychological point of view, the Old Testament stories would remain a mystery to us if we were to reject the proper starting point. But how wondrously the Scriptures open themselves to us when we focus on the Mediator! The acts and motives of Old Testament people, which are often so puzzling in themselves, then become clear to us.

If you don't sense what I'm driving at, think of the difficult book of Esther. The name of God doesn't even occur in this book. But try reading Esther once to see how the Mediator is revealed right from the start of the book. Not only do Mordecai's motives then become understandable, we also see the Mediator at work in his life. And although we are still critical of some of Mordecai's actions, we also learn to appreciate them, realizing that every type of Christ is at the same time His opposite or antitype in many ways. At the end of the book we read: "For Mordecai the Jew was great among the Jews and popular with the multitude of his brethren, for he sought the welfare of his people and spoke peace to all his people." Here we have an almost perfect description of the Christ.

Again, I must admit that it is a real challenge to tell Bible stories in this way. First we must be sure that we ourselves have caught sight of the Mediator revealed in the Scriptures and now see Him in the proper light. We may not lift texts from Scripture here and there, using them in an arbitrary way to present a certain view of Christ. Getting to know Christ as He reveals Himself in the Old Testament as well as the New involves careful, disciplined work. Fortunately, we do have the mind of Christ (I Cor. 2:16).

Up to this point I have spoken chiefly of the Old Testament. People generally assume that it is much easier to tell about Christ from the New Testament, which seems to be the most obvious place to look for information about Him. But when we tell the story of Zacchaeus, let's make sure that the self-revelation of the Christ— and not Zacchaeus—is the main point.

Of course we can't avoid talking about people like Zacchaeus. The Lord Jesus Christ Himself said that people all over the world would speak of Mary of Bethany. But we should talk *mainly* of the One who awakened such great love in Mary's heart: we see His love mirrored in Mary's love. We should take the same approach to the story of Judas: Who is this Jesus, that He was able to arouse such great hatred in a man's heart?

We shall have to be much more aware of these matters if we are to avoid talking chiefly about people, presenting their faith as an example to be followed and their sins as a warning. We should talk instead about the revelation of God's grace in Christ.

God's revelation of Himself in His covenant with His people. The Lord Jesus Christ is not only the Mediator but also the Head of the covenant, the second Adam. When we tell of Him, therefore, we should also talk about the covenant (assuming that we want to present Him as Scripture makes Him known to us). Perhaps you're looking for nothing more than a "simple" story about "Jesus and the soul." If so, let me remind you that such a recitation has nothing to do with Scripture, for God's Word is never concerned simply with Jesus and the soul.

For certain people, all the covenant seems to mean is that children are somehow reckoned with their parents in the eyes of God and the church. They then speak of a "doctrine" of the covenant, a doctrine against which they have quite a few objections. Such people really have not understood what the covenant is all about.

This covenant can be compared to a marriage relationship, in which there are rights and obligations on both sides. When a man and a woman recognize those rights and responsibilities, they can share their most intimate thoughts and feelings. In the covenant relationship, God and His people likewise exchange the deepest love of their hearts (Ps. 25:14).

We must also bear in mind that while a covenant is a contract or agreement between two parties, *this* covenant proceeded from

God alone. By giving man certain rights, God elevated him to the status of a party alongside Himself. Although man was unwilling, God bound Himself to man in the covenant of grace, making Himself answerable for the other party in the covenant. He also taught man what it means to be faithful to the covenant and gave him the Christ as covenant Head, as the One who would say yes to God in our place. Through His Spirit, we also learn to say yes to God. The certainty of the covenant of grace thus rests on what one of the parties has done and continues to do.

There is no conscious fellowship possible between God and man except in the covenant. Outside the covenant we are without rights before God, and there can be no question of fellowship or of man offering his very heart to God and receiving blessings in return. The notion that the covenant was first established with Abraham is an absurdity to anyone who has discovered the meaning of covenant in the Scriptures.

In the covenant God always draws near to His *people* as a whole—never just to individuals. Because of the covenant, the entire people rests secure in God's faithfulness, and every individual member of the covenant shares in that rest as a member of the community. We need not always use the word *covenant*—the beginning of the Bible does not—as long as the children are told about the covenant relationship.

I'm afraid this does not always happen—not even when we talk about the Christ. We may be inclined to introduce Him as the Redeemer of certain individuals, but when we do so, we can no longer present Him as the Head of the covenant. Yet it is as covenant Head that He appears in Scripture.

I have already referred to the story of Joseph. The main point of that story is not what God meant to Joseph but what He meant to His people through Joseph, a people whose development was just beginning in the tents of Jacob. When we turn to the story of David, we see that Scripture does not focus on him as a person. David is presented instead as the head of his people. The story of Nehemiah is to be read as the story of the restoration of the people of Israel. The story of Zacchaeus, in turn, is to be understood as a self-revelation of Christ to His people. The story of Ananias and Sapphira is about the people's communion in the Spirit and God's revelation to and in that people in Christ. People always serve as the *background*, even in the stories that at first glance appear most personal.

This fact, too, makes it difficult to tell the stories. The stories will be hard for the children to understand not because their minds cannot grasp them but because their hearts do not accept them. Because sin has driven us apart, every child is a born individualist. We stand in the world as separate beings and form our opinions on our own.

If you play up to that individualism in telling the stories, the children will readily accept what you say. But can we allow ourselves to be governed by a situation imposed on us by sin and sell the gospel the way an advertiser sells beauty soap? Or should our storytelling try to shatter that individualism?

When you talk about the covenant and Christ as its Head, you need not drag the Church into it, for you will automatically be telling of the Church. This resolves a certain difficulty that we sense very strongly today, namely, how we are to tell children about the Church as the people of God. Awareness of the Church is encouraged through such storytelling. As a result, the children will no longer have a hard time seeing the meaning of baptism. The children who have been baptized will sense its significance, and those who have not will long for it, provided that they receive God's blessing.

It is not true that you cannot talk about the covenant to children who were born outside it and do not bear its seal. The Lord Jesus Christ demonstrated this Himself. When Christ was asked to heal the centurion's servant, He replied: "Shall I come and heal *him*?" In effect He was saying: "Shall I help a heathen who does not belong to the covenant?" The centurion then acknowledged the covenant in his answer: "As a heathen I am not at all worthy to have You under my roof." Christ therefore proceeded to help him. We see the same pattern in the story of the Canaanite woman. When she acknowledged that the dogs have no right to the children's food, Christ gave her His help. He always sought an acknowledgment of the covenant, and we should do the same in our teaching. Those who have been born "within" should be aware that this privilege is a benefit of grace and acknowledge the calling and election of God. Those who were born "outside" the covenant should honor it and show that they desire it, so that they will be able to enter it as well.

In setting out these conditions for telling children about Bible history, I am not withdrawing my earlier contentions about how to tell Bible stories. As we tell a story, it should come alive; it should draw the children in and get them involved. The children should get wrapped up not just in the adventures of certain people but especially in the historical unfolding of God's self-revelation and man's response to it. We must tell the children of God's great deeds. I do not claim that the following outlines meet all these requirements, but I can assure you that I have tried to keep them in mind.

The purpose of these outlines. Although these outlines are not intended to serve as actual exegetical material, solutions to some particular exegetical difficulties have been offered. Those who wish to take up the exegetical problems at greater length will have to turn to Bible commentaries for further help.

These outlines are indeed written in the form of stories. But I must emphasize again that they cannot be told just as they appear in print. Such a procedure would be entirely unsuitable in the case of younger children. My suggestions for using these outlines are to be found in the Preface. The storyteller must adapt them to the world of the child's experience. I did choose the narrative form, however, to close the gap between these outlines and the actual telling of the stories. I hope this makes it easier to use the outlines.

To keep this large work from growing even larger, it was often necessary to deal with a considerable amount of Bible history in a single chapter. I trust that each subdivision within the chapters contains enough material to allow for a separate storytelling session if so desired. The chapters have been arranged into larger groupings to provide an overall picture.

The First World

1: The Kingdom of God

Genesis 1—2:3

In this first section of Genesis we are not just told that God created all things. What is revealed to us first and foremost is the Kingdom of God. At this point we cannot speak of this Kingdom as the Kingdom of God's grace, for by *grace* we usually mean the favor to which we have lost all claim, i.e. the favor of the forgiveness of our sins. To avoid confusion, therefore, we should speak here of the Kingdom of God's favor.*

The institution of the Kingdom of God is central to this chapter. In preparing the earth in six days, God repeatedly brings forth the higher from the lower and makes the lower subservient to the higher. Finally He creates man and makes him king (Gen. 1:26-8). With the creation of earth's intended king, God reaches the culmination of His work. We hear something of His rejoicing when He says: "Let us make man in our image, after our likeness; and let them have dominion." These words give us the impression that God is saying: "Now let Us make man. Now We are reaching the climax of Our work."

When we tell the story this way, we must not glorify man as he is in himself. It was God who made man. Moreover, He made man in His own image so that man would be able to exercise dominion. Man remains completely dependent on God in everything, and in everything he is to serve Him. The Kingdom of God can therefore be described as that Kingdom in which all things have been subjected to man, while man is subjected to God in voluntary obedience.

It is not enough, then, to tell the children that the world was created by God. They must learn more than that. If a child's heart has been

---

*There is a distinction to be made between a favor that originally proceeded from God to His entire creation and a favor forfeited by man's fall but now given on the basis of Christ's reconciling work. The latter favor is called *grace*. In Dutch the distinction is between "gunst" and "genade," the latter being "verbeurde gunst." —TRANS.

29

touched by the Spirit of the Lord, he will also long to hear more; he will want to hear about God living in constant communion with the entire creation. This communion was present in the Kingdom of God: man, exercising his dominion, served God.

God gave man the day of rest as a sign of that communion in His Kingdom. In the first chapter of Genesis, we read repeatedly that God saw all He had made and pronounced it very good. Moreover, this chapter tells us that God's good pleasure encompassed His entire creation. In Genesis 2, which continues the narrative, we read about the sabbath. God blessed and hallowed that day of rest, and through it He blessed and hallowed everything He had made. He gave Himself to the world He had made to serve His glory. The serenity God bestowed on His Kingdom came to special expression in the day of rest.

Central to this section, therefore, is the institution of the Kingdom of God. The surrounding and supportive context of this central point is the revelation that all things are from God, through God and unto God. This is exactly why God was able to institute His perfect Kingdom. Man, as king, was to direct all things unto God, that is, to God's glory. Man could do so only because all things, himself included, are from and through God.

There is another point we must not overlook: God takes *direct* pleasure in the works of His hands, for His glory is reflected in them. There are so many things that no human eye has ever seen, things for which man has never offered praise to God. All the same, these things, too, exist to glorify God. What God has created is just too wondrous and profound ever to be grasped by the mind of man. We must also remember to tell of the direct pleasure God takes in the glory of those works of creation.

But the founding of the Kingdom of God is the central point. Therefore we can already speak of Christ as we tell this story. The Kingdom of God on earth was ruined by the fall of the first Adam, but it was restored by the second Adam—Christ.

Main thought: *The Kingdom of God is instituted.*

The first day. There was a time when there was nothing of what we now see all around us—nothing at all. God alone was. Yet He was not lonely, and He did not long for something to love and cherish, for God eternally has His Son, whom He loves in the Holy Spirit. God did not need this world, but He decided to create it all the same. That was a free decision on His part (Rev. 4:11). He could just as well have decided not to do it, for He is not "served by human hands as though he needed anything" (Acts 17:25). He did not need us then, and He does not need us now.

When He decided to create the world anyway, He did so because He wanted to glorify Himself in it, because He wanted to see His glory reflected in the world as in a mirror. Moreover, He wanted men to share in His blessedness; He wanted them to partake of His joy.

Once, at the beginning of the time in which we live, God brought forth heaven and earth out of His fullness. Heaven is His throne and the dwelling place of the angels, whom He created at the same time (Job 38:4-7). It is in heaven that His glory is revealed most openly. He also created the earth, making it dependent on the blessing of heaven. Heaven and earth were made for each other. Today many people are content with just the earth. They lose sight of heaven, and then the real treasures of the earth escape them too.

At first the earth and all that was under heaven was an undifferentiated mass lacking order and form. It lay in darkness. Yet God was at work there; His Spirit was moving over the waters. Under the cover of darkness God was preparing what he was about to bring to light. Yes, God works even in darkness and in secret; the fruit of His work becomes visible later. In the same way God is working at this very moment in the hidden depths of many a human heart. Perhaps He is at work in your heart, teaching you to have faith.

Then God called the light into being. He calls to things that do not exist as though they do, and suddenly, there they are! That was how He created the light. In that light He cherishes the earth with His favor. How wonderful the light is! It is a sign reminding us daily of God's favor and of His concern for this world. God also separated the light from the darkness, calling the light *day* and the darkness *night*. Each has its own value. There is much that is hidden in God and His works. This, too, is reason to adore Him and look to what He does. But there is also much that He brings to light, for which we praise Him as well.

A time of darkness and a time of light had passed. That was the first day.

The second day. Again a time of darkness set in. Then the second day began. In the darkness God was preparing what He meant to bring forth on that second day.

By creating an atmosphere around the earth, God made a partition between the earth and the rest of what He had created under heaven. Then He made the sky above the earth, where the clouds are suspended. When we look up into the night sky, we also see the stars. God called the sky *heaven*. It reminds us of that first heaven in which the angels adored Him. When we look up at the sky, we are struck by the immensity of the space beyond the earth. How far away the home of the angels must be! How highly exalted God must be!

This atmosphere includes the air we breathe in order to live. God did indeed create immense distances, but at the same time He is very close to us with His Spirit. He is the strength of our life.

The third day. Again there was darkness. God was preparing for His creative work on the third day.

The earth itself was still unformed. God had already separated the light from the darkness and made a partition between the earth and the rest of creation. On the third day He gave order to the earth itself and separated the water from the land. Then the deep seas and high mountains appeared. God revealed Himself in the creation of the seas and mountains: His thoughts are unfathomable, and His intentions and faithfulness are firm as the mountains.

A second wonder occurred on that third day. Out of the earth plants and trees shot up. Where did they come from? No seed had yet been sown in the earth. On this occasion, God caused the earth itself to bring forth those growing things. As the Almighty, this fell well within the range of His omnipotence. Those particular plants had to die, of course, but within them were the seeds from which new plants would grow. In this way God remains faithful to the works of His hands as He provides for the wondrous life He has created, a life so weak and yet so strong because He upholds it.

God adorned the face of the earth on that third day. What a gorgeous array of flowers He made! There are so many flowers no eye has ever seen, flowers for which no man has ever praised God. Yet they have not blossomed in vain, for God has beheld them and seen His glory reflected in them. What a delight the earth could become for man! At the same time, God provided food for man and beast by way of these plants.

The fourth day. In the darkness which again followed, God prepared what He intended to bring forth on the fourth day.

He wanted to bind the light to firm laws and patterns that would dominate the life of man. He therefore created the sun, moon and stars to give and reflect light. Now day and night follow each other in strict regularity. No one can escape this order, which teaches us to number our days.

No one can stare into the sun, for its intensity is like the brilliance of God's countenance. What tranquillity and comfort a look at the stars can give us! Do you ever look up at the starry heavens? Sometime you should take a good look at all those distant, mighty worlds. How small you then seem to yourself. Can't the God who takes care of all those worlds also take care of our little problems and concerns?

The fifth day. There lay the waters of the earth, without anything to move in them. In the forests there was no song of birds to break the silence. In the darkness of the fifth day, God was preparing a new wonder.

Just as His wondrous power caused the earth to bring forth plants, He now made fish appear in ponds, streams, lakes, rivers, and oceans. Great fish moved slowly through the waters, and tiny ones glittered as they darted in all directions. When we visit an aquarium, we are amazed at all the new varieties of fish we see. The variety is almost endless! How great God must be! How rich and varied are the ways of the Creator of all those species of fish and all the different kinds of birds, each kind with its own distinctive song!

God sees it all and delights in the fullness of life in His creation. That fullness of life is our delight too.

The sixth day. God still had not reached the culmination of His work as Creator. For the sixth time darkness came, as God prepared to make the crown of His creation.

In the light of the sixth day, He first filled the earth with all sorts of wild animals and creeping things—the enormously large and imperceptibly small. Each animal was given a nature of its own and a distinct purpose for its existence. In each of them a distinct thought of God is revealed. We do not know which animal to admire most—the lion for its majesty, the bull for its power, the horse for its spirit, the deer for its swiftness, or the fox for its slyness. The making of those animals was the last step before the creation of man.

Then God took counsel with Himself to make man. He meant to give man dominion over all He had made. Man was to rule the world in God's name and glorify God in the process. For better or worse, the world had been placed in man's hands. If man continued to adore God, the world would be blessed through him. Because man was expected to rule the world in a God-glorifying way, the Creator made him in His own image, giving him wisdom, a heart full of love, and the will to do the right. Man was created in the likeness of his heavenly Father.

Furthermore, God gave man His creation to *use*. There was nothing man could call his private property; everything belonged to God, who had made it. Man had no natural rights given with his nature, so to speak. God even gave man the food he ate. Just as He had given the animals green herbs to eat, He designated the fruits as food for man.

The seventh day. Thus God had established a Kingdom on earth in which all things were subject to man, who exercised dominion over them in God's name. This Kingdom was a Kingdom of Peace. The world was like a great temple which God chose to inhabit and favor with His blessing.

God wanted to demonstrate this in a special way. Therefore He brought the creation week to a close with the seventh day. On that day He did no more creating. Instead He rested from His work; that is to say, He delighted in what He had made and sent His good pleasure and blessing out into the world. On that seventh day He instituted the day of rest and blessed the world through it. The day of rest has become an enduring sign that God remembers this world in His favor.

The world blossomed and exulted before God's face. Its future—for better or worse—was in man's hands. What an honor, and what a responsibility! Man had received rich gifts from God so that he would be able to rule the world in God's name. But because he was man, he was also capable of resisting the will of God. And that's exactly what he did. When he fell, he dragged the world down with him. God's work of creation was ruined.

But it was not ruined for good. There came another man, the man Jesus Christ, who is also God. He restored the world from its fall and was obedient even unto death. The world's future now rests in His hands. In *His* hands it is safe. The day of rest has since become a sign of God's favor, a favor that will never pass away.

2: The Covenant of God's Favor

Genesis 2:4-25

In Genesis 1 we are told about the institution of the Kingdom of God. In Genesis 2 we read about the establishment of a covenant. The objection that there is no literal or explicit mention of a covenant in this chapter carries no weight, for all the elements of a covenant are to be found here. Even more decisive is the fact that God is here called Yahweh, the God of covenant faithfulness.

We must never lose sight of the great significance of the covenant. Without covenant, there is no religion, no conscious fellowship between man and God, no exchange of love and faithfulness.* Without the covenant, man would be just an instrument in God's hand. When God created man, He had more than an instrument in mind: He made a creature that could respond to Him. Only if man was capable of responding would he be able to assume his position as partner in a covenant. Without a covenant, God would have only claims and man only obligations. But as soon as God gave man a promise, man also had a claim on God, namely, to hold God to that promise. And God then had an obligation toward man, namely, to fulfill that promise. Once the promise is given, we can speak of a covenant, for a covenant, after all, is an agreement between two parties in which the claims and obligations are spelled out. Of course we must never forget that the covenant was initiated by God and that God's promise elevated man to the rank of covenant partner. Because the covenant is tied to God's promise, the calling described in Genesis 1 (which also includes a promise) prepares the way for it.

---

*The Westminster Confession of Faith puts it this way: "The distance between God and the creature is so great, that although reasonable creatures do owe obedience unto Him as their Creator, yet they could never have any fruition of Him, as their blessedness and reward, but by some voluntary condescension on God's part, which He hath been pleased to express by way of covenant" (Chapter 7, Section 1).—TRANS.

We are accustomed to speaking of this covenant as the covenant of works. However, we should not take this name to mean that man was expected to earn eternal life as a reward for doing good works, as though eternal life was man's payment for services rendered. Because man owes everything he is and has to God, we may never speak of man earning wages paid out by God. Therefore it might be wiser to speak of the covenant of God's favor. *Grace,* in general, also means favor, but in the Scriptures *grace* always has the special meaning of favor that forgives guilt. We could express the difference by saying that God made a covenant of favor with Adam and a covenant of grace with Christ. The only demand made of Adam was that he choose consciously for the favor given him by God if he and his posterity were to abide forever in that favor. In this way, too, the contrast with Christ is clear: Christ had to continue to choose for God's favor even when that favor had completely forsaken Him. In this way Christ had to reconcile and redeem what Adam had ruined.

God's specific test-command* was intended to bring man to conscious obedience, that is, to conscious acceptance of the covenant. Before that, man did what was good because his heart suggested nothing else to him. Only by facing the possibility of a conflict could he learn to choose consciously.

He was given this opportunity by way of a specific command. There was a certain tree in the garden whose fruit was obviously good for food, but man was ordered not to eat its fruit. In this way he came to know— *know* here means *distinguish*—that "good" is what God commands and "evil" what He forbids. It was not a matter of human judgment, then. The point at issue was how man was to distinguish good from evil—in dependence on God by not eating or in disregard of God by eating. That's why God says later: "Behold, the man has become like one of us, knowing [i.e. distinguishing *for himself* between] good and evil."

Eating the fruit of the tree of life, which was yet another tree, can best be compared with taking the sacrament in our time. When man ate the fruit of this tree and thereby affirmed the covenant, his faith that God would bring him to eternal life, that is, to full, eternal dominion in His Kingdom, was confirmed. However, the comparison with the sacrament is not a complete parallel, for at one time the entire creation spoke of God's favor. The revelation of this favor then reached its climax in the tree of life. In our own time, by contrast, wrath is revealed from heaven. God therefore sets apart bread, wine and water for use in the sacraments that witness to His favor. Before the fall, the "sign" and the "thing signified" were so closely linked that the one was unthinkable without the other. Hence the way to the tree of life had to be closed to fallen man, or he might eat and live forever.

---

*A term frequently met with is *probationary command.*—TRANS.

In this chapter the description of history begins. In history, the fullness God laid down in creation is opened up and developed. In history man is given his calling. The process of opening up and developing is to take place in fellowship with the Lord. This covenant fellowship is to govern history. Thus the beginning of history is bound up with the initiation of God's covenant. The covenant includes a cultural task for man: man is called to "cultivate"* the garden (Gen. 2:15). Man's task is already suggested earlier in the words: "There had not yet been a man to cultivate the ground" (vs. 5).

Main thought: *The covenant of God's favor is established so that man can live in fellowship with God.*

The special creation of man. God did not intend that everything in heaven and earth remain just as He had made it. He included much in this world that was still hidden but would one day be disclosed. Think of the tiny seed: the whole flower lies concealed in it and will develop from it. In the same way, the world contained hidden treasures placed there by God, treasures that would one day be revealed. But those treasures would not be unearthed automatically. Man had a role to play in bringing this about. The beginning God gave this world was at the same time the beginning of history: what He had laid down in creation was to be brought to light in that history.

That was what God desired of this world, to which He had given so much. Now the world would have to respond by bringing to fruition all that He had created in seed form. This response was first and foremost a matter of man's labors. But man would not be able to reach the intended goal unless God gave the world—especially man—His blessing and fellowship. God in His love would reveal Himself to man in an ever greater way, and man would then give God all that was in him and in the world. That's what God had in mind when He chose to live in covenant with man.

When two people make a covenant, they take upon themselves the obligation to give each other something, to engage in some sort of exchange. In the marriage covenant, the greatest covenant on earth, each partner surrenders his entire heart to the other. God

---

*The Hebrew verb means work as service of God.—TRANS.

wished to enter such a covenant with man; God would give man His love in ever greater measure, while man would give God all that was in his heart and in the world.

That's why God made man different from all the other creatures. When He made heaven and earth, the plants and all the other creatures, He also made man—as one of the many. There was a time when the plants with which we are acquainted simply did not exist. Up to that time it had not rained, and there were as yet no human beings to take care of any plants. There was only a mist that moistened the earth. But out of that moistened earth God brought forth the plants—the shrubs and bushes, the plants that live for several years, and the herbs of the field that come up anew each year.

God then made man as one of the creatures, but He gave him a special task. Man was to look after the world; he was to cultivate (i.e. keep and dress) the world and all it contained. Man was indeed different from all the other creatures, for he was privileged to live in conscious communion with God in the covenant. Therefore man's creation took place in a special way. True, he was created out of the earth just as all the other creatures were, but it was by a special act of God that he began to live: God Himself breathed the breath of life into his nostrils. With that beginning God gave man a special place among the creatures.

The revelation of God's covenant favor. God selected a special place for man on earth. To be sure, the whole earth was a marvelous place, but in one particular spot He had caused the most wonderful trees to grow, trees that produced particularly nutritious fruit and were a delight to the eye. A river flowed through this area and divided into four branches.

This garden in which man lived was indescribably beautiful. We do not know exactly where it was situated, but we do have an approximate idea since we can identify two of the rivers. The earth, after all, has changed a lot. As a result of sin, the garden has completely disappeared from the earth.

You can be sure that man enjoyed himself in this garden. He delighted in the shade of the trees and the rippling water of the rivers. But most of all he enjoyed the favor of his God, who had chosen for him the most wonderful spot in all of creation. The whole garden spoke to man of God's favor. To man that was the most important thing.

Of course man had not been placed in that garden to live an idle life. From the outset he had a task: he was to cultivate and maintain the garden. Indeed, there was much to do. At the time man was far from being able to see all his task involved. Moreover, he had to keep (guard) the garden. Evidently there was a hostile power in the world. (I'll tell you more about that in the next chapter.) But for now, man had to keep the garden for God and give the Lord the treasure of the earth and the grateful love of his heart.

Testing and strengthening in the covenant. Man, then, lived as God's child, sharing in His love. But man still had to choose. God had let His favor rest upon man, but would Adam and his posterity want to live in that favor forever? Would man still want that favor if someone else came along to make another proposal in an attempt to lead him down a different path? If man chose for God's favor, he and his children would be allowed to live in that favor forever. If not, death awaited him.

To settle this matter, God put man to the test. In the middle of the garden He had made a tree which He called the tree of the knowledge of good and evil. God told man that he was permitted to eat from any tree in the garden except that particular one. The fruit of that tree was undoubtedly delicious; man's mind told him that it would be good to eat. Yet God forbade it, and man therefore had to learn to distinguish between good and evil. Good is not what my own mind—ignoring God—suggests to me; good is what God commands, while evil is what He forbids. God's will alone is good, and I must obey that will without question. If man wanted to remain forever in God's favor, he had to choose for God and His favor by subjecting himself to God's will. The day he ate from that special tree, he would die. The fellowship with God would then be broken. For man that would mean eternal death.

The test would be a hard one. Yet God had provided man with something to strengthen his faith that he would possess God's favor forever if he remained obedient. In the middle of the garden there was another important tree, namely, the tree of life. Although the whole garden spoke to man of God's favor, this favor was particularly evident in the fruit of that tree.

Those two trees standing in the middle of the garden represented opposing directions. If man ate from the tree of life, he would be choosing God's everlasting favor and rejecting the fruit of the other tree. If he ate from the tree of the knowledge of good and evil, he would be rejecting the fruit of the tree of life and would never again be able to eat from it.

The marriage covenant. The Lord gave still more to man. To be sure, he enjoyed living in covenant with the Lord, but in the entire creation there was no one with whom he could have true fellowship. God first made man aware of this when He brought him all the animals to be named. Then man saw something of the riches of creation, as he correctly grasped the nature of each animal and gave it a name to fit that nature. However, there was no animal that could return the love of man's heart. This made man aware of the need of another human being who would also be man and yet be different from him.

God wanted to fill that need. After causing man to fall into a deep sleep, He took one of his ribs and fashioned it into a woman. While man was unconscious, God prepared the greatest earthly treasure for him. He made woman out of man's own rib so that she would truly be part of him; only then could the two become one. The man was to be the woman's head, just as he was the head of his race. For her, as for his race, he had to choose for God's favor.

As soon as man woke up and God brought his wife to him, he saw that she was different from all the other creatures. She was his peer, and therefore he could give her all of his heart's treasure. And he knew that she had been taken out of him, which made it possible for the two to become one. That's why he called her *woman*. In their marriage, which was also a covenant, his heart opened to her and hers to him. He could therefore bring out what was hidden within him. Man then gained an even deeper understanding of what God intended with that covenant in which man was privileged to live with the Lord. God and man were to give each other what was within them, without fear, without reserve, without shame, just as the man and his wife felt no shame even though they were naked. In their hearts there was only love.

I am running a bit ahead of the story when I tell you that things did not stay that way. The covenant was broken by sin. Do we no longer know anything of that covenant, then? Must we now live outside all fellowship with God?

The covenant that was broken by the first man was taken up again and restored by the Lord Jesus Christ—but in a different form. Now we no longer have Adam as our covenant head. The Lord Jesus Christ, who chose for God's favor in much more difficult and wretched circumstances, has taken his place. Through Him, we still have eternal life if we believe. In that new life, God gives us His love ever more richly, making it possible for us to offer Him all that is in our hearts and in the world.

3: The Covenant of God's Grace

I have deliberately entitled this chapter "The Covenant of Grace" instead of "The Fall." The fall certainly merits our attention, but if we put too much emphasis on it, the revelation of God's grace might become a mere afterthought. When we read through Genesis 3, we see that the fall is described in just seven verses, while the rest of the chapter is devoted to God's grace. Even more important for our purposes is the fact that Scripture is not a book of the acts of men but the book of the revelation of God. Here in Genesis 3, God shows us how He opposed sin and conquered it by His grace when it entered His creation. This chapter reminds us to speak to the children in positive terms by telling them about God's grace. Therefore the fall should not receive the primary emphasis.

Once again we see that God turned to the works of His hands when He should have turned away from them. What can we do to make the children realize what that free act of God meant? He could have used His judgment to destroy sin, thereby allowing the world to perish. In His onmipotent grace He chose another route instead. Here again He gives us abundant reason to praise Him.

We should note that before the revelation of God's grace, Adam and his wife offered excuses for what they had done—but did not confess their guilt. The revelation of God's judgment does not lead us to repent and confess our guilt; for this we need the revelation of His grace. When the element of grace comes through in the judgment pronounced upon the serpent, Adam and Eve show that they believe—by confessing their guilt. Faith in God's grace always involves the confession of guilt.

Genesis 3 does not tell us about the *establishment* of the covenant of grace, for this covenant was established not with Adam but with the Christ. Therefore we must speak here of the *revelation* of the covenant of grace. (This covenant was already dealt with in the previous chapter.)

43

Main thought: *The covenant of grace is revealed to man so that he may believe.*

The world lost in the fall. God had created the heavens and the earth perfect. He subjected the earth to man and established a covenant with him. But God had an enemy in the world, an angel who had fallen away from Him and become a devil. With this fallen angel, who had earned the name *satan*, many other angels fell away from God as well and became devils.

Satan's whole existence is hatred of God. His sole aim is to destroy everything God has made. Thus he was eager to see the world ruined. But he knew that the world had been subjected to man. He therefore decided not to direct his attack against Adam, who had received God's command directly and bore complete responsibility as the world's head. Instead he approached the woman first, hoping to reach Adam through her.

But how should he tempt the woman? At that time he could not do what he does now, namely, suggest sinful thoughts directly. Now our hearts are open to his influence, but the hearts of those two sinless human beings were locked against him. Thus he was forced to try an indirect approach.

In what form should he show himself to the woman? How could he speak without immediately being recognized as God's enemy? He decided that the serpent must speak for him. He certainly could not destroy earth's creatures as long as man was still king, but he could use a creature for his own ends. He chose the serpent because it was the shrewdest of animals. It was doubtless very different in appearance then. The serpent may well have been a familiar part of the human environment, a part of the woman's daily life. Perhaps the serpent had responded to man's love for the lower creation. Even today there remains some interplay and mutual understanding between man and the animals. In any event, satan decided to speak to the woman through the serpent.

Satan knew about the test-command, which we discussed earlier, and seized on it as his opportunity. God Himself led man to the test; satan now took it upon himself to encourage man to break with God. If successful, he could ruin the whole beautiful world through man.

The serpent approached the woman by asking: "Has God placed you in this garden and not allowed you to eat the fruit of those wonderful trees?" Here satan was intentionally misrepresenting God's purposes by making that good command seem an oppressive restriction. He hoped this would arouse the woman's desire to disobey the command. But the woman quickly set him straight: "Of every tree we may eat except one. If we eat of that tree, we shall die." Yet the attempt had been made to arouse in her a desire for what God had forbidden.

Satan then proceeded to contradict the Word of God directly: "You will surely not die." He was trying to separate man from his God by arousing unbelief, for man is bound to God through his faith in God's Word. Unfortunately, this approach succeeded, and now man's heart is open to every lie satan suggests to him.

"You will be as God." In other words, there could be a world in which God is not God, a world in which man is the highest authority. Just imagine such a world. Satan plays on the gift of imagination given to us by God. Because we can imagine such a world, and because satan convinces us that it could become a reality, we stumble into a world of make-believe. As long as we think we can live without God, we have not left that make-believe world behind. Most of mankind lives in this illusory world. We feed on this world of fantasy every day, for it offers us much that looks inviting.

The woman then saw the fruit of that tree in an entirely different light. When it seemed that eating the fruit in disobedience would lead to her complete independence, the fruit suddenly became much more desirable. Satan misleads us by shedding a false light on things, making the wrong appear much more desirable than it might seem on its own. Do you know what feeling first hits us after we have sinned? Not remorse, but great disappointment. The moment we commit the sin, the false light goes out, and the sinful act no longer appears so attractive.

The woman took the fruit and ate it. How wretched she must have felt afterward! Yet she did not face up to what she had done. How foolish we are in our sin! Where was the wonderful result satan had promised? She deluded herself by thinking that the promise still awaited fulfillment because Adam had not yet eaten of the fruit. Once he freed himself from bondage, she would be free in him. She therefore repeated to Adam what the serpent had said to her. (Note that Adam later argues that the woman "gave" him the fruit, while the woman says that the serpent "deceived" her. The temptation of the woman by the serpent was deception, while the temptation of Adam by the woman was foolishness or self-deception. This is the fundamental difference between satanic and human sin.)

Eve made Adam choose between God and herself. Adam, too, disobeyed God and allied himself with satan against God.

Now they both felt wretched. They no longer dared look at each other, for their misery was written all over their faces. Now that they had changed, they realized that their hearts were full of unrighteousness.

Adam and Eve were suddenly ashamed to be naked in each other's presence and therefore covered themselves with fig leaves. They had become strangers to each other, and the whole creation had become strange to them; dangers seemed to threaten them on every side. There was hostility even in the animal kingdom. They were fearful of everything—especially God, although they had earlier loved Him deeply and felt very close to Him. Not only was man lost to his God, the whole world was lost to God as well.

The victory over sin. God saw what Adam and Eve had done. What should He do? Should He allow the world to perish under His judgment? He certainly could have. Instead He turned toward His creation, the work of His hands. Was there something in that creation that still attracted Him or moved Him to be merciful? Certainly not, for the whole world was ruined for Him. All the same, He wanted to glorify Himself by saving the world. That's why He chose to be merciful. It was only in grace that He turned to the world again, intending to conquer and destroy sin.

Shortly after the sinful deed, God came to the garden intending to talk with the man and the woman. The breezes brought them the sounds of His approach. They had often heard Him approach, but this time they were frightened! They concealed themselves anxiously among the trees of the garden, thinking that man can hide from God. Foolish as this may seem, we try the same stunt repeatedly ourselves, as we seek to conceal the evil in our hearts from God's eyes. But why? If we confess, He will hear us.

When God called Adam, Adam confessed his fear of God by hiding himself on account of his nakedness. Without realizing it, he was giving expression to his misery. He did not dare show himself before God any more than you or I do. Fortunately, God still came looking for him.

God asked about the change in the man's attitude toward Him. He wanted to know what had happened, and whether Adam and Eve had eaten of the forbidden fruit. But Adam could not confess and take the blame. He saw no way of escaping judgment. He did not yet know of any deliverance or grace, and therefore he could not confess. If God had never revealed His grace to us, would we be able to confess our sins? "The woman You gave me—she made me eat the fruit!" But the woman then pointed to the serpent.

God therefore made satan feel His wrath, for satan had used the serpent in his plot to ruin God's work. God's curse, which affected the entire world, placed a sign on the serpent. Its crawling through the dust became a sign of its humiliation and of satan's humiliation as well.

Satan will be conquered—by a Man! Just as a man destroyed the world in the beginning, another Man will rebuild it. To that end God destroyed the alliance between man and satan, replacing it with enmity. Again drawing man to His side, God entered into a covenant with him against satan. That enmity between man and satan will last forever. Although satan would go on to do man much harm, a Man would one day be born who would completely overcome satan and rescue the world.

The words of this curse upon satan promised deliverance and grace for man. When God addressed Himself to the man and the woman, there was no curse, nor did God undertake to condemn them. He did come down hard on the life of man, but only as a means of driving him back to God. The woman was told that she would bear children in pain. This would be her lot, and she would learn to cry out to God. She was also subjected to the rule of her husband. If she ever disobeyed by trying to liberate herself from her husband's rule, she would find out what it means to suffer! Only by obedience could she again become truly free—as her husband's helpmeet.

Man's life became hard. He bore an almost unbearable responsibility for the life of the family. It would be difficult for the man to provide the necessities, for the earth, which he had once ruled, would now turn against him by bringing forth thorns and thistles.

Life itself would be filled with thorns and thistles of all sorts. In addition, life would now be clouded by the fear of death, for man was destined to return to dust. God used the sentence of death to clip the wings of man's foolish aspirations, forcing him to turn to his Creator and cry out for deliverance.

Living by faith. As soon as man heard the promise, he believed. He understood the element of grace contained in the judgment. Human life on earth would continue—but in pain. Now that man's wings had been clipped, he might learn to call upon the Lord, his ally in the struggle against satan. Therefore Adam called his wife Eve.* By choosing this name, he demonstrated his belief in the promise.

Adam and Eve realized the immensity of what they had done, and they were broken. The Lord clothed them both by giving them garments made of the skins of animals. He also provided them with means for quenching the fires of sin.

Adam and Eve were still in Paradise,† where everything testified to God's unbroken favor. The tree of life was a special symbol of uninterrupted fellowship. But the fellowship had in fact been shattered. Even though God once again looked upon man with favor, the original, perfect relationship had been lost.

Man now had to learn to live by faith: our sin and the misery in the world had made it appear that man could expect no favor from God. To be sure, man had also lived by faith in Paradise, but then his belief made perfect sense. After the fall, man had to live *by faith alone*. God drove man out of Paradise and appointed an angel to guard the way to the tree of life. At that point the trials of life by faith alone began. All the same, man still enjoyed the privilege of faith in God's continued favor.

---

*The Hebrew word we know in the form *Eve* is closely related to the Hebrew word for *life,* as in the toast *'L Chaim*—To life! —TRANS.

†*Paradise* is an ancient Persian word for a royal park or a pleasure garden.—TRANS.

4: Living Seed

Genesis 4

The content of this chapter is not the life and death of godly Abel or the life and development of godless Cain. Think for a moment what happens when you make either of these themes the focus of the story: you wind up excluding the Kingdom of Heaven. This Kingdom is taught not by examples—although examples doubtless have their value—but by the Word of grace. If God's speaking and acting is not the primary consideration, the examples lose all their meaning.

The main purpose of this chapter is furnishing us with the key to the Kingdom. Adam named his wife Eve and thereby showed that he accepted the promise. In Genesis 4 the promise is fulfilled in the birth of children, which confirms God's Word. But the faith of Adam and Eve is soon put to the test: it turns out that Cain is not genuine, living seed, and Abel is murdered. Hope is then revived in the birth of Seth.

The line must be drawn from Seth to the Christ: Christ would be born of Seth's line. But when we recognize this, we are still not saying enough about the revelation of the Christ in this chapter. In his death Abel is a type of Christ and of all God's people—but he is also Christ's opposite or antitype. Abel's blood—unlike Christ's blood—cannot remove sin; it merely cries out for justice and vengeance. The blood of Christ, then, speaks of better things than Abel's blood: it raises the hope of reconciliation.

But this chapter does not point only to the death of Christ. In the birth of Seth there was new life. That birth pointed ahead to Christ's victorious resurrection.

Evidently Adam and Eve taught their children to offer sacrifices. For those who accepted God's grace in faith, sacrifice became a way of practicing that faith. Through sacrifice as a response to God's favor, man could dedicate himself to the Lord and be strengthened in fellowship with the Lord.

In the case of Cain, however, we already see degeneration setting in. Because he stands apart from the Lord and does not accept the promise in faith, he lives in fear. He then tries to ward off God's judgment and buy His blessing through sacrifice. His worship, like the worship of anyone without faith, is bribery.

Main thought: *The promise receives its initial fulfillment in the birth of living seed.*

Two kinds of seed. After they were banished from Paradise, Adam and Eve had their first child. What a blessing children are to parents who believe! Not only are parents enriched through the lives of their offspring, they also feel God's favor in the blessing of children. The son given to Adam and Eve brought them a special bliss, for his birth was an indication of God's favor in their new life, the life they had begun after their old life was destroyed by sin. In this new life they now saw a fulfillment of the promise God made to them when they were banished from Paradise. That promise they had accepted in faith.

Because Eve had received her son from the Lord, she named him Cain, which means *the one obtained.* Cain's birth was God's way of giving Himself to Adam and Eve and fulfilling His promise.

When her second child was born some time later, Eve appears to have been in a different mood. Perhaps the second child was not born as healthy as the first. In any case, her outlook on her condition had changed. The name she gave the child was not a denial of her faith, but it did reflect a deeper awareness of the trials and struggles of life, from which she, as a believer, had not been spared. Since life's burdens, which are a result of sin, weighed heavily on her, she called her second child Abel, which means *a triviality, insignificance, a mere breath.*

Adam and Eve talked to their children about the Lord and told them about the first sin in Paradise. For parents to reveal their own sins to their children is a bitter pill to swallow. Adam and Eve also told their children about God's grace and the complete deliverance to come. Then they waited for the children's reponse. Would the hearts of the children open? Would they join their parents in believing in the promise of deliverance? Would they come to love the Lord? Adam and Eve prayed that their children would respond positively to God's grace and deliverance. This is always the main concern of believing parents.

Believing parents are very perceptive. Adam and Eve could not help noticing that Abel believed the promise and gave his heart and life to the Lord in a simple way. But it did not escape their attention either that Cain wanted to live for himself. Deep in his heart Cain despised the Lord's promise and felt no need of deliverance. He was sure he could make it on his own. Yet he knew that the Lord was there and could punish him. Consequently his life was filled with fear, as our story demonstrates.

Adam and Eve had taught their children to offer sacrifices to the Lord by burning animals or the produce of the earth. These sacrifices were to be offered wholly out of faith, as a way of saying: "Lord, You have shown us Your favor and given us everything. Therefore we want to devote ourselves and all that we have to Your service. We offer You these sacrifices as tokens of our intent." This pleased the Lord, for He saw that the people were offering their very hearts through their sacrifices. Man became all the more pleasing to God because of the sacrifices offered.

Adam and Eve offered sacrifices, then, and Abel did so as well. But Cain could not join in, for he did not believe. He did not give his heart to the Lord and did not confess that the Lord had given him everything he had. Yet he, too, offered sacrifices. And when he did, it was as though he was offering something of his own to the Lord in expectation of a gift in return. He thought he could buy the Lord's favor and ward off His punishment by offering Him sacrifices. Such behavior is an abomination to the Lord.

One day both Cain and Abel were engaged in sacrificing to the Lord. Because Cain tilled the soil, he offered the Lord the produce of his field. Abel was a herdsman and therefore offered one of the first-born of his sheep. God looked with favor on Abel and his sacrifice—but not on Cain. In some way unknown to us, the Lord made His response known to them. Perhaps He spoke to them directly. (In Hebrews 11:4 we read that Abel "received approval as righteous.")

Now was the time for Cain to come to his senses and confess that his sacrifice was really a lie. Instead he became angry with Abel, who always seemed to be favored, and accused God of being unjust. Because he was the oldest child in the family, Cain thought too highly of himself.

Even at this point, the Lord warned him. If only he would change his ways, he would rise in the Lord's favor. But if he refused to break with his sin, he would be completely overpowered by it. How patient the Lord is!

Life ruined. The power of sin grew stronger in Cain's life instead of weakening. Not only did he hate his brother, he also developed a growing hatred of the Lord's promise and covenant, which required living by faith. Although he had rejected grace himself, he was angry at his brother for possessing it. That's how foolish sin makes us.

Once when the two brothers were together in the field, Cain expressed all his anger and hatred. Abel must have responded with surprise and sorrow, displaying the grace he had received through faith. This aroused Cain's wrath as nothing else could: he attacked his brother and killed him.

Human blood had now been shed for the first time. Abel was the first human being to die. Cain was guilty of fratricide; he had murdered his brother. And that wasn't even the worst of it. More terrible still was his hatred of the Lord's covenant and promise. Cain had killed Abel because Abel was a believer.

Abel typifies all the human beings after him who have been oppressed, persecuted and put to death for their faith. He is also a type of the Lord Jesus Christ, who was put to death because of His love for His father. Yet there is a difference between those two deaths. The blood of Abel could not make propitiation for Cain's crime. Instead it cried out from the ground for God's justice to avenge it. The blood of the Lord Jesus Christ, on the other hand, is indeed a propitiation for the crimes and misdeeds of those who believe in Him.

Since God still hoped to stop Cain on his downward path, He asked him about his brother. Cain pleaded ignorance: "Am I my brother's keeper?" God then told Cain that He knew about the crime and proceeded to curse him. The earth would no longer give Cain its fruit, and nowhere on earth would he find rest. Did Cain then beg God for forgiving grace? No, grace was out of the question as far as he was concerned: "My crime is too great to be forgiven." His only request was that his life be spared for a while. Full of his usual fear, he declared: "I am under a curse. I no longer have Your protection. Anyone who finds me will kill me."

God spared Cain and reserved the right to pronounce judgment on him. He therefore declared that if Cain were murdered, he would be avenged sevenfold. To make sure Cain would not be killed by his fellow man, the Lord put a sign on him. What this sign was we do not know. Apparently everyone who encountered Cain was repelled and turned away in disgust.

That was the last conversation between the Lord and Cain. Cain left the land of Eden and its Paradise, where God had revealed Himself to man. He turned his back on the covenant circle, the people on whom God had bestowed His grace, and settled down in the land of Nod, which was east of Eden.

The faith of Adam and Eve was severely tried. Abel was dead, and Cain was lost to them. They thought they had seen a joyous fulfillment of God's promise, but what had come of it now? All the same, they continued to cling to the promise. Faith can cling steadfastly to the Word of the Lord even when everything looks hopeless. That power of faith was won for us by the Lord Jesus Christ, whose faith did not collapse during His darkest night of suffering.

The sinful grab at life. Why had God spared Cain and given him protection? He had His reasons, but they went beyond Cain's comprehension. The faithful may understand something of God's purpose for their lives and even glorify Him for it, but unbelievers are blind to God's purposes, even if He still chooses to use them for His own ends. Cain was no different from any other unbeliever in this respect.

Cain was married to his sister. In the land of Nod she bore him a son, whom he named Enoch. Cain also built a city with walls to keep himself safe. All his life he was haunted by fears. He had many descendants, including Lamech, who became one of the great figures in Cain's line.

Lamech took two wives and thereby started the abominable practice of polygamy. He wanted to make sure he would have a large family and many descendants. Parents with many children enjoy the Lord's blessing if they have begotten their children for the Lord. Lamech, however, wanted a large family so he could be great and strong against the Lord.

The descendants of Lamech were a highly developed people. Jabal introduced living in tents so he could drive his flocks and herds anywhere he wished. Jubal enhanced life and opened up some of its beauty by inventing musical instruments. And Tubal-cain was the first to make utensils of bronze and iron.

Cain's descendants appeared to be flourishing, then. Had God not said that man was to subdue the earth and make use of its treasures? That was precisely what Cain's descendants were doing. Yet they were doing it not in the service of the Lord but to make themselves more and more independent of Him.

It should not escape our attention that from the very beginning, the greatest development is to be found not among those who fear* the Lord but among unbelievers. Apparently the unbelievers' drive for independence from the Lord is stronger that the believers' drive to serve the Lord. Yet the Lord, who directs all things, is also behind this development in unbelieving circles. Without meaning to do so, unbelievers serve God's purposes with their discoveries and inventions. Believers, too, make use of those discoveries. The treasures God created are disclosed, even though the unbelievers do not thank Him for them.

That was God's reason for sparing Cain's life and protecting him. But Cain's line did not think of the Lord. Instead his descendants lived lives of selfishness, revenge and pride. They reached out for life and tried to enjoy it, but true enjoyment escaped their grasp. This is evident especially from Lamech's song, in which he brags about his self-seeking and revenge. The spirit expressed in that song is still the mainspring of the unbelieving world, which is a world lost to the Lord.

---

*This is the Biblical use of *fear*, meaning *love, reverence, obey authority.*—TRANS.

New hope through the birth of Seth. The faith of Adam and Eve was severely tested by the death of Abel and the spiritual downfall of Cain. But the Lord did not forget His promise. Eve was still to give birth to the genuine, living seed. The Lord fulfilled the promise by giving Adam and Eve another son. Eve recognized that her new son was a substitute for Abel and hoped he would seek the Lord as Abel had done. Therefore she named him Seth.

In Seth their hopes were not disappointed, for he and his line did fear the Lord. In time Seth had a son of his own, whom he named Enoch.

In those days people began to gather together and publicly call on the name of the Lord. That was the beginning of what we now call worship services, although the services then did not have the same form as our services. The life of faith needs that public act of calling upon the name of the Lord. Partly because of the worship services, the fear of the Lord stayed alive in Seth's line. Eventually the Lord Jesus was born of that line. God would surely fulfill His promise.

There is no denying that the faith of Adam and Eve was sorely tried when they lost both Cain and Abel, but in Seth they were given new hope. True life seemed to have been lost for good, but it was now resurrected in Seth. When the Lord Jesus died, it also seemed as though true life had been destroyed for good, but in His resurrection He was revealed as Victor. In that revelation, God's promise to Adam and Eve attained its complete fulfillment. Because of the power of the Lord Jesus Christ, life lived by faith will always be victorious.

The Second World

5: Saved by Water

The flood, like every other judgment during the time of the covenant of grace, took place for the sake of our salvation. According to I Peter 3:20, Noah and his family were *saved* by the waters of the flood. The flood removed unrighteous men from the face of the earth so that Noah, his family, the animals, and the whole world might be saved. The flood points ahead to baptism. Even the final judgment is for salvation's sake: the world will be renewed through it. We are to tell the children about that salvation, showing them how God saved the world in grace through the flood.

Noah appears in Scripture as a type of the Christ, for through him the world was saved. Just as Christ was in the grip of death, Noah was in death's clutches while he was in the ark during the flood. It was God who saved him from death's embrace. Noah was also like Christ in many other ways. Adam's genealogy in Genesis 5 ends with Noah: at the time of the flood, Noah was the head of Seth's descendants.

This Noah was a righteous man. Through Christ's Spirit, he lived before God's face in the covenant. The Christ in his loins was God's link with the world. God established a covenant with Noah to preserve him together with his family in the ark. (In Genesis 6:18 we find the first occurrence of the word *covenant* in Scripture, but the covenant mentioned there is not to be identified with the Noahic covenant first described in Genesis 9.)

After Noah was rescued from the flood waters, he offered a sacrifice. On behalf of the entire world, he sought fellowship with God in the covenant relationship. Because of that sacrifice, the Lord gave Noah a promise about the future of the earth by establishing the Noahic covenant.

Noah also prophesied about his sons and the future of the world. He indicated that the descendants of his three sons would follow different paths. Yet we must remind ourselves again and again that the Christ is to be presented as the central figure in this story. Otherwise we may wind up

59

talking about Noah as a man righteous in himself.

In Genesis 6:3 we read that man's days "shall be a hundred and twenty years." This text must not be taken to mean that man's life-span was being shortened. What it means instead is that God intended to punish the world with the flood once 120 years had passed.

The Noahic covenant is commonly called the covenant of nature. There's nothing wrong with this characterization, provided that we regard man as part of "nature." This covenant was established not only with the earth and the animals but first of all with man. (There can be no covenant with the earth and the animals alone.) God said: "Behold, I establish my covenant with you and your descendants [seed] after you, and with every living creature that is with you, the birds, the cattle, and every beast of the earth with you, as many as came out of the ark" (Gen. 9:9-10).

This covenant includes every creature under man's dominion. Man, the head of the covenant, is to abide in God's grace, which was established through the sacrifice that Noah offered to Yahweh, the God of the covenant, after he emerged from the ark. Noah and his descendants were to live in that covenant of fellowship brought about by this sacrifice. To make sure that man's development of the creation could unfold in that fellowship of faith, God promised that He would never again interrupt that development as He had by way of the flood. The development could now proceed uninterrupted right to the end. It would continue in a straight line right down to the crisis of the final judgment in the future of Jesus Christ. This "covenant of nature" is therefore to be regarded as a renewal of the covenant of grace revealed by God after the fall. This renewal of the covenant reflected the changes in man's circumstances.

Main thought: *The world is saved by water to make a new fellowship with the Lord possible.*

Judgment and salvation revealed. In general it can be said of Seth's descendants that they preserved the knowledge and fear of God for a long time. Doubtless there were children who did not want to walk in their parents' footsteps, but most of the members of this line were faithful to the Lord. Notable among them was Enoch, a man who was dear to the Lord. Enoch did not suffer death but was taken up by the Lord.

As time went on, the descendants of Seth changed. Evidently they were attracted by the seemingly wonderful life lived by Cain's descendants, among whom all kinds of arts flourished. Cain's people were becoming a strong race of men, but violence was the order of the day in their circles. Because they regarded power as all-important, some of them developed into giants. Young men of Seth's line were attracted to girls descended from Cain and married them instead of the God-fearing girls of their own race. The two lines began to mix, and Seth's race was infected with the ungodliness of Cain's people.

None of this escaped the Lord's attention. Sometimes the Lord can endure sin for a long time, but there finally comes a point when He holds sin up to the light of His countenance. Such a time had now come for mankind. God saw that the human beings He had placed on earth to serve Him had instead filled the earth with their sins. There was no stopping them in their wickedness, for their thoughts were completely sinful.

The Lord now turned His back on humanity. For a long time He had carefully protected mankind, for the human beings on earth were the works of His hands. But the time was near when He would let them go: after 120 years, He would wipe them off the face of the earth. Before the judgment struck, they would be given a certain amount of time to repent. The Lord decided to exterminate the animals together with man. The animals would share in the curse upon mankind, for God found everything that lived on earth repugnant.

Yet God could not and would not abandon the world and man completely. Had He not established His covenant with man? Had He not promised that the Savior would come some day to redeem the human race? That promise He would fulfill.

As He surveyed the earth in those days of widespread apostasy, He found one man who still feared the Lord. In that one man, God saw evidence of the Spirit of the Lord Jesus Christ. For Christ's sake, the Lord still felt a bond with mankind and the world through that one man. Thus, although He had decided to destroy the world and mankind, He would save that one man and his family—and thereby save humanity and the earth. He intended to wipe sin from the face of the earth without destroying mankind completely. If God had not given His promise to send the Lord Jesus, this judgment would have meant the end for mankind.

That one man was Noah, who was the head of Seth's line. Noah had three sons—Shem, Ham and Japheth. Like Enoch, Noah lived close to the Lord. When he was born, his father prophesied: "Out of the ground which the LORD has cursed this one shall bring us relief from our work and from the toil of our hands." This was a way of saying that Noah would save mankind from the curse sent by God because of sin. To be sure, Noah *himself* did not save mankind. Mankind was saved instead by the Lord Jesus Christ, who was to be born of Noah's line. Christ's Spirit already lived in Noah. For His sake, Noah was saved—and mankind through him.

The Lord told Noah that He was going to destroy the world with a great flood. Noah was to build a huge ark and make it waterproof. He was to divide the interior of the ark into various compartments, for the Lord was going to send him a pair of each kind of animal and seven pairs of the "clean" animals, i.e. the animals that could be used for sacrifices. God did not wish to wipe out the animals completely. For Christ's sake, the animal world, which shared in the curse upon man, was also to share in man's salvation.

The destruction of life to save life. Noah did what the Lord had commanded. This was an act of faith on his part, for he believed that the Lord would do what He had said. How he was ridiculed for building the ark! In the name of the Lord, he told the scoffers what was going to happen, but they did not believe him. Who would be so foolish as to believe that the world could be destroyed? The course of our lives is so sure and steady!

God tells us in His Word that He will destroy the world by fire when the Lord Jesus Christ returns. Men ridicule that judgment too. Who really believes that sort of thing nowadays? Hasn't the world existed for millions of years just as it does today? Surely it will always continue to exist!

But Noah went on building the ark as a witness against that unbelieving generation. By the time he was finished, the 120 years had passed, and Noah himself was 600 years old. At the Lord's command, he and his family went into the ark. The Lord then caused the animals to come to him there. Now the moment had arrived for the Lord to cut the ties between all those who were about to be destroyed and the one man who would be preserved with his family. What an awful moment it was when the Lord cut the people off from Noah! In the same way, the Lord will one day separate the unbelievers from the Lord Jesus Christ and His chosen ones for all eternity. That, too, will be an awful moment.

The Lord opened the floodgates of heaven and released a ceaseless downpour upon the earth. Water also came up out of the ground. The water level rose steadily for forty days until the whole earth (including the mountains) was covered. The water rose more than seven meters above the highest mountains. Every creature living on the earth was wiped out.

Inside the ark Noah no doubt called upon the Lord, who had brought His world down in ruin. Was there no mercy with Him? Didn't He care about the world He had created? It was as though Noah was also lost and the end of the world had come. But Noah continued to cling to God's promise.

This reminds us of the Lord Jesus Christ, who perished under the wrath of God for our sins. He, too, held fast to God in faith and was glorified in His resurrection. For Christ's sake, Noah and his family were saved by God. After forty days the downpour ended, and God stopped up the fountains of the earth. For a long time the water remained at the same level. Finally it began to subside.

The ark ran aground on one of the highest mountains, Mount Ararat. God had not left Noah without any possibility of rescue. But Noah did not only long for rescue; he also wanted to see the earth again! It wasn't just that he wanted to be free of the confines of the ark. He loved God's earth and wanted it to be saved.

If only his eyes could once again look upon that earth! At first it would be very lonely on the earth, for at one stroke God had wiped out all the life that had arisen on the earth over a period of centuries. Noah and his family would have to build up a new world. This time man would build with God and enjoy His favor.

How Noah longed to get going! In his eagerness he opened the window of the ark and sent out a raven. After circling over the ark for a long time, the raven flew away and stayed away, having found it possible to live on the earth again. God was kind to His world. After seven days Noah sent out a dove. It returned. Seven days later he sent it out again, and this time it brought back an olive branch. When it was sent out once more after another seven days, it did not return. Yet God made Noah wait a little longer.

Finally the day came when the Lord allowed him to leave the ark and walk upon the earth once more with his family. Now the new development could begin in the fear of the Lord.

The Lord had indeed been wise to decide on judgment. The evil had to be removed if the world was again to live in fellowship with Him. It was as though the earth had been reborn through the water.

The lesson applies to our lives too: the evil must die, and we must be born again. The Lord will give us new life. Our existence will then find meaning in Him. That's what the sacrament of baptism signifies. In baptism, too, we are buried under the water and emerge from the water as new creatures. The flood points ahead to baptism.

One day the Lord will destroy the world by fire. That judgment, too, will lead to a new world. God saves the work of His hands for Christ's sake.

Covenant blessing upon the renewed world. What was the first thing for Noah to do on that renewed earth? There he stood as the head of a new world that he was now to begin building. On behalf of that world he offered a sacrifice to the Lord, seeking God's fellowship and favor for mankind. The world would now have to undergo a development in fellowship with God, a development that honored Him. Thus Noah acted very much in the Spirit of the Lord Jesus Christ, who offered Himself as a sacrifice for the world.

Noah used the clean animals and the clean birds for his sacrifice. The Lord was pleased with Noah's offering, in which He recognized the Spirit of the Lord Jesus Christ, the One who would one day sacrifice Himself to remove the curse from the earth and sanctify the world's life.

God remembered His covenant at that point and promised that He would never again interrupt the world's development in such a terrible way. Never again would the earth be covered by flood waters. God would permit the development of the world to run its course to the end. He confirmed this in a covenant with Noah and his sons, blessing them in that covenant and telling them that the human race was to develop again on earth and rule the world. To that end He protected humanity from the wild animals by instilling in the animals a fear of man.

Now men were also permitted to use animals for food. Evidently human life had been weakened and needed such strengthening. God also protected man from himself: He ordered that every murderer be punished with death. In this way God protected human life and blessed it. He did not want to abandon the creature created in His own image. One day the Lord Jesus Christ would come as God's perfect likeness. He would then restore God's image in believers. In man, God once again blessed the whole creation, the work of His hands.

God decreed that the rainbow would be a sign of this covenant made with Noah. Every time the rainbow appears, God is reminded of His promise to allow the development of the world to continue uninterrupted. We may count on this promise. God will surely bless us.

The divergence of the lines of Noah's sons. If only the human race would develop in fellowship with God, in a way pleasing to Him! If only mankind would abide by the spirit of Noah's sacrifice, which is also the spirit of the sacrifice to be offered one day by the Lord Jesus Christ!

Unfortunately, it soon became clear that this hope would not be realized. Noah became a farmer and planted a vineyard. He let some grape juice ferment and enjoyed the wine he had produced. But he drank too much and became completely drunk. There in his tent lay the head of the human race, naked and without shame! Once again sin was taking its course. And that wasn't even the worst of it.

Doubtless Noah had not intended to go that far—although this does not excuse his conduct. When Ham entered his father's tent and found him drunk and naked, he had no compassion. In fact, he scoffed. There lay the father of mankind, the man who had offered the sacrifice! Ham wallowed in his father's disgrace; he took pleasure in the debauchery and trampled the fear of God underfoot. Today there are still people like that, people who do not care how evil their acts are. All they want is to wipe out the fear of God.

In his obscene pleasure, Ham told his brothers what he had

seen. Fortunately, they did not share his mentality. With their backs to their father, they covered his nakedness. What would become of the newly developing human race if the spirit of Ham were to prevail?

When Noah woke up from his drunken stupor, he should have bowed before the Lord at once because of his sin. Ordinarily he would have done so. On this occasion, however, the Lord's Spirit made him a prophet and judge: Noah uttered a curse and a blessing. Speaking in the name of the Lord as a prophet, he laid out the future of his sons' descendants. He did not curse Ham's entire line, but he did not bless it either. For the time being, it stood apart from the blessing pronounced on the other two lines.

Ham's son Canaan, who had perhaps been amused by his father's behavior, was cursed. He was to be a lowly slave and serve the races fathered by his brothers and his uncles. Noah's words were not in vain: the Canaanites were subject to the rule of other peoples until they were entirely wiped out.

Noah also pronounced a blessing: "Blessed by the LORD my God be Shem." Apparently the line of Shem was destined to have a very special relation to the Lord. In the conflict between the seed of the woman and the seed of the serpent, the line of Shem would achieve victory for the Lord. The Christ would one day be born of Shem's line.

Noah also asked God to bless Japheth and assign him an important role. He asked God to give Japheth many children and make his line dominant, so that Japheth would dwell in Shem's tents and share in the blessing of Shem, i.e. the salvation of the Christ. The development of the world would be governed not by the spirit of Ham but by the Spirit of the Christ.

Sometimes it seems otherwise. Sometimes it looks as though wickedness will prevail. But because of Noah's prophecy, we know better. One day Christ will be recognized as the Victor, with all the world's progress pointing to and serving the coming of His Kingdom. On which side will we stand?

After the flood Noah lived another 350 years. He was 950 years old when he died. During his lifetime, the families of his sons multiplied and the development went on. In which spirit?

6: The Emergence of Distinct Peoples

Genesis 11:1-9

It was fear that led to the building of the tower of Babel. The people on earth were afraid of being scattered and sought safety in concentrated strength. They feared that the human race might be wiped out. Apparently they no longer believed the promise given in the Noahic covenant, the promise that God would preserve the human race on earth and would one day provide a perfect salvation. Protection against man and beast had indeed been promised by God. In faith, the people should have dared to spread out across the earth and subdue it. That was their calling in the covenant.

Even as a dispersed people, they could have remained one in spirit. Faith can cope with the formation of separate human communities, which would have come about naturally if mankind had spread across the earth as intended. Unbelief is afraid of dispersal because unbelievers are not spiritually bound to each other or to God. That's why unbelieving people always seek an outward unity to signify human power.

God used the confusion of tongues at Babel to force mankind to spread across the entire earth. After Babel there were many human communities, but those communities were not one in spirit. Instead of solidarity there was estrangement and loneliness.

It is true that this scattering of mankind, this shattering of the human community, made it possible for the many-sided abilities of the human race to come to light and the earth to be subdued. Thus the scattering of the peoples involved both a curse and a blessing. It cried out for the coming of the Christ and the outpouring of the Holy Spirit. Only then could unity be created among the separate communities, a unity in which the blessing would be preserved and the curse conquered.

Through the confusion of tongues, God broke up the false unity to

67

make room for true unity in Christ. Thus there was grace in the scattering of the peoples.

Because Christ has come and the Holy Spirit has been poured out, the separate peoples today may once again seek true unity with each other in faith. Indeed, they *must* do so. However, this freedom and calling is again being misused in a bid for a false, outward unity. This movement toward unity is ultimately a quest for power. History's development is leading to the kingdom of the Antichrist on the one hand and the Kingdom of Christ on the other.

The Biblical account of the story of the tower of Babel includes a curious phrase that should not escape our attention: we read that the Lord "came down" (Gen. 11:5). Apparently God had lived on the earth up to the time of the flood. (Could it be that His home was in Paradise?) After the flood, God again sought a dwelling place on the earth. The first evidence of His desire to dwell on the earth again was His "appearance" to Abram. For Abram, at least, God was again nearby. In time the tabernacle became God's dwelling place, and later still the temple. Today there is once more an abiding dwelling place in Christ and in His Church through the Spirit.

It was as though God was biding His time after the flood. Life was being eaten away by sin, and the people were spreading across the earth. God finally chose Abram to enjoy His full fellowship. In Abram's great Son, the unity and fellowship with God was restored.

Main thought: *The outward unity is torn down to make room for true unity in the Christ.*

Disobedience born of fear. In the mountainous territory of Ararat, where the ark had come to rest, the human race expanded. The people spread from mountain to mountain but did not wander far away from one another. Since the mountains closed them in, they were not afraid they might lose contact with one another.

At a certain point, however, the people felt the desire to pull up stakes and migrate. Perhaps the mountains could no longer provide them with enough food. In any event, they migrated eastward together. They found a plain in the land of Shinar, and there they settled down. They learned how to build houses of bricks and spread gradually across the plain. In the mountains they had used stones for building; here they found clay, which they could turn into bricks by baking. They also found bitumen, a kind of asphalt that could be used for mortar. The presence of these materials made their life easier.

There seemed to be no limit to the plain; they could easily spread out farther and farther. But the people were afraid of being scattered across the earth and losing contact with one another. Wouldn't they be in greater danger of disappearing from the earth if they were scattered? If they became estranged from one another, wouldn't they wind up fighting and killing each other? Wouldn't the animal world overpower them? Wouldn't they be struck by all kinds of calamities before which they were helpless separately but might be able to face if they were united and strong?

Such were their fears. Driven by those fears, they decided to build a city with walls, a city to which they could flee for protection. They also decided to build a huge tower in that city, a tower that would reach into the clouds. That tower would become their land-mark and rallying point. The tower would help them remain together without ever becoming estranged. Then they would never perish from the earth!

What nonsense! Why did they count on togetherness to provide them with strength and protection? Was there any need for them to fear that mankind might disappear from the earth? Hadn't God promised in the covenant with Noah that He would not allow mankind to perish before the end came? Had He not protected men's lives from their fellow men and from the animals? But the people no longer believed the Lord's Word and promises. And when men no longer believe the Word of the Lord, they become afraid. They then forget that the Lord's help is their only sure protection.

Building that enormous tower to keep themselves together was a direct act of disobedience against the Lord's command. The Lord had ordered the people to spread out, fill the earth, and subdue it. Everything God had put on the earth was supposed to be uncovered and developed by man.

If the people had believed the Word of the Lord, they would have dared to explore the earth and subdue it. They would then have ventured forth under the Lord's protection and would have remained spiritually united through their faith in God's Word and their expectation of the promised Redeemer. But they preferred to rely on outward unity, planning to found a world empire based on human strength.

The Lord's descent. Should the Lord let them go on building? The entire proposal and the purpose behind it were directly opposed to what the Lord wanted to accomplish in His grace. That's why we read in the Bible that the Lord "came down" to see the city and tower being built by the sons of men.

The Bible uses a peculiar expression here. Surely the Lord is present everywhere, in heaven as well as on earth, and does not need to "come down" to see what men are doing. Yet we should not read over this phrase quickly as though it adds nothing to the story, for it does contain a definite message.

In His grace, favor and love, the Lord had kept His distance from men after the flood and did not immediately allow them the privilege of full fellowship with Him. Mankind first had to learn to desire the Redeemer, through whom the people would again enjoy God's full communion. But instead of desiring the Redeemer, the people rejected the very idea of faith and went their own way. The Lord therefore had to do something to arrest the growth of unbelief, for it was still His purpose to preserve and redeem mankind through the Christ. He asserted that purpose by opposing the growth of human strength and power symbolized by the city and tower of Babel. That's what the Bible means when it says that the Lord "came down." He viewed the colossal building project in the light of His purposes and grace. It then became obvious that man's course of action was completely opposed to His own plans.

What was the Lord to do about it? The people could not be allowed to continue this building program, for then the whole earth would never be filled and subdued. Worse still, the people would become completely estranged from the Redeemer and would no longer await His coming. Their lives would become so contaminated with sin that God would again have to annihilate them completely, as He had done in the flood.

But the Lord did not want to send another flood. Moreover, He had promised never to do that again. God therefore announced His intention of scattering the people across the entire earth. They would then be forced to fill the earth and would not grow strong together in evil. Certain people here and there might have to die because they had allowed sin too much room in their lives, but never again would mankind be destroyed. This course of action on which the Lord decided would allow Him to send the Redeemer in His own good time.

Thus when the Lord "comes down," it is to expose men's actions to the light of the purpose of His grace. He then makes short work of human intentions. How fortunate for mankind that He does! Our own wisdom would only serve to ruin our lives. Fortunately, the Lord carries out His intentions with a single goal in mind. Often He still works this way, allowing men's projects to fail in order to show them His grace.

The emergence of distinct peoples. At that time all human beings still spoke one language. (We do not know which one.) The Lord now broke up that linguistic unity. The people began to think differently and express their ideas in different words, with the result that they no longer understood each other. More and more they became strangers to each other. Finally, the various groups and families were compelled to go their separate ways. The Lord always carries out His intentions. When will man ever realize that?

Now the various races of men finally spread across the earth. The work of filling the earth began. Eventually the different peoples lost their knowledge of each other and scarcely remembered that they had once been one people. They even tried to destroy each other in warfare. Fortunately, the Lord kept His promise and prevented the peoples from destroying the human race in a great war.

What a variety there was among men! More of the richness of God's creation was revealed. Red and yellow, black and white—all were made in God's image. What diversity in the development of the peoples scattered across the earth! God had attained one of His goals. But His primary goal still lay ahead: He wanted to redeem man.

The human race did indeed develop and fill the whole earth. But in the midst of this development, there was deep spiritual poverty and hunger for true happiness, love and fellowship. Did God scatter the peoples so that they would remain estranged from one another for all time? No, He broke down the outward unity of unbelief to show mankind the true unity that comes about through faith in the Redeemer.

Now the Redeemer has come and has sent the Holy Spirit so that the peoples can again be united. This does not mean that all differences are now to be erased. On the contrary, the various peoples must retain their own characteristics, but there is no longer any need for the peoples to be estranged from one another. They may know and love one another through faith in the Lord Jesus Christ.

Have the various peoples of the earth taken this step? Are they once again seeking one another? Are they trying to understand and love one another? What about it? Do we, however much we may differ from one another, love each other for Jesus' sake? All too often we don't. And if that true unity for the sake of the Lord Jesus Christ is not found, won't men again seek the appearance of unity that they sought in Babel?

The Lord tells us in His Word that in the future there will be another situation like Babel. One day the worldly empire of the Antichrist, the great enemy of the Christ, will be established on the basis of unbelief and enmity against the Lord.

Will it then turn out that all of God's efforts, including the sending of the Redeemer, were in vain? Of course not! Now there is a people truly one in faith—the people of God, the Church of the Lord. Even though God's people are not entirely free of sin, they are believers and are united in their hearts. Among God's people are human beings drawn from every nation and race, all living together through faith in the Christ. Someday God's people will overcome.

To be sure, the kingdom of the Antichrist will indeed come, but it will be destroyed when the Lord Jesus Christ returns. Then the Kingdom of the Lord Jesus will be established in glory. In that Kingdom, those He has purchased out of every race and language and people and nation will be truly one.

Abraham

7: Blessed in the One

Genesis 12

The need for unity was felt even more keenly because of the division and dispersion of mankind after Babel. What was needed was not just a Spirit-led unity of faith but the one Root by which the whole of mankind would be supported. The One spoken of as the Root would prove to be a blessing to all peoples. Abram was now set apart to be His provisional type.

Life through the Spirit of the One in whom the world would be blessed is completely different from the life of the flesh. Believers before Abram's time were well aware of this, of course, for then, as now, no one who had not been born again could see the Kingdom of God. The contrast or antithesis between faith and the life of the flesh, between the Christ and everything that is of the flesh, had to stand out clearly if faith was not to be confused with the "religious" life of the flesh (idol worship). This was achieved by separating Abram from his country, his kinsmen and his father's house. The contrast also came out later in the miraculous birth of Isaac. The "miracle" of grace had to be made manifest. Christ is the miracle.

All the same, Abram's calling to leave his land and people did not contain the slightest suggestion that grace as the "wholly other" would continue to stand over against human life, as though life on earth was not to be sanctified. On the contrary, Abram was promised that he would become the father of a *nation,* that he would have a name *on the earth,* and that in him all the nations of the earth would be blessed. Grace entered life and sanctified it. Eventually it entered the life of every nation. In the promise to Abram, there was a strong emphasis on *the land* that would someday be his.

From the very beginning, Christ's grace has been bound up with the earth and human society. The One in whom all nations will be blessed is the One who is bound to God. He is the Christ, in whom God and man are joined. This, too, is reflected in the story of Abram. Abram was the first human being to whom God appeared after Babel, the first one to experience God's nearness. At Babel God "came down," but here we read for the first time that God "appeared" in the land of promise. In Israel's history, God's appearing and His dwelling with men became richer and richer in content.

The One, together with all that belongs to Him, is a divine sanctuary. This became clear to Abram when Sarai was saved from dishonor in Egypt. It wasn't just Abram's wife or marriage that was at stake; the promised seed to be born of their union was threatened as well.

When we tell the children the story of Abram's calling, we should stress these deeds on God's part and not emphasize Abram's faith in itself. Nurturing faith is God's work too. Remember that while we cannot live on the basis of someone else's faith, we *can* live out of the revelation of God.

Main thought: *The blessing for all is given in the One, so that all might cling to the One in faith.*

The call to go out and follow. By building the tower of Babel, the people on earth had shown that they did not want to live by faith in God's promise to preserve the human race and one day send the Redeemer. This promise gave them no strength. They were afraid and therefore took steps to ensure themselves of protection in the face of all danger. Because they did not want to obey God's command to fill the earth, He had to scatter them. Now idolatry and superstition gradually became prevalent on the earth—which should not surprise us. Without faith in God's Word, the people began to believe their own ideas about God instead of clinging to what He had revealed about Himself.

God then let them follow their own path, just as a wise father sometimes lets his child go his own foolish way: if the child refuses to listen, he will have to learn his lesson the hard way. God decided to allow the nations to find out for themselves where disobedience would get them. But this is not to say that He abandoned them. As a matter of fact, He was good to them. He gave them rain and allowed them to prosper, but He also punished them frequently when their sins became too much for Him to bear. Yet He sent no prophets to preach His Word to them, nor did He give them any new revelations.

Even after He had scattered the peoples across the earth, He did not abandon them. In spite of everything, He still intended to send the Redeemer, through whom the nations would be saved. The Redeemer would not echo the ungodliness of the nations. He would do God's will in everything, and His hope would be in the Word of God. He would be obedient for all and take away the sins of the world.

The nations could not and would not live with the Lord. All the same, God would send the Redeemer to save them, as a miracle of His love. Then they would all have to come to Him and abandon their ungodly lives.

To teach the nations and the people in all subsequent ages that the Redeemer would be completely unlike us in our ungodliness, God caused the nation from which the Redeemer would be born to live a completely separate life. To that people He would indeed send His prophets. Within that nation He would preserve the knowledge of His name. Because His chosen people would dwell apart, they would have to realize that their faith in the Redeemer required breaking with the ungodliness and idolatry of the other nations. This would eventually teach the other nations to forsake those sins as well.

But that nation was not yet born. It would come forth out of one man. God looked around for someone to become the father of that nation, and He settled on Abram, a man of Shem's line living in Ur of the Chaldeans. As you recall, the Christ was to be born of Shem's line.

Why did God choose Abram? Was his tribe any better than the other tribes? Not at all. In fact, idols were worshiped in the house of his father Terah. We simply do not know why God turned to Abram. When God allows someone to have fellowship with Him and inherit eternal life, it is not because that person is better than others. All we can say is that it was God's will.

Terah and his family left Ur of the Chaldeans. They moved away from the land of Babylon and settled in Haran. The idea of pulling up stakes had probably been planted by God in Abram's heart while he was still living in Ur. This may well have been part of Terah's reason for moving on in search of a land for himself, a place where his descendants could multiply.

While they were in Haran, God made it clear to Abram that he was to leave even his father's house and family and land; he was to move on to another land that the Lord would show him. We do not know how God passed this message on to Abram. However it happened, Abram was completely convinced that it was *the Lord's* command.

The Lord certainly made a heavy demand on Abram when He asked him to break with everything familiar and dear to him. This demand was to teach Abram that life with the Lord is entirely different from the sinful life to which he was accustomed. The Redeemer would not share in the spirit of the peoples of Abram's time; He would be a gift from the Lord.

We no longer need to break with *everything* dear to us in order to serve the Lord and love the Redeemer. But there is no escaping the necessity of breaking with the sinfulness in our lives and hearts. Through faith in the Redeemer, Abram was able to make the break. Through that faith, we will be able to do the same.

Abram did not yet know where he was to go. The Lord may have pointed out the direction to him, but He did not name the land. Thus Abram faced an unknown future. He was simply to follow the Lord. All Abram could do was move ahead in faith, trusting the Lord in everything. We are to follow the Lord in the same way. He sometimes leads us along paths that puzzle us, but if we continue to follow Him in faith, we will eventually receive a blessing.

The promise of blessing. The Lord strengthened Abram in his obedience by giving him a promise. Abram had to trust the Lord and follow Him simply because the Lord called him. All the same, the Lord wanted to make it easier for Abram by way of a promise. Like Abram, we must follow the Lord because He calls us. Even so, we have wonderful promises to sustain us.

What did the Lord promise Abram? Abram was now alone; he had to leave everything behind. The Lord then promised him that he would not always remain alone. In fact, the Lord said He would make a great nation of Abram. In other words, a great nation would come forth from his loins. Abram might appear to be a forgotten man once he had left the others behind in Haran, but the world would one day realize that he was not a forgotten figure at all. The Lord would see to it that his name was honored.

When Abram departed, it did appear as though he amounted to nothing. Why else would he want to live in an unknown land? All of this was to change; Abram was to become a blessing for many because the Lord would always be on his side. All who chose Abram's way were in effect choosing the Lord's way and would therefore experience His blessing. By the same token, all who cursed Abram were rejecting the Lord and would be cursed by the Lord. Eventually all the nations of the earth would be blessed in Abram; he would be a blessing to all peoples.

Didn't the Lord fulfill His promise to Abram in a wonderful way? He became the father of the people of Israel, and out of that people was born the Christ. If we believe in the Lord Jesus Christ, we are actually spiritual children of Abram. In that case we belong to the great nation that was to come forth from Abram's loins.

Abram has not been forgotten, then. We still speak of him often because the Christ was born of his line. Through the Redeemer, Abram became a blessing to all peoples. The Lord always keeps His promises.

Strengthened by the promise, Abram left everything behind as he departed from Haran. The Lord gave him faith. It must have hurt Abram to break all those ties, but he obeyed the Lord's command anyway. He surrendered himself to the Lord and put his life and future in the Lord's hands. At work in his life was the Spirit of the Lord Jesus Christ, the One who surrendered to His Father in all things—even to the point of giving up His life.

The only one who left Haran with Abram and his wife Sarai was his nephew Lot, the son of Abram's brother Haran. Why Lot decided to accompany his uncle Abram we do not know. Perhaps he sensed something of the glory of following the Lord's call. Or it may be that he was attracted by the novelty of Abram's enterprise, which might have seemed an adventure too exciting to pass up. Scripture does not reveal Lot's reason for joining Abram. Later on, as we shall see, there were difficulties between Abram and Lot.

The Lord's appearance in Canaan. At the Lord's bidding, Abram moved on and came to the land of Canaan. At this time the land was inhabited by several tribes of Canaanites, an ungodly people. Even when Abram was deep within Canaanite territory, he still did not know what land the Lord was to designate as his. The Lord had promised to show him the land, but Abram surely must have wondered what form this revelation would take. When he arrived at Shechem, which is in the very heart of Canaan, the Lord appeared to him and told him that this was the land He was going to give to Abram's descendants.

We do not know how the Lord appeared to Abram. Was it perhaps in a dream or a vision? However it happened, it must have been an unusual event. Earlier the Lord had planted certain convictions in Abram's heart as to what he should do, but now he actually *heard* the Lord speak to him and *saw* something of the glory of the Lord.

The Lord had not appeared to any human being since the flood. In Canaan He now appeared to Abram. Moreover, He appeared to him again on several later occasions. The Lord wished to dwell with man again. For Abram, the Lord was not just a faraway God but someone very close to him. And this was only the beginning. Later on, the Lord appeared to Abram's descendants in glory; He even lived in their midst. The most glorious divine appearance of all was the Lord Jesus Christ.

How wonderful it is that God wants to live in intimate fellowship with man—despite his sins! God intends to overcome sin and atone for it. How glorious His appearance must have been to Abram! To us it seems even more glorious, for we know of the appearance of the Lord Jesus Christ! Through His Spirit, God now wishes to dwell in our hearts.

In gratitude Abram built an altar at Shechem. Later he built altars in other places as well. He wanted to offer sacrifices to the Lord and thereby magnify His name. The setting up of those altars was significant, for they pointed to a tie to be established someday between the Lord and the people living in the land of Canaan. Men would reverence God in that land, despite the ungodliness of the people living in Canaan in Abram's time.

Abram's marriage as a sanctuary. When Abram and Sarai left Haran, they had no children, and it looked as though they would never have any. Yet the Lord had said that Abram was to become a great people. How could that be? Was Sarai really to become a mother? Or would the Lord fulfill His promise to Abram in an entirely different way?

Abram soon received a sign, even though it came to him in the midst of his sin. While he was traveling through Canaan, a famine struck the land. He therefore decided to move on to Egypt, which was then the breadbasket of the area. On the way a disturbing thought occurred to him: What if the Egyptians noticed Sarai's beauty and desired her? Abram might then be murdered so that Sarai could be taken as a wife. Hence the two agreed that Sarai would be presented as Abram's sister. (She was in fact his half sister; such marriages were not forbidden in those days.) If the Egyptians took Sarai for Abram's sister, they would probably treat him well for her sake.

When Abram introduced Sarai as his sister, he was telling a white lie, for the fact that they were married was deliberately being concealed. We may never expect God's blessing when we do wrong.

What Abram and Sarai had feared came to pass. Some Egyptians spoke of Sarai's beauty at the court of Egypt's Pharaoh, and she was taken away to become Pharaoh's wife. Pharaoh then overwhelmed Abram with gifts but did not seek his permission to marry Sarai. Were Abram and Sarai now to be torn apart? If so, how could Sarai ever become the mother of the promised child and the promised people?

Fortunately the Lord had other plans. He afflicted Pharaoh and his house with plagues before he could make Sarai his wife. The Lord let him know that the plagues were a result of his plan to take another man's wife. Pharaoh then reproached Abram for his white lie, and Abram had nothing to say in defense of himself. Pharaoh gave Abram his wife back and ordered his soldiers to escort Abram and Sarai out of Egypt before the land was struck by more curses on Abram's account. Because the power of the Lord had been revealed to him, Pharaoh was afraid.

Thus the Lord protected Sarai in her marriage to Abram. After all, she was to be the mother of the promised child and the promised people. One day the Redeemer would be born of that people. For the sake of the Christ, the marriage of Abram and Sarai was inviolable. Everything connected with the Lord Jesus Christ is under God's protection.

8: Christ Alone

Genesis 13

Abram and Lot apparently went their separate ways because of purely earthly factors: the land could not support them both. But history (especially the history of redemption) is in God's hand. Christ reigns supreme in history and reveals Himself in it. The parting of Abram and Lot is also governed by the Christ, who disclosed something of Himself in this event.

This immediately becomes clear when Genesis 13 is read against the background of Genesis 12, which tells us about the calling of Abram. Abram was not cut off from his land and kindred and father's house just to keep him safe from the idolatry that had penetrated his father's household. The question of idolatry is incidental: the real issue was that Abram had become a symbol (type) of an entirely new community being established. Christ dwells apart from all that is called flesh. Therefore Abram also had to dwell apart.

Out of the Christ arises the new community, which is another reason why Abram received the promise of a seed. Lot represented Abram's last link with his kinsmen. It was a link that had to be severed, for the new line would be produced not out of Abram *and* Lot but out of Abram alone. That new community was rooted not in any human bond but solely in the Christ of God.

This also applied to the land. Canaan was promised to Abram—not to Abram *and* Lot. Our inheritance among the saints is secure in Christ alone. That inheritance is Canaan. When we make this affirmation, we must remember that Canaan is not heaven but the new earth under the new heaven. In the light of that future inheritance, we may already regard this earth as Canaan and the life we now live as life in the land of promise.

It was the Christ, therefore, who brought about the separation of Lot and Abram, although Lot's sin also played a role. It seems that at the time, Lot did not appreciate the significance of the promise given to Abram. He wanted to possess Canaan apart from the promise, that is, apart from the Christ. That was his chief sin. We can also point to his lack of modesty, which let him choose the better part for himself, although this sin must not be overemphasized. This lack of modesty is closely related to his failure to appreciate the promise given to Abram, which was his greatest sin.

It is not for us to ask what Lot should have done differently, how he could have shared in the promise to Abram. We are left in the dark about such matters. Nor are we to try to reason out the wondrous ways of the grace that Lot might have received if he had chosen differently. Those are the wrong questions to ask.

In the previous chapter, we saw that there was something very special about the calling of Abram. This point should also be emphasized as we tell the story of Abram and Lot. We are not asked to break with "blood and the soil," but we are indeed called to abandon our original state, in which we lived apart from the Christ, in order to possess Him alone. Once we have come that far, everything else will be returned to us and will seem even more wonderful than before. "There is no one who has left house or brothers or sisters or mother or father or children or lands, for my sake and for the gospel, who will not receive a hundred fold now in this time, houses and brothers and sisters and mothers and children and land, with persecutions, and in the age to come eternal life" (Mark 10:29-30).

Main thought: *Only in Christ do we participate in the communion of the saints and receive our place among the saints.*

The necessary separation. When Abram was sent out of Egypt, he returned to the places where the Lord had appeared to him in Canaan and where he had erected altars. Once he was back in Canaan, he remembered God's promise that out of him an entirely new people would arise, a people that would inherit the land. He and his descendants would be set apart from all other peoples, which was why he first had to leave his own country and people behind. The nation to issue from his loins would be a new people, a people different from all the others, for the Lord would dwell in the midst of that people. Abram's descendants would have to be different and separate because our life in the Lord Jesus Christ must be completely different from human life apart from Him. Abram with his family and descendants were called to symbolize the new life to be given by Christ.

But Abram was still not alone: Lot had come with him. This, too, would change, for the new nation would not come forth from the loins of both men, nor would the combined families of Abram and Lot inherit the land. The Lord Jesus Christ is the One to whom we owe everything. Since Abram was to be a type of the Lord Jesus Christ, he had to part company with Lot and live alone.

The occasion for separation soon arose. Abram and Lot were both wealthy and had many cattle. From time to time, there were conflicts between their herdsmen. Therefore they could not continue to live side by side. There was also the danger that the Canaanites and Perizzites living in the land might cause a clash between Abram and his nephew Lot. Thus Abram proposed that the two go their separate ways. Even though the separation came about in an ordinary way, the Lord's hand was behind it. The Lord wanted Abram to be utterly cut off from everything with which he had been connected.

Abram generously suggested that Lot choose first. "The whole land is before you," he said to Lot. "If you take the left hand, then I will go to the right; or if you take the right hand, I will go to the left."* How kingly Abram acted here! It was as though the whole country was already at his disposal, while in actual fact he did not yet own a single acre of it. Abram regarded Canaan as his own. He was so certain of God's promise that he already possessed the land in his mind. We may likewise lay spiritual claim to all that God has promised us, for He will surely keep His promises.

After the separation. Lot immediately agreed to the separation. From the heights he looked down over the Jordan Valley, which was then the most fertile and wonderful valley in the land of Canaan, and chose it for himself. The rest of Canaan he left for his uncle.

---

*Right is regularly the south and left the north, because one faced east in the act of "orientation."—TRANS.

Why did Lot agree so readily to a separation? Didn't he see anything of the calling and promise that were Abram's? Didn't he think of the promised seed, which would be a blessing to all peoples? And did he forget that the entire land had been promised to *Abram's* descendants? God was to be with Abram. Was that of no importance to Lot? Evidently he did not attach much weight to the promise. His concern was to use Canaan in his own way without regard to the promise and blessing given to Abram. Thus he became immodest and chose the best part for himself.

A Canaan separate from the promise made to Abram is a Canaan separate from the Christ who would issue from Abram's loins. Anyone who possesses something apart from Christ and without giving thanks to Him does not really possess it. He cannot really enjoy it because he is always looking for something better. Lot quickly picked out the best part of Canaan, but he was never able to enjoy it. This is also what happens to people who do not thank the Lord Jesus Christ for everything they have. Peace and true enjoyment are denied them as they try to promote themselves at the expense of others.

Because he already possessed so much in the promise, Abram could wait. His chief concern was that promise. He was not interested in acquiring the largest possible amount of property. All he wanted was to enjoy his possessions in God's favor. Anything he might possess apart from the Lord Jesus Christ had no value for him, which was why he could so easily hand the best part of Canaan over to Lot and choose another direction for himself.

We should not take this story to mean that a believer must put up with anything and everything. A believer can also fight for his place in this life. But he may only fight if he knows that God is with him in what he does.

For Abram, the worst thing about the separation was that he and Sarai would now have to travel through Canaan alone. The last tie with his father's house had been severed. He would now have to rely solely on the promise, that is, on the Christ. God took everything away from His servant so that he could find complete satisfaction in the promise.

Our relationship to the Lord Jesus Christ should be like Abram's. We must also be willing to leave everything behind and be satisfied in Him alone. Although we do not know what He will give us in return when we reach that goal, He must be our main concern. If Abram could continue alone, we should be able to do the same, even though everything might be working against us.

The renewal of the promise. After Lot and Abram parted company, the Lord approached Abram again and spoke to him, probably in his heart. Abram was told to survey the land around him and was promised that all the land as far as he could see would be given to him and his seed. His descendants would be as the dust of the earth. In other words, they could no more be numbered than one can number the dust of the earth.

Abram had certainly left a great deal behind, but he would receive even more in return. He had forsaken his land, but he would be given another. He had turned his back on his tribe, but he would found a great people. The Lord renewed His promise about land and descendants in order to strengthen Abram's faith after the separation. How good the Lord was to Abram!

Didn't the Lord fulfill His promise to Abram? His seed did obtain the land. The generation that came from his loins eventually became a great people. But there was much more to the Lord's intentions. In the final analysis, Abram's seed was the promised Child, the Lord Jesus Christ. In Him the promise to Abram was fulfilled in a much more glorious way. *He* became a great people, a multitude which no man can number, for all who believe in Him belong to that people. For His people, He received not just the land of Canaan but the entire earth. He rules over all of God's creatures and provides a dwelling place for His people on earth. He inspires His people to worship the Lord and will one day give them the new earth as a dwelling place. He turns the entire earth into a Canaan for His people.

Abram certainly could not foresee all that was involved in the promise, but he knew that it was a glorious promise all the same. Because it was a promise given by God, it involved much more than he would ever have guessed. At God's command Abram joyfully moved on through Canaan, even after the separation. It was *his* land, although he was not recognized as the owner of as much as a small field. In the same way, we are to regard the earth as ours, even though we do not possess very much of it yet. The earth is ours if we believe the gospel when it tells us that the Lord Jesus Christ possesses this earth right now despite the fact that His rule escapes men's eyes. From the gospel we know that He will one day show His power.

9: Blessed by the Greater

Genesis 14

Abram was a symbol (type) of the Christ, but he was not himself the Christ. He was indeed the bearer of the promise, but salvation did not reside in him. The origin of grace and the basis for Abram's hope lay apart from him and above him. Therefore it was necessary for Abram to meet his superior in Melchizedek, who then became a type of the Mediator between God and man. Even Abram had to look to someone else. In that fact lies the significance of the encounter between the two. This is apparent from the way the New Testament talks about this encounter in Hebrews 7: the lesser was blessed by the greater.

Abram was to be rich only in that blessing. In the circumstances, the blessing had a special significance for him. When he freed Lot, he played an important role in the lives of the Canaanites for the first time. And what a splendid role it was! Now they would be prepared to recognize him as one of them. Abram must have felt tempted to consider himself one of them and live in Canaan as a Canaanite. The Lord helped him overcome this temptation when Melchizedek blessed him.

That Abram sucessfully resisted the temptation is clear from the fact that he refused the booty. This action signified that he wanted no part of life among the Canaanites. He did not want to be dependent on them or be considered one of them. Therefore all the doors of Canaanite life remained closed to him. Life was to open up for him and remain open in a different way: the Christ would be a blessing to humanity. We may expect life's doors to open for us in the same way. If we want life's enjoyments only for ourselves, those doors will remain closed to us. It is love that opens them.

Chedorlaomer, the king of Elam, was in command when the four kings undertook their joint campaign. Elam was the world power of those days. Yet the name of Amraphel, the king of Shinar, is mentioned

88

first. Could this have anything to do with Shinar's past? (See Gen. 10:9-10.) Or was it perhaps because Babel, under Amraphel, would soon free itself from Elam's dominion?

In their campaign, the four kings apparently followed the customary route: from Mesopotamia northwards, then westwards to Syria, then southwards along the eastern side of the Jordan valley to northern Arabia. In the course of this campaign, they defeated all those who might be able to assist the kings of the Valley of Siddim. Then they swung around and did battle with the five kings of the Valley of Siddim after winning several more victories.

Main thought: *Abram, the lesser, is blessed by Melchizedek, the greater, to make Abram recognize that only the Lord's blessing makes man rich.*

The temptation arising from Chedorlaomer's defeat. After Lot parted company with Abram, he went southward into the Jordan Valley and pitched his tents under the smoke of the city of Sodom. Perhaps he already sought the protection of the city's walls. In any case, he came to share in the fortunes of the Sodomites because he sought close association with them.

After Lot's arrival, Sodom suffered a catastrophe. Together with four other cities, Sodom had been paying tribute to Chedorlaomer, the king of Elam, who was trying to extend his dominion over the entire known world. The five cities of the Valley of Siddim seceded from Chedorlaomer's domain and refused to pay tribute to him any longer. This powerful king then advanced on the area with his army and three other kings to subdue all the peoples who lived near the Valley of Siddim. The five kings resisted Chedorlaomer and his allies—a battle of five against four. The five were defeated, and everything in their cities was carried off, including goods and provisions, wives and children. Lot and his family were also taken captive.

Lot had left Abram voluntarily and had not really appreciated the value of the promise made to Abram. Instead he had sought the friendship of the Canaanites. Hence he was no longer protected by the promise to Abram. Yet the Lord remembered Lot—for Abram's sake and because Lot was a believer, a child of God.

Someone who had escaped when the battle was lost informed Abram of Sodom's defeat and told him what had happened to Lot. Abram at once armed the 318 men of his household and joined three heads of the Canaanites (Mamre, Aner and Eshcol) in pursuing Chedorlaomer.

One night he divided the men into various units. He then surprised the enemy forces in their own camp, routed Chedorlaomer's men, and pursued them a long way in their retreat. After gathering the booty and the wives and children, they headed home again.

Obviously the Lord had been with Abram. He and his small band of men had defeated Elam, a world power. How Abram must have thanked the Lord for delivering his enemies into his hands! He must have given thanks for Lot too, whom he had been able to save from slavery.

Yet that victory involved a temptation for Abram. He was honored among the Canaanites, who would now be happy to accept him as one of them. Would Abram therefore grow closer to the Canaanites, just as Lot had already begun to do? After all, he had won considerable prestige. He was the one blessed by the Lord; he was the bearer of the promise.

If Abram had succumbed to this temptation, he would have been putting his faith in *himself*, in the *bearer* of the promise. He would then have exalted himself and thereby become blind to his utter dependence on the Lord's blessing and favor. He would have wound up thinking he was something in himself. That's a great danger for all believers. They begin to set themselves up as no longer dependent on the Lord.

Abram was not free to join in the life of the Canaanites. Those doors had to remain closed for him if he was to receive glory of another kind, a glory that would open other doors.

The encounter with Melchizedek. Abram must have struggled with that temptation. In any event, he managed to overcome it. To lift Abram completely above the temptation, the Lord prepared a strange encounter. As Abram was returning from the battle, he came near Jerusalem. Melchizedek, the king of that city, came out to meet him, which was rather unusual. Melchizedek was king of (Jeru)salem, that is, king of peace. His name meant *king of right-*

eousness. This man feared the Lord, the God of heaven and earth, and was His priest. How amazing that in the midst of those ungodly, immoral Canaanites, the knowledge and fear of God had been preserved!

The Lord had seen to that, for this Melchizedek had a very special role to play in the midst of the Canaanites. Melchizedek went out to refresh Abram and his men by giving them bread and wine. He met Abram as a priest of the Lord and blessed him. This must have felt strange to Abram. Wasn't he the bearer of the promise, the one specially favored with God's grace? How could he now be blessed by someone else, a priest who was at the same time a Canaanite king?

Still, Abram did not hesitate. After all, salvation resided not in him but in the Lord, who blessed him. Here the Lord was sending out His priest to bless him. In faith Abram bowed his head under Melchizedek's hands and received the blessing. Abram humbled himself before God, giving no indication of pride. And this blessing removed the temptation to seek status and importance in the eyes of the Canaanites.

In Melchizedek Abram undoubtedly saw a foreshadowing of the Redeemer who would one day be born of Abram's line. Abram was nothing in himself, but he wanted to be blessed by the Redeemer, the Mediator between God and men. That Redeemer would be the true and holy Priest of God, the true King of peace and King of righteousness.

We must not make the mistake of looking inward either, for we are only sinners; we are worth nothing in ourselves. All we can do is look to the hands of the Mediator extended to us in blessing, hands in heaven that bless us. That blessing will make us rich, regardless of our earthly poverty.

Now Abram was not one bit concerned that the doors to life in Canaan were closed to him; he enjoyed a different kind of happiness—the blessing of the Lord. In faith we must desire to be rich in that blessing.

The giving of the tithe. What did Melchizedek say when he blessed Abram? "Blessed be Abram by God Most High, maker of heaven and earth; and blessed be God Most High, who has delivered your enemies into your hand!" Melchizedek first blessed Abram in the name of God, who has all things in His hands. He then proceeded to bless and praise and glorify God Most High. The Lord was pleased to be honored in the blessing of Abram.

Melchizedek had seen something wonderful, and he spoke of it in a lofty and marvelous way. God would honor Himself through the redemption of His people and the sending of the Redeemer. If this was so, redemption was a certainty. God still derives pleasure and honor from saving sinful men. How certain our salvation is when we surrender ourselves to God and pray: "Save me too!"

This was the vision of the Lord shared by Melchizedek and Abram. That they were united in faith is evident from the fact that Abram gave a tenth of all the loot to Melchizedek, considering him to be God's priest. When he gave Melchizedek this tithe, he was actually giving it to the Lord.

Abram was within his rights in disposing of the booty in this way. According to the laws governing warfare in those days, it was his to dispose of. For Abram nothing was too marvelous to give to his wonderful God. Indeed, there is nothing too wonderful to give to the Lord. If only we would recognize how wonderful God is and behold His glory in the sending of the Lord Jesus Christ for our salvation! Then we would give Him everything—our hearts, our lives, our very selves. Then it would be our desire to serve Him with all our abilities, with everything we have.

Declining the booty. The king of Sodom had joined Melchizedek in coming out to meet Abram. This king was the successor of the king who had fought against Chedorlaomer and fallen in battle. Like so many others, the previous king had not been quick enough to escape from the Valley of Siddim with all its slime (asphalt) pits. The new king now said to Abram: "Just give me the wives and the children and keep the booty for yourself. You're entitled to it, for you have taken all that loot by the sword."

Was Abram to let one of those Canaanites make him wealthy? He already had enough goods for himself and did not want to befriend the Canaanites or even have a place among them. He did not wish to be considered one of them in any way, which is what would have happened if he had lived off their goods. Therefore he swore by the Lord that he would not take even a thread or the thong of a sandal for himself.

Abram knew only too well that his refusal to keep the booty would be taken as an affront. He would always be a stranger to the Canaanites, and the doors of their life would be closed to him for good. But Abram did not want to have anything to do with the Canaanites. His wealth lay in the fact that he himself was blessed by the Lord, that one day he would be a blessing to all peoples through the Redeemer to be born of his line. In the name of the Redeemer, he was privileged to be a blessing to others, a channel for God's love. Other doors in life opened to him, and his life became good and full and rich.

If we want to be God's children and serve the Lord, we, too, will face doors closed to us. We cannot live life as unbelievers do, but that does not make us any poorer. Unbelievers do not know the true joys of life. Life's true joys remain beyond their grasp, but they are available to us if we surrender ourselves for the sake of Jesus and then become channels for God's love, channels through which He blesses others. Then we can begin to enjoy life properly, for we will be rich in this life and still be independent of others.

10: The Lord in the Covenant

Genesis 15

The Word of the Lord came to Abram "in a vision." All of Genesis 15 deals with what Abram experienced in that vision. It is true that Abram's trance-like state changed into a deep sleep that the Lord sent over him (vs. 12), a sleep like Adam's slumber during the creation of Eve, but this gives us no reason to assume that the vision came to an end at verse 5, for example.

It is likely that Abram's trance-like state with all that happened in it did not last from one night (vs. 5) to the next (vs. 12). In other words, it does not seem to have taken any longer than twelve hours. In a vision, as in a dream, we can live through several days in a short period of time.

A further argument for including all of Genesis 15 in the vision is the abrupt ending of the story: we do not hear what happened to the slain animals. The events in this chapter are no less significant because they were experienced in a vision. In the same way, John's communication with the angel and thereby the Lord (in the visions of the book of Revelation, the last book of the New Testament) is not to be called unreal.

We should not look to Genesis 15 for the origin of the covenant between the Lord and Abram. The covenant between them already existed by virtue of the calling and promise recorded in Genesis 12. In Genesis 17 we hear the Lord saying: "I will establish my covenant between me and you." In Genesis 15, the chapter with which we are now concerned, the Lord shows Abram who He is in the covenant. What it boils down to is that the Lord is everything to Abram. "I am your shield, your very great reward." The Lord does not propose to reward Abram in material terms, for He Himself is Abram's treasure, the reward he receives through faith.

That God is everything in the covenant and represents the other party to the covenant is also apparent from the fact that Abram does not follow the Lord when He passes between the pieces of the slain animals. Only the Lord passes between the pieces, which is contrary to certain customs then prevalent. In the case of covenants between people, the pieces of the slain animals represent both parties to the covenant: just as the animal pieces belong together, the parties to the covenant belong together.

A second idea behind this ceremony is that if anyone breaks the covenant, he is to be slain just as the animals were slain. In the covenant between the Lord and Abram, the pieces stand for the second party only, i.e. Abram and the people of God. The Lord wishes to pass between those pieces; He wants to dwell in the midst of His people and make Himself one with them. Thus this sign receives its ultimate fulfillment in the Christ, in whom God and man are one.

The Lord is in the midst of His people as a smoking fire pot out of which leaps a flame. Often He is also in their midst in darkness and terror, as a purifying fire. As the Lord indicates in Genesis 15, this sign is first fulfilled in the oppression of Israel in Egypt. Its ultimate fulfillment is the terrible agony of the Christ and the purification of all God's people. Through that cleansing, He is our light, our salvation.

We must bear in mind that in the covenant, God is everything to His people. That's why we are told that Abram believed the Lord, and that the Lord regarded this belief as righteousness. Neither in these words nor anywhere else in Genesis 15 do we find any trace of the Arminian idea of justification *on account of* faith, the idea that faith, as a meritorious act on man's part, is regarded by God as a substitute for the fulfillment of the law.

In the covenant, the Lord gives man everything—including faith. In Romans 4:1-5, where these words from Genesis are interpreted by Paul, faith is balanced against works. Paul shows that there is no room for any thought of reward or praise. It was by *faith* that Abram entered into fellowship with the Lord. That fellowship was considered a sign of his righteousness. The Lord was Abram's righteousness. That justifying communion between the Lord and Abram was possible because of what Christ would do one day. In His own power, He would struggle for the fellowship of God's favor and atone for our sins.

This living out of faith, this abiding in things not seen, is fully manifest in Abram, who clings to the promise despite all appearance and opposition. That's why he is called the father of believers, the father of the faithful.

Main thought: *In the covenant, the Lord reveals Himself as the One in whom all promises are fulfilled.*

The promise of the seed. After his alliance with certain Canaanites in the rescue of Lot and his rejection of further contact with their way of life, Abram was alone again. The Canaanites had their land and houses and expanded greatly, but Abram remained childless. He was a stranger in Canaan and did not own as much as a single small field. No wonder his faith was sorely tried and at times grew weak.

One day the Lord sent Abram a vision. Instead of seeing and hearing what was around him, he had some extraordinary sensations. This vision was not a dream, for he was not asleep, but it did contain some dreamlike images. In the vision the Lord said to him: "Don't be afraid, Abram. Don't worry about being a stranger in this land, for I am a shield for you. I am your security in this land, your great reward. I am your treasure and your possession, for I give you My love completely."

Abram was overjoyed and felt privileged to receive this revelation. What bliss! But for Abram, this awareness was not everything. He was not concerned exclusively with his personal happiness: he still wondered what to make of those promises the Lord had given him. The Lord had told him that he would have many descendants, that he would become the father of a great people that would carry the banner of the knowledge of the Lord into the world. He had been promised that those descendants would serve the Lord and possess the land of Canaan.

Abram therefore asked: "Lord, how can You make me rich if I remain childless? Surely I am not the only one for whom the promise is intended. When I die, how will Your promises be fulfilled? My servant, who is in charge of my household, is from Damascus and is not of my kin. He will inherit everything I possess. Then my name will be forgotten." This was not a manifestation of any lack of faith on Abram's part. Abram was struggling with the Word of God, for the Lord's ways were hidden from him. He begged the Lord to reveal Himself more fully.

The Lord gave him a sign in response. The Lord does not respond with a sign when we ask Him something out of a lack of faith. But it's different when we pray: "Lord, I believe; help my unbelief." The Lord's answer was: "Your heir will not be that man from Damascus but your own son, who is yet to be born."

Apparently this vision came to Abram during the night, for

the Lord brought him outside his tent and told him to look up at the stars in the heavens. His seed would be as innumerable as those stars! There was his sign—up in the starry heavens. From now on he could look up at those stars every evening to strengthen his faith.

Did Abram in fact have a multitude of descendants? Yes, he did. Remember that we are not to consider the Jewish people his only descendants. Out of the midst of that people, the Lord Jesus Christ was born. By faith we, too, are spiritual children of the Lord Jesus and therefore descendants of Abram. All believers are reckoned among Abram's children.

However, those descendants were far in the future. There stood Abram, still completely alone, without a single child. What was he now to say to the Lord? Was he to complain that the promise could not possibly be fulfilled? Abram believed in the Lord. What the Lord says is the truth; He can be relied on. Therefore Abram placed himself in the Lord's hands in faith and rested in Him. He then enjoyed wonderful communion with the Lord, a communion in which the Lord forgave him all his sins, looked upon him as His child, and told him of His favor and love.

How could the Lord look upon Abram in love and forgive all his sins? Only because the Lord Jesus would one day put Himself in the place of all of His own and atone for their sins. Do we, too, believe the Word of the Lord unconditionally? If we do, He will also grant us His forgiving grace for Christ's sake.

The way to the promised land. In that wonderful communion, the Lord also repeated the promise about the land. "I brought you out of the land where you used to live in order to give you this land. I do not intend to leave you in this world completely at a loss as to what to do." Once more we see how Abram had to struggle in faith. Now he asked for a sign of this promise.

Here again Abram's request for a sign did not result from unbelief. The Lord gave Abram what he longed for—the most wonderful sign possible. In the ancient Near East, it was customary for two people who had made a covenant with each other to cut animals into two halves and then pass between the halves together. This would signify that the two parties to the covenant belonged together just as the two pieces belonged together.

The Lord commanded Abram to cut up a heifer, a she-goat and a ram. In each case, he was to use a three-year-old animal. The halves of the slain animals were to be laid against each other. He was also to kill a turtledove and a young pigeon.

Abram did what the Lord commanded and then waited to see what else the Lord would say and do. Meanwhile, it had become day in Abram's vision, and he saw birds of prey coming down to devour the pieces of flesh. He drove them away, for to him those signs of God's covenant were sacred. He did not belittle those signs by saying that they were only dead animals. Instead he honored them as signs of God's covenant.

We still have signs of God's covenant today, i.e. baptism and the Lord's supper. Although some people hold these signs in contempt, we are to make use of them and consider them sacred. The birds of prey descending on the pieces of flesh were enemies threatening not only the signs but also the covenant itself and the existence of Abram's posterity as the people of God.

In that vision, Abram lived through a whole day in which he waited for the Lord to come. The Lord deliberately made him wait, to test his faith and his patience. How often the Lord makes us wait too! Let us continue hoping and waiting for Him, for He will not let us down.

Towards evening, the Lord caused Abram's trance-like state to become a deep sleep. Terror and great darkness then came over him. Finally the Lord appeared to him. In that terror and darkness, the Lord already intimated something of what He wanted to say to Abram. He then proceeded to tell him how his descendants would come into possession of the land of Canaan. It would not become theirs until they had passed through great terror and oppression. His people would be oppressed in a strange land for 400 years. Only after this period of oppression could they claim their inheritance.

Wasn't this Word fulfilled in the history of the Jewish people? Abram's descendants were oppressed in Egypt for approximately 400 years. Once this period had passed, the Lord brought them to Canaan.

But it was not only in the history of the Jews that the Word of God was fulfilled literally. We must never forget that the real seed of Abram is the Lord Jesus Christ, and that such passages refer to Him first and foremost. In the death of Christ, this Word received its ultimate fulfillment. Jesus suffered through great darkness and terrible agony on the cross in order to atone for our sins and thereby obtain heaven and earth for us. Even now, believers frequently travel the same route to gain possession of all things with Christ.

The Lord passing between the pieces. In the vision it now became night for Abram. What was to make this covenant between the Lord and Abram official? Should the two parties to the covenant pass between the halves of the slain animals together? If they did, wouldn't they then be equal partners?

Would the covenant last because of the Lord's faithfulness— or Abram's? Did the stability and continuation of the covenant rest on Abram's faithfulness? Could Abram be faithful if the Lord did not make him faithful? Would the covenant be able to endure if the Lord did not ensure Abram's faithfulness? Obviously, only the Lord could pass between the pieces. Thereby He would signify His eternal bond with Abram and his seed.

That's exactly what Abram saw happen. Before his eyes, a smoking fire pot passed between the halves of flesh and a flame shot up out of the smoke. Why did the Lord reveal Himself in such a sign? Because He is often in the midst of His people as a bright light in the midst of darkness and mysteries.

How little the Lord's people understand of His ways! So often it seems as though He is against them in everything. Yet in His zeal He is really in their midst as a consuming fire that cleanses and purifies them. In this way He is their light and their salvation.

God's people are indeed purified by Him. He is in their midst and protects them in the covenant, fulfilling all the covenant promises He has given them. His people are frequently weak and unfaithful, but the covenant does not depend on their faithfulness.

When the Lord passed between the pieces of flesh, He became responsible for the other party to the covenant. If we belong to that other party (i.e. God's people), He will also hold on to us and protect us in the covenant by making us faithful.

If only we would believe that wholeheartedly and entrust ourselves to the Lord! He will take care of heaven and earth together, making it possible for us to serve Him forever.

11: God Hears

Genesis 16

The great danger we face as we tell the story recorded in Genesis 16 is the temptation to push the history of Abram aside and talk about Ishmael's birth and Hagar's flight as events in which Abram's role is secondary. We then put the emphasis on the mercy of God, who took care of Hagar as one of His children. But we are not told in Scripture that Hagar was in fact a child of the Lord. Whether she was is not of primary importance in this context, for God took care of Hagar not because she was Hagar but because she belonged to Abram's family, because she was part of the covenant circle.

It is significant that the figure who appears to Hagar after she flees from Abram's household is the Angel of *the Lord*, the God of the covenant. This alerts us to the fact that the story of Hagar and Ishmael is a continuation of the history of Abram. There is no separate history of Hagar or Ishmael in Scripture.

When God appeared to Hagar and took up her cause, it was not for her own sake but for Abram's. He wanted to correct the injustice in Abram's tent, where Hagar had suffered oppression.

Hagar was originally a slave, but she was elevated to the status of Abram's wife—although her elevation was only intended to make Sarai more secure. But once Hagar conceived a child, she sinned by wanting to keep the child for her own. She wanted the child for herself and refused to regard it as Sarai's child or even as Abram's, as her subsequent flight shows. Her flight had the effect of removing the child from the circle of the covenant and the promise.

Once she had conceived and shown her contempt for her mistress, she was again reduced to the status of a slave. Abram said to Sarai: "Behold, your maid is in your power." That was an injustice. In this entire situation, Hagar was offended as wife and mother. The right course of action could no longer be found once God's ordinance had been violated. Therefore life within Abram's tent, within the covenant circle, took a turn for the worse.

We must not leave the children with the impression that all of this was in keeping with the requirements of the covenant. God showed it was not when He took up Hagar's cause against Abram for the sake of the covenant, that is, for Abram's sake and for His own sake. God's motive comes to expression in the name of Hagar's son—Ishmael. By ordering her to give the child this name, God was indicating that He hears the oppression of life within the covenant circle.

Explaining the name *Lahai Roi* (vs. 14) is not easy, just as it is far from easy to explain why Hagar asked: "Have I even here seen after him who sees me?" Was Hagar astonished that God looked after her, or that she had survived an encounter with God? Either way, her question is an expression of astonishment coming from a person not accustomed to walking with the Lord.

The God of the covenant appeared to her so that she would not break her descendants' link with the covenant. Her astonishment shows how strongly that calling gripped her. The promise about her son and his descendants *could* still be fulfilled within the framework of God's redemptive purposes. The promise that Ishmael would be a "wild ass of a man," that is, a lover of freedom, could have a redemptive meaning: it could turn out that the freedom he loved would be a freedom within the Christ. Ishmael's opposition to everyone *could* yet turn out to be a struggle for Christ's sake. Still, the words of promise about Ishmael already say something about his attitudes in this life. They warn us that his chief concern would be self-preservation, that he would cut himself loose from the ties of God's grace. Hagar had produced a son for bondage.

Main thought: *God hears the oppression of life within the covenant circle.*

Relationships damaged by unbelief. Apparently Abram and Sarai loved each other deeply. In those days it was quite common for a man to have more than one wife, and Abram certainly had a good reason to take a second wife. Hadn't the Lord said that Abram was to have a child who would inherit the promise? But the Lord had not yet said anything about Sarai being the mother of that child. Abram could have thought, "Maybe the Lord wants me to have a child by another woman." Yet it seems that Abram had not yet considered this possibility. He still expected Sarai to be the mother of his promised child.

As Abram and Sarai grew older, their hopes of Sarai becoming a mother dwindled. Eventually Sarai herself suggested to Abram that he take another wife. She specified that it would have to be Hagar, the Egyptian slave, who was her own property. If Hagar bore him a child, she could consider the child her own.

Sarai longed to see the promise fulfilled. In those days, it was considered shameful to be childless. Sarai hoped her proposal might remove some of her shame. Abram agreed to the plan.

Sarai and Abram had worked out their problem together. But this was purely human planning on their part: the Lord was not given a say. Yet Abram enjoyed a special relationship with the Lord. In such an important matter as the birth of the promised child, he should certainly have waited for a sign from the Lord.

Abram and Sarai had clearly become impatient, and impatience in awaiting the fulfillment of the Lord's promise amounts to unbelief. How could they even suspect that the Lord might forget His promise? Didn't they know that He would surely see to it that the promise was fulfilled? It quickly became obvious that Abram and Sarai were on the wrong track, for their plan brought them all kinds of misery.

After Hagar became Abram's wife and conceived a child by him, she began to look on Sarai with contempt. Because she was about to become a mother, the former slave now regarded herself as Sarai's superior and despised her mistress. Nor did she want her child to be considered Sarai's; she wanted the child for herself! Sarai complained to Abram and even accused him of doing her an injustice. She became unreasonable in her jealousy and demanded that Abram turn the clock back and put Hagar in her place again. This Abram tried to do. Although Hagar had become his wife, he placed her under Sarai's complete command as her slave. Sarai then humiliated Hagar.

This turn of events did nothing to straighten matters out. First Hagar was made Abram's wife, and then she was reduced to the humiliating position of a slave! That simply would not do. Hagar was partly to blame, of course, but we must not overlook the fact that Abram and Sarai had treated her as they pleased, which is not the way to deal with any human being.

And all of this happened within Abram's tent, i.e. within the covenant circle. That the Lord could not tolerate. Within the circle of His covenant, He cannot permit injustice. In their confusion, Abram and Sarai already felt the consequences of their initial wrongdoing, but things were to get even worse, for one wicked deed leads to another and perpetuates the evil.

Hagar's flight. Hagar did not put up with the humiliation. She fled and set out for Egypt, the country of her birth. Clearly she did not want her coming child to be considered Sarai's. It was also apparent that she attached no importance to the fact that it would be Abram's child. She did not appreciate the promise Abram had received or realize what the Lord's covenant with Abram meant for herself and her baby. She only wanted the child for herself—not for Abram or for the God of Abram.

What sorrow this must have caused Abram and Sarai! It did not matter so much that a slave had fled: in a strange way, Hagar had become a member of their family. Her flight had torn Abram's family apart. And what would become of her child once it was born? After all, it was Abram's child too. Would it be lost in the world?

Because of their false start, Abram and Sarai were in complete confusion. What would the Lord do? Could He permit such things to go on? The Lord wanted to be merciful to Abram and Sarai in their confusion, but He also had to think of His honor and His covenant with Abram. Hagar had not only removed *herself* from the covenant circle but had also removed a child that was to be born within that circle. The Lord does not quickly let go of anything He claims as His own. Hagar herself belonged to that covenant family living with the Lord, as did the child to be born. For the sake of Abram, with whom He had entered into a covenant, He did not want to forsake Hagar and the child. Ultimately He was interested in Hagar and her child for the sake of Christ, of whom Abram was to be a forefather and type. It was for Christ's sake that God had made the covenant with Abram. And for Christ's sake, the Lord did not want to forsake Abram or anything belonging to him.

The Lord still feels the same way today. Anything bound up

with the Lord Jesus Christ will never be forsaken. If someone belongs to Christ, the Lord will search for him for a long, long time and only give up when that person has completely hardened himself against the Lord.

Thus the Lord went out looking for Hagar. The Angel of the Lord appeared to her beside a spring on the way to Egypt. This figure was the Lord Jesus Christ, who at that time had not yet come to earth but often appeared to men in human form. He said to her: "Hagar, slave of Sarai, where have you come from and where are you going?" The Lord wanted her to understand exactly what she was doing. She was fleeing from the promise of the Lord and from the Lord Himself so that she could be independent and have her child all to herself. Was she fully aware of what she was saying when she answered, "I am fleeing from my mistress Sarai"?

The Lord then told her that she was to return and submit to her mistress. How could the Lord give her such an order after the injustice she had suffered? Would she have to suffer that injustice all over again? She certainly would. It is better to put up with injustice if it means retaining a link with the promise and the Lord. That link should really be her main concern; she should be willing to sacrifice everything for it. She would also have to bury her pride, which made her want the child only for herself. Instead she should desire the child for the Lord. The Lord would comfort her in times of injustice, but first she would have to submit for the Lord's sake. We, too, may have to suffer injustice now and then, but what we suffer must never lead us to cut our ties with the Lord by turning our backs on His people and Church.

Hagar's blessing. To comfort her because of the injustice she had suffered, the Angel of the Lord told Hagar something about the future. She was to have a son and was to call him *Ishmael*, a name that means *God hears*. That name would show that God had not overlooked Hagar's oppression in Abram's tent, and that He would be with her. That name was also intended to put Abram to shame, for God does not permit the sins of His children to go unpunished. He simply cannot stand the sight of injustice within the covenant circle. Injustice there offends Him more than anywhere else, for injustice has no place within the design of His covenant. Within the covenant circle, man's life must be free to flourish. Thus the name *Ishmael* was an indictment of Abram and Sarai.

The Angel of the Lord also told Hagar that her son would become a very great people, and that he would be a "wild ass of a man," i.e. a man with an unquenchable desire for freedom. He would live in conflict with everyone around him, and the hands of all his neighbors would be raised against him. He would pitch his tent near his kinsmen and would be a constant threat to all the nations related to the nation descended from him.

For Hagar and her child, these words contained a wonderful blessing. They spoke of power and freedom and courage. But how would that blessing be used? Would that freedom be true freedom, i.e. freedom from sin for Christ's sake? Would the conflict be a struggle for the Christ? Or would Ishmael fight against the Christ and the gospel?

Unfortunately, he pitted his strength against the Christ. Out of Ishmael were born the freedom lovers of Arabia, the land where Islam arose. The physical and spiritual posterity of Ishmael has lived in continual conflict with the people of God and the Lord Jesus Christ. Thus the blessing given to that people turned into a curse. It is entirely possible for *us* to change God's blessing into a curse as well—by not accepting that blessing in faith as God's gift but instead wanting to use it against God.

Hagar's return. The appearance of the Angel of the Lord and the words He spoke made a deep impression on Hagar. She seemed to come to her senses and finally realize that she was a stranger to the Lord, who had so richly revealed Himself to Abram. She also seemed to realize how glorious it is to walk with the Lord within a covenant relationship. She expressed amazement that the Lord had looked after her. Would the Lord be willing to extend His grace to her too?

With this in mind, she returned to Abram's tent and submitted to Sarai. There the child was born, and Abram obediently named him Ishmael, bowing under the shame that the name implied for him. Thus the Lord brought about something good for Abram and Sarai and even Hagar by giving them a son.

But had Hagar really returned? Had her heart found the Lord, the God of Abram? Could it be said that she considered the promise given to Abram the most important thing in her life? We do not know for sure. What we do know is that her child later manifested the same proud nature his mother had earlier displayed, and that he also showed contempt for the promise given to Abram.

God does indeed call us to enjoy fellowship with Him, to walk with Him and accept the promise, but do we actually accept the promise in faith? Do we give that walk with the Lord the highest priority in our lives?

12: God the Almighty

When the Lord revealed Himself to Abram in Genesis 17 as God the Almighty, He was pointing to His omnipotence not as the Creator but as the One who turns the covenant promises into reality. What He was really telling Abram in verse 2 is: "I will *give* My covenant." In other words, God would fulfill the covenant promise and make it real. This promise was to be fulfilled through a miracle.

For the first time, God revealed that *Sarai* would be the mother of the promised seed, even though Abram and Sarai had both grown old. In a revelation of His omnipotent grace, He would make the promise come true in a miraculous way.

Balanced against this promise on God's part was a demand made on Abram: "Walk before My face and be blameless." Abram was told that he must keep his conscience clear before God and hide nothing from Him. This was a very simple demand. The same miracle must take place in the lives of all believers—the miracle of dying and rising from the dead. But it can only happen if we lead blameless lives and listen to His Word. Then God Himself makes the miracle occur.

After all, the miracle that happened in Abram's life typifies the miracle of the birth and death and resurrection of the Christ. It further typifies the miracle that happens to all believers, namely, their death for the sake of life. The miracle through which the covenant is realized is prominent in the story of the promise of Isaac's birth.

That miracle is depicted and sealed by circumcision, which symbolizes the removal of the physical means of sin according to the flesh. In that act, our old nature and life is shown to be sinful—especially in its origin. On the other hand, we are shown that life and its origin are also sanctified in the covenant.

107

It makes no difference whether circumcision already existed among
the peoples of the ancient Near East and was taken over by the Lord as
the sign of His covenant. It may well be that circumcision spread from
Abraham and his descendants to the other nations.

That even the slaves purchased by Abraham and the slaves born in
his house were to be circumcised indicates that natural ancestry is not the
only factor determining one's position in relation to the covenant. God's
people will come from the East and from the West. Yet we should not
regard circumcision as completely parallel to baptism in our time. In
Abraham's day, the covenant was limited to the family of the patriarchs
and later to the people of Israel. That's why the neglect of circumcision
was punished by banishment. In our time, the covenant is no longer tied
to those boundaries, although it continues to follow the line of the
generations. To be banished from God's people now means expulsion
from the congregation (excommunication).

Abraham was now told that he would become the father of many
nations. This promise was not a reference to the nations that would come
forth from his loins through Ishmael, the sons of Keturah, and later
Esau. God was promising that He would be the God of Abraham's
"seed." When He spoke of all those nations to be fathered by Abraham,
He must have meant Israel as well as the "remnant" of Israel, i.e. all
who would become believers in the Christ. Abraham's seed would possess
the earthly Canaan, and the believers would go on to take possession of
the spiritual Canaan. This spiritual Canaan, of course, is not heaven but
dominion over the earth. In Romans 4:13 we read that Abraham and his
descendants (seed) will inherit the world.

Main thought: *As the covenant of grace unfolds, God reveals
Himself as the Almighty.*

The father of many. For a long time the Lord did not reveal
Himself to Abram. For thirteen long years, Abram had to live by
the revelation that God had given earlier. During those years he
watched his son Ishmael growing up. How often Abram must have
wondered just how the Lord would fulfill His promise! How
would Abram become a great, God-fearing nation that kept the
Lord's covenant? Would that nation be born out of his son Ishmael,
whose mother was an Egyptian slave? And how would God make
room for that people in the midst of all the idolatrous nations?

Then the Lord appeared to Abram again, although we do not
know in what form. The very first words He spoke must have

answered the questions in Abram's heart: "I am God Almighty." The Lord was telling Abram: "There is nothing I cannot do to make the promise of My covenant a reality. I will show you that I am the Almighty. Events will take a most mysterious turn. Just remain upright before Me and do not hide your heart from Me or withdraw it from Me. If you continue upright before Me, you shall know Me in My ways and see My omnipotence. I will realize My covenant with you completely by making you a great nation."

Abram fell on his face before the Lord and worshiped Him. To believe is to worship the Lord in the greatness of His work and power and glory. If we have faith in the Lord today, we will believe in His power to redeem. His power and wisdom are beyond human understanding. Therefore belief *always* involves worship.

Once Abram had demonstrated his faith, the Lord showed him how He had always viewed him and went on to reveal His plans for him. He changed his name to *Abraham*, which means *father of many*. From the very beginning, then, the Lord had planned to make Abram the father of many nations. And now Abram was allowed to bear the name *Abraham* and know the purpose of his life. This privilege was gained through his fellowship with the Lord.

The Lord is willing to treat us the same way. If we know the Lord and walk with Him, we, too, may come to know ourselves and understand the purpose of our existence.

Moreover, that name was also a confirmation of Abraham's faith. He felt that if the Lord had always regarded him as the father of many and now gave him a new name, he would most assuredly become the father of a multitude of nations.

The Lord was explicit about Abraham's future. Not only did He repeat the promise that nations and kings would come forth from Abraham, He also declared that He wished to be the God of Abraham's seed. God would remain faithful to that seed, which would have the privilege of serving Him. Eventually the Lord would give that seed the promised land.

The Lord did remain faithful to the people of Israel, regardless of their stubborness. The Christ was ultimately born of that people. Through Him there are millions of people privileged to believe in God. All of them are spiritual children of Abraham.

Now we can see how that promise to Abraham has been

fulfilled, for the Lord gave the land of Canaan to the people of Israel. Moreover, He has given the spiritual children of Abraham (the Lord Jesus Christ and all who belong to Him) not just one country but the whole world. It may not look that way right now, for the kings of this earth are not believers. All the same, the Lord Jesus Christ, *the* Son of Abraham, is already King over all things. Therefore the believers cannot be overcome by any power in the world. One day they will rule with the Christ.

The Lord is certainly fulfilling His promise given to Abraham. This shows us that God is indeed the Almighty, the One who keeps His Word of omnipotent grace and gives His people everything He has promised them.

The sign of the covenant. People who have made a covenant often select something as a sign of their union and commitment. If a man and a woman enter a marriage covenant, for example, they exchange wedding rings. Those rings are signs by which they pledge their fidelity to each other and are assured of each other's faithfulness. The members of an association or a labor union, likewise, might all wear the same pin on their lapels as a sign of unity.

In the same way, the Lord wanted some sign of the covenant He had made with Abraham and his descendants, a sign to be borne by all men belonging to that covenant. The sign He selected was circumcision, which involved cutting some skin away from the penis. All male babies had to be circumcised on the eighth day after birth. That was the rule not only for Abraham and his children but also for Abraham's slaves and *their* children. Those slaves, then, were regarded as belonging to Abraham's family. God wanted the entire family to live with Him in the covenant. If any member of God's chosen family or later His chosen people (i.e. Israel) did not bear the sign, it would be assumed that he rejected the Lord's covenant. Therefore he would have to be exiled from the people.

The Lord still wants people to live with Him in the covenant and receive the sign of His covenant. In our time He uses a different sign—baptism. Today, those who do not wish to live with the Lord in His covenant are not longer put to death, as in Abraham's day. Instead they are expelled from the fellowship of the church. We call this process *excommunication*. What will the Lord do with those who have rejected His covenant?

Circumcision was an operation on the body. It symbolized the sinfulness and unholiness of the life we receive at birth. That life must die and be replaced by a different life, a holy life that God plants within us. Through circumcision, God expressed His intention of destroying that old, sinful life in us and replacing it with a different life, a new and holy life. The Lord is saying precisely the same thing to us today through baptism.

Think of the Lord's opening words to Abraham in Genesis 17: "I am God Almighty." God can cause that new life to enter us, for He is the Almighty. The power of His grace knows no limits. Do you believe that? If so, He will plant that new life in you too. He can do whatever He wants—and He will.

Life from the dead. God continued to talk with Abraham, telling him more about His reasons for appearing to him at this time: "From now on you are no longer to call your wife Sarai. Call her *Sarah* instead, which means *princess* or *queen,* for she will be the mother of nations and kings."

Abraham could hardly believe his ears! Sarai a mother? After she had already grown so old? By all human calculations that was completely impossible, yet the Lord had delared that it would happen. And Abraham had learned long ago to take the Lord at His Word. Therefore He fell upon his face before the Lord, worshiping Him in faith and accepting this latest Word of the Lord despite the fact that he could not understand how that promise could ever be fulfilled. Because the promise was so contrary to any human expectations, he burst out laughing. His laughter did not indicate disbelief but the very opposite. The Lord's promise, which he did not doubt for a moment, contrasted so sharply with the normal course of events that he had to laugh. He and his wife were so old that they were practically dead. It seemed impossible that they should have a child.

Indeed, the way the Lord fulfilled His promise did run counter to all human expectations. A child would be born to two old people. This birth of life out of death was an utter miracle, just as God's redemption of the world is a miracle. The birth of the Lord

Jesus Christ, His suffering and death, His resurrection from the dead, and God's turning to the world in grace for the sake of Christ is one great miracle.

That work of redemption runs counter to all human expectations. The Lord uses it to show that He is indeed God the Almighty. Do we believe in that miracle God chose to perform in order to redeem the world? If so, God will also perform the miracle of turning our death into life. The life we received at birth is death before God, for we do not want God's love. But He plants another life within us, a life that drives us to seek Him.

Later on, after the child was born, Abraham must have laughed often. His laughter was an expression of the rapture and ecstasy brought on not only by the child to be born but also by the faithfulness and favor and power of God in fulfilling the promise and redeeming the world. If we believe, we, too, can laugh in ecstasy over the Lord Jesus Christ and the redemption we receive through Him.

When Abraham worshiped the Lord, he was also thinking of his son Ishmael, who was then thirteen years old. Now Abraham finally saw the full value of God's redemption and realized all the more clearly the impatience he and Sarah had manifested. Because of that unbelieving impatience, he had taken Hagar as his wife. Ishmael was the product of that union. Was that boy to carrry the curse of his father's disbelief? And would he now have to live completely in the shadow? Therefore Abraham prayed: "O that Ishmael might live in thy sight!" How eager Abraham was to have Ishmael live in the light of God's presence!

The Lord then repeated His promise that Sarah would still have a child and commanded Abraham to name that child Isaac, which means *laughter*. That name would show how Abraham had laughed about the miracle that God was to perform, just as we laugh in delight as we think of God's miracles.

The Lord also heard Abraham's petition on Ishmael's behalf. God would not keep His blessing from Ishmael. He was to be the father of twelve princes and would become a great nation. But Ishmael would not have as great a future as Isaac. The Lord declared that He would establish His covenant with Isaac, which meant that Isaac—and not Ishmael—would be the father of the Redeemer, in whom the covenant is sure. Ishmael would be allowed to live in the light of the coming Redeemer. The Lord promised to bless Ishmael as long as he cherished his bond with the Lord and accepted Isaac as the bearer of the promise.

This brought Abraham's encounter with the Lord to an end. The Lord went away, and Abraham did not see Him any more.

Walking in obedience before God's face. The Lord had told Abraham that He was God the Almighty, the One who would fulfill the promise by His miraculous power. The only thing the Lord had asked of Abraham was that he be upright and walk before His face in childlike obedience. Abraham quickly demonstrated his desire to obey this command: the very same day, he and all the males in his household were circumcised. Thus Abraham and his son Ishmael underwent this rite together—when Abraham was 99 years old and Ishmael thirteen.

If we believe that the Lord is the Almighty, the One who fulfills His promise, we respond to Him as children. Talking back is then out of the question. Nor do we delay obeying His commands; we obey at once. If we still have a lot of objections, it will be clear that we have not yet gained the faith to see the omnipotent grace of God through which we are redeemed.

13: God's Confidant

Genesis 18

The three sections of Genesis 18 (i.e. the incident of the Angel of the Lord eating in front of Abraham's tent, the Lord's telling Abraham what He planned to do about Sodom's wickedness, and the subsequent intercession of Abraham) all illustrate God's acceptance of Abraham as His confidant. Abraham now becomes God's fellow worker. Genesis 18 shows us a man living in intimate communion with God in the covenant.

In large, clear letters, the appearance of the three angels in Abraham's tent (one of them the Angel of the Lord) and the eating of Abraham's food by the Angel of the Lord spells out the miracle of the communion between God and men. This miracle is shown even more fully in the coming of the Christ in Bethlehem: the Son of God stuck His feet under the tables of men.

When Abraham saw the three men approaching, he recognized the Lord immediately. Of course the Lord had already appeared to him many times. His words "Lord, if I have found favor in your sight" point to more than Eastern hospitality. Moreover, Abraham remained standing as he served at the table of his Lord.

One purpose of the Lord's appearance was to encourage Sarah's belief, so that in faith she could receive the strength to bear the child. The Lord accomplished this by chastening her for her unbelief. Doubt and unbelief cannot be overcome by logical reasoning and proofs. The only treatment for doubt is punishment. Through faith, Sarah would become a fellow worker in fulfilling God's counsel. Here, too, we are shown what covenant fellowship means.

The Lord let Abraham know what He was going to do since Abraham was to found a great nation and bring blessing on all the nations of the earth. Abraham was the bearer of the promise, and in him the victory of the Kingdom of God would be assured. God therefore made him His fellow worker: "I have chosen him, that he may charge his children and

114

his household after him to keep the way of the LORD by doing righteousness and justice; so that the LORD may bring to Abraham what he
has promised him."

Abraham was God's co-worker particularly in his intercession for
Sodom. We are never closer to the God of the covenant than in prayer,
for when we pray, He makes us participants in His governing of the world.
This applies to Abraham's prayer too, despite the fact that Sodom was
destroyed since the conditions were not right for preserving it. Still,
through Abraham, the righteousness of God was proclaimed over the
whole world. Through Abraham's prayer of intercession, the righteousness of God also prevailed after his death, and thereby the promise
was fulfilled.

Balanced against Abraham's assertion that God would not slay the
righteous together with the wicked stands the judgment of Ecclesiastes
that one and the same fate awaits the righteous and the ungodly alike
(Eccl. 2:14 and 8:14). Ecclesiastes sketches life as it appears apart from
faith in the Christ. In fact, if we think in exclusively human terms and
leave God out of the picture, we cannot help but conclude that the
righteous and the ungodly travel the same road on earth. The difference
is that the ungodly perish, filled by their vanity, while the life of the
believer is not lived in vain. Believers are here to be a blessing, to mark
out a trail to the future of the Kingdom of God. The ultimate issue is not
what happens to the believers but how God's cause is furthered in and
through them. Shall not the Judge of all the earth do right in His own
cause? God could not let the believers in Sodom perish without a trace,
for then the lives they had lived would be in vain.

As we survey Genesis 18, we are struck by how the Lord bestowed
on Abraham His most intimate fellowship by eating his food. The Lord
enjoyed Abraham's faith and love, just as He is pleased to enjoy our
faith and love. This communion between God and Abraham led Abraham
to pray. In prayer Abraham was God's confidant. At the same time he
looked up to the Lord and respected Him greatly. This is apparent from
his words: "Behold, I have taken upon myself to speak to the Lord, I
who am but dust and ashes." He was also aware of the motive for God's
actions: "Shall not the Judge of all the earth do right?"

Main thought: *The Lord makes Abraham His confidant.*

Intimate communion. One day when Abraham was sitting at
the door of his tent, he looked up and saw three men standing in
front of him. At once he realized that they were not ordinary people
but angels appearing in human form. One of the three was not like

the other two. Abraham recognized Him immediately: it was the Lord, who by this time had already appeared to him often. Therefore Abraham stood up, went to meet the three men, bowed down to the earth, and asked whether they would like to rest and have some food in his tent.

How did Abraham summon the courage to ask the Son of God, who appeared to him there in human form, to come into his tent? The holy God in the abode of a sinful man! Still, Abraham could not hold himself back. He was eager to serve the Lord and show Him his love after receiving so much favor from the Lord.

The Lord agreed and sat down with the two angels in front of Abraham's tent. Abraham quickly told Sarah to bake some cakes and ordered his servants to prepare the best calf for the meal. He himself saw to it that everything was served with butter and milk and remained standing by the table to serve his Lord.

I hope you can form a vivid picture of this scene. There was the Lord, the God of heaven and earth, eating at the table of His servant. He remained at that table for only a few moments. Not long afterward, He left the earth again. Much later, however, the Son of God actually became flesh and dwelt among men, eating and drinking with them. What a great miracle that was! How close God then came to men! Since then He has ascended into heaven as a man and has sent us His Spirit to dwell in our hearts. By His Spirit He is very close to us still and participates in our life. Do we believe that the Lord wants to be just as intimate with us as He was with Abraham when He sat down to eat in front of his tent?

Why did the Lord sit down at Abraham's table? Not just to grant Abraham His favor but also to receive the love and faith of His servant in return. In the same way He wants to enjoy our love today. The Lord longs for that. When we see what great favor the Lord is willing to bestow on us, we gladly give Him our love.

Sarah brought to faith. While the three men were eating, they asked about Sarah, for they had come mainly on her account. However strange the promise may have seemed to him, Abraham really believed that he and his wife would have a son in their old age. Unfortunately Sarah had not yet come that far. Yet she, too, would have to believe if she was ever to receive the child. Therefore the Lord also wanted to bring her to faith.

Evidently the Lord was sitting in front of the tent with His back to its opening, where Sarah was standing. In a voice so loud that Sarah could not help but hear, the Lord said that she would bear a son in about a year. The Lord Himself was speaking to her. Surely she would believe now! Yet, she laughed at this Word of the Lord, feeling that it was simply impossible for her to become a mother: she was far too old, and so was her husband.

The Lord then asked Abraham why Sarah had laughed. Was there anything too wonderful for the Lord? At this point He repeated His promise with emphasis. Sarah now had to reveal herself, but she denied that she had laughed, for she was afraid of the Lord.

The Lord reprimanded her for her unbelief. Unbelief and doubt are sin in the Lord's sight. We may never doubt whether the Word of the Lord is indeed the truth, or whether we can really depend on it. If we doubt the truth of God's Word, He will reprimand us too.

By means of this rebuke, Sarah was brought to faith. And by that faith, she would receive her baby from the Lord. For her as well as for us, the Lord's promises could be fulfilled by faith alone *(sola fide)*.

The Lord's intention revealed to Abraham. The three men rose from the table and set out for Sodom. Abraham escorted them a short distance. The Lord then said: "Shall I hide from Abraham what I am about to do? Abraham, after all, is the bearer of the promise, and in him all the nations of the earth will be blessed. He knows that through the Redeemer, who is to be born of his line, My blessed Kingdom is going to come. Therefore he may also know what I will do to bring that Kingdom to pass. Here, too, he must be My fellow worker, for he must charge his children to walk in My ways and seek My Kingdom. Therefore I will tell him what I am about to do."

This is what the Lord then said to him: "The sins of Sodom and Gomorrah cry out to Me for punishment. I will go down now and test the peoples of that region, to see whether their sinfulness has any limit."

How wonderful that God wanted to tell Abraham about His

plans! *We* must have friends too, special friends to whom we can tell everything. What closeness we then experience! Just as friends tell each other their hopes and plans, God made Abraham His confidant. Of course God cannot do that with everybody, not even with every believer. But we must make it our goal in our daily walk with the Lord to become so intimate with Him that we understand Him better and better and grow familiar with Him.

Abraham's intercession. The two angels continued on their way toward Sodom, while Abraham stood still before the Lord. Then he realized that the Lord had shown him what He was going to do so that he would have an opportunity to intercede in prayer. Therefore Abraham said: "Surely You will not destroy the righteous with the ungodly! If there were 50 righteous people within that city, would You spare it on their account? Shall not the Judge of all the earth do right?"

Abraham prayed this prayer not because he did not trust the Lord but because he knew that through his prayer, God would fully reveal His righteousness. He pleaded with the Lord and appealed to His righteousness so that even if Sodom were destroyed, God's righteousness would be manifest. Prayer is always an appeal to God's marvelous virtues.

But isn't it often the case here on earth that believers die together with unbelievers? Certainly! Believers are not one whit better than unbelievers and deserve the very same fate. However, God has committed Himself to them as their Father. Since the Spirit of the Lord Jesus Christ lives in them, they cannot die like the ungodly, who simply perish and are forgotten. Believers will be a blessing even in their death and will leave traces behind them.

There stood Abraham, praying not only for those believers as persons but also for the honor and name of the Lord, who was linked with them. In this intercession, Abraham symbolized the Lord Jesus Christ, who continually intercedes in prayer so that God's justice and honor may triumph in this world.

When the Lord agreed not to destroy the city if there were 50 believers in it, Abraham realized that 50 would not be found there. He therefore reduced the number to 45 and eventually to ten. Where did Abraham get the courage to pray with such boldness? His courage had grown because the Lord had just made him His intimate friend and confidant. Only when we know that we receive God's favor through Christ are we able to pray for the Lord's cause. In all his boldness, Abraham did not forget reverence: note his statement that he knew he was but dust and ashes. In our hour of greatest intimacy, we are not to forget the fear of the Lord.

Since it appeared that there were not even ten righteous people in Sodom, judgment was inevitable. Was Abraham's prayer then in vain? No, for God's righteousness in destroying Sodom and Gomorrah now became clearer. Moreover, in rescuing Lot from destruction, God further manifested that righteousness to which Abraham had appealed.

Through Abraham's prayer, that is, through the prayer of the Christ who lived in him, that righteousness became a protecting shield under which Abraham and his descendants and all God's people dwell safely. The Lord Jesus Christ is still praying unceasingly for God's righteousness to become manifest.

The Lord then left Abraham to join the two angels who had gone on to test the people living in and around Sodom and Gomorrah. Soon He would destroy those cities.

14: The Judge of All the Earth

Genesis 19

In his prayer Abraham had said: "Shall not the Judge of all the earth do right?" In destroying Sodom and Gomorrah, the Lord did right. Absolute justice was executed—even in the sense that Lot and his family were saved. God's anger is no uncontrollable passion. In the midst of judgment He spared Lot. Thus His righteousness was glorified in both Sodom's destruction and Lot's deliverance.

In the salvation of Lot, Abraham's prayer had been heard. "God remembered Abraham, and sent Lot out of the midst of the overthrow." God had answered Abraham's prayer and had made Abraham a fellow worker in Lot's deliverance and Sodom's destruction. Through Abraham's prayer, the judgment was shown to be just.

The Lord tested the sinfulness of Sodom's inhabitants by exposing His angels, in whom He was Himself present, to their wickedness. As long as the law of the Lord has even the slightest grip on people, the last tie with God has not yet been cut and men still have not sinned to the uttermost. Up to that time, Lot's words had apparently meant something to the inhabitants of Sodom. Now, however, they cut the last tie. In their unnatural passion, which they now revealed clearly and wanted to give full rein, their ungodliness had come to full bloom. God judges people according to their ties with Him. By punishing Sodom, He avenged His right and honor.

He did the same with Lot. Lot was undoubtedly a believer. This is made clear in II Peter 2:7-8, where we read that Lot did warn the inhabitants of Sodom against their wickedness. He urged the two visitors to spend the night in his house because he feared they would not be safe from the Sodomite sin. All the same, he did not break with the sinful milieu in which he lived. He permitted his daughters to become engaged to Sodomites and even lingered when the angels urged him to flee. Strong ties bound him to his possessions and to the affluence of Sodom. As far as his faith was concerned, he moved at half speed.

In a certain sense, therefore, Lot was also struck by judgment. This is evident from what happened to his wife and posterity: his wife's life ended in judgment, and his descendants became submerged in paganism. The Sodomite way of life lived on in his daughters, who not only committed a grave sin involving their father but revealed that sin shamelessly in the names they gave their children—Moab, which means *from my father,* and Ben-ammi, which means *son of my people.* Lot's posterity was lost, even though he himself was saved as by fire.

Genesis 19 is puzzling in that the angels first speak and act as though *they* were sent by the Lord to destroy the city, whereas Lot later addresses the Lord Himself, who then talks about what *He* is going to do. The Lord, before whom Abraham had remained standing in order to pray, must have rejoined the two angels when Lot was removed from the city by force.

When we tell the children about this judgment, we must point to the righteousness of the Lord, which destroys everything that is no longer tied to Him but also protects everything that continues to cling to Him— not just Lot but also Abraham, his descendants, and all of God's people. For Christ's sake, that divine righteousness by which Sodom was overthrown is at the same time a protecting shield providing a refuge for the life of faith. We see, then, that Abraham was right in worshiping the Lord for magnifying His righteousness.

Main thought: *The righteousness of the Lord is revealed so that believers can take refuge in it.*

Unbounded wickedness. The two angels who had accompanied the Angel of the Lord in His visit to Abraham continued on their way toward Sodom. God wanted them to find out whether Sodom's sin had reached its absolute limit. When they arrived at their destination in the evening, Lot was sitting at the gate. He bowed before them and invited them to spend the night at his house. They replied that they would spend the night in the street, which was possible in that part of the world. If they slept in the street, they would have an opportunity to observe Sodom's sinful night life. Because Lot was aware that no one was safe from Sodom's abominations during the night, he urged the two men to enter his house. This makes it apparent that Lot had resisted the sins of Sodom himself. The men accepted his invitation and ate their evening meal at his table.

Before the two lay down to sleep, the men of the city crowded around the house and demanded that Lot turn his guests over to them, so that they could subject the two men to their sexual abominations. Lot went outside and tried to make the Sodomites see reason. He even tried to distract the aroused men by offering them his daughters instead, but they refused to listen. They rose up against Lot, asking: "Will this alien play the judge, keeping us from doing what we want to do?" They pressed hard in an effort to break into Lot's house.

The two men therefore drew Lot back into the house with them and shut the door. They then struck the men outside with a form of blindness so that they could no longer clearly distinguish what they saw and could not find the door. That's how the Lord punishes His enemies. Those men in Sodom symbolize all of God's enemies, who have all been struck blind: they do not recognize what they see for what it is and are not aware of the Lord's hand in human life.

The men of Sodom had been tested. It was clear that they did not shrink from the most horrible of sins. Lot's words no longer made any impression on them. If we forsake the Lord, He abandons us to all iniquity.

God's righteousness as a refuge. Now the two men revealed their identities to Lot and told him that they had been sent by God to destroy the city. They urged Lot to get all his family together and flee. Lot had only two daughters, but they were both engaged to be married to men of Sodom. Through Lot's laxity, his family was already mingling freely with the Sodomites. When he urged his future sons-in-law to flee with him, they laughed at him. How could they, as men of the sinful world, be expected to believe the Word of the Lord?

While this was going on, the night had passed and dawn was approaching. The two men urged Lot to make haste, since God would destroy the city in the morning. But Lot delayed, unable to part with his life in Sodom and his possessions there. Therefore the two men seized Lot and his family by the hand and led them out of the city, telling them not to look back. They were ordered to flee across the whole valley to the distant hills.

Even then Lot knew better than the Lord, who had since joined the two angels. Lot's life was based not on faith in the Lord but on fear. Thus he asked for permission to flee to the little town of Zoar, which the Lord could certainly spare because it was so little. God's patience was indeed great, for He also granted Lot this wish.

It was perfectly evident that God did not save Lot because he deserved it. Lot continually showed his weakness. Nevertheless, he was a believer and was tied to the Christ. Thus God's name was linked with Lot's name. For the sake of His own honor and name, the Lord spared Lot and covered him with the shield of His righteousness.

The recognition of the Lord's righteousness. As soon as Lot and his family had been evacuated from the city, the Lord sent fire and brimstone down on the entire region. The fire from heaven also ignited everything flammable on the ground. Before long, the whole valley had gone up in smoke.

The members of Lot's household did not share Lot's tie with the Lord. His wife was unable to tear herself loose from what she was leaving behind and could not resist looking back. Therefore God in His judgment took her life. The salt vapors beat against her, and she became a pillar of salt.

The same day, early in the morning, Abraham went to the place where he had stood before the Lord. From there he could see the smoke rising from the valley, like the smoke of a furnace. As he stood there, he did not rebel against the Lord. Instead he must have bowed down before Him and worshiped Him for His righteousness, which on the one hand involves terrible punishment for all the ungodly and on the other hand provides a refuge for believers. When he heard about Lot's deliverance, he must have given thanks to the Lord in a special way and reflected on how the Lord had answered his prayer.

Lot's descendants cut off. Lot could not hold out in Zoar either. Clearly he was filled with the fear that judgment would strike him someday. He thought of his willfulness in asking for permission to flee to Zoar. Therefore he went up into the hills, to which the Lord had commanded him to flee in the first place. There he lived with his two daughters in a cave, far removed from all human contact. Once Lot had sought human contact in the wrong way. Now, as a result of his fear and dread, he was an utter outcast. Those who do not enjoy life in God's way, who refuse to live by faith out of God's hand, will lose even this earthly life.

Would Lot's line then die out? His daughters lived with him far away from other people, and the possibility of marriage seemed out of the question for them. Yet they managed to satisfy their desire for offspring—in an utterly sinful way. Each got a son— through the only available male, their father. Those two sons, of course, were born out of sin and unbelief. They had no part in the blessing of the covenant made with Abraham and grew up like heathens. Out of them arose the Moabites and the Ammonites, two nations related to the people of Israel descended from Abraham. All the same, those descendants of Lot were reckoned among Israel's enemies and became adversaries of Israel's blessing.

Lot was saved, but his descendants were lost before the Lord. Lot himself knew the Lord, but his seed had no part in the blessing of God's people. Things turned out that way in part because of the sins of those descendants, but Lot himself was also to blame for his refusal to surrender completely to the service of the Lord. That sin of the father was visited upon the children. Lot himself was saved as by fire.

The righteousness of the Lord, which punishes sin, was also revealed to Lot. How can this righteousness be a protecting shield for believers if they, too, are full of sin? This is only possible because of the atonement for sin achieved by the Lord Jesus Christ through His death on the cross. God no longer sees any sin in believers but looks upon them as His children. He always defends them and protects them according to His righteousness, for they are His possession. The righteousness of the Lord, which is terrible for His enemies, is the believers' basis for security.

15: The Protection
of the Promised Seed

Genesis 20

When we tell the story recorded in Genesis 20, we are not just to show how the faith of Abraham and Sarah had sunk into a state of depression and then add an admonition to the effect that we are not to do as they did. Where are we supposed to get the strength not to do as Abraham did? Isn't Abraham honored as a hero of faith? Are we any better than he was? And can we expect more of ourselves?

Here again we must begin by focusing on God's revelation in this story, namely, that God upholds the promise of the child to be born and protects that promise even when Abraham no longer shows a living faith in it. Abraham's fear that Sarah will be taken away from him and that he himself will be killed represents an almost unbelievable collapse of faith. Just a short time before, he had been promised that Sarah would bear him a child in about a year's time (Gen. 18:10). Implicit in this promise was a guarantee of the safety of his marriage. In faith he had accepted that promise. (Note that God revealed to him what He planned to do about Sodom, and that Abraham responded by interceding for Sodom by way of a prayer rooted in faith.) And now, just a short time later, he was filled with fear. He had abandoned his faith in the promise of the coming seed and further manifested a lack of living faith in the coming Christ.

All the same, God did keep His promise. He protected the marriage of Abraham and Sarah, thereby saving the promised seed that was to lead to the coming of the Christ. That must have been very humiliating for Abraham, for God showed that He could carry out His plans without Abraham and in spite of his lack of faith. Afterwards, the heathen

Abimelech had to tell Abraham what God had done. From the lips of a *heathen,* Abraham heard the gospel of the promise upheld.

In faith, Abraham had to take hold of the promise anew and learn once again to possess Sarah in faith. That this actually happened is apparent from the next chapter of Genesis, where we are told of the birth of Isaac, who was received by Abraham and Sarah in faith. God kept His promise so that Abraham could claim it again. Once more it is made clear that the power of Abraham's faith, like the power of all faith, lay outside him in the promise.

The connection between this bit of history and our own time is immediately clear, although it is not so easy to bring it out in telling this story to the children. If we do not see the relationships in which we live as sanctified in Christ and do not confess the Christ in those relationships, we are doing the same thing Abraham did.

Indeed, God continues to bind Himself to the Christ—in spite of what we do. Yet this faithfulness is intended to lead us back to belief and to a confession of our sins.

Abraham's fear that Sarah would be taken away from him despite the fact that she was already old raises a question: Did Sarah blossom again with new life after the announcement that she would bear a child in a year? Whether she did or not, Abraham and Sarah were well aware that they were living in the midst of the Canaanites, who were well known for coveting what belonged to others and tearing the lives and relationships of others to pieces.

Main thought: *The Lord binds Himself to the Christ so that we can claim the promise.*

The promise disavowed. The Lord had declared that a child would be born to Abraham and Sarah in about a year. Finally! At first they couldn't believe it. Sarah had laughed at the idea, saying that they were much too old, but eventually they were forced to accept it. What bliss they then experienced! They were now doubly happy with each other. Because of that promise, their love for each other deepened. And they knew that out of them, out of that child soon to come into the world, the Redeemer was to be born. Their love shone in the light of the coming Christ, and their marriage bond became a sanctuary for them. This state of mind brought them intimate happiness.

Abraham was probably looking for greener pastures for his herds. He found them in the south, in Gerar, which was part of the territory of the Philistines. Like the Canaanites in the rest of Canaan, the Philistines were people who felt no awe of God or respect for men. They thought nothing of killing a man and seizing his wife. Their kings were especially bold.

Abraham and his family were now entering the territory of Abimelech, king of Gerar. But there was no real danger to Abraham and Sarah. The Lord had promised that within a year, their baby would be born. Surely the Lord would keep them safe for each other. One thing is certain: He cannot break His promise.

Is that also how Abraham and Sarah looked at the situation? As soon as they were close to Gerar, they were overcome by fear. How was that possible? Didn't they believe that promise anymore? If anyone had asked them, they would surely have claimed to believe the promise. Still, in their hearts they were not sufficiently sure of the promise to be confident there was no danger. In fact, they were terribly afraid. They agreed to say that Sarah was Abraham's sister. There was some truth to that, for she was in fact his half sister, but they were denying that they were also husband and wife. In other words, they were telling a white lie. They were disavowing the beautiful relationship between them, which they had seen so gloriously in the light of the coming Christ. By this act, they were at the same time disavowing the promise. How is it possible that Abraham and Sarah were so quickly filled with fear of the potential dangers around them? Why did their faith succumb so suddenly?

How weak we human beings really are! When we are afraid to confess the Lord Jesus, we do exactly the same thing—in our own way. Though we do not have the same promise that Abraham and Sarah had, God has given us to one another, for Christ's sake, as parents and children, as brothers and sisters. If we do not keep these relationships holy for Christ's sake and do not love one another, we are disavowing the Lord Jesus. We often do just what Abraham and Sarah did. We are often just as lacking in steadfast faith as they were.

What they feared then came to pass. Sarah was seized and taken to the house of Abimelech to become his wife. Abraham and Sarah were torn apart, and Sarah was about to become another man's wife. What would become of the promise now? And how could the Lord Jesus Christ then come into the world? Abraham and Sarah had wantonly gambled away their happiness and the promise through their unbelief and deceit.

The promise secured. When Abraham no longer held on to the promise in faith, God still worked toward its fulfillment. He brought sickness to Abimelech and his house and saw to it that no harm came to Sarah from any quarter. Abimelech could not take her to himself as his wife; she remained Abraham's wife.

God even appeared to Abimelech in a dream and told him that he and his house had been stricken by sickness because he had taken the wife of Abraham. Abimelech pleaded ignorance. The Lord replied that Abimelech's ignorance was the reason he had been spared and then demanded that Sarah be restored to Abraham. Abimelech was to ask Abraham to pray for him, for Abraham was a prophet who enjoyed a special relationship to the Lord. The sickness would then be removed. But if Abimelech did not obey the Lord, he would die.

It was certainly marvelous that God remembered the promise, for Abraham himself could not save the situation. Abraham had lost his faith in the promise, which makes it even more remarkable that the Lord still upheld the promise. He does the same thing today. He will see to it that the Christ will one day be the victor, and that His Kingdom will come with great glory. This will happen even if we despair and no longer dare to confess Him, which would be terrible and shameful for us. In hard times and dangerous situations, Christ will continue to dwell in our hearts by faith, so that we will always rejoice in Him and be strong in Him instead of being afraid. It should be our unshakable conviction that no matter what happens, God will always keep His promise.

Abraham called to account. The next morning, Abimelech told his servants everything the Lord had said to him. Like him, they were afraid of the Lord. There they stood before the majesty of the Lord, whose greatness is revealed especially in His faithfulness to His promise of salvation. Little of this greatness was known among the Philistines. But here God revealed Himself again to the heathens in the sure promise of redemption.

Now Abimelech called Abraham to account: "What have you done by your deceit? Through this act you almost destroyed both my life and my kingdom! What were you thinking of? I have certainly not given you any cause for such meanness. You should never have done such a thing to me."

The *believer* was being scolded by a *heathen* for his unfaithfulness and deceit! If Abraham had only confessed his guilt, he would have been able to testify to Abimelech about God's salvation and His marvelous deeds. But Abraham did not confess his guilt. He still heard nothing beyond the accusation being hurled at him. At this point he had no insight into God's mercy, which had saved him together with the promise.

We are unable to confess guilt if we see only God's judgment and not His infinite grace and forgiveness. Actually, Abraham's conduct was indefensible. Yet he did try to make excuses for himself: there was no fear of God among the Philistines, and therefore he thought he might be killed so that Sarah could be taken as a wife. Moreover, Sarah was in fact his half sister. They had agreed to act as brother and sister when God first led Abraham from his father's house. All these excuses were equally cowardly, which is why nothing was made of this opportunity to testify about God's salvation: all Abraham said about God was that God had "caused" him to leave his father's house.

Believers are often called to account by the world. Why, then, haven't we taken full advantage of the many opportunities to witness? Why haven't we shown by our whole life how much we possess in the Lord Jesus Christ? If only we would honestly confess our guilt when we have sinned! We would not be afraid to do so if we would remember that the Lord remains faithful to His promise anyway, and that His mercy is great.

Divine restoration. God showed Abraham His faithfulness and mercy by having Abimelech pass on to him everything that God had said the night before. Abimelech also restored Sarah to him. This made it clear that God was faithful in spite of Abraham's unbelief, and that God upheld the promise even though Abraham had abandoned it. In addition, Abimelech gave Abraham a gift of sheep and oxen and of male and female slaves. He even gave

130

Abraham permission to pasture his herds anywhere in his territory. He told Sarah that he had given Abraham all those gifts to make up for her dishonor in being carried off by another man when she was Abraham's wife.

Abimelech also asked Abraham to pray for him and his house since Abraham was God's prophet. The Lord heard Abraham's prayer and healed the sickness that had come over Abimelech's house. Thus Abraham heard from the mouth of a *heathen* the good news of God's faithfulness to His promise. A heathen had proclaimed the gospel to him. As the thought of God's mercy filled his whole being, Abraham must have felt deep shame.

Did Abraham now believe the promise again, rejoicing in it and living in faith? Were Abraham and Sarah happy once again to have each other? Did they rejoice in the promise of the child to be given them, the child out of whom the Christ was later to be born? In other words, were they happy together in the light of the coming of the Christ? Yes, they were. We know that they viewed God and each other in faith again, for not long afterward, Isaac, the child they had waited for in faith, was born. Then they lived by faith once again.

God had used Abimelech to accomplish His purpose. When Abraham and Sarah saw that God did not forsake His promise, they were able to grasp that promise in faith again.

It's the same way in our time. Our faith can be awakened by the realization that God does not abandon His hold on the Lord Jesus Christ even when it seems that the whole world is drifting away from Him. If we believe this and also believe that God will bring in the Kingdom of the Lord Jesus Christ with glory, we will learn to be happy and strong and unafraid under all circumstances. Then we will be able to confess the Lord Jesus Christ throughout the whole of our lives.

16: Divine Good Pleasure

Genesis 21

The Lord had told Abraham that Isaac was the promised heir. Once Ishmael found out, he had to subdue his own desires and bow to the Lord's will and decree. If he had been content to recognize Isaac's special role, Ishmael would have received eternal life and the blessing of the covenant. But Ishmael could not bring himself to acknowledge that Isaac was the heir to the covenant promise. Instead he ridiculed him at the feast held to mark his weaning. He was jealous of Isaac and resented the fuss made over him that day, for he sensed that Isaac, as the child of the promise, was held in greater esteem than he was. Evidently Ishmael shared the attitude manifested earlier by Hagar, his mother (Gal. 4:28-30).

Ishmael's struggle is the struggle of all of us when we have to acknowledge that life is not in us but in the Christ. As the child of God's good pleasure, Isaac is a type of the Christ, in whom we seek our life. Christ's greatest appeal ("Come, all of you, unto me") is also the appeal that asks the most of us: it calls on us to view our salvation as lying outside ourselves. We, too, have to bow before God's good pleasure, according to which He chose Christ to be our Head and our Savior.

When Hagar and Ishmael were sent away from Abraham's tent and were forced to live outside the covenant circle, God still did not forsake them. He not only repeated the blessing in which great things were prophesied about Ishmael but also remembered Hagar and her son in their distress in the wilderness. In the story of their distress, however, Scripture speaks of the Angel of God rather than the Angel of the Lord, which indicates that the covenant bond was now broken. From then on, God treated Ishmael the same way He treated all the other nations of the earth. He allowed the heathens to walk in their own ways, even though He was doing good out of heaven. Ishmael enjoyed a special blessing because he was the flesh of Abraham.

131

Still, the Angel of God (i.e. the Christ) appeared to Hagar. Christ was concerned with all the nations and allowed them to follow their own paths only for a short time. Soon all nations would have to find the Christ. Therefore, even in those times of abandonment, God was doing good out of heaven.

Ishmael's contempt for the covenant contrasts oddly with Abimelech's recognition of the blessing on Abraham. The covenant between Abraham and Abimelech, of course, was no more than a bond based on mutual respect: it did not involve a sharing of Abraham's covenant blessing. All the same, that recognition by Abimelech must have comforted Abraham at the time. It implied, however faintly, that the ungodly would recognize the Christ as heir to the promise, the One chosen by God to be the Head of the covenant.

Main thought: *The blessing of the covenant is enjoyed in the recognition of God's good pleasure.*

The birth of the heir to the promise. Sarah had believed the Lord when He promised to give her a child. Through that faith, the Lord now fulfilled His promise: a child was born a year after the promise was given, just as the Lord had predicted.

This child was born *after* Abraham and Sarah had reached the age when people are normally incapable of having children. Thus the child was born by a divine miracle. By his very birth, then, Isaac pointed ahead to Jesus Christ, who was also to be born in a miraculous way.

In accordance with God's instructions, Abraham named the child *Isaac,* which means *laughter*. His birth was so unlikely that those who heard about it could not help but laugh. For believers, however, the laughter was an indication of amazement and ecstasy, just as we laugh in faith at the birth of the Christ. On the eighth day, Abraham gave Isaac the sign of the covenant by circumcising him. By then Abraham was 100 years old. And Sarah, who had once laughed in disbelief, now laughed in amazement and praised the Lord.

The heir despised. When Isaac was more than a year old and no longer lived on milk alone, Abraham gave a big feast. At that feast, in which all of Abraham's household took part, Sarah noticed that Ishmael, the son of Abraham and Hagar, sneered at Isaac and made fun of all the fuss being made over him. Ishmael obviously envied and despised Isaac, for he knew that Isaac would inherit the full promise of Abraham.

Did Ishmael's life fall outside the promise? If he had acknowledged God's choice of Isaac as heir to the promise, he, too, would have shared in the promise. But he refused to bow to God's will. Because he wanted to be his own man, he rejected the covenant for himself. The same spirit had lived in his mother Hagar, who had once fled from the covenant circle.

God decreed that the Lord Jesus Christ would be our Head and Redeemer. We, too, should not seek independence but should acknowledge the good pleasure of God and glory in the Lord Jesus Christ as our Head. If we don't, we will have no part in the eternal blessings of God either.

When Sarah witnessed Ishmael's mockery, she demanded that Abraham send Hagar and Ishmael away. Sarah's jealousy as a mother had been aroused, of course, but she could also see that Isaac, who would have to live within the promise, and Ishmael, who rejected the covenant, would not be able to dwell together. Sarah's request was also the Lord's desire.

Abraham was most displeased, but God told him to do what Sarah had asked. He then comforted Abraham by telling him of His intention to make a great nation of Ishmael, even though Isaac was the heir to the promise. Ishmael had selfishly cut the tie with the covenant. When Hagar fled some years before, God had brought her back again; now that the same spirit manifested itself in her son, the breach was complete.

Early in the morning, Abraham sent Hagar and Ishmael away, giving them some bread and water to take along. This must have been very painful for Abraham, for Ishmael was his own son. Nevertheless, he bowed before the sovereign good pleasure of the Lord. He understood that salvation for him, for his house, and even for Ishmael would be attained only through obedience to the Lord.

Sought by God. Hagar and Ishmael wandered off into the wilderness of Beersheba. They went southward, farther and farther away from the covenant circle of Abraham and his household. The worst thing we can ever do is to break with the people of the covenant, the people of God, for God dwells in their midst and wants to reveal Himself to us.

What would the future hold for Hagar and Ishmael? They wandered farther into the desert and found no water. Soon they were both in imminent danger of dying of thirst. Hagar could not watch her son die, so she left him under a bush, sat down a short distance away, and wept.

God then heard the boy's cries and sent His Angel. Again, the Angel who appeared was no ordinary angel but the Lord Jesus Christ in the form of an angel. He asked Hagar why she was crying. God had heard the boy's voice even though he had rejected the covenant. The Lord remembered His promise to Abraham that He would make Ishmael a great nation.

Why did He remember Ishmael? Why did the Christ come to rescue Hagar and Ishmael? Hadn't God allowed them to break away from His covenant? It was true that at the time, there was a breach between Ishmael and the covenant, but one day, in the distant future, the Redeemer would come and grant His salvation to Ishmael's descendants, as He would to all nations still living outside the covenant. That's why the Christ sought him out in the wilderness.

God opened Hagar's eyes so that she saw a well of water near-by. Quickly she brought her son some water to drink. Apparently the well had been there all along, but she had not seen it. First her eyes had to be opened.

Isn't this the situation in which Ishmael, his descendants, and all the nations would find themselves? Redemption was there all the while, revealed in Israel, but the nations did not see its glory. One day the Holy Spirit would open their eyes. All people are blind to that salvation unless the Holy Spirit heals them of their blindness.

God continued to be with Ishmael, who settled in the wilderness of Paran and became a hunter. His mother found him a wife from the land of Egypt. Thus Ishmael became a great nation, just as God had promised. Centuries later, descendants of Ishmael came to worship the Christ, and the curse upon Ishmael was broken.

The covenant with Abimelech. In those days Abraham was

visited by Abimelech, king of the Philistines, and Phicol, the commander of his army. Since Abimelech had seen clearly that God was with Abraham, he wanted to make a covenant with him. He could see that God would make Abraham powerful and great, and therefore he was afraid for his own people's future. He wanted to reach an agreement with Abraham that the two would not deal falsely with each other. With that in mind, Abimelech reminded Abraham of the friendly reception he had received in his land.

Abraham agreed to the covenant but first wanted to clear up a dispute about a water well which Abraham's servants had dug and Abimelech's servants had seized. Abraham insisted on his rights as the one blessed by the Lord. Abimelech apologized, saying that he had been told nothing about the incident.

When that matter was settled, the covenant between Abimelech and Abraham was sealed, with Abraham giving Abimelech sheep and oxen as security. Of special importance were the seven ewe lambs given to Abimelech, for when he accepted them, he was acknowledging that the well belonged to Abraham. In those days, life in the desert depended wholly on wells and oases. The two men swore an oath and then named the place where they had met *Beersheba*, which means *the well of the oath*.

The covenant with Abimelech must have comforted Abraham, for it came not long after Ishmael's rejection of the covenant of the Lord. In that treaty with Abimelech, Abraham received recognition as the one blessed by the Lord. Even though it was a business agreement, Abraham must have seen in it a hint of the prophecy that one day all the nations would bow before his great Son, the Redeemer, and live with Him in covenant.

For a long time, Abraham continued to live in the land of the Philistines, in the general vicinity of Beersheba. He had planted a tree there in remembrance of his treaty with Abimelech and of the Lord's grace as well, which was reflected in the treaty. There he called on the name of the Lord, the everlasting God, the God who is forever faithful.

If only we would acknowledge the Lord Jesus Christ as the One blessed by God, the One in whom God, in His good pleasure, has chosen to give us salvation! If we acknowledge that good pleasure of God and surrender to the Lord Jesus Christ, we will be saved. Outside of Him there is nothing but everlasting ruin.

17: On the Mount of the Lord

Genesis 22

The story of the sacrifice of Isaac shows us the depth of Abraham's faith. When we tell it, therefore, we must make sure that the children understand something of that act of faith. Yet we must not make the mistake of talking *first and foremost* about Abraham's faith. If we are to view what Abraham did in faith from the proper perspective, we will have to understand—as he did—that in faith we can only imitate God, that we are nothing in ourselves.

Abraham definitely understood this. His sacrifice was only an imitation of the sacrifice God made. This is clear from what he said to Isaac as they climbed the mountain: "God will provide himself the lamb for a burnt offering." That was not just a way to avoid answering a difficult question; for Abraham it was a reality. God always provides Himself with a sacrifice, for when we sacrifice, we are not offering what is ours: God gives us of His very own for our sacrifices.

In a special sense, God Himself was the sacrifice on this occasion. God was sacrificing the child of the promise, the child to whom He was bound by His Word. Ultimately He was sacrificing the Word itself. If God could take such a step, so could Abraham. Abraham saw God offering a sacrifice and then copied Him. Only in this way is such a deed possible.

When we view the sacrifice of Isaac in such terms, we recognize it as a type of the sacrifice of the Christ. The sacrifice of Isaac was not completed, but God did indeed offer His own Son for us. In any case, Abraham saw God offering a sacrifice, and this enabled him to do the same. When we see God's sacrifice at Calvary, *we* will also be able to offer our sacrifices.

There is even more to this story. When God asks us to sacrifice our lives and much that is dear to us, He Himself joins in sacrificing us and

136

what is ours. Because we are His children, He is sacrificing something dear to Him. If we see *God's* sacrifice behind *our* suffering, we will be able to give Him whatever He asks of us.

These considerations shed some light on Genesis 22:14. This text should be translated as follows: "So Abraham called the name of that place *The LORD will see!*" In other words, *God* will see to it that there is a lamb for Him to use as a burnt offering; *He* will choose a sacrifice. The second part of the text should then read: "To this day, it is said, 'On the mount of the LORD He will appear.' " He will appear, then, in that He will be seen as He finds Himself a lamb for a burnt offering; He will be seen offering a sacrifice. On the mount of the Lord, which people can only ascend with clean hands and a pure heart (Ps. 24), after they have sacrificed everything, the Lord will be seen offering a sacrifice. In the first instance, the order is reversed: because we see the Lord offering a sacrifice, we can sacrifice in turn and thus ascend the hill of the Lord. But we can also look at it another way: the more willing we are to offer our sacrifices, the more glorious God's sacrifice at Calvary seems to us.

In the light of the love revealed in God's sacrifice, discrepancies are overcome. It's easy to see what stumbling blocks Abraham faced. The Lord asked him to sacrifice a human being, someone who was his own flesh and blood. Moreover, the person to be sacrificed represented the promised seed. Yet, Abraham's faith remained steadfast. Even in such darkness, he felt sure that God's will would find a way to show His faithfulness to His Word. Abraham believed that God could raise Isaac from the dead, if need be. Figuratively speaking, Isaac did return from the dead (Heb. 11:17-19).

This story points beyond Abraham's own faith, then. Abraham was simply imitating God. When we know that a ram was eventually sacrificed in place of Isaac, our attention is drawn still further from Abraham's personal faith. It is true that Abraham had already sacrificed Isaac in spirit, and that God had asked of him the supreme act of faith. But here again we see that the deeds of men are not sufficient. Ultimately God Himself had to provide a suitable sacrifice.

The two lines (i.e. what man does and what God does) run together in the Christ, who is both God and man. In his act of faith, Abraham was a type of the Christ. Christ, we must remember, is the One given by God, the One conceived by the Holy Spirit. Christ is the substitute, the sacrifice God has provided for Himself. Abraham could only offer a sacrifice through the Spirit of the Christ in him.

We should not be misled by the fact that a burnt offering, which represents a sacrifice of dedication, is spoken of here instead of a sin offering. The burnt offering and the sin offering were indeed different in the later ceremonial ritual, but here and in the sacrifice of the Christ they are one. Because He surrendered completely to God, His sacrifice became a cover for us.

Main thought: *On the mount of the Lord He will appear.*

"Tempting" Abraham to believe. The Lord had fulfilled His promise to Abraham in the birth of Isaac. When Ishmael was sent away, it was made even clearer that Isaac was the child of the promise. The expulsion had been hard on Abraham, but God's favor was still with him in the promised child.

Abraham's way lay in the light. But now the Lord suddenly put him back in the shadows: one day He told him that he would have to sacrifice Isaac, the son he loved, the only son Sarah had been able to give him.

Everything in Abraham must have rebelled against that demand. A human sacrifice? The heathens sometimes offered such sacrifices in hopes of appeasing their gods, but the horrible thought of sacrificing human flesh arose in *their own hearts.* In this instance, however, the thought of a human sacrifice came to man as a command from *the Lord.*

Abraham was told to offer his own son. To make matters even worse, that boy was the child of the promise. Thus he was supposed to become the father of the great nation which the Lord had promised Abraham, the nation that was to dwell in the promised land. How were those promises to be fulfilled if the child was now to be sacrificed? Surely the Lord could not ask this of him! Yet He did.

The Lord was "tempting" Abraham. But He was not tempting him to do evil, for He never tempts anyone to sin. Instead He was "tempting" Abraham to believe. He was looking for something in Abraham, seeking a way to develop Abraham's faith to its fullest extent.

This is what God wants of all of us. In faith we must surrender completely to Him, trust that His will alone is good, and do His will always. Even though what God wills might seem wrong on occasion, we must remember that His will is good. He is the Almighty. Because He is completely wise, He alone can say what is good. When we surrender to Him in faith, we gradually learn to understand something of His wisdom. Thus the Lord "tempts" us too—to get us to believe more fully. We must achieve complete trust in the Lord, even when everything appears to be going wrong.

Imitating God. Still, Abraham would never have been able to meet that demand of the Lord if he had not realized something else. "Am I the only one sacrificing something?" he asked himself. "Surely the Lord loves Isaac too! Since Isaac is the child of the promise, He has bound Himself to that child."

The truth of the matter is that God was making an even greater sacrifice than Abraham: He was sacrificing the child He loved, the child to whom He had bound Himself through the promise. If God was willing to make such a sacrifice, it had to be because it was the only way for Him to reveal His love and favor to the fullest extent possible. If so, then Abraham could sacrifice too. In making the sacrifice, he would let God lead him by the hand, for God Himself was sacrificing something dear to Him. When all was said and done, God would surely find a way to fulfill His Word concerning Isaac, and show His faithfulness to His Word, even though Abraham could not see how. God could raise Isaac from the dead, if need be.

Abraham was indeed correct in thinking that if Isaac was to be offered up, it was really God who was doing the sacrificing. God was sacrificing more than any human being ever could. Later on, God Himself offered the greatest sacrifice that could possibly be made when He sacrificed His own Son. He gave up the Lord Jesus Christ completely—for us. In that supreme sacrifice, He wished to show His love for His world. Since He has now shown us His love, shouldn't we come to Him, trust Him alone, follow Him in everything, and surrender all we have to Him?

People usually complain when they have to suffer. Believers complain too. But when they suffer, God is really sacrificing His beloved children. If we would think carefully about that, we would be more ready to follow Him, even when it means suffering.

Thus Abraham began his journey to Mount Moriah fully aware of what God was sacrificing. That was why he managed to come out on top in his struggle with himself. That also explains how he managed to suppress all feelings of rebellion against the Lord's command during the long journey.

We do not know just what Abraham went through in his struggle with himself. Perhaps he received the command during the night. The following morning, he was already prepared to leave. He made all the preparations for the sacrifice; he cut some wood, saddled his ass, and set out with Isaac, taking two servants with him as well. The trip would take them several days, for the Lord had specified that he was to sacrifice Isaac on one of the mountains in the land of Moriah. The Lord would point out the mountain when they got there.

Finally they reached the mountain which the Lord had designated. Abraham left the servants behind at the foot of the mountain, saying, "Stay here with the ass until we have worshiped." Abraham and Isaac then went up the mountain together. While they were climbing, Isaac asked wonderingly, "But where is the lamb for the burnt offering?" This question must have cut deep into Abraham's soul, but he had an answer ready: "God will provide himself the lamb for a burnt offering." That was exactly how Abraham saw it. God Himself would look after the sacrifice, providing something to lay on the altar. Isaac, after all, was His; he was the child of the promise.

The lamb chosen by the Lord for a burnt offering. At the place of sacrifice, Abraham told Isaac the Lord's command. There Isaac bowed to the will of the Lord. Abraham must have explained how he himself looked at the situation, pointing out that God was sacrificing more than they were, and that God would surely find a way to fulfill His promise about Isaac. Then He bound Isaac and laid him on the altar. Just when Abraham was at the point of slaying his son, the Lord again appeared to him in the form of an angel, as He had done earlier, and told him not to harm his son. The Lord had now seen that Abraham, in faith, would obey Him in everything and follow Him always.

That was enough for the Lord. He asks us to trust Him in all things, but we do not have to provide for our blessedness and salvation by our own deeds. The Lord has taken care of that Himself through an entirely different sacrifice, which He has provided. He has given us His own Son, the Lord Jesus Christ, for our salvation. This is what God wanted to show Abraham.

When Abraham looked around, he saw a ram caught by its horns in the bushes. Abraham sacrificed that ram in place of Isaac, but the ram did not belong to him. God gave him that animal for the sacrifice, just as He would one day give the Lord Jesus Christ in place of us and all that is ours.

How gloriously the Lord revealed Himself to Abraham on that mountain! The mountain was probably named Moriah as a result of what happened there, for *Moriah* means *appearance of the Lord*. The Lord appeared there as Himself, for He provided the sacrifice in a much more wonderful way than Abraham had foreseen or described to Isaac. The sacrifice provided by the Lord took the place of Abraham's own sacrifice. If only we would realize that the Lord has sacrificed His own Son, His most precious possession, for us, we would follow Abraham's lead in trusting the Lord in everything. We would then be ready to do whatever He asks of us and follow Him always, however dark the way, believing that He will surely find a path to the fulfillment of the promise He has made to us.

The promise confirmed with an oath. Because Abraham had not withheld his only son from the Lord, the Lord swore that He would fulfill the promise He had given him. The Lord would bless Abraham and make his descendants as numerous as the stars of the heavens and the grains of sand on the seashore. His people would conquer all their enemies. In Abraham's seed, all the nations of the earth would one day be blessed.

The greatest blessing for Abraham was that the Redeemer would be born of his line. In that Child of Abraham, all the nations would be blessed. Abraham, too, was blessed through that Child, for he could only have displayed such great faith through the power of the Redeemer.

All who possess that faith may call themselves Abraham's children. That faith of Abraham is truly fruitful and is still alive today. The Lord is at work in all believers, fulfilling the promise He made to Abraham. If we surrender completely to the Lord in faith, as Abraham did, that faith will also be fruitful in us and we will become a blessing to many.

18: The Guarantee of the Inheritance

Genesis 23

We now have to tell the children about a burial. This is not a reason to hesitate or shrink back, for a child's life is also caught up in the fear of death and the grave. Only by the Word of the Lord can the lives of children be freed—after that Word has been at work in them for a long time.

We must be sure to speak to the children in such a way that we not only comfort them with the prospect of heavenly bliss but also tell them in Scriptural terms how we will one day live on the restored earth, after the dead rise from their graves. Scripture emphasizes the resurrection and does not speak of death as a joyous transition to a happier state.

Scripture recognizes dying—even dying in Jesus—as a loss. When we die, we break with this visible world of which we were made a part. If we avoid this aspect of death when talking to the children, we cannot offer them true comfort. From beginning to end, Scripture is a book of this earth, although the earth is viewed in the light of heaven. The promise we are given is that we will inherit the blessed earthly kingdom forever. That everlasting link with the earth is typified here by Abraham's tie with Canaan.

It should be noted that from the very beginning of Genesis 23, Abraham speaks of "my dead," and the Hittites likewise speak of "your dead." Abraham clings to Sarah in faith even after she has died, just as we cling to our dead in Christ. Moreover, he loves her earthly appearance and wants to see it restored. That's why he seeks a burial place for her in the inhabited world and does not bury her somewhere out in the fields. For believers, the grave is a symbol not only of humiliation and downfall but also of the part they play in history here on earth and even of their ultimate glorification along with the earth. Because he believed in the resurrection of the dead, Abraham buried Sarah. For him

142

her grave was a guarantee that his seed would inherit the land and possess it forever. One day Sarah and her children would be glorified there.

Still, the path to that everlasting inheritance passes through death. For Abraham there was no avoiding this part of the journey, this dying to everything in order to receive everything. The path all believers have to travel (including Abraham and Sarah) is the path Christ faced, for He passed through death to gain His everlasting inheritance.

In verse 10, the city of the Hittites is called the city of Ephron. Ephron was apparently their head and king. Two chieftans (the head of the covenant people and the head of the people of the world) dealt with each other there. Through their negotiations, Abraham acquired a hereditary burial place, although he had no part in the life or death of the Hittites.

Main thought: *The Lord gives Abraham a place to bury Sarah as a guarantee of his inheritance.*

Mourning for the dead. Sarah died at the age of 127, some 37 years after Isaac's birth. She died at Kiriath-arba (also called Hebron), near the oaks of Mamre, which was one of Abraham's favorite places. Sarah is the only woman whose age at death is recorded for us in the Bible. She was the mother of the promised seed, the Mary of the Old Testament.

Abraham followed the customs of his time when he wept and mourned Sarah's death. No matter how old she was, it still pained him that her life had come to an end, for even 127 years was only a short time. Because we have been created to dwell on this earth forever, death is always a violent break, regardless of the age of the person who has died.

Abraham wept for Sarah, for he loved her deeply; he loved the earthly form that had been so dear to him. How could Abraham have borne this loss if he had not known of a resurrection of the dead, a day in the future when the Redeemer would come? When that day arrived, Sarah would be freed from the bonds of death. How can we endure the loss of our dear ones if we don't believe that some day they will be raised by the power of the Lord Jesus Christ?

Sarah had died and was taken away from him, but Abraham clung to her in faith. Now she was with the Lord, but one day she would be revealed anew, for she, too, would inherit the land. Was Abraham mistaken in this expectation? The Redeemer did come, but Sarah and the rest of the dead were not raised. We know now that the Redeemer will come a second time, when the dead will indeed be raised. Then Sarah will inherit not only Canaan but the whole earth.

Nevertheless, that glorious inheritance will be ours only after we have passed through the death that has already been experienced by the Lord Jesus Christ. He passed through death in order to inherit all power in heaven and on earth. If we believe in Him, He will lead us to our everlasting inheritance.

Acquiring the hereditary property. Because Abraham clung to Sarah in faith, he did not want to bury her somewhere out in the fields. Instead he established a burial place of his own that could be used for her, for himself, and for his descendants, as a sign that his descendants would possess that land forever.

To be buried is to suffer a physical breakdown of the body. But for believers, there is more to the story. Believers are preserved in the earth as a sign that they will one day be glorified along with the earth. Hence Abraham wanted a family burial ground of his own and refused to have Sarah buried with the Hittites. Leaving his dead wife's side temporarily, he went to the men at the city gate and asked for a place to bury her.

The Hittites acknowledged him as a prince of God, as someone who had been made great by God. This acknowledgment, which they could not escape, also compelled them to honor Abraham's God—without surrendering to Him, of course. They wanted to live their own lives and stay away from the God of Abraham. That's why Abraham was not interested in their offer to bury his dead with theirs in their best sepulcher.

Abraham and Sarah and their seed had no part in the life or death of the Hittites. Abraham had been set apart from all the peoples of the earth, to show that in him there was a different spirit than in all the other peoples. Abraham was different because the Spirit of the Christ lived within him. As the Holy One, the Christ has nothing in common with the spirit of sin that dwells in all men. Christ has no fellowship with sin, and therefore He wants us, in His strength, to break with sin. We should not as much as *wish* we could have anything to do with sin.

Abraham approached Ephron, who was apparently a prince of the Hittites, and asked if he could buy a certain field, including the cave in it. In keeping with the manners of those days, Ephron offered Abraham the field and cave without charge. When Abraham politely reciprocated by refusing to accept it as a gift, Ephron eventually named the price he wanted for the field—400 shekels of silver, which was probably a fair price.

Abraham then weighed out the price for the field and gave the money to Ephron. The field and cave had become his property. He had paid for it with money that the Lord had enabled him to acquire. Therefore he had to recognize that the field with its cave was a gift from the Lord, a divine guarantee that he and his seed would one day possess that land.

The burial. Abraham then buried Sarah in the cave of the field of Machpelah, opposite Mamre, where he had so often pitched his tents. As long as he stayed there, he felt as though Sarah was still with him. He had loved her deeply in her earthly form. He knew that Sarah's life was not ended for good, and that one day, when the Redeemer came, she would rise up with all who had believed in Him.

When the Christ comes, all who were one with Abraham and Sarah in faith will rise with them in glory. The Lord Jesus Christ Himself rose from the grave. One day He will break the bonds of death for all who belong to Him. His people can therefore find comfort in the loss of dear ones who died believing in the Lord. The same comfort will sustain them when their own lives draw to a close. To be sure, they will then leave the land of the living, but one day their earthly inheritance will be restored.

Job

19: Loving God for His Own Sake

Job 1

The book of Job originated in a circle of wise men living at the time of Solomon—the same circle responsible for the contents of Proverbs, Ecclesiastes, and the Song of Songs. These wise men were concerned with the ultimate questions of life and death. They sought an answer to those questions in the light given by God, the light of His grace and covenant.

At some point, the long familiar history of Job was put down in writing by these wise men. The book they produced wrestles especially with the "why" of suffering.

Job himself probably lived in the time of Abraham. His home was in the land of Uz, east of Palestine. Job was like Melchizedek in that the pure knowledge of God had been preserved in his environment. He knew God just as many other people did before the scattering of the nations at Babel. Up till then, particular or special revelation had come to all men.

This explains the difference between Job and Abraham. In Abraham's life, we see special revelation developing as more and more light is shed on the covenant relationship. In Job's life, this special knowledge of the covenant is not present. Nevertheless, the wrestling of Job is a groping for the covenant. In fact, the whole book of Job can be read as a clarification of the significance of the covenant.

In the first chapter of Job, which tells us about the dispute between God and satan, the question at issue is whether anyone on earth loves God for His own sake. Satan denies that there is any such love when he asks: "Is it for nothing that Job fears God?" God contradicts him and points to His servant Job as an example.

At the end of the chapter, such love is demonstrated when Job says: "The LORD gave, and the LORD has taken away; blessed be the name of the LORD." Of course, that love was possible only through the Christ, who held on to God even when He was forsaken by Him and by everyone else. It was because of the Christ that such love lived in the heart of Job, behind whom we see the person of the Christ.

149

The angels and satan play a definite role in this story. When we read in verse 6 that there was a day when the angels appeared before God, we realize that their activities are being viewed and described in earthly terms. Still, Job 1 gives us a revelation of the relationship between God and His angels and also shows us how He communicates with satan in His government of the world. In our day, when God's transcendent majesty is receiving heavy emphasis, we seem to have less trouble believing in angels and their work.

In this chapter, we see satan busy denying everything. He claims that there is no one on earth who loves God for God's own sake. Such love, after all, is God's own work. This satanic criticism does not come only from the mouth of satan; we also find it in the world. Opposed to it is a criticism that proceeds from faith. With faith as our starting point, we cannot be critical enough of all the sin in the church and the world. All the same we must be wary of any criticism that only destroys.

Main thought: *God takes pleasure in man's loving Him solely for what He is.*

Job's love for the Lord. In the time of Abraham, there was a man named Job living in the land of Uz, east of Canaan. While all the peoples around him wandered further and further away from the knowledge of God, he carefully preserved the knowledge of the Lord that mankind possessed before the tower of Babel was built. Job served the Lord with all his heart.

God had blessed him in a very special way: He gave him seven sons and three daughters. Moreover, Job had more possessions than anyone else in that whole region. He was rich in cattle and servants.

His sons had dinner together every day. On the first day of the week they ate at the home of the oldest son, on the second day at the home of the second oldest, and so on all week long. They also invited their sisters to eat with them, demonstrating wonderful family ties.

Job was deeply committed to his children. On the first day of each week, he rose early in the morning and offered burnt offerings for all of them, praying for them and rededicating them to the Lord. Job feared that they might have denied the Lord in some way or broken the tie with Him at their meals and feasts.

Why did Job pray so much for his children? For one thing, he loved his children intensely and dreaded the thought that one of them might be lost. But even more, he wrestled with God in prayer for his children for *God's own sake*. He loved the Lord above all else. How terrible it would be if his children did not fear the Lord, for God ought to be served by all men. Such was Job's struggle those days.

Satanic criticism. The Word of the Lord now gives us a glimpse of heaven. There was a day when the angels (sons of God) presented themselves before the Lord. The Lord uses the angels in ruling the world. He acknowledges them willingly in His work, and they must in turn acknowledge Him in their service. Therefore they come into His presence from time to time.

Satan came along with the angels. He, too, is in God's hand and is used by God in governing the world. Satan must also acknowledge God, albeit against his will. Hence he took his place in the presence of God.

The Lord asked satan: "Where have you been?" Of course the Lord already knew all about satan's whereabouts but He regarded satan as a stranger and did not wish to acknowledge him. Hence His question.

Satan replied that he had been traveling through the various regions of the earth. Satan roams through this world and uses the power God has given him for destructive purposes. Still, in his work he is God's own instrument—against his will. One day God will bring forth something good even from satan's work.

The Lord then called satan's attention to Job: "Have you considered My servant Job? There is no one like him on earth, a blameless and upright man who fears God and turns away from evil." God was opposing satan by taking obvious pride in Job. Job loved the Lord, and the Lord rejoiced in his love and enjoyed it. Yet, this love did not originate with Job, for the Lord Himself had aroused it in Job's heart. All the same, the Lord knew His own work and took delight in it. In Job's heart, the true love that seeks God solely for Himself was to be found.

But satan scoffed at this love and declared: "Job seeks You not for Yourself but for what You have given him. You have blessed him in everything. No wonder he wants to serve You! Just take everything away from him, and you will soon see whether he really wants to serve You. Then You will see that he is not Your servant solely for Your sake."

The Lord responded by turning Job over to satan. Satan was permitted to deprive Job of everything, but he was to leave Job himself untouched. Why did the Lord take that step? For His own sake. He wants to be acclaimed and honored for the love He can instil in a human heart. He even lets His children suffer in order to bring out their true love for Him. Through suffering, believers are sanctified in their love.

This struggle between God and satan over His faithful servants goes on day after day and throughout the ages. If we are God's children, we can be sure that a battle is being fought over us as well.

The hour of trial. Job was struck by one calamity after another. A messenger came and told him: "The Sabeans fell upon us and killed your servants, carrying off the oxen and asses." Soon a second messenger arrived and announced: "Fire fell from heaven and struck your sheep and shepherds, burning them up completely." A third messenger reported: "The Chaldeans have killed your servants and carried off your camels." A fourth messenger brought even worse news: "A whirlwind struck the house where your children were eating and drinking. The house collapsed, and they were all killed."

Obviously the Lord had given satan power over the elements. He also allowed him to direct the Sabeans and Chaldeans. Everything Job owned was destroyed by satan.

But we must not lose sight of the fact that *God* granted satan those powers and controlled him in all his destructive acts, even though satan would have preferred complete freedom of action. In our time, too, the calamities are satan's doing, but it is God who controls satan. When God lets satan destroy something, He does so to exalt His own honor and increase the blessedness of those who belong to Him.

The first victory. After all those terrible tidings, Job tore his robe, shaved his head, and fell prostrate on the ground. He had succeeded in controlling himself when the first messengers arrived, but when he heard that his children were dead, he broke down.

Yet his link with the Lord was not broken, nor had he lost his love for the Lord. He bowed down before the Lord in reverent adoration, confessing: "I have no *right* to anything in this world. I brought nothing with me into the world, and one day I will return to the dust empty-handed. But that's no reason to accuse the Lord of wrong, for the Lord entrusted all those possessions to me without my having any right to them. I was never their rightful owner. And even if He now takes them all away from me, I will still praise Him for I love Him for His own sake."

Throughout all this suffering, Job did not sin, nor did he accuse God of doing wrong. He did not complain to God of injustice, and the idea of revenge in God did not occur to him. He fully acknowledged God's right to do as He pleased with what was His, even with what He had entrusted to Job.

Job's love for God had won a great victory. He clearly loved God for God's own sake and not for what God had entrusted to Him. His pure love had been fostered and nourished by God Himself. In the face of satan's attack, the honor of the Lord had won out.

Of course Job was a sinful man, and his love for God did not originate in his own heart. There has only been *one* Man who loved God fully for His own sake and did not betray His love for God even when He was left completely to Himself. That Man, of course, was the Lord Jesus Christ, who emerged from His supreme suffering victorious. Christ gives His Spirit to all who belong to Him. That Spirit was already in Job: it was through that Spirit that Job was able to win the victory. Because the same Spirit lives in us, we, too, can win the victory in the greatest trials and temptations of our lives.

20: The Lord's Involvement in Human Suffering

Job 2-39

It is well known that Job's three friends looked for the cause of his suffering in specific sins he had committed. Everything they said points in that direction.

Their words irritated Job greatly because he did not know what to say in reply. All he could do was deny those specific sins, agreeing in general that sin is present in human life, including his own: "Who can bring a clean thing out of an unclean?" (14:4). Since there were no major specific sins to point to, the reason for his suffering must lie elsewhere. But where?

The more Job was driven by his friends' reasoning to deny such sins, the more he was tormented by the inescapable question: Why, then, this suffering? Beside himself as a result of their arguments, he went so far as to deny that there was any justice with God: "He destroys both the blameless and the wicked" (9:22).

On the other hand, his heart continued to cling to God's justice. He wanted to appear before God's judgment seat and defend himself, for he was aware that God would deal justly with him and not simply according to His power.

Although it was undoubtedly a good thing that Job insisted on God's righteousness, there was still a defiant attitude in him, an arrogant assumption that God had to account for His actions. Here Job revealed his ignorance of the covenant: in the covenant, God can be for us and against us at the same time. He is for us and holds on to us for Christ's sake. On the other hand, when His divine will desires it, He can draw attention to the blackness of our sins. In that sense, He can be against us. It is not that any specific sin makes Him turn against us. He may reveal our sinful nature simply to provide us with a deeper insight into ourselves and to exalt His honor in us. Thus, when He is against us, He is for us at the same time.

Elihu, Job's fourth friend, strikes a different note. He does not speak of suffering as punishment but calls it chastisement for our purification. And he points out that we must suffer in order to discover ourselves.

It is noteworthy that Elihu mentions the Angel of the Lord (33:23-4). Apparently the Angel of the Lord was known to man before Abraham's time: Christ had already revealed Himself to the nations. Elihu observes that the Angel of the Lord can speak of reconciliation or atonement. He takes the place of a man. Here we have an indication that the covenant involves a Mediator.

The Lord, the covenant God, finally answers Job out of the whirlwind. Our first impression of His Words is that the Lord reveals nothing new about Himself, nothing that Job has not already said in principle. Job himself had recognized the majesty of God in the works of His hands. So what was new about this revelation?

When Job spoke, he placed himself at the center. Job was the axis around which everything revolved. On that basis, he was willing to acknowledge the majesty of the Lord. But when God began to speak, things changed. Job was brought low. It was as though Job had said: "Here is Job, and who is God?" Now it became: "Here is God, who is forever faithful, and who is Job?" To bring about the change, God pointed to His great power in nature—especially the animal world.

An underlying theme in the Lord's Words is His involvement in Job's suffering. When God speaks, He acknowledges this world with all its brokenness and suffering as His own. He had once taken this world with all its sin and suffering into His covenant of grace. Therefore He continues to accept the world each day, complete with the works of satan, as we saw in the previous chapter.

In Christ, the Head who was Himself perfected through suffering (Heb. 2:10), God reestablishes this world in the covenant of grace. Christ is the Crucified One, and He still sits upon the throne as the Lamb that was slain. In this dispensation of the covenant of grace, the world will forever bear the mark of the cross.

God wants to sanctify the world through suffering. Through that suffering and sanctification, however, the world will be completely renewed and will once again be perfect. Those who belong to the Lord are well aware of this plan of God's grace, for it has been revealed to them in the central suffering of Christ on the cross. Thus believers can find Him even in their suffering.

Main thought: *The Lord is against us in suffering, but at the same time He is for us in the Christ.*

Inward wavering. Again the angels and satan came to present themselves before the Lord, and once more the Lord asked satan where he had been, as He would a stranger. When satan gave the same answer as before, the Lord again called his attention to Job, who still served the Lord uprightly even though He had turned against him in response to satan's challenge.

Satan now made his ultimate request of the Lord: "But if You touch his body and take away his good health, he will break with You." The Lord decided to subject Job even to this trial, in the hope of revealing the glory of His work in Job. Was Job just a victim, then? No, for one result was Job's sanctification in the Lord's service. Job became an example for all of God's people.

God placed Job in satan's hands but commanded him not to take Job's life. Satan then struck Job with the worst form of leprosy. Soon Job was sitting on his ash heap, scratching himself with a piece of a broken pot.

Job's wife had suffered as well. She, too, had lost all her children. But because she was not bound to the Lord in her heart, her suffering was not the same as Job's. Job's inward pain was much more intense, for his sickness and the loss of his children and possessions were only a part of his suffering.

In the past, Job had assumed in faith that his prosperity was a sign of God's favor. But what was he to think of the Lord now that everything was being taken away from him? He did not understand how the Lord, who surely loved him, could let all this happen to him.

Job's wife ridiculed him because he continued to trust in the Lord. She taunted him, saying: "Break with God—even if it means your death." But everything in Job rebelled against that suggestion. In love born of faith, he bowed before the Lord and said: "Shall we receive good at the hand of the Lord and not receive evil? Isn't the Lord entitled to deal with us according to His good pleasure?"

Still, although Job spoke these words and did not sin with his lips, there was a storm raging in his heart. The questions would not go away: "Why does the Lord allow this to happen to *me*? Don't I share in His love anymore? Is He turning away from me in anger? If so, why?"

Rebellion. When Eliphaz, Bildad and Zophar heard what the Lord had done to their friend Job, they came to offer their condolences and comfort him. But when they saw him, they didn't recognize him at first. Job's plight left them in speechless amazement: for seven days and nights they sat beside him on the ground without speaking a single word.

Their silence told Job not only that they didn't know how to give expression to their feelings but also that they regarded him as accursed. The attitude of his friends only confirmed his own feeling that God was completely against him.

Finally Job himself broke the silence by saying that he wished he had never been born. He even went so far as to curse the day of his birth. Apparently Job could no longer trust in the Lord or believe that good would eventually come of all this evil.

Therefore his friends felt obliged to speak. They addressed Job in turn, and he answered them individually. Job was very irritated by what they said, for they did not admonish him according to the Spirit of the Lord. Their reasoning was: "Every man has his happiness in his own hands. If he lives a good life, God will reward him, but if he does evil, God will punish him." Thus they made God's deeds dependent on man's deeds. For them it is not God who makes the first move, embracing man in His favor and encouraging him to believe.

Job was especially hurt when they argued: "Since God has punished you so severely, you must have committed some particularly grievous sins." Bildad provoked Job most of all, by saying: "All your children have perished. Thus they must have been terrible sinners, for the one thing you can count on is that God is just."

This reasoning made Job rebel against God even more. He knew of no solution and had no answer. He was a sinner, like every other man, but there were no major specific sins anyone could point to. Was God really righteous? He finally reached the point of rejecting his belief in God's righteousness, complaining that God dealt with him in an utterly arbitrary way and allowed him no opportunity to defend himself.

His rebellion against God became so strong that he wanted a mediator between God and himself. Fortunately, his words also struck another note. Out of the depths he cried: "I am still a child of God, but why does He not show any pity for me, a creature of

His hands? Surely God has not forsaken me!" It was as though he was crying out for God's love to appease God's anger. He could not believe there was no justice in God and kept saying: "If only I could defend myself! But God is so exalted, so great in majesty." He did acknowledge God's majesty, then, but not with a willing heart.

Torn apart by his suffering and tormented by his friends, Job could no longer wait in an attitude of faith, trusting that God would still bring forth good from this evil. Job did not understand that God in His covenant can be for us and against us at the same time. From eternity He loves us in Christ (and is thus for us), but He can also turn away from us, to glorify His name in us and sanctify us. He needs no specific sins on our part as an excuse. God can oppose us by examining our sins and the sin of our race (in which we participate) in the light of His countenance.

In his suffering, Job was unable to hold on to the Lord any longer. No one has been able to cling to the Lord in the depths of misery except the Lord Jesus Christ. When everything was against Him and He was utterly forsaken by God, He did not rebel against God. How fortunate that He won the victory! Through His power, He will also make victors of those who belong to Him.

Elihu's speech. Job also received a visit from a fourth friend, Elihu. Because he was much younger than the other three, he had kept silent as long as the others were talking. But when the others were finished, he addressed some words to Job.

Elihu did not look at Job's plight in the same way as the three friends. In fact, he had some encouraging things to say to Job. He was aware that the suffering of believers is not a punishment or any sort of repayment for specific sins committed. Instead he regarded it as chastisement intended to test and perfect them. The Angel of the Lord, with whom Elihu was acquainted, would see to it that the believer did not perish in his suffering, for He would one day atone for the sins of believers.

Elihu also told Job that he should regard his trials and suffering as an encounter with God. If we are believers, then we are indeed God's children and He does love us. But we are not worthy to be God's children, and we begin to realize this when God turns against us.

No doubt Job listened carefully to those words of Elihu. There was a great deal of truth in them, and they could have brought Job closer to a solution to his problem. Unfortunately, Job was so hopelessly mired in his own rebellion that Elihu's words were not sufficient to set him on the right path again. God Himself would have to address him.

That's just what God did. But when the Lord addressed Job, He was also directing His Word at us. Let's be sure to accept it as His Word!

The Lord's answer. The Lord finally spoke to Job out of the whirlwind. The answer Job received was not what he was expecting. Job wanted to justify himself before God and ask Him why He had caused him all that bitter sorrow. In effect he wanted to call God to account.

God let Job see His majesty in that whirlwind. Instead of giving Job a chance to ask questions, the Lord began to put questions to Job: "Can you understand My wisdom in the whole creation?" Then God showed him something of His wisdom in the creation, particularly in the animal world.

God spoke of His majesty, just as Job had spoken of it earlier, but now the situation was completely reversed. Job had begun from himself as the central point and had then proceeded to acknowledge God's majesty. He had not really seen that majesty, nor had he bowed before God with a willing heart. When it was God's turn to speak, He declared: "Here I am in all My majesty. Who are you compared with Me?" Then Job was brought low and put in a proper frame of mind for listening to the Lord. As long as we value our own wisdom, our ears are not open to the Lord's message.

There was so much that Job should hear. The Lord now let him understand that because of the covenant, He was bound to His creation with all its riddles and suffering. Despite all the sin in the world and the misery that comes with it, God was still willing to call the world His own. And because the world was His, He would always see to it that good came from evil.

Then Job said: "I have nothing more to say." Job was silent and began to listen. That was how he found God and His love, even in his suffering.

We also recognize God's love in the most severe suffering the world has ever known, namely, the suffering of Christ on the cross. God let Christ suffer to atone for our sins, to save us. Surely we should then recognize the same love of God in all the suffering He brings into our lives. We can only find this love, however, if we listen to His Word in faith and bow before Him. His Word is the Word of His love for us in Christ.

21: Sanctification unto Renewal

Job 40-42

The history of the world is divided into three periods: before the fall, from the fall to the return of Christ, and after Christ's return. The three periods are reflected in Job's life: before his suffering, during his suffering and after his restoration. The third period has prophetic significance: it points to the glory of the Kingdom of God and should be so interpreted. Otherwise there will be monumental problems.

In Job's case, of course, there could be no question of a total restoration. That Job fathered another ten children did not cancel his sorrow over the loss of his first children. He had to bear that cross for the rest of his life. In this way, too, he imaged the Christ. The world today stands in the shadow of the cross. Still, Job underwent a wonderful restoration of his earthly situation. But even in his case, Scripture does not offer the comfort of a wonderful life in heaven. The Scriptural promise is of a restoration on earth, a restoration of which the story of Job prophesies.

We must not write off the ending of Job's story as a mere Old Testament account, assuming that the story would have ended differently if it had happened in New Testament times. The New Testament, in fact, emphasizes the earth just as much as the Old Testament. The New Testament ends with *the earth's* glorification in heaven, even if this restoration of the earth is delayed until the return of Christ. Thus faith is called on to be patient. Through the indwelling of the Spirit, we learn to wait expectantly.

It should be noted here that Job gained his recognition by holding on to the Lord. The Lord acknowledged His work in Job, who served God for God's own sake and not for the sake of any gifts he might receive. Yet, God crowned this love with His rich gifts. Thus the last chapter of Job is tied to the first, as the book comes to a fitting end. One day the believers will be restored to honor by the Lord, for the sake of the Spirit of Christ within them.

161

God's recognition is also apparent from the command to Job to pray for his three friends. Here Job reminds us of the only High Priest, in whom love of God for God's own sake won the victory, the High Priest who is called our Intercessor because of the atonement He has made on our behalf.

Job's intercession on behalf of his friends was necessary because they had not spoken the truth about the Lord (42:7). As pure Pelagians,* they had called man the master of his own destiny—putting man first and God second. That was a denial of any tie with God through faith, a denial of the covenant relationship and a rejection of the Mediator of the covenant.

Main thought: *The sanctification of this life is a preparation for complete renewal.*

Seeing God. After the Lord spoke to Job the first time, Job promised to be silent. Thus he had learned to listen. But he had not yet humbled himself before God's majesty enough to surrender to the Lord completely, confessing that this majesty of God was also the majesty of His love. Therefore God had to speak to him again.

For the second time, God revealed Himself to Job in a whirlwind and spoke to him, destroying Job's faith in his own wisdom and his ability to stand alone. God seemed to ridicule Job, saying: "Take over the government of the world from Me if you can!" Then the Lord pointed to the hippopotamus (Behemoth) and the crocodile (Leviathan) as two monsters from Egypt's Nile that no man could tame. What, then, would come of any human attempt at governing the whole world?

Job had to recognize that God's power extended over the entire creation, that He ruled the whole world. This God was well within His rights in dealing with Job according to His good pleasure. Now that Job had heard God, who claimed this world and all its

---

*Pelagius, a British monk contemporary with Augustine, traveled through the churches of Africa and the Middle East, teaching that the will of man, in each volition and at every moment of life, is free, i.e. in equipose, able to choose good or evil, no matter what the previous career of the individual. He denied the fall as an event affecting us who come later. In other words, sin is not a matter of our nature but of the will. God helps us to do good, but by external means. We choose the good (or evil) ourselves. We can because we have to.—TRANS.

suffering as His own, and realized that God stayed with him even while He was against him in his suffering, he could surrender to the Lord's rule.

Therefore he said: "I will no longer argue with You. From now on I will only speak to You as a child speaks to his father. Please answer me when I ask You something." The Lord is quite willing to answer us—but not if we challenge Him. Instead we must speak to Him in childlike trust.

Furthermore, when Job surrendered to the Lord, he felt as though he was seeing the Lord close up, while earlier it was as though he had only heard about Him. Now he was in God's presence and found shelter there for his life and his suffering. Therefore he repented of his earlier hostility and rebellion. In this way, God teaches us to surrender to Him.

Called to be an intercessor. The Lord then spoke to Eliphaz: "My wrath is kindled against you and against your two friends; for you have not spoken of me what is right, as my servant Job has." Those friends thought they had seen the relationship between God and man in the right perspective, but they had been badly mistaken: they had put man at the center instead of God. Therefore God was angry with them.

If their view were to prevail, every tie between God and man would be severed. Therefore they were told to offer seven bulls and seven rams as a burnt offering to the Lord. Such a burnt offering would be totally consumed by fire to symbolize that the ones making the sacrifice wanted to dedicate their entire lives to the Lord. In this way the three friends were to proclaim their surrender to the Lord.

But it was not a simple matter, for they had shown their ignorance of the right relationship to the Lord and had spoken improperly of Him. Therefore Job had to pray for them and ask God not to deal with them according to their folly. If Job would intercede for them, God could forgive their sins for Christ's sake.

Job, too, had spoken improperly of the Lord, but he had confessed that in all things God comes first. Job recognized the bond with the Lord, which was why he was able to intercede for his friends.

Strictly speaking, no man is sufficiently worthy to intercede for another—not even Job. There has only been one Man who truly knew and acknowledged God, namely, the Lord Jesus Christ, who intercedes for those who belong to Him. If Job was allowed to perform this act of intercession, it was because something of the Spirit of Christ was in him.

The Lord accepted Job's prayers and did not deal with his friends as they deserved. The Bible does not tell us whether those friends were really converted and came to understand what grace is all about. Job's intercession was intended simply to save them from the danger they faced because of what they had said about the Lord. How much greater Christ's intercession for us with the Father is, for He has actually atoned for the sins of His people!

When the Lord permitted Job to play the role of intercessor, He was also crowning Job's love. This love was not Job's own doing; it was the Lord's work in him. When he prayed for his three friends, this love triumphed, for Job did not blame his friends in any way. In his thoughts he put himself in their place and presented their needs to God, asking for the forgiveness of their sins. In the same way, the Christ puts Himself in our place and brings our needs before God. How ashamed Job's friends must have felt when they saw his attitude, for they had never truly sympathized with him in his suffering.

Job was able to act as he did because his heart was full of love for God Himself. For God's sake, he desired the salvation of his friends, which made it easy for him to overlook what they had done to him.

Restoration. In Job's intercession, his unselfish love for God won a great victory. Now God had made His point to satan: in all Job's suffering and also in this intercession, Job manifested a love of God for God's own sake. God had won the battle with satan, and therefore the Lord could now restore Job's possessions.

The Lord gave him double what he had owned before. His relatives, who had pretended not to know him during his time of suffering, soon came to visit him. They ate with him and gave him presents. We do not know whether their interest in Job was genuine but for Job it was a sure sign that the Lord had turned to him again in mercy.

The Lord not only increased his possessions but also gave him seven more sons and three more daughters. Job let his daughters share in the inheritance with their brothers, thus acknowledging his daughters and their families as true branches of his line.

In spite of his seven sons and three daughters, Job mourned the loss of his first children. This cross he was to bear for the rest of his life. Yet, in his family he once again enjoyed God's favor, and that was always the most important thing for Job. He had known God's favor in his earlier prosperity, then thought he had lost it when everything was taken away from him, and now enjoyed it again to the full in his new blessings.

The blessing of Job is a promise to all believers that God will one day show them His full favor in the glory He will give them. Yet, they already receive His blessings here on earth. True, they have their crosses to bear, but they may still taste God's favor in many, many ways. This provisional blessing is a prophecy about the full blessing which God will one day bestow upon them.

Job lived 140 more years and enjoyed his sons and his son's sons—four generations in all. Then he died, an old man who had lived a full life. Life had given him everything he could ask for. In the resurrection of the dead, he would receive it all again in new glory.

Isaac

22: The Preservation of the Covenant Seed

Genesis 24—25:18

The Lord had called Abraham to live a life apart. Therefore he had to leave Ur of the Chaldeans and later Haran. In setting Abraham apart as a type of the Christ, God revealed that in the Christ, a new principle would have to counter the principle of sin, by which the world lived. This new principle would be introduced into the world by a miracle, of which the birth of Isaac had been a type.

Two dangers constantly threatened—mixing with the Canaanites and returning to Haran. If Abraham chose either of these paths, his separate state would be destroyed. These two dangers loomed especially large where Isaac's marriage was concerned.

Abraham instructed his servant to seek a wife for Isaac in Haran and forbade him ever to take Isaac there. This command was the Lord's doing: the Lord was making sure that Abraham's line would remain separate.

It was the Christ, then, who controlled the quest for a wife for Isaac—Abraham's charge to his servant, his faith that the Lord would use His angel to ease the servant's journey, the guidance the servant received along the way, his attitude of faith, Rebekah's willingness to go back with him, and the meeting of Isaac and Rebekah, which was a meeting in the Lord.

When Abraham set down his last will and testament, he saw to it that Isaac was separated from the sons of Hagar and Keturah (Gen. 25:6). To be sure, both Isaac and Ishmael stood at Abraham's graveside, but the subsequent development of Ishmael's posterity is mentioned intentionally. His line developed in a different direction than Isaac's.

Isaac now had to become independent and take over the promise given to his father Abraham. It is noteworthy that Abraham's servant already refers to Isaac as "my lord" when speaking to Rebekah.

169

Main thought: *The Lord preserves the covenant seed.*

The significance of Abraham's seed. Many years before, the Lord had called Abraham out of Ur of the Chaldeans and then out of Haran. Abraham was to live a life apart from all the other peoples, who were sinking away in idolatry. He and his descendants were to live a wholly different life. In short, he was to be a type of the Christ, the Holy One, who was different from all other men. Through the Lord Jesus Christ, the entire human race was to be renewed.

Abraham understood that the Lord had not set him apart without a profound reason. Hence he was well aware that the separation had to be preserved. Accordingly, he would not permit his son Isaac to marry one of the Canaanite women and would not allow him to return to Haran.

Abraham made his servant swear an oath that he would seek a wife for Isaac in Haran. The servant was afraid that the woman might not want to follow him and asked whether he should take Isaac back to Haran if that happened. Abraham replied that he was not to take Isaac to Haran under any circumstances, and that if the woman refused to come with him, he would no longer be bound by the oath. In faith he added: "The Lord will send His angel before you and grant you success in this venture."

Abraham believed that this separation was the Lord's will, and that the Lord would see to it that the woman followed his servant willingly. The servant then swore the oath.

Abraham's desire in this matter was also the Lord's desire. When we walk in the way of the Lord and understand His will, we may confidently count on His guidance.

The guidance of the Lord's angel. Abraham's servant went on his way. When he arrived in Haran, he asked the Lord to show that He had been with him on the way and let him know by a sign which woman He had designated for Isaac. The servant wanted a sign of the woman's helpfulness and readiness to serve, for Isaac's wife must be a servant of God and a servant of men for God's sake.

When this petition was answered in the way he hoped, the

servant was amazed. He saw this answer as a revelation of the Lord, the God of his master Abraham.

We need not look for such signs today. But at that time, the history of the seed of which the Christ was to be born was still being made. In the course of that history, the Christ often revealed Himself in remarkable ways. He had also made Abraham's servant obedient and taught him to wait for His leading.

The servant found Rebekah, Isaac's wife-to-be, and soon he was at the house of Bethuel, her father. Laban, her brother, made himself rather conspicuous in that household.

Before they sat down to dinner, Abraham's servant told them the purpose of his visit. He also told them about the Lord's marvelous guidance on his journey. Then both Bethuel and Laban bowed before the Lord's calling, which was revealed to them by the words of Abraham's servant.

Rebekah's submission. Abraham's servant wanted to be on his way the very next morning. Bethuel and his family hoped Rebekah would stay with them a few days longer, but they let her decide for herself.

The Lord had a hand in this situation too, for Rebekah was being given an opportunity to display her spontaneous and joyous acceptance of the special promise and particular calling of Abraham's seed. She was ready to go immediately. In her decision to depart at once, she was submitting to the Lord in faith; she was showing her faith in Abraham's promise and calling.

When Rebekah made her choice, she was breaking with her father's house. Such a break is rarely required of us. What we must break with instead is the sinful world, so that we can live a completely new life with Christ. In that sense, Rebekah's submission should be an example to us. The Spirit of the Lord, who put submission in her heart, will work in the hearts of all His followers. Just as the Christ once called Rebekah, He will call all who are His to be incorporated into Him.

The meeting of Isaac and Rebekah. Bethuel and Laban blessed Rebekah and let her go. At about the time that Abraham's servant was arriving home with Rebekah, Isaac happened to be in the field praying. In his prayer he raised the question of his marriage, placing the matter in the Lord's hands. Later on, Isaac often played an all too passive role in relation to others, but here he manifested a proper dependence on *the Lord*.

When Rebekah saw the figure of Isaac in the distance, she asked Abraham's servant who it was. When she heard it was Isaac, she covered herself with her veil and quickly alighted from her camel. She was then presented to Isaac by Abraham's servant.

They had received each other from the Lord and found each other in the Lord. Rebekah was a comfort to Isaac after the loss of his mother Sarah, and he needed her support in his life ahead. When he received Rebekah as his wife, he acknowledged God's favor to him and his seed for the future.

That union of Isaac and Rebekah was rooted in faith. Because of their faith, there was something exceptionally noble about their union. Just as they sought to dedicate themselves in their union to the promise given to Abraham, we, too, must place ourselves at Christ's disposal in all things. Only in this way will all our relationships be sanctified.

Abraham's death and last testament. Later in his life, Abraham had taken another wife, namely, Keturah, and he also had sons by her. Before his death, however, he sent those sons away from his tent, giving them gifts. The Lord had told him that Isaac was to inherit his blessing and promise. Therefore Isaac's seed must not be allowed to mix with the offspring of his other sons—not even Ishmael's.

Abraham finally died when he was 175 years old. His sons Isaac and Ishmael buried him in the grave he had purchased, where he himself had earlier buried Sarah. Abraham's body rested in the same ground as a sign that his seed would one day inherit the land. In a way, Abraham and Sarah were waiting for the great day of Christ, at which time all of Christ's people will inherit the earth.

Isaac and Ishmael did not stand at their father's grave with the same attitude. Isaac believed in the Lord and inherited the promise made to Abraham. Ishmael, on the contrary, had sought his freedom and cut himself off from that promise. Isaac was a child of his father's faith, but Ishmael was alien to it.

The descendants of Ishmael multiplied and acquired great power and influence, but they did not share in the blessing of forgiveness of sins and eternal life, the blessing of complete renewal of life before God.

The blessing of Abraham, which is the blessing bestowed on us by the Christ, is shared by all who are Abraham's children by faith.

23: Flesh and Spirit

Genesis 25:19-34

In this segment of the Biblical narrative, the struggle between flesh and spirit comes out clearly. This struggle is not just a conflict between Esau and Jacob. The struggle was already present in Rebekah. She wanted a child, but at the same time she wanted to bear the child of the promise. This struggle was present in Isaac as well. The flesh came to prominence in his special attraction to Esau. At times Isaac's faith sank dangerously low.

That struggle was controlled by the calling of God, which is rooted in divine election. The Word of God was pronounced over the children in the revelation to Rebekah before their birth: she was told that the elder would serve the younger. By this calling of God rooted in election, a division entered the life of mankind. This led to the struggle between flesh and spirit.

The Christ is the only One truly called. Thus He is spirit. The flesh has always struggled against Him, as we see when we survey the history of God's people. The struggle was especially acute at Golgotha.

Jacob and Rebekah submitted to the calling of God. To that extent, spirit had triumphed in them. Yet the flesh was also at work in them, as we see from the means they used to achieve the calling.

Although Jacob bought the birthright, he never dared to make any claim on it. Because he had obtained the promise in a sinful way, he defamed the promise itself. At the time, he hoped to gain the upper hand by worldly means. Only later was his life purified of the use of such means.

Abraham was still alive when Esau and Jacob were born. Their birth, as a step toward the fulfillment of the promise, must have done him a world of good. Yet the story of the twin babies is really part of the history of *Isaac*. As head of his family, he acted on his own when he prayed for the promised seed. For the rest, Isaac assumed a passive attitude. Of all the patriarchs, his faith was the weakest. He is significant as a type of the Christ mainly in that he was to be sacrificed by his father Abraham.

Main thought: *In the covenant circle, the calling of God awakens the struggle between flesh and spirit.*

The prophecy about the two sons. Isaac and Rebekah had been married for many years, but the Lord had not given them any children. The child of the promise that would one day be born of them would be a child they expected from the Lord; he would be a gift of God.

They longed for a child—especially Rebekah. They wanted to be rich in their posterity, but they desired a child in the first place because it would be the child of the promise, from whose seed the Redeemer would be born. Thus they truly longed for the Christ, although they also displayed a certain selfishness in their desire.

Because the Lord delayed the fulfillment of their desire, Rebekah urged that they pray together for a child. They did so, and the Lord heard their prayer.

The Lord informed Rebekah that she was going to have twins. Rebekah had asked the Lord for a revelation because she was afraid. She certainly wanted a child, but what if the life of that child should have a destructive effect? Then she would rather not have it!

The Lord now told her that two children would emerge from her womb, and that there would indeed be a struggle between them. The Lord even prophesied how the struggle would turn out: the stronger would be conquered by the weaker.

That could only mean that the Lord would be on the side of the weaker and would turn against the stronger. This must have worried Rebekah. Her two children would be locked in a struggle, and the Lord would side with one of them. Thus the Redeemer would be born of the weaker, who would be the child of the promise. The stronger would fight against the Redeemer and reject the promise.

What an awful prospect for Rebekah to contemplate! It's always horrible for believing parents to see that not all their children are united in fellowship with the Lord. Only those whom the Lord calls and who then give ear to that calling will follow Him.

The difference between the two. Just as the Lord had foretold, two children were born. The first one they called *Esau,* which means *the hairy one.* To the second they gave the name *Jacob,* which means *heel-holder,* for he was holding on to his brother Esau's heel at birth. These names contained a prophecy about the lives of the two boys. Esau became the man of brute force, whereas there was a sly, deceitful streak in Jacob's character. When they grew older, Esau became a hunter, a man of the field. Jacob was more of a homebody, someone who stayed close to the tents.

Isaac was proud of his older son, the strong one. Isaac was not strong himself, and therefore his son's strength impressed him and appealed to him. Moreover, he loved the taste of the game Esau often prepared for him. Did Isaac ever think of the prophecy that the stronger would be subject to the weaker? His faith now lessened. In his fondness for Esau, he allowed himself to be guided completely by his own preference.

That preference must have had a bad influence on Esau. Partly because of Isaac's attitude, Esau prided himself on his own strength and did not know what it was to bow in faith to the Lord. He became contemptuous of the promise of the Redeemer, assuming he could get through life on his own.

Rebekah preferred Jacob. That was partly a selfish preference: as a mother, she was drawn to her home-loving younger son. Yet, unlike Isaac, she was also acting on the basis of the prophecy. The weaker, after all, was to be the child of the promise.

She certainly must have revealed that prophecy to Jacob. What a danger that was for the boy! Jacob accepted the promise in faith and struggled for its blessing all his life. He prided himself on that special promise, but he tried to obtain it the wrong way.

The fact is that he was *not* the first-born. The first and chief promise belonged to Esau. But how would Jacob now participate in the blessing of the promise? He should have trusted in the Lord's leading, but he did not.

It is possible for us to be God's children and still use the promise in a completely wrong way. We must never be self-seeking. Instead we should be everyone's servant for God's sake.

The birthright surrendered. One day Esau came in from the field and found Jacob boiling some stew. Utterly exhausted, Esau said: "Give me a gulp of that red brew you've got there." That's why he is often called *Edom,* which means *red.*

Jacob saw his golden opportunity, and quickly replied: "Sell me your birthright." Esau was dead tired, and in his heart he was indifferent to the promise given to Abraham and Isaac. Thus he responded: "If I don't get something now, I'll die anyway. What good would that birthright do me then?" The most important thing for Esau was to live life as he pleased. The promise of the Redeemer had little value for him.

To make sure Esau would not change his mind, Jacob asked him to confirm the sale of the birthright with an oath. In his indifference, Esau complied, swearing to his contempt for the Lord's promise.

Jacob then gave Esau some bread and stew, which Esau quickly consumed. Soon he got up and went his way. He forgot about that transaction, for it did not mean anything to him. Esau despised his birthright—and with it the promise of the Redeemer.

Apparently Jacob could not forget the promise. Yet he wanted to inherit the promise not for God's sake but for his own sake. Therefore he tried to buy it—as though the grace of the Lord were for sale! The deal he made with Esau had no bearing on his eventual possession of the promise. The transaction only served to display his deceitful nature.

All the same, Esau and Jacob are contrasted in this story as the one who despised the promise and the one who accepted it in faith. That's how unbelievers always differ from believers who hold on to the promise. Unbelief is no more eager to receive the Christ, who is the fulfillment of the promise, than Esau was anxious to hang on to his birthright. Faith and unbelief are still locked in a struggle in the world today. What side have you taken in that struggle? The victory belongs to the Christ, who was called by God, and to the believers, who are still being called by Him today.

But believers also have to struggle against the sin within them. In the believer himself, there is much that opposes the Christ, much that could lead him to forfeit the blessing of the promise. Believers must never be self-seeking. With all they have received, they must serve the Lord and each other.

24: Rehoboth

Genesis 26

Isaac's stay in Gerar probably took place before the birth of Esau and Jacob: if there were children playing in Rebekah's tent, it would have been difficult for her to pass as Isaac's sister. Thus, before Abraham's death, God already led Isaac to Gerar, down the route Abraham had taken years before.

Isaac was on his own. Although he had long lived in the shadow of his father, he now had to act on his own as heir to the promise and begin to play an independent role in Canaan. In Gerar he matured to independence.

Isaac was certainly no innovator. He has been described as capable of nothing more than digging up the wells his father Abraham had dug before and giving them the names that Abraham had already given them. Yet the Lord appeared to Isaac in Gerar and passed on to him the promise made to Abraham. In his time of oppression, he would have to learn to live by the promise. God appeared to him so that he would realize that he was indeed the heir to the promise.

In the valley of Gerar, Isaac left well after well in the hands of Abimelech's herdsmen, which showed that he was still not fully aware that he was the heir to the promise. Nor did he dare make any claim on the covenant established earlier between Abimelech and Abraham. (Whether this was the same Abimelech or his successor makes no difference. That covenant would have applied to Abimelech's successor just as it did to Isaac, as Abraham's son.)

The real focus of the struggle was not Isaac as Isaac but Isaac as heir to the promise. The issue at stake was the promise—and ultimately the Christ. As long as Isaac had not grasped that promise in firm faith, he could only retreat. As he was being driven from well to well, he bore the image of all of God's people and also the image of the Christ, who was driven and harried and finally cast into utmost darkness.

178

In time Isaac came to the clear awareness of faith, although this did not yet happen at the third well. When Abimelech's herdsmen did not dispute Isaac's rights with regard to that well, Isaac exclaimed: "Rehoboth! The Lord has made room for us, so that we will be able to expand in this land." But it was only at Beersheba that he really found room, after the Lord appeared to him again. There he built the Lord an altar and called on the name of the Lord in public worship. Then he pitched his tents in peace, and his servants found water. Abimelech sought him out there to make a covenant with him, openly acknowledging him as the one blessed by the Lord. Through his faith, Isaac finally found room.

Main thought: *The Lord appears to Isaac at Gerar so that he will recognize that he is the heir to the promise.*

In Abraham's footsteps. Before Isaac and Rebekah had children, there was a famine in Canaan, which made Isaac consider moving on to Egypt for a while. As a start he went to Gerar, in the land of the Philistines, where his father Abraham had also spent some time earlier. Gerar was the place where the Lord had miraculously protected Sarah. At that time a covenant had been made between Abimelech, the king, and Abraham.

In Gerar the Lord appeared to Isaac and told him not to go to Egypt but to continue living as a stranger in Canaan, for he was the heir to the promise given to Abraham. God intended that land for his seed. Isaac was told that his seed would be as the stars of heaven, and that all the peoples of the earth would be blessed through his seed.

This was the Lord's first appearance to Isaac. Of course Isaac knew he was to inherit Abraham's blessing, but up to this time he had always followed in his father's footsteps. Now he would have to act on his own in Canaan, which meant that his faith would have to mature. At Gerar God gave him the promise in precisely the same words He had used in speaking to Abraham. This time, however, He added that the promise would surely be fulfilled because Abraham had obeyed the Lord in faith.

Thus Isaac followed in Abraham's footsteps and became the bearer of Abraham's blessing. He had to share Abraham's faith and form a spiritual bond with his father. It was the Spirit of Christ in Abraham that had made him obedient, and the same Spirit now wished to dwell in Isaac. The thing for Isaac to do was to grasp that promise in faith and thereby become independent. But he had not yet reached that point.

Isaac also followed in his father's weakness, fearing that one of the Philistines would want Rebekah for his wife and kill *him* to get her. Therefore he had Rebekah pass for his sister. Like his father, he did not dare entrust himself solely to the promise.

But the deceit was discovered by Abimelech when he saw how Isaac and Rebekah behaved toward each other. Abimelech reprimanded Isaac, pointing out how easily one of the Philistines could have taken Isaac's wife for his own and what guilt would then have come over the Philistines. In these words we sense a lingering memory of what God had done to Abimelech and his house when Abimelech had wanted to make Sarah his wife. Abimelech was well aware that there was a special relationship between the Lord and Abraham's son, and therefore he told his people that no one was to marry Rebekah. Thus the Lord protected Isaac and Rebekah in Gerar, for they were to have a child from whom the Christ would eventually be born.

The resistance to Isaac. Still, the struggle between Abimelech and Isaac was yet to come. This Abimelech, who was probably the successor of the one whom Abraham had encountered, had not yet seen the arm of the Lord. God prepared Isaac for that struggle by bestowing special blessings on him. When Isaac sowed seed in Gerar, he reaped 100 times what he had sown, which was very unusual. Normally a farmer would reap 30 times what he had sown, or perhaps 50 times. Under the best of conditions, he might reap 80 times as much as he had sown. But a crop of a hundredfold was very rare indeed.

In this abundance, Isaac could sense the special blessing of the Lord. The earth gave him its rich fruits because he was the heir to the promise, the one whose seed would inherit Canaan—despite the fact that the godless held sway there at the time. Thus his faith was being strengthened.

God also blessed Isaac's livestock—to such an extent that his encampment had to be enlarged. But because of his prosperity, the Philistines envied him. They stopped up all the wells that Abraham had dug and Isaac was now using. Finally Abimelech asked him to leave the country because he had become more powerful than the Philistines. All of this was contrary to the terms of the covenant Abimelech had made with Abraham: in that covenant it had been clearly agreed that the wells Abraham dug belonged to him.

It was a question of Isaac's survival as a man of possessions. With his herds and flocks, he had to live off the pastures and water of the land. But his faith was also involved. His father Abraham had enjoyed the use of that land, which he saw as a confirmation of the promise that the land would one day belong to his seed. But wasn't Isaac the heir to the promise? Now he was being asked to go away. Wasn't that land for him too—for the sake of the Redeemer who would one day come?

Isaac was well aware that the Philistines not only envied him his riches but also hated him because of that special promise. Now they had a chance to hurt him. Here he was fighting the fight of faith. Was the promise really for him? And would he be strong in his faith in the promise?

In the same way, the Lord Jesus Christ was persecuted. Indeed, all of God's children encounter opposition. But that opposition will teach them to live and stand firm in faith. Isaac had to learn that in his own situation.

Isaac's response. Isaac did not yet stand firm in faith. When Abimelech denied him the use of the land, he went off to the valley of Gerar. He uttered not one word of protest regarding the violation of the covenant with Abraham.

Isaac's servants then started digging for water. In time they struck a vein, and the water came bubbling up. But Abimelech's herdsmen, who were also pasturing their herds in that valley, quarreled with them over that well and said it belonged to them. Isaac retreated before their refusal to compromise and called that well Esek, which means *wrangling*. When his servants dug another well some distance away, Abimelech's herdsmen claimed it too. Isaac again drew back and called that well Sitnah, which means *quarreling*. He moved on. At last they were far enough away from Gerar, and there was no quarrel over the third well. Therefore Isaac called that well Rehoboth, that is, *broad places* or *room,* for the Lord had made room for him in that land so that his family and household would be able to spread out.

What do you think of Isaac's attitude? He certainly strikes us as a cowardly figure. He never did become a truly independent person. Thus he could hardly be described as a pioneer or path-finder in the Kingdom of God.

There was little he could do about the infringement on his rights. As long as his faith in the promise was not firm, he could not speak up for himself. The focus of the struggle, after all, was not the rights of a man named Isaac but the rights of the heir to the promise. God's promise of the coming Christ was at stake.

In this troublesome situation, God would lead Isaac to faith. When Isaac moved on to Beersheba, the Lord appeared to him again and confirmed the promise. There the Lord told him: "Fear not. Stand firm in the faith that you are the heir, and that no harm can come to you."

After this period of enmity and oppression, Isaac accepted the promise for what it was. Since the Lord had appeared to him there, he built an altar for the Lord. Together with his entire household, he called on the name of the Lord in public worship. In full confidence, he pitched his tents in Beersheba and told his servants to start digging for water.

The Lord does not appear to us anymore to assure us that we may share in the promises that have been fulfilled in the Lord Jesus Christ or still await fulfillment. This is no longer necessary, for He appeared once in the Christ and then came in the Holy Spirit. He now speaks to us through His Word, telling us that we will share in the promise if we believe. It may be that we first have to suffer oppression, just as the Christ, Isaac, and other children of God have, but we will inherit the promise all the same.

The recognition of Isaac. Believe it or not, Abimelech sought Isaac out in Beersheba. This surprised Isaac, who then asked Abimelech reproachfully why he came to him now if he hated him. By that time, Isaac was aware that he was the one blessed by God. Abimelech then admitted that he and the other Philistines had seen that God was with Isaac and went on to say that they would rather make a covenant with him than be his enemies. Thus Isaac was already attaining the position in the land that his father Abraham had reached: even a king wanted to enter into a covenant with him. Abimelech also made light of what he and his men had done to Isaac, saying that they really had not done him any harm but had sent him away in peace. As if they had not driven him out! Abimelech was finally compelled to admit: "You are the one blessed by the Lord."

Isaac then agreed to the covenant, and therefore they had a feast that evening. The following day they sealed the covenant with an oath. The very same day, Isaac's servants told him that they had found water in the area where they were now encamped. Thus Isaac was recognized by the ruler of the land, while the Lord gave him water as a foundation for life and prosperity. Now Isaac could boast even more than before that the Lord had made room for him and his household.

The Christ was persecuted and cast out in a similar way. Finally He was recognized by thousands as God's Anointed, as the Redeemer of the world. God has now made room for Him on this earth and will one day glorify Him. On that day, everyone will have to recognize Him. Believers, likewise, are still being misjudged and oppressed today, but one day they will be recognized openly by men as well as by God.

Jacob

25: God's Prerogative in Election

Genesis 27—28:9

When we tell the children how Jacob received the blessing of the first-born, we cannot avoid talking about the sin of Rebekah and Jacob. Yet we must not put too much emphasis on this sin, for then we might leave the children with the impression that Isaac's sin was less serious. Although Isaac doubtless knew about the prophecy to Rebekah before the birth of his two sons, he selfishly preferred Esau. He favored Esau so much that he wanted to give him the main covenant blessing in spite of the prophecy. At this stage, Isaac was involved in a battle of the flesh against the Word of the Lord. There is also the danger of overlooking the sin of Esau. In taking Hittites as wives, Esau showed that he rejected the promise of the covenant.

When we tell this story, we will have to take a position above all those human sins. God maintains His prerogative in election. He maintains it first in opposition to Isaac and Esau and later upholds it with regard to the one He has chosen, when Jacob has to flee.

When we adopt this perspective, the sin on both sides can be examined in the proper light. Then we will be in a position to speak of God's grace in maintaining His prerogative in election. We recognize Jacob as a type of the Christ. God maintains this prerogative in the face of those who reject Him as well as those who try to obtain His blessing in the wrong way.

The blessing given to Esau in Genesis 27:39 should probably read as the more recent versions have it: "Away from the fatness of the earth shall your dwelling be, and away from the dew of heaven on high." Thus Esau was not to share in the earth's riches promised to Jacob but would dwell in the barren places. The next verse goes on to say that he would make his living by hunting.

187

When Isaac blessed Esau, he prophesied that when Esau broke loose, he would shake Jacob's yoke from his neck. In subsequent history recorded in the Bible, the Edomites submitted to Israel time and again but also tried on many occasions to free themselves. During the time of the Herods, an Edomite even reigned over Israel.

It is strange to hear Isaac give Esau such a blessing after Esau cried out to his father and begged for a blessing. If Esau had only acknowledged Jacob's blessing and submitted to Jacob's primacy, he, too, would have obtained salvation. But he wanted his own blessing, separate from Jacob's, and that's just what Isaac gave him. All the same, Jacob was to rule over Esau mercifully, as would the Christ. Believers would also be coming out of Edom.

It seems that till the very end, Isaac was not sure whether he was actually dealing with Esau or not. Yet he proceeded to pronounce the blessing on the person who appeared before him and claimed to be Esau. Did he bless Jacob against his will, in response to the urging of the Spirit within him? At first he blessed the heir to the promise in very bleak terms (see Gen. 27:28-9). Not until later, when Isaac again surrendered to the Word of the Lord and acknowledged that Jacob was the one God had chosen, did he communicate Abraham's blessing to Jacob in a fuller and more deliberate way (Gen. 28:3-4). When Hebrews 11:20 tells us that Isaac, by faith, "invoked future blessings on Jacob and Esau," it must be referring to the two occasions together.

Main thought: *God maintains His prerogative in election.*

Sinful scheming by Isaac and Esau. When Esau was 40 years old, he married two Hittite women, which caused Isaac and Rebekah a great deal of spiritual bitterness. By taking this step, Esau showed again that he despised the calling and promise of the covenant, for he was willing to have the holy race mix with the people living in the land of Canaan.

Yet Isaac continued to cling to Esau, his favorite. He knew that Jacob was to inherit the promise of the covenant and was also aware that Esau despised the promise while Jacob desired it. God's will was made clear to him in the way his sons developed. Yet, contrary to God's will, he wanted to give the blessing to Esau. By his favoritism, he opposed God's choice of Jacob.

Isaac had become old, so old that he was almost completely blind. He thought his death could not be far away, but he was mistaken, for he lived many more years. All the same, he thought the time had come for him to bless his sons. He would make sure that Esau got the covenant blessing.

He called Esau and asked him to go hunting. He wanted Esau to prepare some game for him to eat and promised that he would then give Esau the blessing. Esau proceeded to do what his father asked. It seemed that Esau was eager to obtain the blessing. He despised the covenant, but he wanted the temporal advantages that came with the covenant blessing, i.e. the advantage of being the first-born.

Thus Isaac and Esau were united in their opposition to the Lord's decree. They rejected Jacob as the Lord's chosen and tried to thwart God's plans. Apparently they did not want the blessing that can only be received by submitting to God's will. In the same manner, people today still reject the Chosen One (the Lord Jesus Christ) and God's will for Him.

Sinful scheming by Rebekah and Jacob. Apparently Rebekah was aware of what Isaac was planning to do. Isaac may even have talked it over with her earlier, rejecting her efforts to change his mind. Rebekah knew that Isaac's hopes could not be realized. Undoubtedly her preference for Jacob helped shape this conviction, but she was also submitting in faith to the prophecy about her sons. In her fear of what might happen, she eavesdropped on the conversation between Isaac and Esau. Then she called Jacob and told him to deceive his father.

Jacob feared the deception; he was afraid he would be caught. He would then be cursed instead of blessed. But Rebekah took all the responsibility on herself and told him that the curse would only affect her. Of course Jacob should not have let that determine his actions. Instead he should have insisted on taking the responsibility for his own actions.

Rebekah did not fear that curse. She was firmly convinced that everything would turn out right in the end, for it was God's will that Jacob receive the blessing.

It's amazing how faith and sin were mixed together in Rebekah. She was so strong in her conviction that she was able to convince Jacob. She even devised a clever plan to make the deception successful.

All the same, her deceit was deeply sinful. It's true that Rebekah's starting point was correct, but after she had failed to change Isaac's mind about giving the blessing to Esau, she should have left the rest up to the Lord, who would see to it that His Word would triumph. No one may try to obtain the Lord's blessing under false pretences.

A blessing for the deceiver. Jacob did just what his mother told him to do. When Isaac heard his voice, it sounded to him like Jacob's voice, but he finally fell for his son's trick anyway. Was Isaac's conscience bothering him by then? Did he yield to the deceit—perhaps unconsciously—because he knew that Jacob was the one who was to receive the blessing?

The smell of Esau's clothes, which Jacob had borrowed for the occasion, put Isaac in the mood to give a blessing. He promised Jacob the blessings of the earth and power over the nations. He also prophesied that Jacob's descendants would be the center of attention in the world: "Cursed be every one who curses you, and blessed be every one who blesses you."

Thus Isaac gave Jacob the blessing that God had once given Abraham, but in a rather weak form. Everything taking place in Isaac's tent was fouled by sin, but the Lord saw to it that His chosen one received the blessing despite the plans of Isaac and Esau. The blessing cannot be taken away from the one God has chosen. God jealously guards His prerogative in election.

In the same manner, God carefully defends and upholds the choice He made when He elected Christ. As God's chosen one, Jacob was only a type of the Christ. Because Christ is the One God has chosen, God's blessing cannot be taken away from Him. Neither will anyone ever receive any genuine blessing apart from that Chosen One. Someday all the nations will have to recognize the Christ as God's Chosen One and see how God blesses Him.

A blessing for Esau. Jacob had hardly left Isaac when Esau came home from the field. Only then did Isaac understand the deception. He might have been uncertain before, but now he was sure of what had happened and saw how awful it was. He became aware of all the sin in his own household. Perhaps he even realized how sinful he had been in his preference for Esau. Isaac must have seen how the Word of the Lord had crushed his plans and conquered him. That was why he immediately said that Jacob was the one to whom the blessing belonged.

Esau gave expression to his bitter sorrow and annoyance, sneering that Jacob's name indeed meant *deceiver*. But the reason for his sorrow was that the blessing of the first-born had passed him by. Unfortunately, he was not sorry about his contempt for the covenant. On the contrary, he still refused to bow before the Lord. If he had accepted Jacob's election and Jacob's blessing, there would have been salvation for him as well. But that was not what Esau wanted. There will also be an everlasting grinding of teeth about the victory of Christ, the One whom people in this life did not want to acknowledge as God's Chosen.

Esau then asked for a blessing of his own, separate from the blessing given to Jacob. Isaac gave him what he asked for. "Unlike Jacob, you will not receive the fatness of the earth," he said. "You will dwell in barren lands. There you will live from hunting and from spoil. You will be your brother's servant, but when you break loose, you will shake his yoke from your neck."

In reality this was a terrible prediction about Esau's future, for revolting against Jacob meant revolting against the Christ. Unfortunately, Esau's descendants (the Edomites) have been the constant enemies of Israel and of God's covenant with His people. Yet there must have been Edomites who went down on their knees before the Christ. Thus Esau is subjected to Jacob, to the Christ, in an eternal rule of mercy.

The chosen one disciplined. Esau did not submit to the decree of the Lord. On the contrary, he hated Jacob on account of the blessing he had received and planned to kill him as soon as his father died. Apparently there was a peculiar tie between Esau and Isaac. His respect for his father held Esau back as long as Isaac was still alive.

Esau's words were reported to Rebekah, who then ordered Jacob to flee to her brother Laban in Haran. Pitifully she comforted herself and Jacob by saying that Esau's wrath would be short-lived, and that she would soon be able to send word to Jacob to return.

She must have known in her heart that Jacob's absence would probably last a while longer, and that the coming departure could well mean a final good-by. That must have been a bitter thought for both of them. No doubt they felt that the Lord was against them because of their deceit.

Jacob was indeed the one God had chosen, but for that very reason he would have to surrender completely to the calling and promise of the Lord and not walk in his own ways. This flight was the Lord's way of chastising him. Through this frightening chapter in Jacob's life and some other events as well, the Lord would purify him of his wilfulness. Jacob would have to follow the path of suffering. In this respect, too, he was a type of the Christ. Yet Christ followed the path of suffering and the cross not because of any sins He had committed but to atone for the sins of others.

Submitting to God's will. It was easy for Rebekah to find a justification for Jacob's leaving home. She pointed out to Isaac that Esau had married Hittite wives and declared that if Jacob should also get mixed up with the people of that land, her life would no longer be worth living. Here she was giving expression to her faith; she was showing that she lived by the promise.

Isaac therefore commanded Jacob to go to Paddan-aram and get himself a wife from his mother's family. Knowing and believing that Jacob was the heir to the promise, he now urged him never to take a wife from among the Canaanites. Evidently Isaac had abandoned his opposition to the Word of the Lord. When Jacob departed, he gave him the full blessing of Abraham. God had brought Isaac back to a recognition of His divine prerogative.

Jacob went away. He bowed under the cross laid on him because of his sin. He was obedient to his father and mother—and thereby to the Lord. He submitted to God's will and rejected the prospect of mixing with the Canaanites.

Because matters had been straightened out in principle between Jacob and his parents, fresh jealousy erupted in Esau, who now took another wife while keeping his two Hittite wives. His latest wife came from the line of Ishmael, Abraham's son. He probably thought this step would help him make peace with his parents, but he was mistaken. Hadn't Ishmael despised God's covenant with Abraham? Esau did not live by the covenant and thus did not understand what his parents believed and wanted. There is no room for compromise when it comes to the Lord and His covenant. Only complete submission will do, and that was out of the question as far as Esau was concerned.

26: God's Primacy in the Covenant

Genesis 28:10-22

Jacob had received the blessing of Abraham, but God had not yet revealed Himself personally to him. Moreover, when Jacob left his father's tent, his conscience must have bothered him terribly about the way he had obtained that blessing. There was something standing between God and Jacob, who had not been recognized directly by the Lord as the one upon whom the blessing rested.

When we bear this in mind, the meaning of the Bethel episode becomes evident. At Bethel God acknowledged Jacob as the bearer of the blessing and granted him His fellowship for Christ's sake. This acknowledgment came even before things were straightened out between God and Jacob many years later at Peniel. Here again God showed that *He* takes the initiative in the covenant. He was even willing to overlook Jacob's sin temporarily.

Jacob may have thought that he came first and that he had sought God out by reaching for the blessing, but now he learned that it is God who takes the initiative. This was also impressed upon him through the fact that the promise came to him while he was asleep. Jacob was not involved actively in the encounter between himself and God. It was made clear to him beyond denial that the surety of the covenant is rooted solely in the faithfulness of God. When the Lord acknowledged Jacob as the heir to the promise, He assured him that He would always be by his side.

After God appeared to Jacob in the dream, Jacob called the place where he had slept a holy place, a gate of heaven. He identified the gracious revelation of the Lord with that place (Bethel), which was also of special significance to him later in his life. In the same way, God's revelation of grace was later tied to Jerusalem and the temple.

Bethel and Jerusalem find their fulfillment in the Christ, in whom the revelation of God's grace is complete. Yet that revelation of grace was more closely identified with Jacob—as the one blessed by the Lord and as a type of the Christ—than with Bethel. From Jacob the angels climbed up to God, bringing Him Jacob's life and needs, but they also descended to Jacob, giving him the grace and love of God. There was intimate covenant communion between God and Jacob; Jacob gave himself to the Lord because the Lord gave Himself to Jacob and would continue to do so in the future. Thus Jacob was undoubtedly a type of the Christ, who enjoys perfect communion with God. Fortunately, Christ lets us share in that communion.

When Jacob anointed the stone and set it up in faith as a sign, he was accepting God's promise. That act on his part is not to be identified with the idolatrous anointing customary among the heathens. When Jacob anointed the stone at Bethel, he was consecrating Bethel as the place where God had revealed Himself. In Jacob's time and throughout the Old Testament period, revelation was still tied to a particular place. In Christ we can now worship the Father anywhere. Yet we still worship Him on the earth. Thus faith is not separated from the earth.

The consecration of Bethel was a prophecy that one day the whole earth would be consecrated as the house of God. This happened in principle when the Holy Spirit was poured out.

When Jacob declared, "If God will be with me and will keep me in this way that I go . . . ," he was not laying down a condition for consecrating his life to the Lord. If he had thought in terms of conditions, it would have been clear that Jacob did not accept the Lord's promise at Bethel in faith. He lived in the conviction that the Lord would surely do as He had promised. Therefore his surrender to the Lord was genuine. By his vow he accepted the Lord's promise in faith.

Main thought: *As the One who takes the initiative in the covenant, the Lord offers His communion to His own.*

Far from the covenant circle. Jacob did what his father Isaac told him to do: he went to Paddan-aram (Haran) to find himself a wife. The real reason for his departure, however, was the sin by which he had obtained the blessing. Now he had to cut himself off from the covenant circle. When would he be able to return to it?

He had received the blessing, of course, but the Lord had never appeared to him personally. What did the Lord mean to him,

especially now that he had sinned? To be sure, Jacob had gone
after that blessing, but was he interested in it because of the Lord
Himself? That would become clear only through a meeting with
the Lord. Or would the Lord turn away from him because of his
sins? In any case, he must have felt forsaken, cast out of the
covenant circle.

All those questions, which must have filled Jacob's heart,
were answered when the Lord revealed Himself to Jacob. At that
first encounter, the Lord made it clear that although Jacob had
received the blessing in the wrong way, it was truly his. The Lord
then bound Himself to Jacob so that he would not be lonely as he
went farther and farther away from the covenant circle.

The Lord could form this bond with the sinner Jacob only for
Christ's sake. He bound Himself to Jacob to such an extent that
He temporarily overlooked the sin Jacob had committed, by giving
him the promise without chastising him. Fortunately, our lives are
preserved by God's covenant faithfulness—not by our own
faithfulness.

Jacob's ladder. On the evening of the first day of his
journey, Jacob lay down under the bare heavens. He used a stone
for his pillow. In a dream that night, he saw a ladder between
heaven and earth. God's angels were climbing up and down the
ladder, and the Lord stood at the very top. In this dream, the Lord
told Jacob that He was the God of his father Abraham and of
Isaac. What God had been to Abraham and Isaac He now wanted
to be to Jacob as well. From then on the Lord would be bound to
Jacob, and Jacob would be bound to the Lord. There was to be a
continuous communion between the Lord and Jacob. This
communion was symbolized by the ladder in the dream: the angels
climbed up it to carry Jacob's life and the consecration of his
heart to the Lord and climbed down it to declare the blessing of
the Lord to Jacob.

Such wonderful communion cannot properly exist between
God and a sinful human being; it is only possible between
God and the Man Jesus Christ, who was obedient to God in all
things. For Christ's sake, the communion with God enjoyed by
Jacob is now available to all of us—if we believe in the Christ, who

atoned for our waywardness.

In His own voice, God repeated to Jacob the promise made to Abraham. God would give him the land and numerous descendants. In that seed, all the families of the earth would be blessed. With an eye to the journey that Jacob was just beginning, a journey that would take him away from the covenant circle, God promised to accompany Jacob and bring him back to his own land.

God revealed Himself to Jacob while he was asleep, giving him wonderful promises. In that condition, Jacob himself could do nothing but listen to what God was promising. Fortunately, God's promise and covenant do not depend on our consent or our work. They come from God, who enriches us through them. The response He expects from us is faith.

Heaven's gate. When Jacob awoke the next morning, he said: "Surely the LORD is in this place, and I did not know it!" Jacob was amazed that the Lord should seek him out in such a way and grant him this communion, which went beyond anything he could have imagined. God's grace always goes far beyond our expectations.

Jacob was also filled with fear—not in the sense of terror but of holy trembling in the face of God's wonderful grace. "What an awesome place this is!" he said. "This is none other than the house of God and the gate of heaven! God lives here, and I was privileged to commune with Him here."

That spot became a very special place for Jacob, a place that was also to play an important role in his later life. It was holy to him, for there God had communed with him for the first time. When Israel became a nation, there was also a special place where God wished to commune with His people, a place like this gate of heaven, namely, the tabernacle (and later the temple).

We do not have such holy places any longer, for the meaning of those places has been fulfilled in the Lord Jesus Christ. Now He is our gate to heaven, our entryway to God. Yet, in the Lord Jesus Christ we see the grace of God as something so infinitely high and immeasurably deep that we are sometimes filled with holy trembling in the face of the glory of that revelation of His grace.

The vow. Jacob then set up the stone that had served as his pillow and poured oil over it. From that point on, the stone would be a symbol of what God had promised him and also of his acceptance of the promise, his belief that God would indeed give him the land in which he and his seed would serve the Lord.

Jacob made a solemn promise at the site of the stone: if the Lord would bring him back to his father's house in peace, he would serve the Lord as his God. That stone would be like a temple to him, to remind him that he was to give the Lord a tenth of everything he received. He would also worship the Lord at that place.

When Jacob promised to serve the Lord if the Lord would bring him back in peace, he was not laying down a condition. He believed without a doubt that the Lord would indeed bring him back, and that he would then offer his life in that land to the Lord. By giving the Lord one tenth of his possessions, he was showing that he surrendered his whole life to the Lord.

To Jacob, that holy place was a symbol standing for the entire country. He wanted the entire land to be a holy land in which the Lord was served. That one Bethel (i.e. house of God) marked the whole land as a Bethel.

We who live after Christ's ascension see a still broader meaning in that name: we have learned to view the entire earth as a Bethel in which we serve the Lord. All of the earth can become a Bethel because the Lord has poured out His Spirit. Since we have the Spirit, we may serve the Lord anywhere on earth. After the renewal of heaven and earth, the earth will be a Bethel in the full sense of the word, for then God will dwell among men forever.

27: The Word Becomes Flesh

Genesis 29-30

In Genesis 29 and 30, the promise that there would be many descendants is brought to partial fulfillment in the birth of eleven sons. (Jacob's twelfth son was born later.) Because Jacob received so many sons and also became wealthy, we can speak here of the Word becoming flesh. The promise was taking shape.

Of course there is more involved in this talk of the Word becoming flesh, namely, the sanctification of man's sinful nature. Because of this sanctification, the Child to be born of Mary could be called the Holy One. In this segment of Bible history, then, man's sinful nature was being sanctified according to the purposes of God's grace.

This process already began when Laban and Jacob reached an agreement that Jacob would serve Laban seven years for Rachel, and later on another seven years. Laban had no noble intentions: he sold his daughters to his nephew Jacob because of the advantages Jacob could bring him. Jacob was not taken into Laban's heart or his house. Thus, because Jacob remained a stranger in Haran, there was no danger of his settling there permanently and becoming involved in the life of the local people.

The deceit of Laban and the jealousy between Leah and Rachel were factors in Jacob's becoming the father of twelve sons. This is an illustration of the sanctifying power of the Word of the promise. When Abraham fathered a child born in unbelief (i.e. Ishmael), that child was cast out. In Jacob's case, however, all the sons became heads of tribes and heirs to the promise. The Word of the promise was at work here, overcoming the sins of men and sanctifying all those sons.

When Leah named her first four sons, she spoke each time of the Lord, the covenant God. Apparently the unhappiness she endured because of Jacob's love for Rachel had sanctified her. In faith she became preoccupied with the covenant promise given to Jacob.

When Rachel named her servant's sons, however, she spoke of God without using His covenant name. It appears that the covenant, with its promise, was still meaningless to her at that time. Later on, Leah's faith also dwindled away, because of jealousy; when she named her servant's sons, she spoke only of her happiness. When the light finally dawned in Rachel and she received a child, she, too, confessed the Lord.

It appears as though the Lord punished Jacob for taking more than one wife—hence all the misery in his household. On the other hand, He seems to have used the misery as a way of revealing Himself to Leah and Rachel.

After Laban tricked Jacob into marrying Leah, Jacob agreed to Laban's sinful proposal and took Rachel to himself as well. The deceiver had been deceived. In all that happened afterwards, Jacob must have seen the hand of the Lord against him many a time.

It is not completely clear when the two weddings took place. The second one came one week after the first, at the end of the week-long wedding feast. (Laban told Jacob to wait until the week of the marriage festivities was over.) However, it is not certain whether that double wedding took place at the beginning of those fourteen years or in the middle. In any event, the double wedding did not come at the end. Most of the evidence suggests that it took place after the first seven-year period.

Jacob increased his wealth by means of the trick of putting peeled rods in the watering troughs of the flocks. Again a sinful intent lived in his heart. But an angel of God came to him in a dream to inform him that the blessings came from the God who had appeared to him at Bethel (see Gen. 31:10-13). Here, too, sinful human nature was being sanctified through the Word of the promise.

Main thought: *The promise receives its initial fulfillment when Jacob is blessed.*

Serving for wages. From Bethel Jacob traveled on in the direction of Haran. After many days' journey, he arrived at a well in the field, where he found three flocks of sheep accompanied by shepherds. The well was covered by a stone that could hardly be rolled away by one man. Therefore the shepherds often waited for each other at the well.

When Jacob questioned the shepherds, he learned that they came from Haran. It soon became obvious that they knew Laban,

Jacob's uncle. They told him that Laban's daughter would soon be coming to the well with some sheep.

Jacob wanted to be alone with his cousin when he met her. Hence he tried to persuade the shepherds to leave, pointing out that it was still early in the day. They replied that they could not leave, for no shepherd or shepherdess was to be alone at the well.

While they were still talking, Rachel came along with the sheep. Jacob immediately rushed to help her, singlehandedly rolling the stone away from the well's mouth and giving water to her sheep. He then told her that he was the son of Rebekah. Therefore she took him back with her to Laban's house.

Jacob quickly made himself useful by helping with the pasturing of Laban's flocks. We do not know whether Jacob told Laban why he could not return to his home. In any case, Laban must have been aware that Jacob wanted to stay on. Moreover, he must have noticed that Jacob had fallen in love with Rachel, his younger daughter. Laban wanted to make the most of these circumstances, for he had discovered that Jacob was a good shepherd. Therefore he proposed that Jacob serve him for wages.

In this way, Jacob's stay in his uncle's house was assured. Unfortunately, he was not made a member of the family or taken into the family circle. Because of his greediness, Laban lacked sensitivity. Yet the Lord deliberately let things develop in this way, for he did not want Jacob to feel at home in Haran. Jacob had to remain a stranger so that he would eventually return to Canaan to await the complete fulfillment of the promise there.

Jacob took Laban up on his offer and agreed to serve his uncle seven years for Rachel. This service was not meant to take the place of a dowry, for Jacob was paid wages. All the same, it was hardly a fitting way to deal with such a matter as marriage. Greedy Laban was happy to accept Jacob's proposal.

The seven years that Jacob served for Rachel seemed but a few days to him, for he loved her deeply. At the end of seven years, the marriage ceremony was to take place. But when the wedding night came, Laban brought Leah to Jacob instead of Rachel. Jacob did not realize that he had been tricked until the next morning. In the face of Jacob's accusation, Laban tried to excuse himself by saying that it was not customary in that region to marry off the younger daughter before the first-born. If this were true,

Laban should not have made such a promise to Jacob in the first place. Laban then proposed to let Jacob have Rachel as well once the week-long wedding feast was over. Jacob accepted. Thereby the wedding state lost its dignity and was degraded.

A week later, then, Jacob was given another wife, which meant that he had to serve Laban seven more years. During all those years, he remained a stranger and a servant in Laban's house. According to the Lord's decree, he was to remain isolated, just as his grandfather Abraham has been set apart. Jacob was set apart for the sake of the Christ, just as Abraham had been. The Christ was set apart from everything sinful in this world and was therefore a stranger on earth. God's great Son governed Jacob's life in Haran.

If we are Christ's, we are not called to separate ourselves from life, but we must indeed see to it that we live apart from the sin of the world. As far as sinful life on earth is concerned, we are strangers for Christ's sake.

The birth of the children. It did not take long for the misery caused by the double wedding to become apparent, for Jacob loved Rachel and neglected Leah. That's why the Lord was concerned about Leah. How often God takes the side of those who are oppressed on earth! He finds the oppression of life intolerable especially within the covenant circle. Thus the Lord gave Leah four sons, while He withheld children from Rachel.

During the early years of her marriage, Leah turned to the Lord, the God of the covenant and the promise, who reigned over the household of her husband. That she sought Him in her suffering is obvious from the names she gave her sons: Reuben, Simeon, Levi, and Judah. Each of these names contains a mention of the covenant God. She praised the Lord especially and displayed her bonds with Him when her fourth son was born—by calling him Judah. The Christ was later to be born of Judah's line. The great privilege of becoming mother to the line that would lead to the Christ went to Leah instead of Rachel.

At the time Leah's children were born, Rachel was consumed with jealousy, for she did not have any children. Therefore she complained to Jacob, who answered her angrily and declared that he was not responsible for her failure to conceive. Rachel then suggested that he take her servant Bilhah for a wife, with the idea that Bilhah's children would be reckoned as Rachel's. This step damaged Jacob's marriage even more.

Bilhah had two sons, Dan and Naphtali, who were born out of jealousy and unbelief. Yet the Lord accepted them as future tribes of His people. The Lord Himself had decreed it that way. While Ishmael was earlier lost to the people of God, the Word of the promise now overcame the sins of men and sanctified those births, simply because it was the Lord's will.

Leah then stopped having children, so she gave Jacob her servant (Zilpah) for a wife. Only envy of Rachel made her decide on this measure. Zilpah likewise had two sons, Gad and Asher. By then Leah's spiritual life had almost dwindled away. When she named these two sons, she spoke only of hope and good fortune.

Later on, the Lord again thought of Leah, who was still being neglected by Jacob, and gave her two more sons, Issachar and Zebulun. When she named them, she spoke of God but did not use His covenant name. She also had a daughter, Dinah.

At last God turned to Rachel in His covenant grace, giving her a son whom she called Joseph. In that name, she showed that God had removed the shame of her past, and that she hoped that the Lord would someday give her another son. Thus she now mentioned the name of the Lord, the covenant God. Apparently happiness had opened Rachel's eyes to the blessings of the covenant.

While Jacob lived in Haran, then, the Lord gave him eleven sons. Though they were born in the midst of envy and jealousy, the Lord in His grace overlooked all that sin, for He now wanted to begin fulfilling the promise that a great nation would be born of Abraham's line. By the power of the grace of Christ, who was to atone for our sins, God saw to it that those sins led to no fatal consequences.

Sly calculation. At the end of the fourteen years, Jacob wanted to leave. But Laban realized that the Lord had blessed him for Jacob's sake and therefore asked Jacob to stay. He wanted Jacob to work for wages, but Jacob told him that he was not content with mere wages; he wanted a part of the blessing which

God had given Laban for his sake. He told Laban that he would settle for a small portion of that blessing. He wanted all the speckled and spotted animals—all the black sheep and the speckled and spotted goats. This was to take effect at once: Jacob would also share in the blessings God had already given Laban, for he would receive all the speckled and spotted animals in Laban's flocks as his own. If all the animals were divided along such lines, there could never be any misunderstanding about who owned them.

Laban agreed, and the flocks of the two men were separated. Jacob's flock would be pastured by Laban's sons, while Jacob would take care of Laban's flock. Moreover, Laban stipulated that Jacob's flock was to pasture three days away from his own, so that his animals would not see any spotted animals and have opportunity to mate with them. He believed that no spotted animals would be born in his own flock.

But Jacob played a trick on Laban. He put partly peeled rods in the watering troughs of the flock, which led to the birth of many spotted animals in Laban's flock. He also drove young spotted animals in front of Laban's main flock from time to time. The resulting matings led to the birth of more spotted animals, which Jacob could then claim for himself. Thus Jacob's flock grew, and he became rich. In time he had many servants of his own.

Here Jacob showed that his deceitful nature had not changed. But the grace of the Lord overcame human sin: Jacob was blessed for the sake of the Word of the promise. Yet all of Jacob's sins were uncovered later, when the Lord turned against him because of them. But for the time being, the blessing won out for Christ's sake. The Lord even showed Jacob in a dream that many spotted animals would be born because of the Lord's blessing. How ashamed Jacob must have felt then! God can overlook our sins temporarily because He directs them to the Christ, but He will confront us with them eventually.

28: Separation by the Word

Genesis 31

It was at God's express command that Laban and Jacob went their separate ways. Of course the attitude of Laban and his sons and their envy of Jacob were factors in the separation. Yet the Lord deliberately ordered Jacob to leave. God saw to it that Jacob never developed close ties with the people of Paddan-aram, for if he had, he would not have been able to leave so easily.

At the end of his stay in Paddan-aram, God spoke to Jacob again, just as He had spoken to him at Bethel. God reminded Jacob of that earlier encounter. When God spoke, light again entered Jacob's life.

The dream of which Jacob spoke to his wives can only be understood as a direct revelation from God (see the connection between verses 13 and 3 of Genesis 31). In that dream, the Lord showed Jacob that the increase of his flock was not just the result of his tricks but the Lord's doing. Because of this revelation, Jacob must have looked at his stay in Haran in a different light.

God had safeguarded Jacob from the greediness of Laban, and now He was separating the two men. In this context Laban is referred to as "the Aramean." Laban wanted the fruit of Jacob's blessing—but not its essence. Thus he was hostile toward the one blessed by the Lord. The danger of which Jacob spoke, namely, that Laban might send him away empty-handed, was by no means imaginary.

Even though the parting came about by the Word of the Lord, it was not complete: Jacob's sons carried much of the Aramean character with them, and Rachel stole her father's household idols. Was she hoping for another son through the blessing of those gods? Why would she take those idols if she had given her heart fully to the Lord?

The separation between man and sin is complete in the Christ. This separation between Jacob and Laban was also governed by Him.

Main thought: *Jacob and Laban are separated by the Word of the Lord.*

The flight. Laban's sons saw Jacob's flocks, which they had to pasture, increasing steadily. Jacob had become richer than Laban. Jacob heard Laban's sons talking enviously about his prosperity and realized that Laban's attitude toward him had changed to hostility.

Jacob wanted to break with Laban, but this was also the Lord's will. Through Jacob's desire, the Lord brought about a separation, so that Jacob would not get involved with life in Haran. One night the Lord came to Jacob in a dream and told him to leave that land.

Jacob called Leah and Rachel together in the field and complained about Laban. He told them about Laban's hostility and pointed out how Laban had changed his wages time and again in the six years that Jacob had served him after the initial fourteen years. Jacob also told his wives that he had been shown in a dream that the Lord had protected him from Laban's greediness. It's not likely that Jacob told them about his own tricks, but what he did say was no lie. He also informed them that the Lord had commanded him to leave that land.

Leah and Rachel immediately agreed with his plan. Through his greediness, Laban had also alienated his daughters. They complained that their father had *sold* them to Jacob. Moreover, the things he should have given to Jacob in the form of a dowry he tried to keep for himself. (Jacob eventually acquired them anyway.) This estrangement, too, was the Lord's doing.

One day, when Laban was busy shearing his sheep, Jacob fled with his wives, children, servants, and all his possessions. Jacob had not dared to tell Laban about the Lord's command to leave. Yet, if he truly believed it was the Lord who had spoken to him, he should have done so, for then the break with Laban would have been seen openly as a break for God's sake. Instead Jacob had fled in secret.

Jacob's departure was not a complete break—especially not where Rachel was concerned. Rachel left not for the Lord's sake but for the sake of her own future. She even stole the household idols from her father's house. Apparently her heart still clung to them. She expected another son with their help—instead of leaving that matter in the Lord's hands. Thus Rachel did not surrender wholly to the Lord's calling.

By His Word, the Lord had separated Jacob and Laban, so that Jacob would live only for the Word of the Lord and await the fulfillment of the promise in Canaan. Events had to take this course for the sake of Christ, who is completely removed from the sinful life of the world. Since Jacob's separation was not complete, the cleansing of his house would have to continue later.

The Aramean. Not until the third day did Laban find out about Jacob's flight. Laban was beside himself with anger, not because he loved Jacob but because he wanted the fruit of Jacob's blessing. He had started to hate Jacob because of the promise and the covenant of the Lord. This hatred was the hatred of an unbeliever for the heir to the promise.

Now Jacob had escaped, disgracing Laban's house by his secret flight. Therefore Laban got all his kinsmen together and pursued Jacob. After seven days he overtook him in the hill country of Gilead, in Transjordan.

The night before Laban caught up with Jacob, God appeared to him in a dream and told him that he was not to try to make Jacob return—neither by flattery and promises nor by angry words. God upheld the separation, and Laban had to submit to it.

It was the Lord who had sent Jacob away and protected him in the separation. The Aramean encountered God, who watched over the heir to the promise. For a long time, his greediness had made things hard for Jacob, but at last the trap had been sprung and Jacob had escaped.

In the same way, the evil one hates the Christ and is hostile to Him. Yet, in His resurrection and ascension, Christ has broken all the bonds. Those who belong to Christ are being persecuted and oppressed on earth, but someday there will be an escape for them too. The day will come when the Lord confronts the enemies of His church.

Settling the differences. When Laban spoke to Jacob, he

reproached him only for his secret flight. Hypocritically he added that he had wanted to hold a great feast for Jacob before he went away. He admitted that he had the power to harm Jacob but had been forbidden to do so by the God of Jacob's father. With a sneer he asked why Jacob had taken along the household idols belonging to Laban if the separation was for the Lord's sake and would lead to Jacob's inheriting the promise.

Jacob answered that he was afraid Laban would have stripped him of all his possessions and sent him away empty-handed. But he also turned immediately to the motive that he regarded as most important: he declared that the separation was for God's sake. He went on to promise that the person who had stolen Laban's household idols would be killed. (Jacob did not know that Rachel was the guilty party.)

Laban then searched all the tents, but he did not find the idols, for Rachel had hidden them in a clever way. Jacob became angry that Laban had pursued him and had dared to accuse him of stealing the idols. Jacob did not know that while his house was cleared of suspicion in the eyes of men, it was not blameless before God. Yet Jacob showed that he was only following God's calling, and that he had had no part in the sin of the Aramean. Thus the Lord restored what Jacob's secret flight had spoiled.

Now he could also point out to Laban how he had served him faithfully, while Laban had profited from the fruits of his labors without ever really accepting him. The God of Abraham, the God whom Isaac also feared, had watched over Jacob. In reality, Laban had been opposing the Lord.

When Laban heard all this, he became ashamed. He knew that everything Jacob had—wives and children and possessions— had come from him. What was he to do about that? He would let Jacob have all of it and would acknowledge him as rightful owner. To be sure, this step of Laban's part was long overdue. Moreover, Laban had been forced to take this step.

Thus Jacob and Laban finally settled their differences. Laban acknowledged Jacob—albeit unwillingly—as the one blessed by the Lord. Won't all men someday have to acknowledge the Christ as the One blessed by the Lord, even though many will only do so unwillingly? The Lord had bestowed an honor on Jacob for Christ's sake.

The covenant. Laban even wanted to make a covenant with Jacob, and Jacob agreed. He set up a stone as a sign and asked Laban's kinsmen, who were also his kinsmen, to gather stones. Together they made a heap of stones as a witness to their covenant and called it Mizpah, which means *watchman*: that heap of stones was to see to it that the covenant was enforced.

Laban demanded that Jacob not take any wives besides his daughters. Neither he nor Jacob was allowed to pass that heap with hostile intentions against the other. Both men took an oath to abide by the agreement, with Jacob swearing by the God whom his father Isaac feared. Afterward they had a meal together to confirm their agreement.

However, this agreement involved a sharp demarcation between Jacob and Laban. There was no spiritual bond between them; they were lined up against each other as the heir to the promise and the man who hated the blessing of the promise.

Jacob never passed that heap of stones with a hostile intent. The boundary was respected by his descendants as well. Later the Christ went beyond that boundary with His gospel—not with hostile intentions but to bring salvation to Aram (Syria).

Believers are never to cross the boundary between themselves and unbelievers for hostile purposes. They are to go to unbelievers not to destroy but to bring the message of salvation.

Early the next morning, Laban said good-by to his grandchildren and daughters. With his kinsmen, he then returned to Haran.

29: Israel's God

Genesis 32-33

Up to this point, God was willing to bless Jacob while overlooking his sins. But when Jacob returned to Canaan, God confronted him with those sins in order to purify him. To that end, he used Jacob's fear of his brother Esau.

From the very beginning, Jacob's struggle was a quest for the Lord's blessing, for the promise of the covenant. That was clear even at his birth, when he held on to his brother's heel. (The Bible makes this point in Hosea 12:4.) Yet the manner and means used by Jacob were often clearly of the flesh, which was why he was in need of purification.

The big turning point in his life came at Peniel, where God gave him the name *Israel*. At that point he became the wrestler who no longer struggled with men for the blessing but with God—the wrestler armed with spiritual weapons, with faith.

Of course that victory over the flesh was not complete. The flesh continued to intrude in his household, which is why Scripture still refers to him often as "Jacob" after the change in his name. When he returned to Bethel, the change of name was confirmed.

The wrestling match at the Jabbok was God's idea. Scripture tells us that a "man" wrestled with Jacob, but that "man" was no one other than God.

When we tell this story, we should place the emphasis not on what Jacob did or on his kingly bearing toward God and man but on what God did. God purified Jacob in that struggle and brought him into Canaan as a renewed person. This Jacob acknowledged in the name he gave to the altar at Shechem: he called it "The God of Israel is God." The One with whom he had wrestled, the One who had allowed him to prevail, was the mighty God who had brought him to Canaan.

The wrestling match at the Jabbok was a real event—and not a dream. The Man Jacob faced, his opponent, was God. This quickly became clear to him. His fear of Esau was his fear of the sin by which he

210

had deceived Esau. And his fear of that sin was ultimately a fear of God, who confronted him in that sin. He recognized God in the Man wrestling with him.

On Jacob's part, the struggle was a matter of holding on in prayer and supplication (see Hosea 12:4). Jacob submitted to the Lord in His hostility and anger, but at the same time he clung to the Lord for His covenant and promise. In the power of the promise, he could prevail against the Lord in His anger and wrestle on to win the blessing.

Jacob's struggle was only a slight shadow of Christ's struggle in Gethsemane and on the cross. When Christ held on to God in his utter abandonment—while God was completely against Him—He was laying the foundation for the covenant. Yet the wrestling of the Christ and all the struggles of believers who feel forsaken remind us of Jacob's wrestling match. Because of Christ, believers are assured of victory.

Main thought: *The Lord reveals Himself as a wrestler.*

Jacob's fear. After Laban's departure, Jacob traveled on toward Canaan. Along the way he met God, who had bound Himself in a particular way to the land of Canaan. By his deceit, Jacob had sinned against God. He thought of Esau, but this immediately led him to think of the Lord too. What was Esau to him? Even more important, what was the Lord to him?

While thinking these thoughts during the journey, he saw a multitude of angels. His eyes had to be opened so that he could see them. It was as though they were coming from Canaan to meet him. The angels were the Lord's messengers, but he did not know whether they were for him or against him. There had been no confrontation yet. The army of angels and his army were still separate. Therefore he called that place Mahanaim.

Then he sent messengers to his brother Esau, who was living in the mountainous country of Seir in the land of Edom, south of Canaan. Esau, the hunter and fighter, found in those barren mountains the surroundings that suited him. He had not forgotten Canaan, but he was willing to leave it to his brother Jacob. Many men of valor were with Esau, who had apparently acquired power and wealth.

Esau gave Jacob's messengers no definite answer but set out to meet Jacob himself, accompanied by 400 men. Apparently Esau

had not yet made up his mind how to approach Jacob. His earlier
anger had subsided, but he felt that he now had Jacob in his power
and could do with him as he pleased. Esau's attitude would depend
on what Jacob said and did.

Jacob's messengers told him that Esau was coming with 400
men. This upset Jacob greatly. In his fear, he divided his family,
servants and animals into two companies: if Esau attacked one
company, the other would have a chance of escaping.

Then he turned to the Lord and called upon Him as the God
of his father Abraham and his father Isaac, the God of the
covenant, the God whose promise he had received. He appealed to
the Lord's own assurance that Jacob would return. He confessed
his sin before the Lord and declared that he was not worthy of all
the blessings he had received. He begged God to deliver him now
from the hand of Esau, for Esau might kill him together with his
family and servants. The Lord had promised that Jacob's seed
would be too numerous to count. How could that promise then
be fulfilled?

Jacob prayed fervently, but he found no rest. He still sensed
that the Lord was against him, and that the sin between himself
and God had not yet been removed. He stayed right where he was
instead of advancing to meet his brother.

Yet he was eager to do whatever he could to appease his
brother. Therefore he sent servants ahead with cattle to present to
Esau. He hoped that a series of gifts would put Esau in a good
mood. The presents were intended to still his brother's anger over
Jacob's deceit. As he took these measures, however, his eye was on
the Lord.

The wrestling match. Jacob was restless when night came.
Finally he got up and made the company that had remained with
him cross the ford of the Jabbok. He himself stayed behind to be
alone with God.

There he met a Man who wrestled with him. In that Man he
recognized the Lord, whom he feared. Jacob was afraid not just of
Esau but also of the Lord, who had turned against him because of
his sin. In wrestling with the Man, Jacob was clinging to God in

hopes of appeasing Him. It was possible that God would turn to him again in favor!

During the wrestling match, Jacob was terribly afraid. All his sins and his deceitful nature rose up before him. Yet he had a basis on which to make his plea, namely, that God would be faithful to the promise He had made.

Much more fearsome was the struggle of the Lord Jesus Christ, against whom God turned because of our sins. Christ had no promise to appeal to. He first had to provide the basis for the covenant and the promise by His work of reconciliation. Yet Jacob's wrestling match pointed ahead to Christ's struggle. All believers have something to learn from that struggle.

When dawn was breaking, the Man with whom Jacob was wrestling touched Jacob's thigh and put it out of joint. Jacob was to keep this injury as a remembrance of his struggle. For the rest of his life, he walked with a limp, as a permanent reminder that he must never again seek the fulfillment of the promise in his own strength and by his own means.

When the Man asked Jacob to let Him go, Jacob felt he had won. The blessing of the Lord was his; the Lord had allowed Jacob to gain the victory over Him. Therefore he said: "I will not let You go unless You bless me."

The blessing took the form of a change in Jacob's name. From then on he would be called Israel, for he had borne himself like a king toward God and men—and prevailed. All his life—even in earlier days when his gaze had been fixed mainly on people—he had struggled for the promise. Now his struggle had become a wrestling with God, for God had chosen Jacob as His opponent. In that struggle Jacob had prevailed, by basing his plea on the promise.

When Jacob asked the Man His name, He refused to tell him. God can never pronounce His name all at once. God's revelation always comes to us as a surprise. Jacob, too, would find that out.

Jacob called that place Peniel, for there he had seen the face of God and survived the encounter. From that time on, he walked with a limp. Because of this aftereffect of Jacob's encounter with God, the Jews refuse to eat the nerve of the hip. Thereby they honor the struggle of their father Jacob.

Reconciliation with Esau. In the light of the night's events, Jacob took an entirely different attitude toward his meeting with his brother. Now he was sure of God's favor and could lay his fears to rest.

Early in the morning he saw Esau coming. He put the maids with their children at the head of his party. Then came Leah with her children, and last of all Rachel with Joseph. Jacob himself walked ahead of all of them, bowing to the ground as he met his brother. Thus he approached his brother, for whom he had earlier set so many traps, as the lesser. Then Esau, the man of spontaneous, natural feeling, was overcome. He went up to Jacob and embraced him. This, too, was the Lord's doing, for the Lord guides the hearts of men like streams of water. It was His will that Jacob should enter Canaan in peace.

After Jacob had introduced his family to Esau and shown him his blessings, Esau accepted the gifts Jacob had sent ahead—but not without repeated urging. Worried about his little children and the nursing sheep and cows, Jacob declined the escort Esau offered. He didn't even want a small contingent of Esau's men along. Jacob promised to come to Seir later, but first he would have to go on to Canaan. Therefore the brothers said good-by to each other.

From Succoth to Shechem. Jacob went on to a place in Transjordan. Apparently the Jordan River could not be crossed yet. Therefore he built himself a temporary house and erected shelters for his cattle. He called that place Succoth, which means *huts* or *hovels*.

Transjordan, however, was not yet Canaan. His heart longed for the other side of the river, where his father Isaac lived. At last he crossed the Jordan with his whole company and camped near Shechem. He was finally back in Canaan again. God's promise at Bethel had been fulfilled.

From Hamor, Shechem's ruler, Jacob bought the piece of land on which he had pitched his tent and there erected an altar for the Lord. To be sure, this was not yet the complete fulfillment of the vow he had made earlier to return to Bethel and worship the Lord. Yet, in erecting this altar he was acknowledging the Lord, who had led him, who had wrestled with him, whom he had been privileged to defeat, and who now made him return to Canaan. Therefore he called the altar "The God of Israel is God."

We should likewise acknowledge the Lord. Although He must be against us because of our sins, He also allows Himself to be overcome by our prayers and gives us His compete blessing.

30: Holy is the Lord

Genesis 34-36

After the history told in Genesis 34-36, decadence crept into Jacob's house. His sons did not live in abiding covenant fellowship with the Lord.

Jacob himself postponed his return to Bethel and the fulfillment of his vow. The Lord had to remind him to live up to his vow, which he finally did after a number of years had gone by. All that time he had lived near Shechem. By staying there, he ran the risk of the Shechemites mixing with his family, as the story of Dinah's violation dramatically illustrates. To be sure, Jacob's sons avenged Dinah's defilement, which averted the danger of a fusion of Jacob's family with the Shechemites. Therefore the break with the Shechemites must be seen as the Lord's doing, but the behavior of Jacob's sons in this matter was shot through with injustice.

Not until Dinah was dishonored and avenged in a sinful way did Jacob make his family destroy all traces of idol worship. Had he previously looked the other way when Rachel bowed down to her household idols? Surely he must have found out about them sooner or later!

The danger of degeneration in Jacob's family in Canaan continued to grow. It was this part of Jacob's history that made a temporary stay in Egypt necessary. Later on, a period of isolation became even more imperative because of the sins of Judah's sons and of Judah himself.

At Bethel the Lord renewed the promise, and Jacob renewed the covenant. In the story of Jacob's return to Bethel, we read a curious statement: "Then God went up from him" (Gen. 35:13). Did this mean that God then removed Himself further from Jacob and his house, subjecting them to even greater temptation?

Later on God's holiness was made manifest to Jacob, both in his sorrow over Rachel's death and in his bitterness at Reuben's shameful

216

deed. Thus, when the Lord was nothing but holiness to Jacob, he returned with all his family to visit his father Isaac in Mamre. Jacob had undoubtedly visited his father before then, but now he brought his whole household to Isaac for the first time.

Finally we are told of Isaac's death, which did not follow immediately. Isaac was still alive at the time Joseph was sold into slavery by his brothers. Some years after that, he died.

Main thought: *The Lord's holiness is made manifest to Jacob.*

The break with the Shechemites. Jacob had lived in the vicinity of Shechem too long. His stay there must have lasted several years. (This we deduce from Dinah's probable age.) Jacob's house and the inhabitants of Shechem got used to each other and sought each other's company.

Dinah, too, sought the company of the girls from Shechem. A young man named Shechem, who was the son of Hamor, the prince of Shechem, desired her and raped her. However, he had fallen in love with her and wanted her to be his lawful wife, with Jacob's consent. Therefore, with his father Hamor, he went to Jacob to ask for Dinah in marriage, offering to give Jacob whatever he might demand by way of payment.

Since Jacob's sons were with the cattle in the field and could not be consulted, Jacob did not give Hamor and Shechem a proper answer. As soon as his sons returned, he told them what had happened. For some strange reason, Jacob then retreated to the background. Had he been defeated by this humiliation of his house? He lacked the strength to take action and make decisions.

His sons were outraged by the shameful deed. How did this ungodly man dare take their sister by force? They were concerned about the honor of their family as the covenant family and therefore decided to avenge the violation of Dinah's honor. Thus they were zealous for the covenant of the Lord, but the means they used were sinful through and through. Theirs was no sanctified zeal. The Christ, too, was zealous for the name of the Lord, but His zeal was holy.

Jacob's sons deceived Hamor and Shechem by telling them they did not want any payment for Dinah. All they asked was that

Hamor, Shechem, and the other men of their city let themselves be taken into the covenant circle by circumcision. Thus they chose to play an unholy game with the covenant and its sign.

Hamor and Shechem succeeded in persuading the inhabitants of Shechem to go along with this proposal. Thus all the men were circumcised. However, on the third day after the circumcision, Simeon and Levi, in whom the unholy fire evidently burned stronger than in the other brothers, gathered a band of men and made a surprise attack on the men of Shechem, killing them all. Jacob's other sons joined in carrying away from Shechem everything they could lay hands on, including the women and children. In the process Dinah was rescued.

The news hit Jacob hard. He had lacked the strength to take action himself. Had he lost his resolve by reproaching himself for staying in Shechem too long? In any event, he would now have to deal with his sons' betrayal. Did he see his own former deceit reflected in their treachery in an intensified form? He was defeated and without strength, and he feared that all the Canaanites would turn against him to destroy him and his household.

Through the treachery of Jacob's sons, the Lord brought about the separation that Jacob himself should have brought about long before. Thus the Lord saw to it that Jacob's posterity was set apart—in a manner that was awful for Jacob. In all of this, the Lord was manifesting His holiness to Jacob.

Back to Bethel. The Lord gave Jacob no peace either, for Jacob still had not fulfilled his earlier vow to worship the Lord at Bethel. Finally the Lord called him back to Bethel. There he would once again stand on the spot where the Lord had appeared to him at the top of the ladder and had promised him His guidance. There he would be close to God, closer than anywhere else.

Jacob was deeply impressed by the thought. Full of emotion, he told all who were with him that they were going to Bethel to build an altar to the God who had answered him in the days when everything was going against him. Therefore he demanded that all the idols be removed from his household. Rachel's household idols, which Jacob had tolerated in his great weakness, were probably still around. There were also traces of idol worship which the women from Shechem had brought into his camp. All the graven images and magic charms were handed over, and Jacob buried them under an oak tree near Shechem. Thus his camp was finally purified. Within his household, only the Lord was holy.

The Lord safeguards His honor, then. Our sins, which Christ took upon Himself, were judged in Him. In His suffering, Christ was made holy unto the Lord. One day all believers will be holy unto the Lord for Christ's sake. Since He is faithful in the covenant, He also requires faithfulness of us.

God's appearance at Bethel. After Jacob had fulfilled his vow and erected an altar at Bethel to worship the Lord, the Lord appeared to him again. God blessed him and confirmed the change in his name: Jacob had become Israel. This was the Lord's way of letting Jacob know that He remembered how the sins that had stood between Himself and Jacob were removed. He also renewed the blessing of Abraham and Isaac, to which Jacob was heir.

This appearance of God to Jacob was something marvelous. Once more it was made clear that the security of the covenant is rooted exclusively in the faithfulness of God. This also made the future look brighter, despite all the dangers threatening Jacob's posterity. For the sake of Christ, God can keep giving Himself to His people in spite of their sins, for He is able to overcome those sins time and again by His grace.

Then God went up from Jacob. For a long time afterward, He did not appear to Jacob but left him and his kin to be tested in Canaan. After this confirmation of His faithfulness, they had to hold on to that faithfulness and develop the strength to withstand temptation.

From his side, too, Jacob renewed the covenant. He erected a stone memorial, over which he poured oil. The pillar of stone would be a witness to the covenant between God and Jacob's house. In a special sense, that place would be holy to Jacob.

From Bethel to Mamre. From Bethel Jacob traveled to Mamre, where his father Isaac lived. His mother Rebekah was already dead. He had undoubtedly visited his father before, but he had never yet taken his entire household to meet Isaac. His whole house would now come under the blessing of the promise he was to inherit from Isaac.

On the way to Mamre God tested him: Rachel died giving birth to her second son. As she was dying, she gave him the name *Benoni,* which means *son of my sorrow.* Apparently Rachel was only concerned with her own grief, and not with the covenant, through which this son had been obtained.

But Jacob looked at this event in a different light, calling the baby Benjamin, which means *son of my right hand.* In that name he expressed his joy for God's sake, for now he had twelve sons. Yet he must have been overwhelmed with grief. He buried Rachel on the way to Ephrath and put a pillar on her grave. In his sorrow he must have bowed before the Lord and acknowledged that the Lord is God and does all things according to His good pleasure. In this grief, too, God manifested His holiness to Jacob.

That holiness was also manifested in the bitterness Jacob felt when his oldest son Reuben dishonored him through sexual relations with Bilhah, one of his father's wives. At the time it happened, Jacob kept silent, but on his deathbed he showed how deeply he had been hurt, for he rejected Reuben as his first-born (Gen. 49:3-4). It must have been a struggle for him to bow before the Lord in this matter too.

Without Rachel and with fresh dishonor on his house, he finally arrived at Isaac's place at Mamre. Through his sorrows he had learned to acknowledge the Lord. Isaac and Jacob must have understood each other better than before.

Years later Isaac died and was buried by his sons Esau and Jacob in the grave Abraham had bought. Then the promise was transferred fully from Isaac to Jacob. Esau left Canaan for good and settled in Edom, where his seed multiplied while continuing to live outside the covenant. But Jacob and his house waited for the fulfillment of the promise in Canaan.

Joseph and Judah

31: Sold for Twenty Pieces of Silver

Genesis 37-38

At the beginning of Genesis 37 we read: "This is the history of the family of Jacob." Genesis told us earlier that Jacob had returned to the tent of his father Isaac after spending many years in Haran. But now that Isaac was dead, Jacob was the patriarch. Yet, the next chapters of Genesis belong under the heading "Joseph and Judah." The same thing happened in connection with Isaac: the history of the family of Isaac is the story of Esau and Jacob. The pattern is that Scripture speaks mainly of the coming patriarch while the former patriarch is still alive. It is as though Scripture were hurrying from one generation to the next. History hastens toward the birth of the Christ.

At this point in the Genesis narrative, the first four sons of Leah (Reuben, Simeon, Levi, and Judah) become prominent along with Joseph, the son of Rachel. It is evident that the struggle between Leah and Rachel was continuing. That struggle was also carried through in later centuries, in the opposition between Judah and Ephraim.

We cannot say that Joseph is the dominating figure in the last part of Genesis. In Genesis 38 we are told about the history of Judah, i.e. about Judah's shame—but also about the birth of his son, from whose line the Christ was to be born. Furthermore, Judah was the one who pleaded that Joseph be sold rather than killed. Eventually Judah's history takes a turn for the better: he gives his father a guarantee of Benjamin's safety. All those stories end with the blessing of Judah by Jacob: "Judah, you are the one!"

The Christ was to be born of Judah's line. Yet, during this period it was not Judah who headed Jacob's house and thereby typified the Christ. There was shame on all those sons of Leah. The light falls fully on Joseph, Rachel's son. Hence it is clear that the Christ was not born of Judah's line because of any intrinsic worthiness on Judah's part. In fact, it's just the other way around: Judah became the greatest of Jacob's sons because the Christ began to prevail in him. Before Judah's rise, the one without equal was the son of Rachel, who typified the Christ for a time.

Joseph's dreams most likely had something to do with the opposition

223

in Joseph's tent between Leah and Rachel. Rachel was dead, and Benjamin didn't count for anything yet. Thus Joseph stood alone against the powerful sons of Leah—except, of course, that he was his father's favorite. Therefore it is significant that we are told in Genesis 37:2 that while he was a boy, he was assigned to assist the sons of Bilhah and Zilpah. Because of the jealousy between Leah and Rachel, Jacob did not dare entrust Joseph to Leah's sons.

The revelation in Joseph's dreams was connected with the struggle in his mind. That there was revelation in those dreams is not to be denied: the light of God was shining on Jacob's tent. The dreams represented the latest special light. However, Joseph received and communicated that revelation all too eagerly. In the process, his jealousy and pride as Rachel's son got mixed up with the divine light.

There is no need to tell the children about every detail recorded in Genesis 38. Yet the main points should certainly be brought to their attention.

As we deal with these chapters, the emphasis should not fall exclusively on Joseph, or it will look as though Joseph was matchless in himself. Joseph recedes into the background before Judah.

Main thought: *Joseph is banished from the community so that he will be able to save that community one day.*

God's revelation in Joseph's dreams. Rachel was dead, and Jacob had returned to Isaac's tent. Jacob's sons had grown up and were pasturing the herds by themselves. Once there had been jealousy between Leah and Rachel, and now there was bad feeling between Leah's sons and Joseph, the son of Rachel. Joseph was still young—only 17 years old.

The jealousy on the part of Leah's sons was aggravated by Jacob's special love for Joseph. It was as though Jacob now gave Joseph the special love he had for Rachel. He didn't even try to hide it! He gave Joseph a special robe, which had the effect of elevating him above his brothers. In a normal household, *every* child has a special place in his father's heart. There should be no thought of a father favoring one child at the expense of others.

There was jealousy in Joseph's heart too. The jealousy on both sides was so strong that Jacob did not dare entrust Joseph to Leah's sons. Instead he assigned him to help the sons of Bilhah and Zilpah in pasturing their flocks.

Evidently the morals of Jacob's sons had become more and more coarse. After living near the Canaanites for so long, they adopted their ways and sought their companionship.

Joseph reported the rumors about his brothers' wrongdoing to Jacob. The Spirit of Christ in Joseph's heart was protesting against that mixing of the holy line with the Canaanites; in Joseph's complaints, the Spirit of the Lord was bearing witness against Jacob's sons. Still, Joseph's sin of pride and jealousy was also involved in what he said about his brothers.

In that struggle between Joseph and his brothers, the Lord sent His light. He revealed Himself to Joseph in a dream: the sheaves of his brothers bowed down to his sheaf. In another dream, the sun, moon and eleven stars bowed down to him. Joseph told these dreams to his father and his brothers.

Joseph's hopes made it easy for him to assume that God was revealing Himself in those dreams. It was his hope that God would entrust him with the leadership of his father's house, so that he could lead that house into righteousness. But this hope also resulted in part from jealousy.

Joseph's brothers were extremely irritated by those dreams. As a result, they began to hate him and did not greet him anymore. They rejected not only Joseph's dominion but also the reign of righteousness and God's light in the revelation to Joseph.

Jacob was alarmed by those dreams. He was disturbed by the thought of Joseph's lordship—especially by the thought that he and Leah would also have to bow before Joseph. Yet, in the course of his life he had found out first hand how amazing God's ways sometimes are. Therefore he kept an open mind.

The lordship of Christ, who was the most despised man on earth, is also amazing. All the same, we shall have to bow before Him. God is free in His election and chooses the One He wants as Redeemer. We will all have to acknowledge that there is light only in the Christ.

Getting rid of Joseph. On a certain day, Joseph's brothers were together in the field pasturing the flock. Jacob had kept Joseph home with him, apparently more concerned than ever about his safety. Yet he sent him to his brothers to inquire about their well-being.

After a long search, Joseph found them in Dothan. They saw him coming from afar and decided to kill him and throw him into a pit, agreeing to tell Jacob that Joseph had been devoured in the field by some animal. Only Reuben refused in his heart to go along with that plan—but not because he bowed before the revelation of God in Joseph's dreams or before God's election of Joseph or before the punishment which that election involved for all of them. If he had bowed to God's will, he would have rejected his brothers' plot entirely and would have reprimanded them for it. He was against the plan only because he did not dare take the responsibility as the oldest son. Therefore he advised the brothers not to kill Joseph but to throw him into the pit instead. He would die there anyway, but the brothers would be able to say that they had not taken his life with their own hands. Secretly Reuben intended to rescue Joseph later on.

The brothers did as Reuben advised. After they had thrown Joseph into the pit, they sat down to eat. The men who had been prepared to kill Joseph with their own hands showed their complete indifference to his misery by eating peacefully. Their wickedness was rooted not just in hatred of their brother but in their contempt for him as a believer. They hated Joseph as God's witness, for God had spoken through Joseph.

How the holy line had fallen! What a dreadful thing to happen in the covenant circle! When the Lord Jesus Christ witnesses against our life, our flesh hates Him for it. What would have to happen to those sons of Jacob before they would acknowledge God's election again and His grace in that election?

While they were eating, they saw a caravan of Ishmaelites or Midianites coming from Gilead on their way to Egypt. (The peoples descended from Abraham's other sons, such as the Ishmaelites and the Midianites, intermarried in northern Arabia.) Judah then hit upon the idea of selling Joseph to these traders. He argued that there was no need for them to kill Joseph, for they could get what they wanted without taking such a step: Joseph would be gone from their father's house for good.

It was as though the evil one himself had led them on. The real goal they were pursuing was getting rid of God's witness. If they had gotten their way completely, they would have wound up destroying the entire covenant circle. How great God's grace must be if it can conquer such an attitude!

The brothers took Judah's advice: Joseph was sold for 20 pieces of silver. They paid no attention to his cries. Joseph, they assumed, was banished from their circle for good. They could not possibly have known that Joseph's banishment from their midst was God's doing and would one day serve to preserve their community—not just by keeping their family from starvation but also by turning them again to the Word of the Lord and to each other. In the same way, the Christ was sold and banished from the community of His people in order to save His people.

Darkness in Jacob's tent. When Reuben returned to the pit after his brothers had gone away, he did not find Joseph there. Evidently he was not present when Joseph was sold. After Reuben was told what had happened, he reproached his brothers for their crime—not because he sided with the Word of God but because he did not dare look his father in the eye and tell him that Joseph was dead.

The brothers had not given the traders Joseph's special robe. They now smeared blood on the robe and showed it to Jacob as evidence that Joseph had been killed by a wild animal. They claimed they had found the robe but had not seen Joseph. That way Jacob could never blame them for what had happened to Joseph. That robe of Joseph's, which symbolized his special place in his father's heart, played a peculiar role in this story. It was as though the hatred of the brothers was focused on that robe. Joseph was torn apart by his brothers' hatred of his dominion in grace.

When he was shown the blood-stained robe, Jacob became convinced that Joseph was dead. He tore his garments and mourned for a long time. His hypocritical sons tried to comfort him, but Jacob refused to be comforted. The joy had gone out of his life.

Worse yet, the members of the covenant had rejected God's witness, the Christ, the Head of the covenant. Because *that* light had departed from Jacob's tent, complete darkness descended. How would the light ever return to Jacob's house?

Judah's shame and honor. How could the life of faith and fellowship be preserved in the covenant circle when that circle lived in darkness? It soon became evident that Jacob's family was going downhill. Judah retreated from the company of his brothers and associated with Canaanites. He even married a Canaanite woman and had three sons by her.

The sins of the Canaanites took over so completely in Judah's family that the Lord struck down his two oldest sons. Even Judah himself fell prey to Canaanite waywardness. Through his sin, he became the father of twin boys, Perez and Zerah. Thus Judah's line seemed to be losing its holy character completely. Would Judah's house be utterly submerged in the life of the Canaanites?

God's ways are wonderful! From the line of Perez, the Christ was later to be born, even though Judah did not realize it at the time his twins came into the world. Judah was chosen to become a forefather of the Christ, but not because of any virtues or good conduct. On the contrary, the Spirit of the Lord was far more in Joseph at the time.

Judah was chosen simply because it was God's good pleasure. Not even the great sins in Judah's life managed to block his election. When God chooses us to be joined to the Lord Jesus Christ and inherit salvation, it is not because of our superiority but because of God's good pleasure. Later on, the Spirit of the Christ was manifested in Judah and his offspring, as God brought Judah to the fore. In him and in his descendants was the Light. Judah became Israel's hope, and Joseph receded into the background.

32: God's Word in Egypt

Genesis 39-41

In the story of Joseph in Egypt, we can almost identify Joseph with the Word of God—in the sense that the Word of God came to Egypt with him. In Egypt he suffered humiliation (like the Christ, who is the Word of God), and he was also exalted. Christ's states of humiliation and exaltation are typified in Joseph's life.

First the Word of God was in the house of Potiphar, where Joseph spoke out against sin. Then there was the prophecy in connection with the dreams of the butler and the baker. (Whether God also used dreams at other times to reveal Himself to the heathen world does not concern us here.) The dreams Joseph interpreted were divine revelations, and he discerned their meaning through the Spirit. In the same way, God's revelation was present in the dreams of the Pharaoh. With Joseph, the Word of God came to Egypt to prepare for Israel's arrival in Egypt.

It is quite clear, then, that we are not to speak of Joseph merely as a person. Here again we have a revelation of the Lord's counsel for His people's redemption. Scripture relegates Joseph's personal life to the background. "He had sent a man ahead of them, Joseph, who was sold as a slave" (Ps.105:17)

This revelation to Egypt prepared Egypt for receiving Israel. In the seven years of plenty and the seven years of famine of which Joseph prophesied, the God of Israel, who alone is God of heaven and earth, revealed Himself to Egypt. This revelation had no other significance for Egypt; there was no intent to convert Egypt at that time.

This relation between Egypt and Israel should not become the basis for conclusions about the relation between the world and the Kingdom of

God in our time. Then God was still letting the peoples choose their own paths, but now the presence of God's people in the world has a much broader significance. Egypt's only role at that point in history was to preserve Israel for a while.

Main thought: *The Word of God prepares Egypt for receiving Israel.*

In Potiphar's house. The Ishmaelite traders who had bought Joseph and brought him to Egypt sold him to Potiphar, a member of Pharaoh's court and a captain of the guard. In his father's house, Joseph had been a witness for God, which was why his brothers sold him. He did not lose this calling in Egypt. The Lord soon showed him that it was a special calling: Joseph found favor with Potiphar, who made him an overseer responsible for all of his household. This must have strengthened Joseph's belief in the Lord's favor and in the special calling God had revealed to him in dreams.

That position in Potiphar's house also involved dangers. Potiphar's wife was attracted to the young man and tempted him to commit a sexual sin. How could Joseph remain steadfast in that temptation? Only because of the fact that he had to be a witness in the world, that is, only because of the Spirit of Christ within him. He certainly would never have had the strength to resist her advances on his own.

Thus Joseph brought the Word of the Lord to Potiphar's wife. After all, the Word of the Lord asks us to be faithful in all relationships. He pointed out to her that Potiphar had given him his complete trust, and that he would be violating that trust by getting involved with her sexually. Above all, he made it clear that what she had in mind was sin before God. Through the Spirit of Christ, Joseph was witnessing against Egypt's sin on God's behalf.

When Potiphar's wife did not get her way, she switched roles: she screamed and accused Joseph of trying to seduce her. Her husband, who was also the overseer of the king's prison, angrily put Joseph into prison.

Thus Joseph suffered for the sake of God and His Word. In this respect, too, he was a type of the Lord Jesus Christ, who likewise suffered under false accusations. He also typified believers who suffer oppression for the sake of the Word.

In prison. How easy it would have been for Joseph to doubt God's intent for his life once he found himself in prison! What would now become of his dreams? Yet the Lord gave him strength to hold on to his calling: He strengthened Joseph's faith by letting him find favor with the prison guard. Earlier God had blessed all the work Joseph undertook for Potiphar, with the result that his master had prospered because of him. Now God blessed his life in prison, so that he received a position of trust there too.

One day the chief butler and chief baker in Pharaoh's palace were put in prison by the king, for suspicions about them had been raised. Potiphar, who was in charge of this royal prison, entrusted these special prisoners to Joseph. Apparently Potiphar's anger had subsided. Did he ever fully believe his wife's accusation?

While they were in prison, the butler and baker each had an unusual dream. Joseph, who noticed their restlessness brought on by the dreams, felt much more conscious of his calling. Therefore he asked them about the cause of their unrest. After they told him their dreams, he interpreted them. He foresaw reprieve for the butler and punishment for the baker.

It was for Joseph's sake that God spoke to the people in Egypt at that time. Joseph interpreted the revelation contained in their dreams. Since he was the light of the Lord in Egypt, attention had to focus on him, for in those days God was busy preparing a divine work. He wanted to set Israel apart for a while in Egypt, for Israel was in danger of being overwhelmed by the ways of the Canaanites. Joseph had only been sent ahead so that God could use him to prepare Egypt for the reception of Israel.

But how long would it take before the attention of all of Egypt would be focused on Joseph? The butler had promised to put in a good word for Joseph with Pharaoh after his restoration, but he forgot his promise. That Joseph had made such a request of the butler showed that he did not doubt his calling. But the butler had not heard the Word of God in his dreams as Joseph interpreted them. When he finally did speak up about Joseph, it was not for Joseph's benefit but for his own sake and Pharaoh's sake.

This does not alter the fact that Joseph brought God's Word in prison, promising deliverance to the butler and judgment to the baker. After all, Joseph had given them a divine revelation about their lives, just as the Christ reveals God's truth to us. If we search for that truth in faith, we will walk in the light.

The elevation of Joseph. About two years later, Pharaoh dreamed two dreams that seemed to have the same meaning. From the fact that he dreamed twice, Pharaoh concluded that his dreams had an unusual significance. The dreams affected him deeply, and he called on all the magicians and wise men of Egypt to interpret them. They failed. It was as though God had blinded them, for they should have been able to understand something of the meaning of those dreams through common sense.

Then the butler remembered Joseph and told Pharaoh what had happened to him in prison. Joseph was summoned from prison. After he was cleaned up, he was brought before Pharaoh.

Joseph told Pharaoh that he did not personally possess the power to interpret dreams. But because he was aware of his high calling and convinced that God was now speaking to Egypt for his sake, he declared that God would make the interpretation known to him.

Pharaoh told him the dreams, and Joseph interpreted them. Then he advised Pharaoh to make provision for the seven lean years during the seven fat ones. Pharaoh elevated him to the second highest position of authority in his kingdom.

Joseph, the bearer of God's testimony, was elevated in Egypt as a type of the Christ, the Word of God, who was elevated and is now seated at God's right hand. One day all who have suffered oppression for the Word of God will be exalted.

Joseph's faith in his calling was not misplaced. He was now more certain than ever that he would someday be a blessing to his father's house. Yet he did not send messengers right away to inform his family about his new position. He understood that God's way, which had been mysterious so far, would also bring him into contact with his father's house again. The crime in that house would have to be dealt with in God's way.

Just as Joseph's faith was justified, the faith of all who surrender to the Word and calling of God will be justified. If only we would learn—in faith—to live for the Word of God alone!

Ruler in Egypt. Pharaoh had given Joseph the name *Zaphenath-paneah*. That name would prove to be very significant, for it meant *redeemer of the world and preserver of life*. Joseph would one day become the preserver of life not just in Egypt but also in his father's house. Moreover, Pharaoh gave him Asenath, the daughter of Potiphera, priest of On, for his wife. Thus Joseph was accepted into the highest circles of Egypt's wise men.* That was doubtless a great honor, but it also involved certain dangers.

That Joseph did not forget his special calling with regard to his father's house is evident from the names he gave his two sons, who were born during the years of plenty. The first son he called Manasseh, by which he meant to say: "God has made me forget all my hardship and all my father's house." He did not mean that he had now cut himself off from his father's house; all he was saying was that he was no longer depressed by its hardship and troubles. Since he had become independent through God's favor, he could be a blessing to that house. In principle his dreams had come true. All the other things would follow.

He called his second son Ephraim, which means *double fruitfulness*. This was his way of saying that God had made him fruitful in the land in which he had been persecuted. Thus he still regarded Egypt as the land where he had suffered oppression. His heart went out to his father's house.

In the seven fat years, he stored grain in Egypt. When the seven lean years came along, Pharaoh referred the Egyptians to Joseph, who then began to open up the storage bins. Soon people from other countries came to Egypt to buy grain.

Joseph's path had indeed been a dark one, but now God placed him fully in the light. He was a blessing in his humiliation as well as in his high estate. Thus he bore the mark of the Christ,

*On was the most important seat of learning in the country, where the chief temple of the sun god Re was located. The Greeks later called it *Heliopolis*, which means *city of the sun*. —TRANS.

who is an eternal blessing both in His humiliation and in His exaltation. We, too, must be willing to bear the mark of the Christ, so that we will be a blessing for Christ's sake whatever befalls us.

33: Restored Unity

Genesis 42-45

Joseph's course of action restored unity to Jacob's house. We must not look for a desire for revenge in Joseph's behavior. The Bible tells us why Joseph brought accusations against his brothers: "Then Joseph remembered his dreams about them; and said to them, 'You are spies' " (Gen. 42:9). He acted in full realization of his calling, which God had already revealed to him in dreams. Joseph was called to be the leader of his father's house and bring it back to the paths of righteousness.

Joseph was not looking for revenge, nor did he punish anyone. However, his brothers had to find each other through suffering and thereby come to themselves. They had to admit their crime to each other openly. They also had to show that their attitudes had changed, and that they had overcome their jealousy. That these changes had indeed taken place is apparent from their attitude toward Benjamin, the other son of Rachel.

Everyone in Jacob's house played a part in the reconciliation. Joseph sacrificed his revenge and acted through the power of the calling of God. By letting Benjamin go, Jacob forsook his fearful habit of holding on to anything connected with Rachel. The moment he agreed to let Benjamin go, he surrendered himself and his house to God the Almighty. (After this victory over his special preference for Rachel and her sons, Scripture calls him *Israel,* the one who wrestled with God.) Judah sacrificed by putting his life on the line for Benjamin. And Judah was speaking for all the brothers, each of whom had been humbled before the others in the family. Thus unity was restored in Jacob's house.

Over them all was the Spirit of sacrifice of the Lord Jesus Christ, who gave Himself for His own. His sacrifice was to atone for sin, and that atonement was at the root of the reconciliation between the various members of Jacob's house. Through Christ's atonement, the Spirit of

His sacrifice affected them all in such a way that unity was restored.

In this sense, Joseph was already the preserver of Jacob's house. That was the most important thing he was called to do. In addition, he gave his father's house a place in Egypt and maintained it there, as we read in Genesis 46. In preserving the house of Jacob (especially in spiritual respects), Joseph was a symbol of the Christ.

Main thought: *Unity is restored through sacrifice on the part of everyone.*

Joseph's sacrifice. Joseph probably expected his brothers to be among the many people coming to Egypt from other countries to buy grain. Thus he must have guessed something of God's plan for bringing about reconciliation in Jacob's house. In any case, Joseph decided to oversee the trade with the foreigners himself.

One day his brothers arrived in Egypt to buy grain. When they bowed before him, Joseph remembered his dreams, but he felt no vicious satisfaction at having his brothers in his power, nor did he want revenge for what they had done to him. Instead he sensed that it was his calling to lead his father's house in righteousness.

However, he could not make himself known to his brothers right away. First they would have to admit their crime. And Joseph also had to find out whether their attitude had changed. That's why he told them that he suspected them of being spies. When they defended themselves by saying that they were all brothers and by explaining their circumstances at home, Joseph replied that he would keep them in prison, allowing one of them to go back and get Benjamin.

He then put them all in prison, where they would have an opportunity to turn to God and come to themselves by remembering their former sin. God was against them now as they had been against their brother Joseph in the past—and thereby against God Himself.

After they had spent three days in prison, Joseph spoke to them in a somewhat different tone: he did not want to be unjust, for he feared God. In his position he was subject to God, and therefore he did not act arbitrarily. Only one of the brothers would remain in prison. The others would be allowed to return home with the grain and get Benjamin. The brothers talked the situation over and agreed that this was the result of the sin they had committed against Joseph. This official at least treated them fairly, whereas they had shown Joseph no mercy. Reuben once more reproached his brothers for their crime.

Joseph understood what they were saying without his brothers realizing it. For a while it was too much for him. But he pulled himself together and had Simeon, who was the second oldest, bound before their eyes. He did not keep Reuben, the oldest of the brothers, for Reuben had wanted to save Joseph's life. When the brothers saw Simeon being bound, they must have remembered how Joseph had been bound.

When the brothers left with their grain and provisions for the journey, the money they had given Joseph for the grain was back in their sacks. When one of them found money in the mouth of his sack during the journey, they were all shocked. They were even more frightened when they all found their money in their sacks after they got home.

They told their father what had happened in Egypt, and Jacob lashed out at them in anger. They must have felt that their father was justified in his anger and sorrow. However, for Jacob himself, who did not know about the crime the brothers had committed, this anger was rebellion against the Lord. Reuben offered Jacob two of his own sons in case they should fail to bring Benjamin back from the next trip to Egypt, but Jacob declined his offer.

Apparently there was no unity yet in Jacob's house in Canaan. The brothers were divided against each other. Because their crimes had not been confessed, they could not yet be united.

Joseph's heart went out to his father's house. He sacrificed his vengeance and self-satisfaction to seek what was best for Jacob's house and bring it to reconciliation. In the process he showed that the Spirit of the Christ was in him, for it is Christ's desire to unite and preserve His own. It was for that purpose that He gave His life to atone for our sins.

Jacob's sacrifice. Driven on by hunger, Jacob's sons had to go back to Egypt, but they could not go without Benjamin. When Jacob, still angry, blamed them for admitting that they had another brother, Judah stepped forward and pointed out to his father that he was being unfair. He also gave Jacob his personal guarantee that no harm would come to Benjamin.

With that assurance, Jacob gave in. He no longer kept apart from his other sons because of his grief over the one son of Rachel. Instead his heart went out to all his house, and he surrendered himself with his entire household to God the Almighty. Jacob had once more become Israel, the one who wrestled with God and prevailed. His entire attitude had changed.

The brothers set out for Egypt with gifts for the official with whom they had dealt and twice as much money as before. When they arrived in Egypt and were brought to Joseph's own home, they feared that it was because of the money. But the overseer at Joseph's house put their minds at ease and brought Simeon out to them. He gave them water for their feet and took care of their animals.

The sight of Benjamin was too much for Joseph when he entered. But he quickly pulled himself together and seated the brothers at a table according to their age. They regarded him as a seer able to divine the relationships between them in their father's house. Then they had dinner at Joseph's home. They ate at a separate table, but they were accorded the highest honor, for food was brought from Joseph's table to theirs. And Benjamin's portions were five times as large as his brothers' portions.

There they were eating again, the twelve of them together! By now the brothers were no longer envious of Benjamin, Rachel's son, because of the privileges he enjoyed. The light was shining on Jacob's house once more! However, Joseph had not yet taken his place among them; his brothers were not aware that it was Joseph who was eating with them.

Judah's sacrifice. The next morning they left with their grain and their money in their sacks. Apparently Joseph did not want to accept money from his father's house. Moreover, in Benjamin's sack was Joseph's cup, the cup from which he himself drank, the cup that seemed to enable him to foresee the future. (That was how the Egyptians viewed this cup, in any event.)

When the brothers were overtaken and the cup was discovered in Benjamin's sack, they did not surrender Benjamin but returned together to Joseph. This made it clear to Joseph that the jealousy between Rachel's sons and all the other sons had been overcome. They all offered to become Joseph's servants, and they confessed that they had no defense. Appearances were completely against them; God had found them out in their sinfulness. At this point they were already sacrificing themselves for Benjamin's sake.

Because Joseph proposed to keep only Benjamin as his servant, Judah went up to him. He acknowledged Joseph's sovereignty but spoke in a moving way of his father's sorrow. He also told Joseph that he had given his father a guarantee of his brother's safety, and he offered himself as Joseph's servant in Benjamin's place. Now it was completely clear that the former sin had been overcome and rooted out. Instead of causing their father more sorrow, the brothers were now weighed down by his grief. Instead of abandoning a son of Rachel, as they had done before, one of them stepped forward to sacrifice himself in place of Rachel's son.

In all of them—especially Judah—the Spirit of the Lord Jesus Christ was apparent, that is, the Spirit of the One who sacrificed Himself for all, even though He was the least of all men and was everyone's servant. Christ sacrificed Himself to atone for the unrighteousness of all of us. If there is something of His Spirit in us, we, too, will give our lives for one another. Only in this way is true unity possible.

Reconciliation. Joseph could no longer contain himself. He ordered everyone to leave the room except the brothers. Then he revealed his identity to them. The brothers almost fell over in amazement and feared that he would punish them for their sinful deed. They were utterly dismayed. The spirit of humiliation in them was genuine.

Over and over Joseph told them that *they* had not sent him to Egypt; it was God's own doing, to keep Jacob's house alive during the years of famine. They should no longer worry about their guilt. Joseph assured them that he was no longer preoccupied with it either. Instead the brothers should look to God, who had made things turn out for the best. We may do the same if we first confess our sin and receive forgiveness.

Joseph told the brothers to return to Canaan. They were to tell their father everything and then come to Egypt to live. Joseph was so highly regarded in Egypt that even Pharaoh insisted on bringing Joseph's family to Egypt. Pharaoh was willing to send wagons to Canaan for the women and children in Jacob's house. If necessary, they could leave their household goods behind.

Joseph gave his brothers presents, especially Benjamin, and he sent along some wonderful gifts for his father as well. He also urged them not to talk about their crime anymore during the journey. Neither were they to blame themselves or each other, for the wrongdoing had been erased. Together with Joseph, they would believe in forgiveness. In that belief, they would be one.

The brothers went back to Jacob and told him everything. Jacob's heart almost failed him, and he could not believe it. The brothers told him all that Joseph had said, including his words of reconciliation. At the same time, they must have confessed their crime to their father. Jacob noticed the spirit of unity in the words of Joseph and his other sons. It was the same spirit of unity that lived in his own heart.

When he heard all of this and saw the wagons from Egypt accompanying the words of reconciliation spoken by Joseph, he believed. Jacob's spirit was renewed. He shook off the gloomy spirit of all the years since the loss of Joseph and said: "It is enough! Joseph, my son, is still alive! I will go and see him before I die!" Then God's light shone on the house of Jacob again in all its fullness.

The members of Jacob's house had found each other through the Spirit of the Lord Jesus Christ, which was at work in all of them. This Spirit of sacrifice, this Spirit of willingness to be less than the other, first conquered Joseph. Through Joseph it then took root in all the others as well. Fortunately, this Spirit is still at work in the world today! What we must do is seek fellowship with the Lord Jesus Christ through faith in His sacrifice. That Spirit is evident in our time too. It overpowers us in such a way that we can find each other again and be truly one.

34: The Preserver of Life

Genesis 46-47

For Egypt and especially for the house of Israel, God made Joseph a preserver of life. His role was a revelation of the blessing of the Christ, who is the preserver of the life of the whole world—especially the life of His people. The people of God are the focal point as the Lord's counsel is fulfilled in the history of the world.

Joseph was also the preserver of the life of the house of Israel, by getting Jacob and his family to leave Canaan, where they were in danger of being submerged in the ways of the Canaanites. He saw to it that when they came to Egypt, they lived in isolation. He stressed to his brothers the importance of telling Pharaoh that they were shepherds, for then the Egyptians would not want to associate with them.

Leaving Canaan was a sacrifice for Jacob and his house. For a time, they would be letting go of the land promised to them as an inheritance. They continued to cling to that land in faith, for Jacob made Joseph swear that he would bury him in Canaan. Thus Joseph, who had made the house of Jacob leave Canaan, had to promise to bury Jacob in Canaan, as a sign that Jacob's descendants would possess that land someday.

The lordship of Christ is likewise our guarantee that we will possess the new earth under the new heaven. Thus, for the believer it does not go without saying that life is good wherever God is with His favor. The believer longs for his fatherland, his spiritual home, where all things are tokens of God's mercy.

Jacob's house lived in Egypt for a while, then. We should be careful, however, not to draw parallels between that stay in Egypt and the

241

Church's presence in the world. In Joseph's time, there was a difference between two kinds of places. Those who lived in God's grace made Goshen their home, while the heathens lived in the rest of Egypt. God allowed the heathens to follow their own paths, although He blessed them in many ways in His goodness toward them.

This distinction between two kinds of places cannot be transferred to our time. Nor is the relationship between the Church and unbelievers in our time to be identified with the relationship between Israel and the Egyptians, for today God is no longer content to let unbelievers follow their own paths. Instead He has opened up His covenant to all peoples. We should be especially wary of comparing the two kinds of places in Joseph's time to sacred places and secular places, by distinguishing between the life of faith and the Church, on the one hand, and the life of the state and society, on the other.

What does remain is the contrast between a life lived by faith and a life of unbelief. To a believer, everything is grace. He even sees his daily bread as the fruit of God's eternal grace in Christ. By eating his bread, he exercises covenant fellowship with his God. That bread, too, he receives from the hand of Christ, just as the house of Israel received its provisions in Goshen from the hand of Joseph, who belonged to that house. Despite his power, Joseph was a stranger to Egypt.

An unbeliever is not acquainted with the covenant or with the Head of the covenant. He does not know God's grace in Christ. He only receives the gifts that stem from God's goodness to unbelievers, which He allows them to enjoy as long as they live in the covenant of this world.

In His grace in Christ, God will also sanctify all suffering and will show us His favor there too. Accordingly, Genesis 46:4 is especially noteworthy, for Jacob was told that when he died, Joseph's hand would close his eyes. When we die, the Christ will be present—and with Him the grace of God.

Yet, knowing all of this does not make this present earth our fatherland. In faith we accept God's favor in all things, even in adversity, but we do not see all things clearly yet. There is still adversity and suffering. We are still embroiled in conflicts, and we still have the body of this death to contend with. Therefore we have not found our fatherland yet.

According to Hebrews 11, that fatherland is "heavenly." But we must not make the mistake of identifying it with heaven. Our fatherland is the new *earth* under the light of the new heaven, that is, the New Jerusalem that will come down from heaven. When that day comes, all things will be clear, and we will see directly. God's favor will then be evident in all things. There will be harmony between the covenant fellowship with God in our hearts and what our eyes see.

Thus it was not enough for Jacob's sons to make it clear to Pharaoh that they wanted to remain strangers or guests in Egypt. Jacob himself confessed to Pharaoh that he was a stranger on earth even while he was in Canaan. Only the full possession of the land of Canaan by the people of Israel would be a prophetic proclamation of the possession of the new earth by the people of God.

Because of the peculiar relationship which then existed between Israel and the other peoples, it would be wrong to draw conclusions about the relationship between church and state from the relationship between Jacob's house and Pharaoh. Pharaoh is rather to be viewed as the ruler of the world and Egypt as the house of bondage. Accordingly, in the conversation between Jacob and Pharaoh, God's people met the ruler of the world.

Pharaoh enviously asked Jacob his age. (The patriarchs still lived to an old age under God's special blessing.) Jacob responded in faith by confessing that he was a stranger on earth. He was a stranger especially to Pharaoh, who sought his fatherland in the here and now.

Neither does the relationship of Joseph to the house of Jacob parallel the relationship of the state to the church. It should be viewed instead in terms of the relationship of Christ to the Church.

It is doubtful whether all the measures Joseph took as a ruler in Egypt were right in the long run. If we proceed from the notion that Pharaoh was a son of the gods, everything Joseph did as ruler made sense, for Pharaoh would then be the rightful owner of everything, even the land and the people. Joseph's policies led to a loss of freedom.

In Israel, the holy theocracy, the land and people belonged to God, Israel's King. He then parceled out the land and goods to the people according to His good pleasure. All God's people now belong to Him because Christ has purchased them for God with His blood.

Main thought: *Joseph is given by God as a preserver of life.*

Leaving Canaan. At the invitation of Joseph and Pharaoh, Jacob decided to go to Egypt with his house. For a while, then, he would live outside Canaan. That was not easy for him. He did not say: "Wherever God is with me, I am happy. It does not matter to me where I live." He clung to Canaan, which had been promised to his seed.

At Beersheba, which was on Canaan's border, God appeared to Jacob. This was God's first revelation to him since Joseph's dreams. Now that Joseph had been found, now that the unity of Jacob's house was restored, now that Jacob's spirit was renewed, God spoke again. He told Jacob that it was good that he was on his way to Egypt. God would go down to Egypt with him and would one day allow his offspring to return. God would show Jacob

His favor in his life in Goshen. Even in death, God's special favor would be with him, for Joseph's hand would close his eyes.

Jacob traveled on to Egypt with all who belonged to him, using Pharaoh's wagons. Scripture tells us that Jacob came with 66 souls. Counting Jacob and Joseph and his two sons, the number of people in Jacob's house was exactly 70 (not including his sons' wives). They are all mentioned in Genesis 46, but that doesn't mean that all 70 were already part of Jacob's company. Some of those mentioned would be born in Egypt. Scripture mentions all the heads of tribes and of households, all those through whom Israel would become a great nation.

Jacob entered Egypt believing that God's favor would be with him there, and that he would return one day to Canaan. In the same way, we may believe that God's favor will be with us in this life for Christ's sake, even though we have not found our father-land here. We long for the new earth, which will receive the full blessing of heaven.

Leader of Jacob's house. Jacob sent Judah ahead to get directions from Joseph about the land and the road. Then Joseph got his wagon ready and rode out to Goshen to meet Israel, his father. When they met, they threw their arms around each other's necks and wept for a long time. Jacob had his beloved son, the son of Rachel, back again.

But the house of Jacob had received something more in Joseph: Joseph's dreams were fulfilled, for he had become the leader of Jacob's house. Joseph would support his father's house in Egypt; it was because of him that Jacob and the brothers had been led out of Canaan, where they were in danger of mingling with the Canaanites. He also saw to it that Jacob and his house did not mix with the Egyptians. He stressed to his brothers that they were to tell Pharaoh they were shepherds, for all shepherds were despised by the Egyptians. Pharaoh would then give them a separate place to live. Goshen would be assigned to them as the best pasture country.

The Lord gave Joseph back to Jacob's house as a preserver of life. In this role Joseph was a symbol or type of what the Lord Jesus Christ is for us today. God gave us Christ as a preserver of life. He will see to it that we do not become submerged in the life of unbelievers, in the sins of the world.

Israel and Egypt. After his father's house had arrived in Egypt and Pharaoh was notified, Joseph presented five of his brothers to Pharaoh. When they told him they were shepherds, Pharaoh promised them Goshen. Therefore Jacob's house remained separate from life in Egypt.

Later there was a meeting between Jacob and Pharaoh. Jacob was presented at court. As the bearer of God's promise, he blessed Pharaoh when they met. During their conversation, Pharaoh asked Jacob his age, for Pharaoh must have noticed how old the patriarchs became under God's special blessing and envied Jacob for it. Jacob confessed that he felt he did not have very much longer to live. Moreover, his 130 years were fewer than the years of his fathers' lives. He went on to point out that his days had been evil.

He confessed that he had been a stranger in Canaan. He longed for the time when his descendants would inherit Canaan. But even that possession of Canaan would only be temporary; it would be a prophecy about the everlasting possession of the new earth by the people of God.

Jacob longed for the new earth above all else and expressed this longing to Pharaoh, who hoped to find his fatherland in this life and therefore envied Jacob for the many years he had already lived. It is indeed a privilege to live for a long time, but only if we value our life on earth as a prophecy about our dwelling forever on God's new earth.

Preserving Israel and Egypt. Because of the orders given by Pharaoh and Joseph, Jacob's house lived in the land of Goshen. There Joseph provided for the needs of his relatives, even as they increased in number. That house of Jacob was God's main concern as He governed the world. Therefore it was Joseph's primary concern too.

However, Joseph also took care of the rest of Egypt. The year after the hungry Egyptians had sold their cattle to buy grain, they were forced to sell all their land. As a result, the whole land of Egypt became Pharaoh's property during the years of famine. Joseph brought many people together in the cities so that he could provide for them better. Yet he also gave seed to the people and decreed that one fifth of the land's harvest would go to Pharaoh. Thus all of Egypt became subservient to Pharaoh in a special sense.

It is doubtful whether so much power could safely be entrusted to a sinful man like Pharaoh. Later on, Israel's King (i.e. God) was indeed the sole owner of the people and the land, but He gave the land to all His people according to His good pleasure. In that sense, God is our King too.

How thankful Joseph must have been that he was allowed to prepare a place for his father's house in Egypt, where he could provide for the families of his father and brothers. Jacob's house, after all, was Joseph's main concern.

Holding on to Canaan. Although Jacob and his house lived in Egypt, Jacob's heart was still in Canaan, the promised land. When he felt he was close to death, he called Joseph and made him swear that he would bury him in Canaan rather than in Egypt. His grave in Canaan was to be one more bond between his descendants and that land. It would serve as a sign that they would inherit the land someday.

Joseph swore that he would do what his father asked. Since God had made Joseph the preserver of Jacob's house, Joseph would see to it that Jacob's grave would be among his people. Jacob believed in that future blessing for his descendants. Therefore he bowed in faithful devotion at the head of his bed. His portion of the promised land—through his descendants—was secure in God's promise. Joseph's oath had confirmed him in this belief. When we believe, our portion among the saints is likewise secure.

35: The Bringer of Peace

Genesis 48-50

In all prophecy there is perspective; the lines of prophecy are drawn further and further into the future. Thus Jacob must have seen immediately that the people of his line would possess Canaan. But he also saw further into the future. Behind Israel's possession of Canaan lies something greater: the people of God will one day possess the entire world. That background is what made Israel's possession of Canaan so wonderful.

This perspective in Jacob's prophecy about his sons is evident especially from the prophecy about the coming of Shiloh, that is, the bringer of peace. The fulfillment of that prophecy began with the building of the sanctuary in Shiloh; peace for Israel radiated from that place. But the meaning of the Shiloh prophecy was further fulfilled in the house of David, especially in David's son Solomon. (*Solomon* is derived from the same word as *Shiloh*.) But Solomon, as the king of peace, prophesied about the coming of Christ and thereby the outpouring of the Spirit: in that "dwelling of God with man," peace has been given. And behind all of this lies the second coming of Christ, through which His Kingdom of Peace will be established.

The same perspective is found in the words of Genesis 49:1, where Jacob speaks to his sons of "what shall befall you in the days to come." Actually, the verse should read "in the last days." Here prophecy is concerned with the last days; in other words, it is dealing with the future.

Jacob adopted both of Joseph's sons as his own. In so doing, he took Joseph's posterity to himself to save it from the danger of being absorbed in Egypt. He also gave Joseph a double portion, which equaled the portion of a first-born and was greater than the portion given to any of his brothers. Thus the first-born's portion went to the first-born son of Jacob's beloved wife Rachel instead of to Reuben, Leah's first child. This was in keeping with Joseph's significance for Jacob's house as the preserver of life.

Yet Joseph did not inherit the first-born's right to head his father's house in the future. That right was given to Judah. Here, too, it is clear that the determining factor was not Joseph's superiority but God's election. Thus, no one was in a position to boast before God. Before long, the leadership would pass from Joseph to Judah, but the scepter would never depart from Judah. Jacob did not yet see the special meaning of the tribe of Levi in Moses and the priesthood.

After Jacob's death, the promise that Shiloh would arise from the tribe of Judah would sustain Israel's house, keeping its faith and hope alive. That promise was intended to help preserve the unity of Israel's descendants and keep them from mixing with the Egyptians.

Main thought: *The prophecy about Shiloh brings light to the house of Israel.*

Joseph's double portion. After a few years, Joseph learned that his father was ill. Since it was obvious that his sickness would lead to death, Joseph took his two sons Manasseh and Ephraim to Jacob's bed.

Although Joseph was governor of Egypt, he did not wish to be considered an Egyptian. He thought of himself as belonging to the house of Jacob. But what would happen to his two sons, who were born of an Egyptian woman? Would they be lost to Israel and have no part in the promise of the covenant? Joseph believed otherwise, which is why he took his two sons with him to his father's deathbed. He wanted them to receive their part of his blessing.

When Jacob heard that Joseph was coming, he summoned all his strength. At this point Scripture again calls him *Israel*, the bearer of the promise. He received Joseph sitting on his bed and said to him: "God has given me His promise, and now I pass it on to your two sons Manasseh and Ephraim. Therefore they will be reckoned as my own sons. Along with my sons, they will be heads of tribes of Israel." Thus Joseph would have not one but two tribes in Israel. The sons who would be born to Joseph after these two would be counted as parts of the tribes of Ephraim and Manasseh.

This must have come as quite a surprise to Joseph. Not only were his sons to share in Israel's blessing, they were even given the same degree of honor as Reuben and Simeon and all the others. God's grace was indeed great, for Jacob did this in the name of the Lord. Joseph himself was also honored by this blessing. Through his sons, he had received the portion of a first-born, twice the size of his brothers' portions. The greatest portion went not to Reuben, Leah's oldest son, but to him, Rachel's first-born.

Through this special blessing, Jacob's beloved wife Rachel was being honored. Therefore Jacob also mentioned Rachel. He imagined himself standing once more at her grave, just as he had stood there long ago with Joseph, who was about 16 years old at the time.

Not until that point did Jacob see Joseph's sons, for his eyes were dim with age. When Joseph told him who the two young men were, Jacob embraced them. Then he praised God because he had not only seen Joseph again but had also been privileged to see Joseph's sons and was allowed to adopt those sons as his own.

The moment had come for Jacob to bless Joseph's sons. First Joseph bowed to the ground, for it was as though they were in the presence of God Himself. Joseph had put Manasseh by Jacob's right hand and Ephraim by his left hand, but Jacob crossed his arms and laid his right hand on Ephraim and his left hand on Manasseh. In that posture he passed on the blessing of God's covenant.

When Joseph saw Jacob placing his right hand on Ephraim, the younger son, he tried to correct his father, but Jacob said he had done so intentionally. The seed of Manasseh would be great, but Ephraim's seed would be even greater. This, too, was according to God's election. But in both instances, the blessing would be so great that later Israelites would say: "May God make you like Ephraim and Manasseh."

What a tremendous privilege for Joseph and his posterity! They had received the blessing, and Joseph's sons, young men about 20 years old, had accepted that blessing in faith. They wanted to be Israelites rather than Egyptians.

With regard to that double blessing for Joseph, Jacob also promised Joseph's descendants a special part of the land of Canaan. He spoke of "a piece of land which I took from the hand

of the Amorites with my sword and my bow," by which he meant
a piece of land which his descendants would one day take from the
Amorites. To him God's promise was so certain that it was already
a reality. In spirit, he was present there himself to see the land
taken from the Amorites.

Thus the promise of the covenant was confirmed once again
to Joseph. And Joseph was strengthened in his hope that he and
his descendants would belong to the people of Israel. For us, too,
the most important thing is to belong to the covenant people and
to bear the sign of the covenant through baptism.

Judah is the one! Then Jacob called all his sons around him to
bless them and tell them what would happen to them in the future.
He said that he had expected much of Reuben because he was his
first-born, but it turned out that Reuben was not superior: he had
violated his father's honor. Although Reuben was indeed the first-
born, he was not called to be the leader of the people.

Neither did Simeon or Levi receive that honor—because of the
abomination they had committed against Shechem. At that point,
Jacob looked at Judah and called out: "Judah, you are the one!"
Judah was called to be the first-born, the one who would lead
Israel.

It was true. Joseph had been given a double portion, the
portion of a first-born, but Judah had received the calling. His
brothers would bow down before him, for the Christ would be
born of his line. Judah would conquer his enemies and would rule
until the coming of the Christ, the King. But the Christ would be a
King of Peace; He would be Shiloh, that is, the King who brings
everlasting peace with God. Therefore the tribe of Judah would
receive rich earthly blessings as a sign of the blessings to be brought
by the Redeemer.

Then Jacob went on to bless his other sons, including Joseph,
whose tribe would receive special blessings from God. While he
was blessing his sons, Jacob exclaimed: "I wait for your salvation,
O Lord!" In his mind, he already saw the blessings that the
Redeemer would bring.

The house of Israel would have to live in the light of the

promise that Shiloh would come one day to reign in peace in the land of the promise. Therefore Israel would have to remain apart and not mix with the Egyptians. In Shiloh, all the tribes would be blessed, including Joseph.

Has that promise been fulfilled? The Christ did come, and He brought peace to the hearts of those He calls His own, but He did not reign in peace in the promised land. One day, however, He will come again. Then He will establish His Kingdom of Peace on the new earth, of which Canaan is only a prophecy. Since we believe that He did come once, we must live in expectation of His return.

Jacob showed his sons how sure he was of the fulfillment of God's promise by ordering them to bury him in the land of Canaan, in the cave of Machpelah, where Abraham, Sarah, Isaac, Rebekah and Leah were buried. He wanted to be with his own in death. At the same time, his grave in Canaan would bind his posterity once more to the land of Canaan. Then Jacob died peacefully, believing God's promise.

Jacob's burial. Joseph had his father embalmed. After 70 days of mourning, he and his father's entire household went to Canaan to bury the patriarch. A long procession of Egyptians accompanied them.

They traveled through Transjordan to prevent a clash with the people living in the southern part of Canaan. Beyond the Jordan they lit a great bonfire as a sign of mourning, so that the surrounding people could see why they had come. Then they crossed the Jordan River and laid their father to rest in the cave of Machpelah. There Jacob's sons stood united around his grave. They were reconciled and were again bound to Canaan. Jacob had not believed in vain, for the future of his descendants was now clear. The procession then returned to Egypt.

Joseph's end. While Jacob was still alive, he had told his other sons that once he was gone, they should ask Joseph's forgiveness again for the wrong they had done him. Hence they told Joseph what their father had said and bowed down before him, asking forgiveness for the sake of the God whom they all served together.

That was indeed a wonderful witness. It moved Joseph deeply that they were still afraid. He told them that he had put that sin out of his mind a long time ago and preferred to focus on God's hand behind those events: through that sin, God had brought about good for Israel. Thus Joseph comforted them and remained their support in Goshen.

Joseph lived to the age of 110 and saw his race increase greatly. This was a fulfillment of the blessing of which Jacob had spoken, for all those children's children were Joseph's. They all belonged to Israel—and not Egypt. All of them were included in God's covenant.

When Joseph died, he was embalmed and put in a coffin in Egypt, which was to be taken along to Canaan for burial when the Israelites returned someday. That coffin, too, kept the thought of Canaan alive for the house of Israel and strengthened the Israelites in their belief that there would one day be an exodus, a deliverance.

Eventually the Israelites would take possession of Canaan, and there Shiloh would appear. Since they lived in the light of this expectation, they were able to wait for God. Now that the Christ has come, we must also learn to wait for the complete deliverance.

Deliverance from Egypt

36: I Am Who I Am

Exodus 1-4

From the very beginning, the book of Exodus presents us with different circumstances than Genesis. Exodus gives us the history not of a family but of a people. The transition is made in the first verses of Exodus.

The people of Israel would have to enter into the Lord's covenant as a people. That's what the book of Exodus leads up to right from the start. The establishment of the covenant at Sinai is the real content of this book.

Therefore we should guard against overemphasizing the deliverance of the people from Egypt. This deliverance was only a means of reaching the goal—establishing the covenant. In a spiritual sense, the covenant comes first; the deliverance from Egypt must be seen as following from the covenant. Here, too, the Word of God holds: "Seek first his kingdom and his righteousness, and all these things shall be yours as well" (Matt. 6:33).

When the Lord asked Pharaoh to let Israel go on a three-day journey into the wilderness to offer sacrifices to Him, He was not making an unjust demand. Such sacrifices to the Lord would show that Israel was a free people, but the decisive factor, of course, was that Israel was God's people—not Pharaoh's people. "Israel is My son, My first-born." Pharaoh and Egypt were called to be Israel's preserver—but only temporarily. Now Pharaoh would have to decide whether to acknowledge that Israel was God's people.

In these chapters of Exodus, the Lord meets with His people by speaking to Moses. Because the Lord chose to speak to him, Moses was called to be the head of the people. The elders were to say to Pharaoh: "The Lord has met with us." Thus the calling of Moses was not initially a call to lead Israel out of Egypt. Moses was to be a mediator between God and the people, so that the Lord could meet the people through him.

The Lord had dealt with the patriarchal *family* through the patriarch himself or through one of the members of his family. Now that there was a covenant *people*, someone would have to serve as head of that people. This development is a clear foreshadowing of the Christ. Thus it is also curious that the Lord here refers to Aaron as "the Levite," which is an indication of the house of Levi's future calling to serve as mediator. We must not overlook the fact that alongside Moses there was the high priest, who remained the spiritual representative of the people before God when their earthly ruler was gone.

In addition to the need for a leader of the people, there is another revelation in the early chapters of Exodus, namely, the necessity of atonement, which is shown a bit further on by the institution of sacrificial worship. This, too, is a clear foreshadowing of the Christ. The necessity of atonement also influenced the history related in the first chapters of Exodus. To be sure, some indication of the need for atonement had already been given to the patriarchs—in the institution of circumcision, for example. But burnt offerings were not yet distinguished from sin offerings, as they were in the laws given at Sinai. And the element of atonement in the rite of circumcision comes strongly to the fore in the threat to Moses' life, which led to Zipporah's circumcising her son.

This element also dominates the beginning of this Bible book. Israel's oppression in Egypt must not be seen first of all as persecution on the part of Pharaoh. If Pharaoh were the major obstacle, we would not be able to explain the vision of the burning bush, in which God unmistakably showed that His zeal and righteousness lit the fire of purification among the people, and that it was only by grace that they were not consumed. The persecution in Egypt was to teach Israel that it was a people under sentence of death. By means of their miraculous increase even during times of oppression, the Israelites were to learn that the miracle of grace gives life. In telling the children of this oppression, we must direct their attention not to Pharaoh first of all but to the Lord.

Against this background, the significance of the name *Yahweh* becomes clear: "I am who I am." What this expression conveys first of all is that God is Himself, governed by nothing outside Himself, and that He chooses His people by sovereign grace, even though they deserve death. The name further indicates that God will remain the same through all eternity since He can never be overcome by anything outside Himself, that He is faithful in His covenant, and that His grace is not overcome by the sins of the people. This name is now made fully known. God has elected His people in the Mediator, and for the sake of the Mediator He grants them the forgiveness of their sins.

That the establishment of the covenant is the goal from the very beginning of the book of Exodus is apparent from the Lord's meeting with Moses on Mount Horeb. The Lord gives Moses a sign: after the deliverance from Egypt, the people would serve the Lord by that very mountain. What the patriarchs and Joseph saw in their prophetic visions was mainly the exodus—and not the establishment of the covenant. Yet it is the latter event that dominates the story of the deliverance of Israel from Egypt. The book of Exodus helps us understand the actual purpose of this deliverance.

Main thought: *The Lord meets His people in the mediator.*

In Egypt's fiery furnace. During Joseph's life and the years shortly after his death, the people of Israel multiplied at a tremendous rate. Their numbers grew continually, and it was obvious that the Lord's blessing rested on them.

Indeed, the Israelites were the people that possessed the promise: God wanted to be their God. Yet the Israelites were just as sinful as any other nation. Only by the Lord's grace could they continue to exist and live in covenant with Him. But before the Lord took the entire people into His covenant, He wanted the Israelites to understand that they deserved death because of their sins, and that they remained alive only because of His grace. To accomplish this, the Lord brought about the oppression in Egypt.

Pharaoh feared the growth of the people and thought he could use cruel oppression to stop them from multiplying. It didn't work. Instead, a miracle happened: the more the people were oppressed, the more they increased in number. This miracle struck fear into the hearts of the Egyptians, who began to dread the Israelites (Ex. 1:12). Nevertheless, they continued to persecute the Israelites and thus opposed God. Pharaoh even commanded the midwives to kill the baby boys of the Israelites. But the midwives did not obey Pharaoh's orders, and God blessed them for it. Their behavior was an indication that God was on Israel's side. Finally Pharaoh decreed that all the newly born male children of the Israelites were to be cast into the Nile River. If the Israelites had nothing but daughters, they would have to intermarry with the Egyptians and would then merge with them.

On the one hand, God was against the people of Israel, for the oppression of Pharaoh was His own work. God was simply using Pharaoh as His instrument. Yet the fact remains that Pharaoh unleashed that oppression against the Israelites out of hatred, even though God intended it to be a blessing for them. Therefore Pharaoh was guilty all the same.

On the other hand, God was favoring His people and blessing them. In this period of testing and oppression, the people had to learn that they had earned death and were allowed to go on living only because of God's mercy. The entire people of Israel typified the Lord Jesus Christ, who was laden with our sins and died to restore us to God's favor. In the same way, we must die unto sin to live in God's grace.

The mediator's preparation. After Pharaoh gave the order that all the male Israelite babies were to be thrown into the Nile, a baby boy was born to Amram and Jochebed as their third child. This baby was exceptionally beautiful. By faith his father and mother regarded him as a special favor from God. They could not reconcile themselves to the thought that their child had been born only to die in infancy. Therefore, in faith, his mother hid him for three months. And when she could hide him no longer, she cleverly placed him in a basket of bullrushes and set him adrift in the Nile at a spot where Pharaoh's daughter often bathed.

Just as Jochebed hoped, Pharaoh's daughter found the baby and decided to keep it. Jochebed was even allowed to nurse and rear the child for Pharaoh's daughter. The king's daughter named the child Moses, which means *drawn out of the water*. Once he was grown, she adopted him as her son.

The one whom God had chosen as mediator for His people was threatened with death from the day of his birth. In this regard he was a type of our Mediator Jesus Christ, whose life was threatened from the very beginning on account of our sins.

In that child, God had provided the future head of Israel. If the people of Israel were to live in covenant with the Lord, they would need a head to represent them before God. Our Head is the Lord Jesus Christ, who was also the real Head of the people of Israel. Moses was only a type of the Christ.

At Pharaoh's court, Moses was instructed in all the wisdom of the Egyptians. Yet this education did not incline his heart toward Egypt. He continued to consider himself a member of Israel and felt the urge to take up the cause of his oppressed people.

One day, when he was about 40 years old, Moses killed an Egyptian who had beaten one of the Hebrew men. The next day he tried to separate two Hebrews who were fighting. Moses' action revealed the urge of God's Spirit, who bound him to Israel and made him take up the cause of his own people. But if Moses hoped to represent that people before God and be God's representative to that people, he would have to wait for God's time. A person who holds such a position will only accomplish something if he follows God's calling.

Up to this point, Moses' actions had been entirely *self-*motivated. Therefore he did not even shrink from committing murder. The means he chose were unholy. When he found out that people knew about the murder he had committed and that Pharaoh was trying to kill him, he did not return to Pharaoh to confess his guilt but fled from Egypt. He gave up his privileged position at the court because he was bound to his people. Thus his flight was undertaken in faith.

Moses fled to the land of Midian and wound up in the household of Reuel or Jethro, a priest who probably lived in the Sinai peninsula. This peninsula bordered on Egypt and extended just a bit past Mount Sinai or Horeb. There he herded Jethro's sheep, and Jethro gave him his daughter Zipporah in marriage.

During his years in the Sinai peninsula, Moses learned to wait. The urge to take up his people's cause was very much alive in him, but he was far away from them. He suffered there from homesickness, which is evident from the fact that he called his oldest son *Gershom,* saying: "I have become a stranger in a foreign land." Because he waited and waited with no solution in sight, his reliance on his own strength was broken. Moses learned to surrender to God, which was the only way he could become a mediator for his people and a type of the Lord Jesus Christ.

Called by the Lord. After a long time, God remembered His people and mercifully turned to them for the sake of the covenant He had made with the patriarchs. He felt there had been enough oppression by then. He adopted the people of Israel in the sense that He wanted Israel, as a nation, to learn about His covenant. Therefore He wanted Israel to experience His favor as a people.

The time had come for the Lord to call Moses to lead the people. One day, when Moses was with the flock at Mount Horeb, the Lord appeared to him in a flame in the middle of a bramble bush. The bush was on fire, but it was not consumed. When Moses came closer to get a better look at this remarkable sight, God told him that He had come down to deliver His people. God now wished to dwell in the midst of His people with His special favor, and Moses was to lead the people out of Egypt.

Later Moses would have understood the meaning of the burning bush. God, with His zeal and justice, was among His people during the time of oppression in Egypt. Yet, because of His grace, Israel was not consumed.

Now Moses had become a different person. He did not feel worthy of standing before that people in the service of God. Therefore God promised Moses that He would be with him. To show Moses how sure it was that the goal would be reached, God declared that the people would serve Him at that very spot.

Neither the people nor their deliverance was the main thing in this revelation. Most important of all was the name of the Lord, on which the people would call at Mount Horeb. For the sake of the Lord's name, their deliverance was sure. That's why the prediction that the people would worship God at Mount Sinai could be a sign for Moses.

Then Moses asked the Lord by what name he should announce God to the people. He sensed that a new revelation of the Lord was about to come and wondered what it would be like. The Lord responded by telling Moses His name—Yahweh, that is "I am who I am," or "I will be what I will be." What God was now revealing was that He would let the people of Israel live with Him in covenant out of His sovereign grace, and that His grace would never be overcome by the sin of the people. Thus they would learn to know Him throughout their generations. God also told Moses that Pharaoh would refuse to let the people go, that God would perform miracles in Egypt, and that eventually the people would be free to leave, loaded with the riches of Egypt.

But how could Moses expect the people to believe him? By now Moses understood that God Himself would have to prepare a place for him and his message in the hearts of the people. And that the Lord intended to do. He not only gave the mediator to the people, He also gave the people to the mediator. In the same way, the Lord wants to prepare a place in our hearts for the Christ, our Mediator, and wants to give us to Him.

The Lord gave Moses three signs by which he could demonstrate his calling. Moses was the mediator. Therefore he would be able to change a staff into a dangerous snake and then change the snake back into a staff, as an instrument of blessing. He could summon sickness and curse, but he could also cause the curse to give way to blessedness and life. The water of the Nile River, which was worshiped in Egypt as a god, could be changed by Moses into blood, which would cause Egypt to perish along with its idols. Through these signs, the people would understand by faith that God's grace was with Moses, the mediator.

Moses questioned the Lord further about his calling. He pointed out that he was not eloquent but slow of speech. How, then, could he be the Lord's prophet to the people and to Pharaoh? The Lord responded by promising to teach Moses what to say.

Until then, Moses had accepted the calling with which the Lord came to him. His questions concerned the Lord's position toward the people in that calling. But when it came time to make his commitment and say, "I am ready," Moses shrank back and asked the Lord to send someone else. Then the Lord became angry and simply commanded Moses to proceed.

Moses became the mediator, then, for the Lord Himself saw to it that Moses was ready and willing. To meet him halfway, God promised that Aaron would do the talking for him. But that was the end of the matter. The Lord said: "Go now, and take this rod in your hand." To Moses the rod would signify God's presence.

Shouldn't anyone shrink from being a mediator between God and His people? No one is fit to assume such a responsibility. Only the Lord Jesus Christ was able to step into that role. But through Christ's Spirit, Moses was far from powerless. That staff he was leaning on was a sign to him that God would be with him through Christ's Spirit.

Moses' return as head of his people. Moses then went to his father-in-law and asked his permission to return to Egypt to join his kinsmen. Apparently he did not mention his calling to him; that was something Jethro would not have understood yet. Jethro let Moses go.

The Lord also reassured Moses by telling him that the Pharaoh who had once sought to kill him was dead. Riding on an ass and taking his wife and possessions with him, Moses set out for Egypt. In his hand he carried the rod that symbolized God's presence.

At the beginning of this journey, the Lord told Moses that he should ask Pharaoh to let the people of Israel go so that they could serve the Lord. But Pharaoh would harden his heart and refuse. Then Moses was to tell him that Israel was God's first-born son. It was true that all peoples were the Lord's possession and would be adopted by Him in due time as His children, but at this time Israel was still the only people He had adopted.

If Pharaoh should choose to keep this eldest son from God and refuse to allow the people of Israel to serve the Lord according to His will, God would slay Pharaoh's first-born son. This would make Pharaoh realize what he was doing when he denied the Lord His son. Pharaoh would find out the hard way how much God loved His people.

It was strange that the Lord should raise this matter of His love for His people at the beginning of Moses' journey to Egypt. Circumcision was a way of indicating that a certain people belonged to God. Through that ritual of circumcision, God's people bore the seal of His covenant. Yet, Moses' second son had not been circumcised! Most likely Moses had circumcised his first son against the will of Zipporah but had lost the battle when the second son was born.

Thus Moses' own family, as a whole, did not bear the sign that it belonged to the covenant, even though Moses was called to be the head of the people. When the Lord raised this matter, Moses must have felt oppressed. The Lord came to him at a place where he had stopped for the night and sought to take his life, perhaps because of this feeling. God may take the life of any man who does not respect the sign of His covenant, who does not ensure that his children bear the sign of being hidden away securely with the Lord in His covenant, whatever the cost. How lightly people today often treat the sign of baptism!

After these events, Zipporah circumcised her second son with a sharp flint. Then the danger that threatened Moses' life disappeared. But this did not win Zipporah over to the covenant and the sign of the covenant, for she accused Moses of being a bridegroom of blood to her. She had received him back, as she had once received him when they were married—but only through the bloody operation of circumcision. How little Zipporah understood of what she said!

Through this circumcision of his son, Moses had not only been given back to his wife but was also given to his people to be their head. In the same way, the Lord Jesus Christ has been given to us to be our Head. That, too, happened through the spilling of blood, but in Christ's case the Mediator's own blood was shed. Thus Christ is a bridegroom of blood to us.

Apparently Moses sent his wife home after this event. He would have had to tell her about God's covenant and about his own calling as head of the people. And at that time, Zipporah was not able to share his life in that calling. Later, after the exodus from Egypt, she joined him again (Ex. 18:1-9).

Moses continued on his way alone. At Mount Horeb his brother Aaron met him, for the Lord had also revealed Himself to Aaron, telling him to go and meet Moses. By divine instruction, Aaron could already acknowledge the calling of Moses.

Together they traveled to Egypt and spoke with the elders of Israel. Moses showed the elders the signs which the Lord had told him to use. The Lord opened the hearts of those elders to receive His Word, which came to them by Moses. Moses was given to the people as their head, and the people were in turn given to Moses by the Lord. They received Moses in this light and believed that God was visiting His people to deliver them from oppression.

At that time, their belief was only a belief in the deliverance which the Lord would give through Moses. Therefore, when affliction came, their faith would be severely shaken. But the first tie had been established between the people and Moses, their head. That tie existed because of God's own Word, spoken by Moses.

In the same manner, God has given us the Lord Jesus Christ as our Head, but we must also be given to Him. We must accept Him at God's Word as our Head and Redeemer.

37: Freedom to Serve the Lord

Exodus 5-11

In the previous chapter we saw that the main issue with regard to Israel was not freedom and the promised land but the covenant and the service of the Lord. Therefore the Lord made an important demand of Pharaoh: "Let My people go so that they can serve Me." Pharaoh was the temporary guardian of Israel, but his guardianship did not include the right to interfere with Israel's freedom to serve the Lord, who was Israel's Father.

The whole struggle between God and Pharaoh in the first nine plagues concerns that freedom. God spared Pharaoh for a long time to give him a chance to recognize that the Lord is God, and that His people are free to serve Him. This struggle had nothing to do with the deliverance of Israel out of Egypt.

The struggle typifies the struggle that goes on throughout the world's history. The Lord's *rights* were at stake in this struggle about the freedom of His people to serve Him according to His Word. That freedom may not be interfered with either by people or by governments.

It was only when Pharaoh refused to the very end to acknowledge that freedom that Moses left his presence in anger. The anger of Moses, the mediator, was a revelation of the Lord's anger at Pharaoh, which settled the case. Not only would the Israelites be free to serve the Lord, they would be led out of Egypt for good. Moreover, the power of Egypt would be destroyed through the death of all the first-born.

That final conflict and the exodus of Israel were a prophecy about the day of the Lord, the end of the world, when the people of God will be delivered and the power of the world will be broken. But before that end comes, God demands that His people be given the freedom to serve Him. Whatever else God promised Israel was not important at that po'nt. Anyone who denies the Lord the right to make this initial demand is denying God's absolute sovereignty in general.

In that struggle we also see the significance of the mediator. God put Moses in His own place in relation to Pharaoh, with Aaron serving as Moses' prophet. God placed Pharaoh in this position to prove His power to him. Moreover, Moses later held a high position among the whole of Egypt's people. In a similar way, the world is in the hand of Christ, the Mediator. Through Christ, God demonstrates His power in the world, in the struggle for freedom to serve God.

When Paul refers to this segment of Bible history in Romans 9:17, he quotes Exodus 9:16. God raised Pharaoh up for a certain purpose, namely, to make him an example to the whole world in the struggle for the freedom to serve Him. In the nine plagues, therefore, we see an important sequence of events. The first three plagues lead the magicians of Egypt to admit: "This is the finger of God." This showed that they realized they were not dealing with a magical power in the hands of Moses and Aaron but with a power that went beyond the capacities of men. But Israel suffered through those first three plagues as well.

In the following six plagues, there is a distinct difference: Israel was spared. This showed that the Lord was in the midst of Egypt, distinguishing carefully and choosing for His people.

The fourth, fifth and sixth plagues, namely, flies, pestilence among cattle, and boils, still involved the earth alone. But in the last three the Lord revealed Himself as the God of heaven and earth, who rules over all the powers of nature, commanding the wind and hail by His Word.

The seventh plague was the hail storm. The eighth plague, the locusts, was caused by a wind from the east that brought swarms of locusts, carrying them over the Red Sea. The ninth plague, darkness, was probably also the result of the wind: it may have been a sand storm such as the Egyptians had never experienced before. In the last three plagues, the Lord was revealing Himself as the supreme and exalted God.

When Pharaoh hardened his heart again and again, he was not fighting against an arbitrary divine power that chose for some people in Egypt and against others; he was opposing the supreme God. It then became a personal conflict. Although Israel lived in the shelter of the Most High, Pharaoh rejected His dominion of grace. That made the judgment on Pharaoh inevitable: the tenth plague had to come.

Main thought: *The Lord struggles on behalf of His people so that they will be free to serve Him.*

The mediator revealed in Egypt. Once the people of Israel believed in Moses' calling, Moses and Aaron went to Pharaoh to ask him in the name of the Lord, Israel's God, to let God's people go into the wilderness to hold a feast for the Lord. God made no other demand on Pharaoh; He was not asking that Israel be allowed to leave the land of Egypt for good. The main thing was for Pharaoh to acknowledge the freedom of the Lord's people to serve Him according to His Word.

Pharaoh had only been appointed by God as a temporary guardian over Israel. Therefore he would have to acknowledge the rights of God, who was Israel's Father. Instead he replied proudly: "Who is this Lord, whose voice I should obey and let Israel go?" Pharaoh did not want to know the Lord or acknowledge His rights.

When Moses and Aaron spoke of their mission and urged Pharaoh to obey for God's sake, he accused them of trying to distract the people from their work. Pharaoh then demanded that a heavier burden be laid upon the people, to make them suffer even more. From then on they would have to find their own straw for the bricks they made.

The people of Israel suffered physically under the misery of that heavier workload, and soon they blamed Moses and Aaron for making Pharaoh dislike them, arguing that the two leaders were responsible for Pharaoh's evil thoughts about the Israelites. Thus Israel's faith in Moses' calling was tested and immediately found wanting.

The reason this faith succumbed so quickly was that the people still looked to Pharaoh and valued his good will. They did not yet dare entrust themselves completely to the Lord, even though deliverance had to come through oppression. Sadly enough, this is often the attitude of the covenant people: again and again they look back. Therefore the severe oppression that followed only served to estrange Israel from Egypt completely.

At this reproach by the people, Moses turned to the Lord and asked Him why He had dealt with His people in this way. His question did not stem from doubt; he was simply seeking an understanding of the Lord's ways. The Lord answered that He would demonstrate His power to Pharaoh. Now the Lord would be fully revealed as Yahweh, the God who declares, "I am who I am," the God who rules the world and the nations in sovereign power in a way that even the patriarchs had never seen. This would teach Israel even more to seek refuge with the Lord. Once again the Lord promised deliverance out of Egypt.

Although Moses conveyed these words to the people, they did not listen to him. Because of their cruel bondage, they could not believe, nor could they wait for the Lord. They did not possess the faith that overcomes the world, and they no longer saw in Moses the mediator in whom God had come down to His people.

In times of oppression, God's people still waver often. Yet Christ, the Mediator, has come down to us and remains with us so that we can believe. Thus God's mediator stayed with Israel. God's faithfulness is not destroyed by our lack of faith.

The mediator revealed to Pharaoh. Again the Lord sent Moses to Pharaoh. But this time Moses himself objected. If he had failed to persuade the people of Israel, how could he ever persuade Pharaoh? He blamed his failure on the fact that he was not an able speaker—as if his mission were dependent on the art of human persuasion rather than on the revelation of the Lord!

The Lord answered that Pharaoh was willfully hardening his heart to the Lord's calling, and that at the same time the Lord was hardening Pharaoh's heart because of the sins of the world. Thus the Lord would show His power to Pharaoh, so that the whole world would see how God deals with those who oppose the service of the Lord.

Therefore the Lord delivered Pharaoh into the hands of Moses. By Moses' hand, the plagues would come over Egypt. Moses was made as God to Pharaoh, and Aaron would serve as Moses' prophet, speaking the Word in God's name. In the same way, God has exalted our Mediator and has placed all power in heaven and on earth in His hands.

God also told Moses to give Pharaoh a sign to prove that he was sent by God. Thus equipped, Moses went to Pharaoh. Standing before the king, Moses told Aaron, who carried Moses' staff in his hand, to throw the staff down. The staff immediately turned into a serpent.

The magicians who surrounded Pharaoh also threw their staffs down, which likewise turned into serpents. No doubt they thought this made them Moses' equal! God's staff, carried by the mediator, was intended for leading Israel and was a means by which God could also lead the nations. Yet it became a serpent that would bite Egypt.

To show that God's miracle was different from what the magicians had done, the serpent that had been Moses' staff swallowed up the other serpents. This was a demonstration that the Lord, the God who redeems, possessed greater power than the magicians in Egypt.

But who can see God and His miracles except those who believe? Thus Pharaoh did not acknowledge the Lord or Moses, and he refused to listen to the Words of the Lord. How often God reveals Himself when man refuses to see!

The finger of God. At the Lord's command, Moses struck the waters in Egypt and they turned to blood. This happened in front of Pharaoh and his courtiers when they were on their way to the river, probably to worship the Nile, the god of Egypt. The fish died and the river stank. Thus Egypt and its idol were defeated. This plague lasted seven days. But the magicians managed to duplicate the plague, and Pharaoh did not listen.

Then the Lord commanded Moses to stretch out his staff over the streams of Egypt. The result was that frogs appeared everywhere. Pharaoh then deceitfully promised to let the people go if Moses would take this plague away and pray for him. Perhaps for a moment Pharaoh was deeply impressed. But it is also possible that he deliberately deceived Moses, whom he considered an imposter. To show that he had control over Pharaoh, Moses left it up to him to decide the time when the plague would be removed. When Moses prayed, the frogs died, but Pharaoh still did not believe, for the magicians were able to do the same thing—except that they did not have the power to remove the plague.

When Moses stretched out his staff over the dust of the earth, the dust turned into gnats—perhaps mosquitoes with a dangerous sting. This was a plague that the magicians could not duplicate. The Lord put an end to their power, and therefore they had to admit to Pharaoh that there was a divine power in this sign surpassing the magical powers of men. Nevertheless, Pharaoh hardened his heart. He had been shown divine power, but he still refused to acknowledge the Lord.

The Lord in Egypt's midst. The Israelites had also suffered under the plagues. Even the Lord's own people deserve the wrath of God unless God forgives their sins. In their sin, they are one with the life of the world; only by God's grace are they distinguished from the world. That grace of God would now be made manifest in Egypt, so that Pharaoh could see that it was not simply a divine power that was at work but the Lord Himself, who looks after His people.

A mixture of vermin sprang up in Egypt—probably swarms of dogflies. But they were not found in Goshen. Defeated by this plague, Pharaoh told Moses and Aaron that the Israelites would be allowed to worship the Lord—in Egypt. When Moses refused, arguing that the Egyptians would take offense, Pharaoh promised to let the Israelites go, provided they did not go too far away. Pharaoh still imposed a condition on the Lord. Moses warned Pharaoh not to be deceitful again, but Pharaoh once more hardened his heart as soon as the plague was lifted through Moses' prayers.

Then the Lord sent a pestilence to strike the cattle of the Egyptians, but not a single animal of the Israelites died. Although Pharaoh was aware of this, he still hardened his heart.

When the next plague struck, not even the magicians could stand before Moses. Ashes which Moses had taken from a kiln and thrown toward heaven in the sight of Pharaoh became boils on men and beasts. Again God spared Israel from the plague, but Pharaoh still did not believe. Without faith it is impossible to recognize that the Lord treats His people in a different way than those who do not believe in Him.

The God of heaven and earth. When Moses gave the word, God caused a heavy hail to fall. Among the Egyptians there were some who feared the Lord's Word and had brought everything inside beforehand. The cattle out in the field and the crops that were already ripe were destroyed. Again Pharaoh promised to let the people go, but he did not keep his promise.

Then the Lord sent locusts carried on by a strong east wind. Again Moses had warned Pharaoh, and his courtiers urged him to give in. Didn't Pharaoh see that Egypt was being ruined? Pharaoh was ready to let the people go, but first he wanted to know just who would be going. When Moses told him that everybody and everything would go along, Pharoah sneered that the Lord would be no more favorably inclined toward their plan to make such a journey than he himself was. Moses and Aaron were then driven from Pharaoh's presence. That was why the plague came.

Pharaoh seemed to humble himself before the Lord and acknowledged his sin. In answer to Moses' prayer, the locusts were driven into the Red Sea by a west wind. But Pharaoh then hardened his heart again.

Finally God caused a thick darkness to cover the land of Egypt, but in the homes of the Israelites there was light. In those latter three plagues, God revealed Himself as the God of heaven and earth, against whom Pharaoh was struggling.

Pharaoh's sin had finally reached the point of no return. Before Moses went to Pharaoh again, summoned because of the darkness, the Lord revealed to Moses that God would no longer be lenient with Egypt. If Pharaoh changed his mind once more, God would slay all the first-born and lead Israel out of Egypt.

Equipped with this knowledge, Moses went to Pharaoh, who did say that the Israelites could leave, provided that the cattle remained behind. But the Lord would not allow that either. Who was Pharaoh to impose conditions on the Lord? Moses also told Pharaoh that the Israelites had no way of knowing in advance which of the cattle they would have to sacrifice to the Lord.

Then Pharaoh became angry and declared that Moses and Aaron would die if they ever appeared in his presence again. Moses answered that Pharaoh had chosen the right words, for the two brothers would not see his face again. Moses left Pharaoh's presence burning with anger. God's wrath had turned against Pharaoh.

Before the seventh plague struck, God had said that He would direct His plagues toward Pharaoh's heart. In the last three plagues, God did speak to Pharaoh's heart in an effort to reveal Himself as the supreme being, the God of heaven and earth, in whose hiding place Israel was secure. But Pharaoh hardened his heart against that revelation too, which meant that the decisive point had been reached for him and for Egypt. God's patience with those who turn away from Him is great today too, as He demonstrates His power in the world, but at some point the hour of decision arrives.

The Lord is a glorious God for His people. The One who provides a hiding place for His people is certainly very high and exalted. It is by faith alone that we abide in that hiding place. He will see to it that there is freedom on earth to serve Him according to His Word.

38: Resurrection

Exodus 12—13:16

The Israelites were in imminent danger of becoming enslaved to the life of Egypt. Already they had built the treasure cities there. Along with Egypt, they were bound to perish. To a certain extent, they were ensnared in the death of Egypt; Egypt threatened to become Israel's grave. Thus Israel's deliverance from Egypt was a resurrection from the dead. In that sense, the deliverance was truly Easter (resurrection). Easter is the fulfillment of Israel's Passover.

The Lord laid claim especially on all the first-born of Israel, for He had spared them in Egypt. However, through those first-born, God claimed the entire people for Himself as His first-born son. Those first-born, and thereby Israel as a whole, had fallen under His judgment, but God accepted them in grace. Here we have the ban* in the sense of setting apart, either to God's judgment or to His service. The redemption of the first-born was to be a constant reminder to Israel that it had been set apart not for judgment but for service. For Israel, that meant resurrection.

The Passover was both sacrament and sacrifice for Israel. We must be sure to distinguish these two elements clearly. The lamb, whose blood was smeared on the doorposts, was the sacrifice that covers and makes atonement. The Passover supper, the supper of communion with the Lord, is based on the sacrifice.

That not one part of the lamb was to be broken symbolizes the unity of Israel, a unity Israel experienced in its fellowship with the Lord. That none of Christ's bones were broken points to the same thing.

At the Passover supper, the Israelites were to eat unleavened bread. They had eaten unleavened bread during the days immediately after their departure from Egypt because they left in great haste. Apparently it was not until later that God instituted the feast of unleavened bread.

---

*The Old Testament uses *ban* for setting apart (devoting) to the Lord for either curse (destruction) or blessing (life).—TRANS.

The announcement of that institution, however, was immediately connected with the announcement of the institution of the Passover itself. The unleavened bread stands for the new life, which is free from the leaven of sin.

Main thought: *God raises Israel from the dead.*

Sacrifice and sacrament. God had already performed many miracles in Egypt, but Israel was still in bondage. Israel contributed to Egypt's greatness by building its cities. Egypt was under judgment of death because it did not fear the Lord, and it looked as though Israel was destined to perish one day along with Egypt. In Egypt, Israel was seemingly ensnared in death and the grave. Yet the Lord had promised to lead the Israelites out of Egypt, as though raising them from the dead. Now, after the ninth plague, that was finally going to happen. This God had told the people through Moses.

Now He gave the people a strange command: they were to make the present month the first month of a new year, for a new time was beginning for Israel, a time in which Israel would rise from the dead, as it were. On the tenth day of that month, each family was to set apart a lamb from the flock, choosing one without blemish. And on the fourteenth day, they were to kill that lamb and prepare it without breaking any of its bones or over-cooking it, roasting it whole on the spit. The blood of that lamb was to be smeared on the lintel and the two doorposts, using a sprig of hyssop. Afterward the Israelites were to eat the lamb. If the lamb was too much for one family to eat, they were to share it with another. There were not to be any leftovers; whatever was left was to be burned. Moreover, they were to eat unleavened bread and bitter herbs with the lamb.

This was indeed a strange series of commands. What did it all mean? During the night of the fourteenth, the Lord was going to visit Egypt in judgment by slaying all the first-born. Now the Israelites, of course, were just as sinful as the Egyptians. When God saw the blood on the doorposts, the angel of death would pass over them. That blood of the lamb was a sign of the blood of the Christ, by which they would receive atonement for their sins and be saved from the wrath of God.

When their sins were forgiven for Christ's sake, God would be able to dwell in their midst, and they would be privileged to have supper with the Lord at one table. When they ate that lamb, it would be as though God was the host in their home, giving them His food and His fellowship.

Those bitter herbs were to remind them of the bitter oppression in Egypt. But now the Lord would lift their affliction and show them His favor through their deliverance from Egypt. From then on, they were to celebrate that supper every year. Time and again they would enjoy the privilege of having supper with the Lord at one table. How close God and His people would be!

To this day that sign has never been abolished. Even now we have a supper in the church at which the Lord is host, where believers sit with Him at one table, namely, the Lord's supper. We no longer eat lamb with unleavened bread and bitter herbs. Instead we eat bread that has been broken and drink wine that has been poured out, as signs of the broken body and shed blood of the Lord Jesus Christ. At this supper, God is as close to His own as He was to the Israelites.

The Lord had also instructed the Israelites to eat that meal standing up, dressed for travel, each man with his staff in his hand. After the meal they would leave Egypt in haste.

When Moses informed the elders of all of this, they bowed their heads in faith, in adoration of the grace of the Lord, which was now going to be manifested to them. They believed that what the Lord had promised was about to happen. Without faith, that supper would not have had any significance for them, but through their faith, they could view it as a sign of God's favor. Without faith, no one will benefit from the Lord's supper either, but for believers, it is still a sign of God's faithfulness in His covenant.

When the Israelites celebrated that supper in later years, they were to tell their children what it all meant. What joy that must have brought them, especially when they believed, for only then did they understand that the blood of the lamb was a token of the forgiveness of their sins. The lamb, served whole, symbolized the fact that they were privileged to be one as a people if they remained in fellowship with the Lord.

Egypt and Israel set apart. The Israelites did as the Lord commanded them. There they were that night of the fourteenth, standing and eating the lamb. In spirit they were close to the Lord, and the Lord was near them.

While they were eating, the Lord's angel of destruction was going through the land of Egypt, slaying the first-born of both man and beast. The Lord set those first-born apart, consecrating them to His judgment. The consecration of the first-born to judgment was a sign that the entire land of Egypt was under judgment. One day that judgment would come, just as it will come for all unbelievers at the end of the world. Then God will consecrate them to His wrath.

When the angel of death saw blood on the doorposts of the Israelites, he passed over those homes. In those homes, the first-born were also set apart—not for God's wrath but for His favor and love. *They* were privileged to serve the Lord—not because they were better than the first-born of the Egyptians but because God had forgiven their sins on account of Christ's blood. And when those first-born were set apart for the Lord, the entire nation of Israel was consecrated to Him through them.

Later the Israelites would always remember what happened in Egypt. Every oldest son had to be ransomed because he was really designated for special service to the Lord. Moreover, all the first-born among the animals were to be consecrated to the Lord. In the case of an unclean animal, the first-born would either be redeemed with a clean animal or be killed (by having its neck broken).

Everything and everybody must be consecrated to the Lord, that is, set apart for His wrath and judgment or for His favor and love. When we have received forgiveness through Christ's blood, we may be consecrated to the Lord's favor in the whole of our lives.

A new life in freedom. There was a lot of weeping that night in the land of Egypt, for all the first-born Egyptians were dead, even the oldest son of the Pharaoh. No one slept that night, and Pharaoh summoned Moses and Aaron to tell them that the Israelites could leave immediately and take all their possessions with them. This was a farewell for good. Pharaoh understood this very well, for he said: "Bless me also!" In other words, he wanted Moses and Aaron to pray to the Lord on his behalf. He sensed that a curse had come upon him.

All the Egyptians urged the Israelites to leave their land in a hurry, for they feared they would all die. In their haste, the Israelites did not have time to let the dough which they had prepared for the journey rise. Therefore they ate unleavened bread during those first days outside Egypt.

The Lord had told them that at the time of their departure from the land of Egypt, they should demand silver and golden vessels and clothes from the Egyptians. After all, they had served the Egyptians with their hard labor. And God saw to it that the Egyptians gave them what they asked for, in return for leaving in a hurry.

The Egyptians drove the people of the Lord out of their land not because they wanted them to be free but because they feared them. The Lord, through His people, is a curse to those who do not believe in Him. The Israelites left the land of bondage laden with the treasures of Egypt. In this way the Lord honored them, not because they were better than the Egyptians but because they were His people, whom He had granted forgiveness through the blood. One day, at the end of the world, we, too, will go forth crowned with honor, when by faith we have received full forgiveness of our sins.

The Israelites journeyed to Succoth, where they set up the first camp and spent the night. Moses immediately gave them several ordinances concerning the Passover, the night when the angel of destruction "passed over" them, the night when they were raised from the dead. Among other things, Moses told them in the name of the Lord that although they were now eating unleavened bread because of their hasty departure, from then on they were to eat it every year for a whole week during the Passover celebration.

The eating of unleavened bread was also a sign to them. Leaven always contains an element of decay. That all leaven had to be barred from their homes for seven days was a sign to them that all corruption of sin was to be excluded from their lives. They were to live a new life before the Lord.

As many as the Lord our God shall call. Thousands upon

thousands of men aged 20 or older left Egypt that night. When we add the women and children, we see that the Israelites were indeed a large army of people. This shows us how God had made them increase in Egypt. In addition, a mixed multitude of people left with them. It is possible that these people tagged along because they had seen something of the honor and grace of Israel's God. Perhaps some of them came simply because of blood ties with the Israelites.

These people certainly would not be the only strangers living among the Israelites in the future. How were the Israelites to deal with them all? Were they also supposed to participate in the Passover? Would they be permitted to enjoy God's favor in His covenant?

If the strangers were willing to receive the sign of the covenant, i.e. circumcision, they would count as covenant people. These people were a prophecy of the many people drawn from all the nations who were outside the covenant at first and therefore did not belong to the people of God but were later incorporated into that people because they acknowledged the Lord Jesus Christ as their King. It is wonderful that we may belong to that people, that by faith we may receive the forgiveness of sins through the blood of Christ and also take our places at the table of the Lord.

Consider the Passover in Egypt, the "passing over." The angel of death passed over the homes of the Israelites. Every first-born in Israel, indeed, every Israelite was raised from the dead, as it were. Every Israelite was delivered from the death that reigned in Egypt. Although all Egypt would perish one day, the Israelites were raised up to a new life in freedom.

Israel was saved from death and raised to a new life through the blood of the true sacrificial Lamb, i.e. the Lord Jesus Christ. Christ would die one day in place of His people. But He would also rise from the dead. Therefore, at our Passover (Easter), we remember the resurrection of the Lord Jesus Christ. The deliverance of Israel out of Egypt was a prophecy of Easter.

By the power of the Lord Jesus Christ, the Lord will also raise up His own to new life in our day. By faith in Christ, we experience the resurrection even now. If we live in our sins, we are bound by the bonds of death, in which we will certainly perish. Through faith in the Lord Jesus Christ, we are saved from that death. Thus we receive eternal life here and now. This life we will never lose —not even when we die. One day we will be glorified with Christ forever.

39: The Day of the Lord

Exodus 13:17—15:21

The day of the Lord is the day the Lord comes. From a prophetic standpoint, we could say that it is the day on which the Lord came in judgment, or the day of Christ's first coming, or the day of the outpouring of the Holy Spirit, or the day of Christ's return. Actually, all these facets are included in what is meant by *the day of the Lord,* for the one is an extension of the other. Scripture itself indicates that we are to think of the day of the Lord in connection with Egypt's fate when it tells us that the song of Moses will be sung during the final plagues (Rev. 15:3).

The day of the Lord is the day on which the Lord reveals the rights of His love. On the one hand, He reveals those rights in the destruction of the ungodly, when He avenges their rejection of His just rights. We read that the Lord was glorified through Pharaoh and Egypt: the rights of His love were glorified. That began with the hardening of Pharaoh's heart and continued with Pharaoh's pursuit of Israel. Not only Pharaoh's sins but sin in general, the break with God, was being punished in this hardening of his heart.

Thus it is not enough to point out Pharaoh's individual sins as we tell this story to the children. Pharaoh was neither willing nor able to know the God whose dwelling was with Israel. But this is natural to all of us. The judgment on sin in general is seen in Pharaoh's destruction. The hardening, the willful closing of the heart to the revelation of the Lord, is a judgment upon the first (original) sin.

On the other hand, God revealed the rights of His love by proclaiming that His people were for Himself alone. The Lord placed the Red Sea between Israel and Egypt, keeping Israel in the wilderness as in the hollow of His hand. This deliverance of the people of Israel was a prophecy of the ultimate deliverance of all of God's people on the day of Christ.

By asserting the rights of His love, God received from the people what His grace first supplied. By the Red Sea, He caused the people to surrender to Him in faith. Then, on the opposite bank, He had them sing of the Lord's victory. In this song, they sang only of the Lord.

The song of Moses in Exodus 15 can be divided into the following four parts: (1) The theme, which appears in verse 1 and is repeated again and again by Miriam and the women. (2) In verses 2-5, the first strophe,* the Lord is praised in a general way as warrior and victor. (3) Verses 6-10, the second strophe, tell that the real struggle was between the Lord and His enemies, who persecuted Him through His people. (4) The third strophe, verses 11-19, sing of the deliverance of the people and of the salvation the Lord has reserved for them.

Main thought: *The day of the Lord is a revelation of the rights of the Lord's love.*

Led by God Himself. From Succoth, their gathering place, the people set out under Moses' leadership. They carried with them the bones of Joseph, in accordance with the oath his brothers had sworn a long time ago. Before his death, Joseph had prophesied about the deliverance from Egypt. By taking the bones of Joseph with them, the Israelites not only fulfilled the oath once sworn to Joseph but also showed that they viewed this exodus as a fulfillment of the promise God had given their fathers many years before. By faith they apparently expected to be led to Canaan.

Yet the Lord did not bring them to Canaan immediately. The shortest route would have been along the Mediterranean coast through the land of the Philistines, a journey of only a few days. But the Israelites were not yet ready for war with the Philistines. Furthermore, the Lord had other things in mind for them first.

The Israelites, as a people, still had to enter into a covenant relationship with the Lord. This would have to happen in the wilderness, before they arrived in Canaan. And God had to make the separation from Egypt final, showing His people that He kept them in the hollow of His hand.

Strophe is a term borrowed from ancient Greek drama. The word itself means *a turn,* and in drama indicates, for example, the song of a chorus during one turn or figure of a dance, as, for instance, in moving from the right to the left of the stage. An opposite movement, with accompanying song, is the antistrophe. In the present instance it is practically identical with a "metrical unit."—TRANS.

Therefore they took another route, from Succoth to Etham, a more southerly road. Thus they were leaving Egypt to enter the wilderness. On this journey the Lord went before them. During the day, the pillar of cloud was in front of them, often providing shade. At night this pillar glowed with fire, lighting up the desert.

Here again the Lord was revealing Himself in a fire. He had used a flaming torch to reveal Himself to Abraham and a burning bush to reveal Himself to Moses.

The Lord was with His people in the covenant, but they still had to be purified as silver is purified. Sin had to be removed from their midst. That they were not consumed by the fire was a result of the fact that the Lord Jesus Christ would one day stand in their place in the fire of God's judgment. God's wrath against our sin would one day be kindled in all its fullness against Him. He would die in that fire to atone for us and be raised from the dead afterward. All who are united with Him in faith will be purified by that fire—but not consumed. Yet unbelievers will perish in that fire.

By the pillar of cloud and of fire, the Lord Himself led His people on their journey through the wilderness. The people saw in that pillar the burning zeal of His love and His protecting hand.

God still precedes His people down through the centuries in the Lord Jesus Christ. In Him, the One who was crucified only to rise again, we behold God's love sanctifying us, saving us, and pointing the way for us in this life.

Hardening and testing. When the Lord went before the Israelites from Etham, He was not leading them out of Egypt but along the wrong side of the Red Sea, i.e. the west side. Those who noticed this must have been surprised, but they followed obediently. The Lord had told Moses that He would bring glory to Himself through Pharaoh by means of this strange route. What this meant would soon become clear, although at the time the Israelites did not understand it.

In the meantime, Pharaoh and his servants had already gotten over the first shock of the death of all the first-born. For a brief moment, they had trembled before the God of heaven and earth. Yet the effects of such an experience usually do not last very long if the experience does not lead to true repentance. Again

Pharaoh closed his heart to the Lord. This hardening of his heart was sent upon him by the Lord as a judgment, for man had once turned away from the Lord in sin.

Today, people who do not fear the Lord are still willfully blind. We must recognize this blindness as a judgment on that original sin. We, too, deserve this judgment in all its severity. Only God's grace opens our blind eyes.

Now Pharaoh assembled his army, his chariots and his horsemen to pursue the Israelites in an effort to bring them back by force. He overtook them by the time they reached Pi-hahiroth. Here the people seemed to be trapped: in front of them (to the south) and along the right side (to the west) were mountains, while to their left (to the east) was the Red Sea and behind them (to the north) were the Egyptians.

The Lord had led His people into a corner so that they would have to surrender completely to Him; there was no help for them other than from the Lord. Now He would show them how they were wrapped in the power of His love.

The people were not yet ready for that kind of faith. They rebelled against Moses and reproached him for bringing them out of Egypt to die in the wilderness. The Egyptians, on the other hand, rejoiced when they found the Israelites in such a position, for they assumed that they had simply gotten lost in the wilderness. Now the Israelites would be easy prey.

Moses told the people not to be afraid but to wait upon the Lord, who would show them His salvation. The Egyptians, whom they now saw behind them, they would see no more. God would separate them from the Egyptians once and for all.

Moses cried out to the Lord and the Lord answered: "Your salvation is already decided. Let Israel go forward. Stretch out your hand over the sea, and it will divide in two. Israel will pass through, but the Egyptians will die in the sea."

It was terrible for all those Egyptians to perish. That would mean their eternal destruction. It is also terrible that all unbelievers will perish one day. However, that judgment is rooted in God's love. Didn't He have a right to the Egyptians in His love? Weren't they the work of His hands? But since they had rejected His love, He pronounced judgment on them.

It was night when the Egyptians overtook Israel. The pillar of fire stood in front of Israel, lighting the way. Those who believed would have understood: the Lord was testing and purifying His people, even in that time of anxiety. But then the pillar of fire and the Angel, who used it to guide Israel, moved, taking up a position between Israel and the Egyptians. Israel stood in the light, but darkness surrounded the Egyptians, who did not dare come closer to the Israelites. Still, the Egyptians did not repent. Their hearts were hardened.

Separated for all time. Over the sea Moses stretched out his staff, which was a sign of the presence of God's power. The Lord then sent an east wind that separated the waters and opened up a dry path through the sea. This event we cannot explain. It was the doing of the Lord, who was close by with the power of His grace, just as He came very near to us in the birth of the Lord Jesus Christ.

For Israel, however, it was an act of faith to advance along that path. The waters could close again at any moment and drown them, which was just what they deserved because of their sins. It was only because they were saved by Jesus Christ that this did not happen. One day Christ would pass through the waters of God's wrath into death and prepare a way for His people through those waters. By faith, the Israelites were now able to walk this path, certain that there was deliverance for them.

The Egyptians followed them, showing the ultimate folly of their blindness. They still did not see the God of Israel who was going to pronounce judgment on them. They were led to the slaughter like sheep. As soon as the Israelites had reached the other side, the pillar of fire turned around and the Lord looked wrathfully at the Egyptians, who were then overcome with terror. Finally they woke up to the fact that Israel's God was fighting against them. They were thrown into a panic. Their chariots were destroyed, and they wondered how they could possibly escape.

At the Lord's command, Moses again stretched out his staff over the sea, and the waters returned, first on the west side. Thus the Egyptians, who now wanted to turn back, were confronted with a wall of water. Quickly they were all swallowed up; not one of them survived. In the same way, the Lord will one day judge all His enemies, as His love claims its rights. On the day of Christ's return, all His enemies will perish before Him.

Israel felt secure in the power of His love. It seemed as if that power had encircled the entire people. God had used it to separate them from the land of Egypt forever, showing that the people of Israel belonged to Him. Now He would soon be able to establish His covenant with them.

One day, when the Christ returns, all of God's people will be freed from sin and the evil powers that still oppress them here. Then He will encompass them forever in the power of His love, showing that His love has rights over His people.

The song of Moses. Moses and all the men of Israel then sang a song, with Miriam and the women responding. Together, the men and women sang only of the majesty of God, who had destroyed Pharaoh and his army. Thus God had led the entire people to worship His name. For a moment, they saw Him in His perfect glory. That's how the Lord wants His people to worship Him.

They sang of the Lord as the warrior against whom no earthly power can prevail. Who would be able to lift a finger against Him? And they sang of the Lord as the One who had defeated His enemies in His wrath—not just for the obvious crimes they had committed against Israel but because they did not want to fear the Lord, who has a right to them in His love. They also sang of the Lord as the One who has demonstrated the rights of His love for His people and has saved them. That God would prepare a dwelling place for them in the promised land, where He would also prepare a sanctuary among them for Himself.

At the end of time, the redeemed will sing of the Lord's victory and of the rights of His love, by which He brings His enemies to destruction and prepares an eternal dwelling place for His people.

At Mount Sinai

40: Borne on Eagles' Wings

Exodus 15:22—17:16

In Exodus 19:4 we read: "I bore you on eagles' wings and brought you to myself." The Lord brought Israel to Himself at Mount Sinai in order to establish a covenant there with Israel as a people. The journey to Sinai was the avenue along which God showed how He would provide for the Israelites. More than once He overlooked their murmurings. They still had to learn to trust Him in faith. After Sinai, God's wrath was kindled against the people because of sins He had overlooked before Sinai.

At Marah the Lord made a statute and an ordinance for the people. The statute was that He would provide for the people in all their needs, and the ordinance was that they would rely on Him. He tested them there, encouraging them to believe in Him. They were to accept the special promise that the Lord would be their healer. This was symbolized in the restoring of the water at Marah, where Israel was threatened with death (see II Kings 4:40). The tree that Moses threw into the water did not itself restore the water; it was simply a sign intended to provoke the people to faith. An ordinary piece of wood—and not Moses' staff—was the means employed, to make certain the Israelites would not get the idea that the staff had magical power.

The Lord put Israel to the test at Marah and again in the Wilderness of Sin. The rain of manna was to teach Israel to live one day at a time, by faith, eating out of the Lord's hand. All the Israelites had to do was gather what was at their fingertips, and there would be enough for everyone. Their Father in heaven was looking after them.

It seems strange that the sabbath commandment should come up in connection with this miracle. Apparently Israel had not kept the sabbath in Egypt. Well before the proclamation of the ten commandments on Mount Sinai, the significance of the sabbath was made evident. At the root of the people's work was their rest in God, which resulted from Christ's atonement. Thus they were to eat the manna not just as food to

287

satisfy their hunger but as God's favor in the form of food. Thus the manna was a revelation of what Jesus Christ is for us, namely, manna from heaven, the restoration of our whole life in God's favor.

In the story of the faultfinding when the people ran short of water, it was not the Lord who put the people to the test. In fact, it was just the other way around. Israel was testing the Lord, saying: "Is the Lord in our midst or not?" This challenge was to force the Lord to show His love in the way *they* saw fit. Such a challenge was born of unbelief, not of faith.

Yet the Lord gave Himself to the Israelites there in spite of their challenge. In a most humble way, He became their servant. Notice how the Lord replied: "Behold, I will stand before you there on the rock at Horeb" (Ex. 17:6).* The Lord was willing to stand before Moses and the elders—and thus before the people—as a servant stands before his master! Through this humbling experience, the people would learn that God would show His love in His own way. They would also learn to serve Him.

At Rephidim, the Israelites got to know the Lord as their banner. The battle was the Lord's. That meant not just that the Lord would fight for Israel but also that it was the Lord's battle rather than Israel's. As the first of the heathen nations that Israel encountered on its way, Amalek had turned on the Lord. For this reason, all memory of Amalek would be blotted out.

Moses' raised staff was a sign of the people's communion in faith with the Lord in battle. This is probably how the difficult words of Exodus 17:16 are to be explained: "A hand upon the throne [or: banner] of the LORD! [Or: The LORD has sworn.] The LORD will war with Amalek from generation to generation." That the hand was upon the throne of the Lord meant not only that the people's help was from the Lord but also that Israel saw its cause as the Lord's cause. In this battle, Israel had to be the Lord's; then the warfare would not cease.

Main thought: *The Lord bears His people on eagles' wings and in His covenant brings them to Himself.*

Israel's healer. When the Lord led Israel out of Egypt, He intended to gather the people to Himself at Mount Sinai, as He had told Moses in advance (Ex. 3:12). There He would take them as a nation into His covenant. On the way to Sinai, in an effort to

---

Horeb was the name for the entire mountain range of which Sinai was a particular peak.—TRANS.

teach His people what He would be to them, He constantly over-looked their sins and showed them His love. The only thing He asked of them was that they trust Him and expect all good from Him. Later He would also punish them for their sins, but for now they were to learn the power of His grace.

For three days they marched from the Red Sea through the wilderness. Then all the water they had taken with them was gone. They saw some water in the distance, but it turned out to be un-drinkable. It was so bitter that they feared it might poison them.

Suddenly they realized that the wilderness was full of dangers. They thought of the diseases that might befall them. And there were no physicians available, as there had been in Egypt. They began to murmur against Moses, saying: "What shall we drink?" Did they think *Moses* would be able to supply them with drinking water?

On this occasion, too, Moses was the mediator between God and the people. He passed the people's complaint on to the Lord. At the Lord's command, he threw a log into the bitter water, and it became sweet.

The log itself did not change the water. Nor did the Lord want Moses to lift up his staff over the water, for it might begin to look as though there were some magical power in that staff. The staff was not magic; the power belonged to the Lord. The log was only a sign. At the Lord's command, Moses was to throw it into the water in faith. This sign was to provoke the people to faith. We are to listen to God's Word, observe His signs, and then wait expec-tantly for the Lord. That's how He comes to us.

At the same time, the Lord said that the restoration (Hebrew: healing) of the water was a sign to them that they could always count on Him in the wilderness. He would preserve them especially from the diseases they had known in Egypt. The Lord would be their healer. By this sign and promise, the Lord was testing them, seeking to awaken their faith.

This promise still holds, for He comes to us just as He came to the Israelites at that time. He gave Himself in His love in the Lord Jesus Christ and still gives Himself in Him every day. Thus He heals our lives too. It is He who forgives all our sins and heals all our diseases. That does not mean that He shields us from every disease and heals each sickness that strikes us, but He does save this temporal life so that we do not live it in vain.

Because the sweet water was originally bitter, the Israelites called that place *Marah*. From there they moved on to Elim, where there was a large oasis with twelve springs of water and seventy palm trees. There the Lord showed them that He would also bestow on them the gentler, more pleasant signs of His favor.

Bread from heaven. From Elim they journeyed to the Wilderness of Sin. They had to move slowly, for with such a large army of people, there were many delays. Thus it was already the fifteenth day of the second month. All the food they had taken along with them from Egypt was gone. Would they now have to slaughter all their cattle?

Again they began to murmur against Moses and Aaron: "We should have died in Egypt, where we had plenty of meat and bread. That would have been better for us than wasting away slowly in this wilderness!" Evidently they had not yet let go of Egypt entirely in their hearts. What shameful ingratitude!

When Moses once again brought their complaints to the Lord, he was instructed to tell the people in the name of the Lord that they would receive what they had asked for. Again the Lord overlooked their sin, but before He gave them food, they would see His glory. They would have to learn to fear the Lord, that is, show Him reverence, for without such fear there can be no trust.

At Aaron's command, the people left their tents and looked toward the wilderness. There the glory of the Lord appeared as a shining pillar of cloud. He is a God of grace, but in His grace He is full of glory, exalted far above anything we can imagine.

That evening the wind brought a flock of quails into the camp; all the Israelites had to do was pick them up. The next morning dew lay round about the camp, and when it had vanished, they saw on the ground little round kernels or seeds (see Ex. 16:31), fine as hoarfrost. The Israelites thought the seeds were of no importance and therefore called them "man."(*Man* probably means *nothing*.) But Moses said that this was the bread the Lord had given them.

They gathered it up, some more and some less, but each time

they measured it there was one omer* (about a cup full) per person. That was truly miraculous.

Moses gave an order that none of the manna was to be kept for the following day. Some of the Israelites saved some anyway, but the next morning the manna had a foul odor and was infested with worms. Israel was going to have to learn to live one day at a time. Every morning the Lord would provide for them anew. This is still the way He does it. Therefore we must not worry about the future.

On the sixth day, when the Israelites measured the manna, they had exactly two omers apiece. They expressed surprise, and Moses explained that the seventh day was the sabbath of the Lord. On that day He would not send any manna. Israel was to rest one day out of seven, to learn to trust the Lord and rest in Him, upon whom they depended for all their needs. For Christ's sake, He would take care of them in His covenant.

Thus they were not only to eat this manna but also taste the Lord's goodness in it. His gracious favor in the Christ came to them through it. In fact, the Lord Jesus Christ is the true bread that has come down from heaven (John 6:31-3). By means of the favor which God bestows upon us in Him, our life is sustained.

Nevertheless, there were some who were disobedient and went out on the seventh day to gather manna. They found nothing. Their disobedience made the Lord sad. Here again He had put them to the test to encourage them to trust in His Word.

Later, at the Lord's command, the Israelites placed a jar with manna in the tent which they made for Him. This jar was to be a reminder not just of the provision made for them in the wilderness but also a prophecy of the Lord Jesus Christ, the true bread from heaven.

Israel's servant. Again they moved on. They came to Rephidim, where there was no water for them. This time they not only quarreled with Moses but also put the Lord to the test, saying: "Let Him now show whether He is in our midst or not." They

---

*An omer is one tenth of an ephah, the ephah being a bit more than a bushel.—TRANS.

wanted to force the Lord to manifest His love. Such coercion is not a mark of faith but of unbelief. Their rebellion was so fierce that Moses thought they might stone him. Did they think Moses had led them out of Egypt on his own authority?

At this point the Lord ordered Moses to take some of the elders of Israel and go out before the people to the rock at Horeb. The Lord would stand before him. He was to strike the rock with his staff, and water would come out of the rock.

This was really putting the people to shame. In their distrust, the people forced God to give evidence of His love. Even then the Lord did not say that He would abandon the people; He gave them proof of His love in spite of what they had done. The Lord is wonderfully good, for He also appeared in the Christ to a world which had put Him to the test. He continually manifests His love in this way.

The Lord said further: "I will stand before you there." The Lord was going to stand in Israel's midst as a servant in the presence of his master. How the Lord humbled Himself here! The Lord Jesus Christ, likewise, came not to be served but to serve, to give His life as a ransom for many. He washed His disciples' feet.

Water gushed forth out of the rock, and the Israelites drank. But did all of them know the love of the Lord? How many were there who tasted the favor of God? The Israelites called that place Massah and Meribah, which means *testing* and *contention*.

Israel's banner. The supply army had stayed behind. Suddenly this army was attacked by the Amalekites, a nomadic people who tended their flocks in that vicinity. They not only saw in Israel a threat to their pasture lands, but hated Israel as the people of God. They had heard what the Lord had done for Israel, for they were descendants of Esau. Esau had hated Jacob because of the blessing of the covenant, and that hatred had smoldered on in his clan.

Thus the Amalekites were the first nation whose hatred the Israelites encountered during their journey. Indeed, the people of the Lord would always encounter hatred—not because of themselves but because of the Lord. For this reason, the Amalekites had to be destroyed as an example of God's ultimate destruction of all His enemies.

Joshua was sent out against them with a select band of warriors. At the same time, the Israelites would have to realize that the battle was the Lord's, that the Amalekites fought not just against Israel but mainly against the Lord, and that the Lord would be fighting the Amalekites through Israel. In this battle, Israel was to be with the Lord.

As a sign of all this, Moses was to climb up to the top of the mountain and lift up his staff to heaven with both his hands. As long as he held his staff up, Israel would prevail, but when the staff came down, Amalek would be the stronger of the two nations. Therefore Aaron and Hur held up Moses' hands. The Israelites defeated the Amalekites and killed many of them.

If we are the Lord's, we must remember that life's contest revolves not around us but around the Lord. If we bear this in mind in our struggle against sin, it will give us a different outlook on our situation. Only then will we be strong, for then we will realize that the Lord Jesus Christ is the victor on our behalf. Because Christ would overcome the devil and his kingdom for His Father, Israel was able to conquer *its* enemies on this occasion. Thus we, too, will be able to win.

When the battle was over, Moses built an altar to serve as a memorial. He called it *The Lord is my banner*. The altar was to impress upon Israel the Lord's decree that Amalek was to be utterly wiped out. Moses was told to record this episode in a book and be sure to tell it to Joshua, his helper.

Because Israel was to be the Lord's, because Israel's hand was to be on the throne of the Lord, because Israel was to confess that its cause was the Lord's cause, the war against Amalek would never end. If we are the Lord's, we must never call a halt to the fight against sin, the devil and all God's enemies. If we make peace, we will lose the battle.

Fortunately, the Lord Jesus Christ never relaxed in that struggle but fought it to the very end. He is still waging war out of heaven. He will make sure that those who belong to Him wage this battle continually. And He will give them the victory, for He has conquered and He will always conquer.

That was how the Lord led Israel through the wilderness during those first days. He went before them in the pillar of cloud and of fire. He was everything to them, providing for all their needs and overlooking their sins. All of this was intended to teach them to believe in Him and thus be prepared to enter into the covenant with Him. Did the Israelites learn their lesson?

41: The Covenant Established

Exodus 18-24

The establishment of the covenant is described especially in Exodus 24. We see that the covenant is two-sided:* the people of Israel were to accept the covenant of their own free will and likewise had to promise to keep the statutes of the Lord. At the same time, we see that Israel *could not* keep the covenant.

Notice that the establishing of the covenant did not take place without bloodshed. The people were protected by the Christ, who was obedient in His life and in His death. The "Yes" voiced by the Israelites on this occasion pointed to the "Yes" voiced by the Christ, who answered for all His people: "Yes, Father, not My will but Yours be done" (Luke 22:42). He protects His people and puts His Spirit in their hearts so that they will learn to respond. Since the Christ was given to us by God, the *plan* of the covenant is one-sided.†

Half the blood was sprinkled on the altar, in the very presence of God, who comes to the people at the altar. Christ, with His own blood, likewise entered the heavenly sanctuary. There He presents Himself to God in His entire life of obedience, for our good.

The other half of the blood was sprinkled on the people. This was a revelation of the application of the work of Christ to the people. Thereby atonement was made before God for the sins of the people.

It is not clear whether the elders representing Israel saw a form: we read only that they saw the God of Israel. It is possible that they saw a revelation in the sense of a very brillant light, although the possibility of a revelation in a specific form is not to be excluded. In this case, God could well have revealed Himself in a form. After all, He made man in

---

*The theological term is *dipleuric*. —TRANS.

†The theological term is *monopleuric*. —TRANS.

His own image.

Whenever we picture God in a particular form, however, we are bringing Him down to our level. Revealing Himself in a particular form is something God does of His own accord. Because of the danger of idolatry that accompanies revelation of this kind, we do not read of it very often. Today, God is revealed to us in the Christ.

Jethro's visit to Moses and the people is taken up in this chapter because it was on Jethro's advice that the people were organized. This organization meant that Israel had become a nation and was no longer a patriarchal clan. As a nation, the Israelites were about to enter into a covenant with God.

In Exodus 19:5 we read that Israel would be God's own possession among all peoples. In this text God goes on to declare: "All the earth is mine." The Hebrew word translated as *my own possession* means *a particularly valuable possession.* It is a word one would use in speaking of something to be stored away and cherished. In adopting Israel, then, God was adopting the entire earth. Therefore in the next verse we read: "You shall be to me a kingdom of priests."

The Israelites were a nation of priests and kings. Although the whole earth was subject to them, they ruled it as priests, praying for the earth and blessing it. The Israelites could only do so because the Christ lived in their midst. Israel was a holy nation, in which God sanctified Himself, making His name great while redeeming His people.

The covenant made here with Israel was a form of the covenant of grace. Notice that God also began by giving Himself, saying: "I am the LORD your God." He made His demands as the God who gives Himself in love.

We must not separate the law from God's giving of Himself. Only in this way is the law able to convince us of sin and arouse a response of love in us. At the same time, the spirit of bondage in which Israel lived at this time was expressed both in the ten commandments and in the laws that followed. But it was seen most clearly in the ten commandments. Almost all of them were prohibitions.

Evil was forbidden as if to disobedient children. Indeed, God's people were still very childlike at that time. When those people reached the stage of adulthood and were made free in the time of the New Testament, the law was written in their hearts, and they no longer lived in fear of prohibitions. Instead they lived out of love for the commandments.

The Angel of the Lord, about whom God spoke in Exodus 23:20ff, was God Himself, the Son, the revelation of Jesus Christ. God's name was in Him, and He would not pardon transgressions. Yet, in thought we are not to separate the Angel of the Lord from the pillar of cloud and of fire, for He appeared in it. That He would not pardon transgressions means that He would not overlook sins without just cause. Not only would atonement have to be made via sacrifices, which pointed to the sacrifice of the Christ, sins would no longer be allowed to pass without punishment, as happened before the establishment of the covenant on Mount Sinai.

The Angel of the Lord had led the people since the exodus from Egypt. But now the people were told that it was God's presence that accompanied them. Through their elders, the people had even looked upon the presence of God, and now, in addition, that accompanying presence was sealed in a promise. By this demonstration of grace, Israel shouldered a greater responsibility.

Main thought: *The Lord takes Israel into His covenant as a nation.*

Israel organized as a nation. In Rephidim, Moses received a visit from his father-in-law Jethro, his wife Zipporah, and his two sons Gershom and Eliezer. Evidently when Moses had said good-by to his wife, they had agreed to meet again at Rephidim.

When Moses heard that his father-in-law was approaching, he went out to meet him, bowing down and kissing him. He received the visitors in his tent and told them what the Lord had done to Pharaoh and the Egyptians for Israel's sake and also about Israel's deliverance along the way.

Impressed by all this, Jethro praised the Lord and confessed that the Lord was greater than any other god. He also offered a burnt offering and sacrifices. He then joined Moses and Aaron and all the elders of Israel in a sacrificial meal. There they had communion with one another in their faith in the Lord. Thus Jethro was a symbol of all the heathens who would come to praise the Lord and live with Israel in the covenant.

The next day Jethro saw how Moses presided over the people, settling disputes and making the statutes of the Lord known to the people. But Moses could not do all that work alone. Moreover, there was a danger that the people would take the law into their own hands if their grievances were not solved quickly. Jethro informed Moses of this danger and made him see that Israel was no longer just a big family but a nation and ought to be organized as such.

On Jethro's advice, Moses appointed able men to be judges of thousands, of hundreds, of fifties, and of tens. Only the difficult cases would be brought to Moses.

Thus the people were organized as a nation. It was with such an Israel that God would establish His covenant. Moses' place among the people had now been better defined. In the same way, the people of the Lord today live under their King, Jesus Christ, and are led by Him. After the nation was organized, Jethro left.

A holy God. From Rephidim the Israelites proceeded to the wilderness of Sinai, to the foot of Mount Sinai. They arrived there in the third month after the exodus from Egypt.

Here the Lord intended to reveal Himself to the people as a nation and take them into His covenant. At the Lord's command, Moses climbed partway up the mountain. From the top of the mountain God spoke to him, and Moses passed on His Words to the people. Now the Lord came very close as He addressed the people, even though He spoke through Moses as an intermediary. God still addresses us that way. Through the Lord Jesus Christ, He has given us His Word. He still speaks to us through that Word and is very close to us.

At the Lord's command, Moses said to the elders of the people: "You know how I brought you out of Egypt and bore you on eagles' wings and brought you here to Myself. I did that because I had something special in mind for you. I have chosen you to be My possession in a very special sense. The whole earth and all the nations are Mine. I do not intend to forsake them. Instead I will hold on to them by drawing you especially to Myself. Then you will be a nation of kings and priests. You will rule on earth; no one will be able to touch you. As priests you will be a blessing to all nations, supporting them in your prayers. I will therefore dwell in your midst and glorify Myself in your deliverance. Because I am great in the midst of you, you will be a holy nation. This you must accept in faith, and also obey Me and keep My covenant."

Surely the Lord was giving Israel a special privilege—but not because Israel was a special people. God's choosing them made them a special people. Furthermore, they did not possess those privileges for themselves alone but on behalf of the whole earth.

When Moses had spoken these words to the people, they said they would do what the Lord asked of them. Thereby they showed that they wanted to enter into the covenant with the Lord. Surely they did not know what they were saying, for who can live in accordance with the intention and will of the Lord?

The Lord is a holy God. There has only been One who could live by His will, namely, the Lord Jesus Christ, who also wishes to instil something of His Spirit in the hearts of His people. Only because of this can His people live in accordance with God's commandments. The people of Israel at this time were still convinced that they could do it by themselves, which made them disobey time and again. Nevertheless, when they responded positively at Sinai, they showed something of the Spirit of the Christ, who would one day say yes for them with His whole life.

Moses now told the Lord what the people had said. Then the Lord wanted to show them who He was in all His holiness. Therefore the people had to consecrate themselves, wash their garments, and confess their sins. Moreover, they were to stay some distance away from the mountain.

On the third day, the Lord descended upon the mountain. There was thunder, lightning, the sound of a trumpet, and a thick cloud. All the people in the camp were terrified. Moses led the people to the foot of the mountain, which was wrapped in smoke and shook tremendously.

When the sound of the trumpet was very loud, Moses asked the Lord what His will was. The Lord answered that Moses was to come up. This was as the Lord had promised Moses. Through this event, the people were to accept Moses as the mediator called by God. In the same way, God spoke to the Lord Jesus Christ out of His glory, telling the people to listen to Him so that they would believe He was the mediator sent by God.

On the mountain God again told Moses that the people were not to touch the mountain—not even the priests, the men who were called to offer sacrifices on behalf of the people for the time being. Moses received the explicit command to impress this on the people again.

How they must have felt the distance between God and themselves! God did want to adopt this people as His special possession. However, Christ had not yet atoned for their sins. Their sacrifice would only be symbolic of Christ's sacrifice, and therefore there was still distance between God and the people.

The Lord comes much closer to us today. He even wants to dwell in our hearts by His Spirit. But even today, He remains the holy God who wishes to sanctify us.

The law of the covenant. When Moses had come down from the mountain, God Himself spoke to the people. He said: "I am the LORD your God, who brought you out of the land of Egypt, out of the house of bondage." The Lord began to give Himself to His people as their God, who would be faithful forever. Because God gave Himself to them, they were also to give themselves in love to Him. That was what the Lord intended to ask of the people. But they were just at the beginning: Israel, as a people, was still an immature child. God addressed Israel as such, speaking as though He were talking to disobedient children who must be forbidden to do evil. God spoke ten Words, the ten commandments, most of which were prohibitions.

God gave those commandments for us as well. But now He prefers to write His commandments in the hearts of His people. His people are no longer like immature children; they are adults who serve the Lord of their own free choice.

When the people saw and heard all the signs accompanying God's appearance and heard Him speak the ten Words, they backed off and stood some distance away. They were afraid they were going to die, for they could not bear it. They asked that God speak to them through Moses from then on instead of addressing them directly.

Moses comforted the people and told them not to be afraid, for they would not die. God would not let them perish. He only wanted to fill them with a deep reverence, so that they would not break with His covenant.

Who could stand before God? Surely we deserve to be struck down by God in His wrath! Because of the Lord Jesus Christ, we need not be afraid. We may have communion with God without fear. As long as we keep reminding ourselves that He is the holy God, what we will fear is sin.

In addition to those ten Words, God gave Israel still other commandments. These He communicated to Moses when Moses went up the mountain again to be with Him. There were laws about worshiping the Lord, laws about the Israelites' relationships with each other, and laws about the festivals in which they would worship the Lord. In all these matters they were to show that they were the Lord's people, a holy nation.

The Angel of the Lord. The Lord also promised that He would send His Angel before them in the pillar of cloud and of fire. In Him they would be blessed and would be able to conquer the peoples living in Canaan. He would see to it that they inherited the land.

While the Lord was speaking, however, He made it known that this Angel was not an ordinary angel but God Himself, the eternal Son of God, who would become flesh one day. Thus He was the Lord Jesus Christ. Because this Angel was God, they would have to be on their guard before Him and fear sin, for their sin could not be forgiven without sacrifice. And He was not going to overlook their sin without punishing them for it: it would be a different story than before they arrived at the mountain where they were taken into the covenant.

In the Lord Jesus Christ, there is an abundance of grace available for us, too, as we are led through this life by Him. However, since He is the holy God, we must live carefully.

Establishing the covenant. Moses told the people all that God had said. Again they declared that they would do what the Lord had asked of them. Moses also wrote all those Words of the Lord in a book.

Then Moses made an altar at the foot of the mountain and arranged twelve stones around it, symbolizing the twelve tribes of Israel. Young men who acted as priests on behalf of the people slaughtered the sacrificial animals. The blood of those animals was collected in basins.

Moses poured half of the blood on the altar, for it was on the altar that the Lord wanted to meet Israel. There the blood confronted Him. Israel, in its sinful life, could not exist before God; it needed atonement provided by another life. Yet, the lives of the sacrificial animals could not accomplish this atonement. Their blood only symbolized the blood of the Lord Jesus Christ, who would guarantee the life of His people with His perfect life.

Without the Lord Jesus Christ's obedience both in His life and in His death, there would have been no covenant. Because of that blood of Christ, God established the covenant with His people. That covenant concerns us, too, for in Christ the covenant was also established with the people of other times and places that belong to Him.

Moses then read aloud all the Words of the book of the covenant which he had just written down. Again the people promised to obey the Lord. Moses took the other half of the blood and sprinkled it on them. It was a sign that God would forgive the people their sins for the sake of Christ's blood, for they could not obey on their own account. Moses said: "See, this is the blood of the covenant which the Lord has made with you in accordance with all those Words."

Following the Lord's command, Moses then went up the mountain with Aaron, Aaron's two sons Nadab and Abihu, and 70 of the elders of Israel. There they saw the God of Israel. We do not know exactly what they saw, but the ground under His feet seemed to be paved with sapphire stones, a sparking dark blue. It appeared as though the blue sky was beneath Him. It was a breath-takingly wonderful sight. They were not consumed by this God; in perfect peace, they ate and drank in fellowship with Him. What God gave to those representatives of the people He was actually giving to the entire people.

Through the blood of Christ there would be full communion between Him and His people. How serenely and peacefully we can walk with the Lord if we, too, are reconciled through the blood of the covenant of the Lord Jesus Christ! When He gave the cup to His disciples at the supper table, He said: "This is the new covenant in my blood." At the Lord's supper we enjoy God's communion in His covenant in a special way.

42: The Mediator

Exodus 32-34

With the restoration of the covenant after it had been broken by Israel, the significance of the Mediator came out much more than at the time the covenant was first established. Notice how Moses wrestled with God for its restoration. Continually we see in Moses the Spirit of the Mediator Jesus Christ.

Following the pattern of Scripture, we should refer to Moses as the mediator of the Old Testament. In the history of Israel, however, and especially in this section of Exodus, the Angel of the covenant emerges—leading Israel in the pillar of cloud, for example. He, too, is Mediator. The mediatorship is the unity of the Angel of the covenant with Moses. Later this combination was perfected in the Christ, when the Word became flesh, that is, when the Angel of the covenant became flesh. But in the story to which we now turn, we see Moses struggling for fellowship with this Angel. That's why he asks God not to send him on from there unless His presence goes with him by way of this Angel. Without His leading, Moses would not know the way.

Furthermore, Moses asked to be allowed to see the glory of the Lord. To be a perfect mediator, he would have to see that glory. God's eternal bond with him and his people would be guaranteed by Moses' seeing that glory and being in communion with God. Still, a man is not allowed to see that glory as long as he is in his mortal body. This privilege was given to the Christ, however. Moses was only allowed to see the back of God and hear the name of the Lord called out. The most a sinful man like Moses can attain is communion with God through faith in His Word. This mediatorship of Moses cried out for the perfect mediatorship of the Christ.

Moses asked to be blotted out of God's book if God would not forgive His people their sins. This was consistent with his position as mediator, for in that position he was also head of the people and therefore shared their guilt. Moses said this to the Lord knowing that the Lord could not do it. Thus God could not reject the people for their sins either.

We must not tell the children that Moses sinned when he dashed the stone tablets of the law to pieces. The people had broken the covenant. In breaking the stone tablets (the book of the covenant), Moses was showing what the people deserved, namely, that God break the covenant. Later God did not provide tablets of stone again, but Moses, through whose mediation the covenant was restored, was permitted to see to it that there were stone tablets to be used. The second time God merely wrote upon them with His own finger.

Main thought: *The Mediator is revealed as the covenant is restored.*

Covenant breaking. For 40 days Moses stayed with God on the mountain, receiving all the commandments God wanted to use to regulate Israel's life-style in the covenant. Because he was gone so long, the people despaired of the Lord and of Moses as their mediator and head. They had learned of God's presence through what Moses had said and done, but now that Moses was gone, they had lost the Lord too.

They wanted the Lord to appear in a visible form before them. They thought that this would enable them to believe in the presence of God again. Therefore they asked Aaron to make them an image of God. No doubt they wanted this man, who would see to it that they got a satisfactory image of God, to become their new leader.

How they sinned when they made an image of God! He had prohibited that very thing in His Word. In acting as they did, they were giving the Lord a form that pleased them, thus pulling Him down to their own level.

Aaron sensed that it was wrong, but he was afraid that the people would completely reject his leadership if he refused. Therefore he put them to the test and said that if that was what they wanted, they would have to give him the gold they were wearing. He was hoping that neither the men nor their wives would be willing to make that sacrifice.

How Aaron was disillusioned! If it's a question of satisfying their own desires and wishes, people are willing to sacrifice a great deal. The Israelites readily brought Aaron what he asked for, and now he had to do his part. Thinking back to a form he had seen in Egypt, he had a wooden likeness of a bull calf made and then had it covered with a layer of gold. When it was finished, those who had made it said to the people, "This is your God, O Israel, who brought you up out of Egypt." What an abomination! Aaron put the final seal on his own sin by building an altar before this calf and proclaiming a feast for the following day. Now the people could worship the Lord in this golden calf.

God looked down upon that feast from heaven. He told Moses, who was with Him on the mountain, what the people had done and informed him that the covenant was thereby broken. "Let Me alone," He said, "that I may destroy the people and cause a new people to arise out of you." Isn't it strange that the Lord should ask Moses to allow Him to do that? But we must remember that Moses had been appointed mediator and head of that people. Hence the Lord did not wish to act without him.

This proposal deeply disturbed Moses, for he was a mediator to the hilt. Moses had given himself to this people and wanted to intercede for them. Here we see in him the Spirit of the Mediator Jesus Christ, who was faithful to His people unto death.

Moses struggled on behalf of the people, pointing out three things to the Lord. Wouldn't all the great deeds He had done for His people be in vain? Wouldn't the Egyptians scoff that He had led His people out of their land only to destroy them in the wilderness? And didn't He remember the Word He swore to His servants Abraham, Isaac and Israel?

Then the Lord turned His wrath from the people. He saw in this intercession of Moses something of the Spirit of His dear Son, who was to intercede and die on behalf of His people. Therefore He wanted to remember His people in His grace and hear Moses' prayer. But He did not tell this to Moses yet. He had Moses return to the people still thinking that God's wrath was fully kindled against them.

Judgment and initial restoration. When Moses went down to Joshua, who was waiting for him farther down the mountain, he could hear the people shouting as if they were making merry at a feast. Once he reached the foot of the mountain, Moses saw the golden calf. In his anger, he cast to the ground the tablets of stone on which God had written the law of the ten commandments. The tablets, which God Himself had given Moses, broke into pieces. Since the people had broken the covenant, Moses broke this book of the covenant. The people deserved to be rejected by God forever.

Next Moses set about putting things right. He burned the image, ground the ashes and gold to powder, and threw the powder into the drinking water, which he then commanded the people to drink. In this way they drank down the curse.

He lashed out in anger against Aaron. Moses did not think the excuse offered by Aaron, namely, that he was a powerless tool in the hands of the people, worthy of a reply. He saw how the people had become unmanageable once Aaron loosened the reins of government. How would the people now be able to stand against their enemies?

The curse they had drunk would have consequences. Moses stood at the entrance to the camp and called out: "Who is on the Lord's side? Let him come here to me!" At this all the sons of Levi, men of his own tribe, rallied to him. The rest of the people still hesitated to confess their guilt. We are never quick to dissociate ourselves from our sinful intentions.

He commanded the Levites to take their swords and go through the camp killing everybody they met—even members of their own families. The Spirit of the Lord took hold of the Levites to let them execute the order, and the same Spirit filled the people with terror so that they were powerless to resist. About 3000 men fell that day.

Before there could be restoration, it had to be made evident that some of the people were still faithful. If there had not been such faithfulness, intercession would have been impossible. The people were being judged as a nation, for they deserved death as a nation. The 3000 fell on their behalf.

Now Moses was able to go up to the Lord again the next day with his intercessory prayer. He confessed the sin of the people, but he added: "If You will not forgive the sin of the people, then blot me out of the book of life. As head of the people, I share in their guilt." Moses knew that God could not do this. For Christ's sake He would be faithful to the Word and office He had given Moses.

In fact the Lord answered: "I will not reject you, nor will I reject the people as a whole, but I will blot out anyone who sins against Me. Go now and lead the people again. I will send My angel before you, and I will punish the sin of the people later."

The Lord said that His angel would go before the people, but He did not say who that angel was, that is whether he was the Angel who is Himself God—the Son of God. He did not say that His own presence was going to be with Israel again.

On the contrary, although He promised to bring the people into the land of Canaan by this angel, He also said that He Himself would not be among them. If He were to be among the people, they would be destroyed. Thus it was clear that the sin was not yet forgiven.

The mediator's struggle. When the people learned what the Lord had said, they were filled with sorrow and took off all their jewelry as a sign of their repentance.

The Lord wanted to continue to meet with Moses, but He could not do so in the camp, which was still in a sinful state. Hence Moses pitched a tent outside the camp, and there the Lord appeared to him. The people then sensed that they were alienated from God.

This tent was called the meeting tent. Whenever Moses went out to this meeting tent, the Israelites watched him from their own tents. Then the Lord would descend upon this tent in the pillar of cloud, and all the people would bow down in worship.

How wonderful it must have been for Moses in that tent! There he enjoyed God's presence as never before. The Lord talked with him just as one talks with a friend. When Moses left the tent, Joshua remained behind on guard. At this time, only Moses enjoyed the glory of this fellowship with God. The Lord Jesus wants to offer such intimate fellowship to His people. Once our sins are atoned for and forgiven, God again wishes to have communion with us as friend with friend.

Moses used this precious fellowship to be a mediator for his people. If God's presence did not go with him by way of the Angel, he could not lead the people. He would only find the way in the light of God's full grace upon the people. The people, too, could only walk in this light.

In response to Moses' intercessory prayer, God promised to restore His covenant and grace fully. Indeed, Moses had said, "Let it appear that I, as mediator, share in Your favor, and that You keep Your promises to me."

Conscious of the restored communion, Moses felt the need to know the Lord even more intimately. How could he lead the people if the Lord did not let him see His glory? Hence he asked, "Show me, I pray You, Your glory."

In asking this, Moses went too far. That full glory would be accessible to the Mediator Christ but could not be seen by anyone in this sinful life. The Mediator should see that glory, but Moses was only a shadow of the true Mediator.

God did promise to proclaim His name before Moses, although along with that promise He stressed that He was doing this out of free grace. Only the Christ would have a right to this glorious revelation. In addition, God promised that Moses would catch a glimpse of His glory when He passed by after first hiding Moses in a cave.

Moses was surely a wonderful mediator for Israel, but the real Mediator far surpasses him. Christ is now our Mediator, and in heaven He beholds God's face. What is there that He cannot do for us?

Promise and demands. At the Lord's command, Moses went up the mountain the next morning with two stone tablets that he had been allowed to cut as replacements for the ones he had dashed to pieces. There the Lord proclaimed His name before Moses, stressing that He was merciful and gracious and would forgive sin. At the same time, He would also punish the sins of those who forsook Him—to the third and fourth generations. Moses then saw something of God's glory. Afterward he prayed for the people.

In reply, the Lord promised that the covenant was restored again, and that He would give signs that would fill the nations with terror. At the same time, the Lord demanded that Israel be a holy nation and not ally itself with Canaan's inhabitants or their idolatry. The people were to serve the Lord as He had commanded them; they were to keep the great feasts, dedicate to Him the first-born of their flocks and their first-born sons, and observe the sabbath.

The Lord wants to give Himself and His full blesssing to us in the covenant, but He also demands that we give ourselves to Him. The specific demands He makes on us are to be found in the law of the Lord. Hence the Lord once more wrote this law on the tablets of stone with His own finger.

When Moses came down from the mountain, his face shone so brightly that the Israelites could not bear to look at him. He had to cover his face. What a wonderful mediator they had received from God! Yet he was less than our Mediator, who does not cover His face from us and does not keep us at a distance but wishes to bestow on us the same glory that He Himself possesses.

43: God's Dwelling Place

Exodus 25-31, 35-40

It would not be wise to discuss the building of the tabernacle in detail, mainly because our primary concern is the revelation of God in Christ. Thus we should not go into the symbolic significance of all the details, although the main features of the tabernacle's construction should definitely be explained one by one.

We must start out from the original situation, a situation that will one day be restored. Once the whole earth was God's dwelling place, and some day it will be His dwelling place again. When the Holy Spirit was poured out, God again began to dwell among men. This happened in the Christ. Through Him, God now dwells in those who are His and in the entire earth. In principle, the outpouring of the Holy Spirit is the sanctification of all creation—even if it is only temporary.

Before Christ had atoned for sin, the sanctuary could not be restored on earth. For this reason, God provisionally gave His people a prophetic symbol of it, namely the tabernacle. Because God's dwelling among men has been made possible in the Christ, the whole tabernacle is a foreshadowing of Him. In Him its meaning is fulfilled.

Moses saw a model of the tabernacle when he was up on the mountain and constructed it in accordance with the blueprint he was given. According to the letter to the Hebrews, the tabernacle—and the model as well—was an image of heavenly things. God's dwelling among His creatures is perfect in heaven, and one day, when heaven and earth have been united, it will be perfect on earth. But we must remember that in heaven there is free access to God, while in the tabernacle this access was cut off. In the tabernacle, Israel was being taught how God was set apart from men.

Thus the tabernacle reflects the situation in heaven, where God's dwelling is among men. In addition, the sacrifice and the high priest's mission with the blood in the Holy of Holies were prophecies of the sacrifice of the Christ and His entrance into the heavenly sanctuary.

It should be stressed that an Israelite could only understand these things by faith. Otherwise this whole arrangement would become a stumbling block to him, a reason to trust in the flesh. In fact, that's just what it became for many in Israel.

Main thought: *God's renewed dwelling among men in the Christ—and, through Him, in the world—is symbolized in the tabernacle.*

The freewill offering. When God created man and the world holy, He wished to dwell in the heart of man. The entire world was like home to Him; it was God's house, that is, His temple. (We call God's house a temple.) As a result of sin, our hearts and the world have been desecrated and we have driven the Lord away from the earth. Nowhere could He find rest; there was no place where He could dwell.

Yet He had resolved to make the earth His temple once again. But in whom would He dwell? First He would dwell in the Lord Jesus Christ, for His heart was a temple. Through Him, through the atonement He made for the sin of men, God could also make the hearts of believers a temple. By His power He could make the lives of believers so holy that they would serve Him together with all that was on the earth. Thus He intended to make all of life and the whole world His temple once more.

Unfortunately, today this is still possible in principle only, for sin remains a reality to be reckoned with. When Christ returns, He will purify the whole creation of sin and its consequences. Then the whole creation will once more be a temple of God.

In principle this happened through the Lord Jesus Christ and the outpouring of the Spirit. Israel had yet to learn about the coming of the Christ. Therefore God could not yet send His Spirit to dwell in Israel. All the same, He wanted to give Israel a sign of what was to come; He wanted to show them by a picture how things would be through the Christ. By means of this picture, He wished to bestow on Israel much of His gracious presence.

A house was to be constructed—or rather, a special tent. This tent would be used as long as the Israelites journeyed in the wilderness. The Lord would dwell in the tent and use it as an example. This special tent or tabernacle would be a prophecy of how God wished to dwell in the whole world in the Christ. Thus the tabernacle was a type of the Christ and of the entire world as it would one day be completely sanctified.

Therefore the tabernacle had to be built exactly as the Lord specified. God gave Moses precise instructions for its construction. You will remember that Moses had been on the mountain with God for 40 days when Israel was making the golden calf below. After that episode, he spent another 40 days on the mountain with the Lord. God gave him detailed instructions for building the tabernacle and also showed him a model. Without this guidance Moses could not have built the tabernacle.

Once Moses had received all his instructions, he called the Israelites together as the Lord had commanded and asked for freewill offerings of gold and silver and copper, finely woven linen of blue and purple and scarlet, animals' skins, wood found in the wilderness, oil, spices, and precious stones. He also asked every able-bodied man and woman to donate some labor to the building of the tabernacle. Bezalel and Oholiab, two men who had received special talents from God in artistic craftsmanship, were called to special service.

Through their offerings, the people would show their desire to have God dwell in their midst and their longing for the still more wonderful and intimate fellowship that God would bestow upon them when the promised Redeemer came. The people brought their offerings willingly, moved by the Spirit of the Lord. They wanted their offerings to show that they had finished with the sin they had just committed. The Lord was pleased to dwell in their midst—not in the form of a golden calf but in the tabernacle. Thus all the people went to work.

The Holy of Holies. The tent was made of wooden frames overlaid with gold. The frames were covered with four layers of cloth; the bottom one, visible in the tabernacle, was of fine linen and was beautifully embroidered. It was rectangular, 30 cubits* long, ten cubits wide, and ten cubits high. By way of this form, the tabernacle represented the whole earth upon which the Lord would one day dwell.

The tent was divided into two parts, with a curtain separating the front from the back. The back was ten cubits long and thus formed a cube. Perfect in its measurements, it spoke of the perfection of the dwelling place of God. That's how perfect our hearts and the world have to be.

The ark, a chest of wood overlaid with gold, with a cover of pure gold, was kept in this area. On the cover of the ark were two angel figures, one at each end, with their faces bowed forward so that the points of their wings touched. This ark with its solid gold cover represented the throne of God—His dwelling place in the midst of Israel.

If an animal was slaughtered as atonement for the sins of the people, its blood was to be sprinkled on this gold cover. The animal was slain for the sins of the people, and the blood, thus sanctified, would now be in God's presence. This sanctified blood would atone for the sin of the people before God. Therefore the cover was appropriately called the mercy seat. Perhaps it could better be called the atoning cover, for atonement means covering.

Of course the blood of the animal was not able to atone for the sins of men. Only the blood of the Lord Jesus Christ, His life freely given on our behalf, could do that. That blood of the animal was nothing more than a sign of the blood of the Christ, of His life and voluntary obedience, which He offered to God in our place. When He ascended into heaven with His holy life, which He had offered in our place, He came before God's throne. This was symbolized by the sprinkling of the blood on the throne of God in the Holy of Holies.

That dwelling of God in the midst of His people was indeed wonderful! Yet He lived there still hidden behind the curtain that shut off the Holy of Holies from the front part of the tabernacle. No one was allowed to enter there or take a look into it except the high priest when he sprinkled the blood there once each year on the great Day of Atonement. How far removed God still was from the

*A cubit was probably about 18 inches or 46 centimeters.—TRANS.

people, and the people from Him! The Lord Jesus Christ had not
yet shed His blood and atoned for sin. Now that His sacrifice is
history, all believers have free access to God through Him and may
enjoy a most intimate fellowship with the Lord. When we pray, we
stand in His immediate presence. He is even pleased to dwell in us
by His Spirit.

The Holy Place. The rest of the tabernacle was the Holy Place.
Even here the people were not permitted to come, although the
priests were allowed to enter. The priests, with the high priest as
their head, represented the people to God and God to the people.
Thus they were mediators between God and the people. Every day
the priests had to be in the Holy Place, for it was there that they
offered incense on the gold-covered altar every morning and every
evening. The incense that rose up to the Lord symbolized the
prayers of the priests for the people. Accordingly, the priest
prayed along with the sacrifice. Because he had been with God and
had asked for God's blessing upon the people, he could bless the
people waiting for him when he came out.

The Lord Jesus Christ is likewise our Intercessor in heaven.
He prays for us daily before God's face. For that reason He can
bless us from heaven.

Also in the Holy Place was the table of showbread, with bread
and wine on it. This bread and wine came from the people's
harvest, but it was as though the Lord Himself were offering bread
and wine to the people. That bread and wine, after all, was not the
fruit of men's labors but a gift from God. God maintained Israel's
life. He also sustained the people unto eternal life. His grace gives
us strength more than choice food.

This Holy Place also contained the golden lampstand with its
seven arms, in which oil was burned at night. The people of God
were to be a light to the world, just as that lamp illumined the
sanctuary. This was only possible because the Lord made it so.
The oil in the lamp testified to the Lord's role, for the oil was a
symbol of the gifts of the Holy Spirit (i.e. faith and hope and love)
by which we become a light in the midst of the world.

How glorious God's intent toward Israel was! Yet, even this
Holy Place was closed to the people. What a great distance there

still was between God and the people! They were not allowed a glimpse of that shining gold and wonderful service; they did not get a chance to see God's majesty and glory there. We are much closer today, for in the Christ we are privileged to behold God's glory in the Spirit.

The outer court. Around the tabernacle there was a large outer court set off by heavy curtains. Here the people were permitted to come. As a matter of fact, they could see quite a bit when they looked with eyes of faith.

In this outer court stood the bronze laver, in which the priests had to wash when they were ready to begin the holy service. Not even the priests, separated from the people for this holy service, were holy men; they were impure because of sin. This they had to demonstrate time after time by their ritual of washing.

Here, too, was the bronze altar of burnt offering, on which the sacrifices were offered. This was the most wonderful thing the Israelites could see in the outer court. Although God lived behind the veil, the Israelites could see a little of His presence at this altar of burnt offering, for here the sacrifices were brought into His presence. From here He would reveal Himself to the people.

Sometimes a slaughtered animal was completely consumed by the fire on the altar. Such a sacrifice was called a burnt offering. Food and drink would be sacrificed with it. When an Israelite watched this in faith, he saw that just as the sacrifice in its entirety went up to the Lord in flames, the life of his people and his own life was given wholly to the Lord.

Thus the sacrifice pointed to the consecration of all of life. Strictly speaking, however, no one can or may dedicate his life fully to the Lord, for it is a sinful life. The only exception was the Christ, who did exercise this privilege—unto death. By His Spirit, He also wants to teach us to offer our lives to God as a burnt offering.

Sometimes only a portion of the slaughtered animal was consumed in the fire. The remainder was then eaten by the priests. This occurred in the case of the guilt offering and the peace offering, which would be brought to atone for the sin of the people. Here the Israelite was to understand in faith that the animal's blood was shed in his place, for he himself deserved eternal death. Thus the animal's blood pointed to the blood of the Redeemer that would one day be shed for him.

At other times it was mainly the fat of the animal that was burned. The one who had given the animal would then eat the remainder at a sacrificial meal in the court, together with the other members of his household. It was as though they ate in the very presence of God, as though God Himself sat at that table as host. What wonderful communion they then enjoyed with the Lord! Such a sacrifice was called a thank offering.

Before the animal would be slaughtered, the one who brought it for sacrifice would lay his hands on its head, as if to indicate that the animal stood there in his place. How beautifully this illustrates what the Lord Jesus Christ is for us! We may lay our hands on Him and say: "He stood in our place in God's judgment."

God's presence in His dwelling place. Thus the tabernacle and all the services performed there pointed to what God wanted to be to His people in the Lord Jesus Christ; it gave the people an indication of how He wished to dwell with His people. But God had not yet come to that tabernacle and filled it with His glory.

On the first day of the first month of the year, exactly one year after the exodus from Egypt, Moses set up the tabernacle. When everything was in place, the cloud covered it. The glory of the Lord filled the tabernacle so completely that Moses could not go into it. The tabernacle now became the meeting tent in which the Lord met with His people through the Mediator.

How wonderfully God then lived among His people! Yet, what a distance there still was between God and the people! It is even more wonderful today, now that the Christ has atoned for the sins of His people and has overcome that distance. In His name, all of us may draw nearer to God boldly, and God will not reject us. He wishes to dwell not just among us but also within us, by His Holy Spirit. In this way our heart and our whole life become God's dwelling place.

By means of the cloud, God also gave Israel the signal to proceed. When the cloud lifted from above the tabernacle, the

people began their journey again, but whenever the cloud continued
to hover over it, they stayed where they were. Thus God Himself
set the tempo of the march.

44: Consecrated to God

Leviticus 8—10:7

It is not exactly clear what the sin of Nadab and Abihu was. Scripture says that they brought unholy fire to the altar. Did they perhaps take fire for the incense offering from the altar of burnt offering? Or did they offer incense at a time when the Lord had not ordered it? We have no way of knowing for sure. In any case, there was evil intent in what they did. They were probably caught up in the enthusiasm of the people when the Lord consumed the offering and then decided to consecrate the joy in the people's sacrifice by using incense in a spontaneous, man-made ritual. However well-intentioned that decision appeared to be, it represented willfulness on their part. This the Lord cannot tolerate in His priests.

In Aaron's silence after the death of his two sons, we see his complete consternation. The question probably arose within his heart too: Who, then, can be a priest? This made the significance of the anointing even greater in his eyes, for the anointing oil was a symbol of the Holy Spirit. Only through the Holy Spirit can a man serve as priest. Through the Spirit, the Christ offered Himself as a sacrifice to God, blameless. Only when we participate in His anointing can we offer ourselves as a sacrifice.

Moses forbade Aaron and his sons to mourn openly. The people's dismay at this calamity could easily turn into murmuring against God. Therefore the priest should not take part in the people's mourning, in order to sanctify them even in this affliction. There has only been One who could participate fully in the people's affliction and still remain completely holy to the Lord.

Main thought: *Through the anointing, the whole priestly service is consecrated to the Lord.*

The consecration of the priests and the sanctuary. Once God's holy dwelling was finished and the Lord had filled it with His glory, the priestly service had to be initiated. Mankind itself was originally intended to be a royal priesthood, revering the Lord in all of life, but because of sin we have all forfeited this privilege. Therefore the people needed a special priesthood to mediate between God and themselves—reconciling the people with God and bringing the whole people back to the service of God.

The Lord chose the tribe of Levi for this priestly service, putting this tribe in charge of the service in the sanctuary. Aaron would be high priest, and after him his oldest son, and then his sons's son, and so on. All of Aaron's sons i.e. his whole line, would be priests. God had not chosen Aaron and his line and the whole tribe of Levi because they were better than the rest of the people: they were no more worthy before God than the others. Only One was holy and could properly serve as priest for the people, namely, the Lord Jesus Christ. It was He who made them worthy of their office and qualified them for it.

On the day the Lord had designated, Moses called all the people to the outer court. Aaron and his four sons stood in front of the sanctuary. There he washed them with water from the laver. Next he dressed Aaron in the white priest's robe with a sash. Over the robe Aaron wore a blue garment, and over it the ephod jacket with its beautifully woven belt. On his breast hung the chestpiece (with the Urim and Thummim* inside).

Aaron stood before the people in all his splendor. On the blue garment hung the pomegranates and the tinkling bells (see Ex. 39:24-6); Aaron was a symbol of the Word of God that rings out from heaven. On his shoulderpiece and on his chestpiece, the names of the twelve tribes of Israel were engraved in precious stones: he would carry these before God's presence when he entered the sanctuary. On his head he wore the priest's turban, and on his forehead was the golden plate of the holy crown with the inscription "Holy to the LORD."

In himself Aaron was not worthy to be a priest, which is why these trappings were necessary. Only in these garments did he

---

*The Urim and Thummim may have been two gemstones enclosed somehow within the chestpiece, which could be cast as lots to find out God's answer to questions of importance to Israel. The matter is still unclear.—TRANS.

become holy to the Lord and wonderful. The Christ had no need of such garments; He was clothed with His own righteousness and holiness. He bore the names of those who belong to Him not on His shoulder or on His chest but in His heart.

After this Moses took the anointing oil and anointed God's dwelling place and all that was in it. Nothing on this earth was fit to be used in the service of the Lord. Everything had been profaned by sin. Therefore anointing oil was used to consecrate the dwelling place to the Lord.

Moses also poured anointing oil on Aaron's head. This oil set him apart in the office of high priest. Moreover, the anointing oil was a symbol of the Holy Spirit, who would qualify him for his priestly ministry.

Our Lord Jesus Christ was likewise anointed with the Holy Spirit—but not because He was in need of consecration. Through His anointing, He was designated as our High Priest and received the power of the Holy Spirit. This enabled Him to accomplish the formidable task of atoning for His people and sanctifying them.

Moses put the white priest's coat with the woven sash on Aaron's sons and placed the priest's turban on their heads. Then sacrifices were offered for Aaron and his sons—a sin offering for their sins and a burnt offering by which they were restored to communion with God and consecrated to the Lord. Moses put some blood from the sacrifice of ordination on the tip of each one's right ear, on the right thumb, and on the big toe of the right foot. Their ears had to be consecrated to hear the Word of God, their hands for their priestly work, and their feet to stand in the sanctuary.

It was a wonderful service. These priests would be mediators between God and the people, making atonement for the people time and again to restore covenant communion with the Lord. Yet, their ministry remained imperfect, for the priests themselves needed atonement and sanctification.

How the ministry of our Lord Jesus Christ transcends theirs! He is now our Priest, making atonement for us and sanctifying us. He wants to make all of us priests, giving us of His Spirit, by which we are consecrated to God and privileged to serve Him. We, too, offer sacrifices, for we give Him our entire lives, our thanks and our adoration.

The initiation of the holy service. After Aaron and his sons had been consecrated to the work, they offered their first sacrifice to atone for the people and consecrate them. For the very first time, Aaron lifted up his hands to bless the people.

Here began Aaron's priestly ministry. Moses was to introduce Aaron to the Lord as high priest, for Moses was the actual mediator between God and the people at that time. Together they entered the sanctuary, and there they prayed for the work of the priesthood and for the entire people. When they came out, they lifted up their hands together and blessed the people once more.

Then the pillar of cloud that rested on the sanctuary changed. The glory of the Lord shone through it, and all the people saw it. It was as though the Lord showed Himself to the people, full of majesty but also full of grace and mercy. This is how He would always look upon the people, because of this priestly ministry.

Fire appeared before the Lord, quickly consuming all the flesh and fat that lay burning on the altar of burnt offering. All the people shouted for joy, for they saw this as a sign that the sacrifice had been accepted, that atonement had been made for them, that they were pleasing to the Lord. They fell on their faces in adoration and thanksgiving.

There is another sacrifice that was completely consumed and accepted by the Lord—the sacrifice of the Christ. Because of that sacrifice, we will shout to God in joyful adoration. By that sacrifice, all who believe have been atoned for and are pleasing in God's sight.

The necessity of perfect obedience. Caught up in the people's enthusiasm, Nadab and Abihu took a censer, put fire in it, sprinkled incense on it, and tried to enter God's dwelling place with it to offer the joy of the people as a sacrifice to the Lord. But before they could step inside, fire came forth from the presence of the Lord and consumed them. Their dead bodies lay in front of God's dwelling.

Horrible! Why did this have to happen? Nadab and Abihu wanted to consecrate the joy of the people to the Lord. Yet they had gone about it in a way and at a time contrary to the Lord's command. A priest may not do whatever he pleases; he must do everything in perfect obedience. The Lord will be honored in the way He Himself chooses—not in our way. Because of their willfulness, Nadab and Abihu could not be priests. In their death the Lord glorified Himself, His will and His law.

Aaron, the father of the two dead priests, was silent—completely crushed. His heart must have been broken! But in his horror he must have asked himself, as the people surely did: Who, then, can serve as priest if the Lord is so strict?

There is indeed no one who can serve as priest—no one but the Christ, in whom there was no willfulness at all. Christ offered Himself blameless to God. His whole sacrifice was in accordance with God's will. The Holy Spirit, with which He was anointed, qualified Him for that sacrifice. Christ also gives us of His Spirit, enabling us to learn to serve the Lord in the way He wants to be served—and not according to our own wishes. Only by the Spirit is such service possible.

In his anointing, Aaron must have found the answer to the question that was in his heart. If he held fast to his anointing, relying on the power of the Lord and asking about His will, he could serve as high priest.

The dead priests, still wearing the garments that had been contaminated by their sins and by the judgment that had befallen them, were carried outside the camp at Moses' command and buried. Nadab and Abihu were not particularly sinful men; it was just that there was a willful streak in them. How often we are guilty of such willfulness as well!

Moses forbade Aaron and his two remaining sons, Eleazar and Ithamar, to let their hair hang loose or tear their clothes in mourning. No matter how much this judgment affected them personally, they had to be priests first of all. This order was not given because God refused to recognize any place for grief in His service; the problem was simply that the grief and lamentation could easily degenerate into murmuring against the Lord. Therefore the entire people should be able to look to those priests standing before God in the worst bereavement with their garments untorn, their sorrow under control.

Only one Man could enter fully into our affliction, sharing our grief but remaining above it at the same time. His lament before God never became an accusation, not even when He cried out, "My God, My God, why have You forsaken Me?"

How readily our complaints become accusations against God! Shouldn't we look to this Mediator of ours, who never accused God? That way we would overcome our grief and at the same time be comforted, for we know that He can share fully in our sorrow.

In the Wilderness

45: Israel's Calling

Numbers 9:15—10:36

With this story begins the journey through the wilderness. Since the Lord had called Israel to go up and possess Canaan, the people had a holy calling to pursue. That's why Moses could say: "Arise, O LORD, and let thy enemies be scattered; and let them that hate thee flee before thee." And when the ark came to rest, he would say: "Return, O LORD, to the ten thousand thousands of Israel."

We should be careful about drawing comparisons between this wilderness journey of Israel's and the Church's life on earth. Canaan, the land where grace rules, was in Israel's *future*, but for the Church today, the Kingdom of God is not purely future. Now all things live under the rule of grace. In principle, Canaan is already here, even though sin is still powerful. Our continual contact with the sin all around us and within us makes life a wilderness. Therefore we can speak of a "going up," a pilgrimage to Canaan. The Church knows no rest until she has arrived at the place where grace has full sway. Thus the Church goes its way in a holy calling, battling for dominion.

The cloud of the Lord controlled the journey, with the Israelites trusting completely in the Angel of the Lord as He went before them. In that pillar of cloud, in the revelation of God's covenant communion in the Angel of the Lord, Israel's calling was to be found.

Indeed, Canaan was not just the land overflowing with milk and honey but the land where the Lord would dwell in the midst of His people. There all the benefits would be proof of His favor, and His people would experience His steadfast love, His covenanting faithfulness.

Our calling, too, is to be found in God Himself, in His covenant communion. This communion is likewise our promise. For God's people, calling and promise come together in Him. That's the approach Moses used with Hobab, his brother-in-law, when he told him about calling and promise.

327

The Angel of the Lord, now become flesh, goes before us. In our struggle here on earth, our calling and promise is to possess the communion of God in Him. The tempo of our struggling pilgrimage on earth is determined by this goal. We must try to help the children understand something of this Angel's leading, both in history and in the present.

Main thought: *Led by the Angel of the Lord, Israel sets out in a holy calling.*

Surrendering to the leading of the Angel of the Lord. Exactly a year after leaving Egypt, the Israelites had set up their tabernacle. In the middle of the first month, they celebrated the Passover for the second time. They remembered their miraculous exodus and gave thanks to the Lord. Now the journey through the wilderness could begin. On to Canaan!

For the believing Israelites, the land of Canaan was not just a land overflowing with milk and honey; it was the land where the Lord would dwell wondrously in the midst of His people. In that land, God would give His favor and fellowship to His people in double measure. This promise was like a call to the believing people, which is why they longed to get on with the journey. The Lord was already dwelling among them in a wonderful way. What would it be like when they obtained the proof of His favor in the rich bounty of that fertile land?

Still, they had to wait for the Lord's sign. Whenever the pillar of cloud lifted, they were allowed to go on, but when the cloud settled on the tabernacle, they had to stay where they were. How impatiently they must have looked at that cloud while they were waiting! How long the waiting seemed to last! For days God would keep them in the same place. All the same, I suspect there were also times when they felt they had to travel much too fast, times when they had to go on almost without rest.

The Lord alone knew how things had to go. He was leading His people by way of these stops and starts; He was putting them to the test. After all, their ultimate goal was neither inheriting that rich land nor living a peaceful life in the wilderness but experiencing God's communion in that land. And that communion could only be received by submitting to Him in faith. In the wilderness it ought to be a delight to follow after Him, and then it would also be a delight to enjoy communion with Him in Canaan. The Lord should always be their all.

If the people followed obediently, they would also be involved with the Lord while waiting in the wilderness—by attending to His service in the sanctuary, worshiping Him and waiting on Him. During the periods of rest, the people sought to know the glory of His service and noted how He wished to reveal Himself to them.

If the Lord is what we want, then we must submit to Him in faith. We must submit willingly to the guidance of the Angel of the Lord, that is, the Lord Jesus Christ, who already offers us God's communion. Under His guidance, we must set forth to do battle with sin. All through our lives, we look to Him to see what He wants to reveal to us about Himself.

The sound of the silver trumpets. Moses was also commanded to make two silver trumpets and see to it that they were blown on certain occasions. When a long, drawn-out sound rang out over the people from one of the trumpets, the elders (i.e. the heads of the tribes of Israel) were to gather. If a long, drawn-out note sounded from both trumpets, the entire people of Israel was to come and meet with the Lord.

The sound of the trumpets rang out above all the noise in the camp: the Lord was calling the people together to meet with Him! Something of the exultation of God's grace and His joy rang out over the people in the sound of the trumpets, drowning out all the other sounds of life.

That sound is still there—if only we can hear it. It is there in the preaching of the gospel, especially on Sundays in church. That sound rings out—for those who are able to hear—above all the uproar in the world.

Whenever Israel sinned, however, there was a threat in that sound. Then believing Israel had to understand that even in His wrath, God was merciful and chastised His people in order to cleanse them. In that way, the gospel goes forth today.

On other occasions, a few short blasts of the trumpet were sounded. Then a shock would go through the camp, a shock of surprise for the believers: it was time to move on, to inherit the land and wrest it from the hand of the Lord's enemies. In the same way, the gospel calls us to battle and summons us to inherit the Kingdom.

Carrying the sacred dwelling place. When the people moved forward behind the cloud, the ark of the covenant went ahead of the army. Then three tribes followed under the leadership of Judah. Behind them were two branches of the tribe of Levi, carrying the tabernacle. Then followed three tribes under the leadership of Reuben. Then came the third branch of the Levites, with the tabernacle equipment. They were followed by three tribes under the leadership of Ephraim. At the end of the procession marched the last three tribes, under the leadership of Dan. In this way, the first two branches of the Levites were able to set up the tabernacle and were ready when the third branch arrived with the equipment.

This is how the Israelites always carried God's holy dwelling place in their midst. The believing Levites must have carried the sacred dwelling place in a spirit of holiness and reverence, for it was their most cherished possession, the sign of God's communion with them. Around this dwelling place, the tribes were drawn up as they journeyed. Moreover, they camped in a set order around it whenever they were to remain in a certain place for a while. God's dwelling place was the center of their lives together.

The presence of that dwelling place was wonderful, but God's people today enjoy an even more glorious privilege: the Lord, by His Holy Spirit, is pleased to dwell in the hearts of His people. That's the real richness of life! Our attitude toward this indwelling must be one of holy reverence. We must not grieve the Spirit of the Lord.

Passing on the calling. Jethro, Moses' father-in-law, had apparently gone away already, but his brother-in-law Hobab was still with him. When the Israelites were about to set out, Moses said to him: "We are going to the place the Lord promised to give us. Come with us and share our prosperity, for the Lord has promised to be good to Israel." How Moses exulted! "We are going to inherit the Lord's salvation in His land! Come with us!"

If we have seen the salvation of the Lord, if we believe in it and have been gripped by it, we cannot remain silent. Then we have to pass on the calling we receive: "Look at what's in store for us! Come with us!"

At first Hobab did not want to go along. He could not yet cut himself off from his land and family, for he had a definite place with them. But Moses said to him: "You have a place among us, and a distinct calling. Since you know the wilderness so well, you can show us where the wells and pastures are, so that we will know where to set up camp. Thus you can be our eyes in the wilderness. And for the sake of this calling, you will be crowned with honor by the Lord. We will be good to you in His name." At this Hobab's heart was gripped. He heard the calling of the Lord and stayed, deciding to go along with Israel on its long journey.

We can say to the people we encounter: "Hear the calling of the Lord. You, too, must have a place among God's people. Join us in the battle against sin and inherit the Kingdom with us." In our enthusiasm, this calling must radiate from us. Then God will also give us people to go with us and serve the Church of the Lord.

From wilderness to wilderness. On the twentieth day of the second month of the second year, the cloud finally lifted from the tabernacle. The blast of the trumpet was heard throughout the camp, and the march began. The Israelites journeyed for three days, resting at night, until they came to a place where they camped for a somewhat longer time. They had traveled from the Wilderness of Sinai to the Wilderness of Paran.

It was a journey from one wilderness to another. Here in Paran, the wilderness was indeed barren. If they had not followed the Lord and camped where He told them (via the pillar of cloud), the terror of the wilderness would certainly have overtaken them. Fortunately, they were proceeding in a holy calling—to inherit a land where God would dwell among them. Knowing this, Moses would cry out whenever it was time for the ark to set out: "Arise, O LORD, and let thy enemies be scattered; and let them that hate thee flee before thee." And whenever the ark rested again, he said: "Return, O LORD, to the ten thousand thousands of Israel."

The Lord was always there, either going before them or

resting in their midst. It should be that way for us, too, and it will be—if only we believe. God is in our midst in the Lord Jesus Christ and is in us through His Spirit.

46: For His Own Sake

Numbers 11

The people already sinned in the Wilderness of Paran, which was the first campsite. In their obstinacy, they sinned again and again. They longed for Egypt, which meant that they rejected their holy calling and were likely to forsake the covenant. In this situation, Moses' mediatorship failed. We read that when Moses heard the people weeping with their families, every man at the door of his tent, he had nothing more to say to them. This rising tide of iniquity made him helpless and paralyzed.

On the other hand, he knew that the Lord's anger was being kindled. But he had nothing more to say to the Lord either; he could no longer pray to the Lord to overlook the people's sin. The Bible tells us that it was also sin in Moses' eyes. He was disturbed and appalled, but he could no longer cope with the situation.

In such a case as this, what could possibly persuade the Lord to forgive the people and turn to them again in His grace? God seemed to be fed up with them. There was nothing in this people that could move Him. Now He could only pity them for His own sake, to glorify His faithfulness and grace to this people. He shamed them by giving them quails while also visiting them because of their sin.

Evidently Moses, as mediator, did not yet see clearly enough that this people's calling lay solely in God's election, that God wanted to glorify Himself in His grace by saving them. In this respect, too, the mediatorship of the Lord Jesus Christ is far superior to that of Moses. On the one hand, He fully identified Himself with the sin of His people, and on the other hand, He can always intercede with the Father.

Because Moses could not carry the burden of this people alone, 70 elders were chosen. To them God gave something of the Spirit that was in Moses. Of course that did not detract from the Spirit that was in Moses, but it did enable them to have communion with him. The 70 elders had a twofold calling: to strengthen Moses in his intercession with God and support him in his influence on the people. This granting of the Spirit to

333

the 70 was a prophecy pointing ahead to the day when all believers would
share in the Spirit with the Christ. That's why Moses rebuked Joshua.

Main thought: *The Lord forgives His people's sin for His own sake.*

Feeling sorry for themselves. After a three-day march, the
Israelites came into the Wilderness of Paran and remained there for
some time. Already they began to feel sorry for themselves. What
a barren wilderness! How long was this to go on? Even with the
Lord, they were not able to face the wilderness. Communion with
God did not mean enough to them to make every place, even the
loneliest wilderness, a paradise for them. It was not enough for
them to possess the Lord. How little we, too, sometimes think of
the Lord and His love!

The Lord heard their complaints. In His great patience, He
sometimes seems not to hear our rebellious, self-pitying complaints.
However, there comes a time when He decides to listen carefully,
and then His anger is kindled. That's what happened to Israel. In
the outlying parts of the camp, some tents were consumed by fire.
If the wind caused the fire to spread, the whole camp would go up
in flames.

Moses saw the danger and recognized it as a sign that the Lord's
anger was kindled against the people. The Lord was letting them
see just what would happen to them if He turned against them.
Therefore Moses fell down before the Lord and prayed. In response
to his intercession, the fire retreated. The Israelites called that place
Taberah, which means *place of the fire.*

The people's craving. After this threat was averted and the
people had seen the glory of God, they began to complain again.
They had not yet rid themselves of self-pity. If we are consumed by
self-pity, we are less and less able to recognize what we have and
become more and more aware of what we do not have. If God is
not our joy, we develop an insatiable desire for the good things of
life. We also feel we are constantly being short-changed and

become miserable creatures deserving of pity.

The complaining started among the aliens who had left Egypt with the Israelites. They stubbornly persisted in their complaints in spite of the revelation of the glory of the Lord in the destruction of some outlying tents by fire and the subsequent extinguishing of that fire. Gradually their spirit infected all the people, so that they all began to complain, "We remember the meat and the luscious fruits we enjoyed in Egypt."

Thus the people despised the manna the Lord gave them. They declared that they were getting sick of the whole business, for they did not see the riches of God's favor.

Faith in the Lord governs the way we receive God's gifts, even down to the taste in our mouths. How blind we can be! The people would rather have Egypt's foods without God's favor than this manna with it. What do we value most in life? We throw away gold for something that does not even have the value of brass.

The mediator's failure. Moses was no longer able to cope with the situation. He heard the people weeping in their tents. They really felt sorry for themselves. The people would not listen to any word from Moses; nothing he said would be able to reach them anymore. On the other hand, he realized that because of their complaints, God could only become more and more angry with them. Yet he had nothing more to say to the Lord either; he could no longer pray for the people. He was no longer master of the situation, for he was overwhelmed and appalled by the iniquity of the people.

The only thing he could do was complain to the Lord that he could not handle the situation, that the burden was too much for him. Moses was indeed feeling sorry for himself—but because of the people. He was near collapse under the burden of their sin. He complained: "Are these my children? Must I carry them all in my arms and bring them to the land You promised them? Can I give them meat to eat? Why have You laid this burden upon me? If You still ask this of me, please kill me now, so that I will not have to witness my own undoing."

Here Moses failed as mediator. There is only one Mediator who could fully bear the sins of His people—Jesus Christ. He always had something to say to God and could pray for His people even when confronted with their most horrible sins. How fortunate that we know of a Mediator who never fails!

The communion of the Spirit. First God met His servant Moses halfway. He ordered him to gather 70 elders of Israel and bring them to the meeting tent. When they were gathered there, the Lord came to them in a cloud, touching them with the Spirit He had given to Moses, so that they prophesied whenever the Spirit rested upon them.

These 70 men were to support Moses in his leadership of the people. Although they were among the people, they shared in the Spirit that was in Moses. Therefore they could strengthen his communion with the people and his influence on them. Moreover, they would stand with him so that he would have more strength to go to God on behalf of the people.

How grateful Moses was for this gift of God! Apparently the Lord had chosen two more men as prophets, for in the midst of the people there were two men prophesying, two men who did not belong to the 70. When Joshua heard about it, he asked Moses to forbid them, but Moses earnestly rebuked him. Why wasn't he glad that two more men had received a portion of the Spirit of the Lord? Would that all the Lord's people were prophets! After all, the prophetic gift had been granted to these two by the Lord Himself. Therefore Moses was delighted.

The Spirit in Moses was given to those elders so that they could support him. At the same time, this showed clearly the unity through the Spirit which would have to unite all of God's people. The Spirit in the Lord Jesus Christ is given to all His people—not to support Him, for He needs no support, but to enable us to serve the Lord in communion with Him.

Satisfaction and shame. Thus the Lord met Moses halfway. But what would He do with the people who despised His covenant and longed to return to Egypt, to reap the benefits of the land there without His grace? Humanly speaking, this faithless abandonment of His covenant should have destroyed God's pleasure in lifting up this people. But how would God now consider them? There was absolutely nothing in them that could move Him to turn to them again. If He still thought of them, it would be for His own sake, to glorify His faithfulness and grace to them. It was for that purpose that He also kept Moses as mediator and gave him the support of the 70 elders.

The Lord commanded Moses to inform the people that on the next day, He would give them enough meat to supply them for a whole month. At the time Moses did not understand it. He was unable to hold on to his faith in the Lord. Hence his doubt: "How will You give this numerous people a month's supply of meat?" Apparently Moses feared this might be too difficult for the Lord!

The next morning the wind brought so many quails that they spread as far as a day's journey around the camp. So many fell to the earth that they piled up about a meter high. The people ate some of the quails and dried others in the sun for future use.

However, as they ate those quails, they were not filled with shame and remorse because of their ingratitude and faithlessness. Instead they acted as though it was simply their due. Therefore the Lord's anger was kindled against them while they were still eating! He brought a great plague on them. When it was all over, they called that place Kibroth-hattaavah, which means *graves of craving,* for those who were buried there had forgotten the Lord in their craving.

The people were to move on shortly. There were many who had to tear themselves away from the graves of dear ones buried there. God is merciful and exalts His grace to His people, but He also disciplines and purifies them.

47: Illegitimate Honor

Moses, the mediator called by God, lived in obedience and faithfulness to the calling that dominated his life. In his life there was no self-seeking, no grasping for more than God had given him. He was aware that no one takes honor upon himself in the Kingdom of God (Heb. 5:4).

Miriam and Aaron, however, wanted more than God gave them. Jealousy of Moses does not account for what they did. Rather, what we see here is the sin of spiritualism and fanaticism. They pointed out that they, too, possessed the Spirit of prophecy. In a pride that was anything but spiritual, they let themselves be driven ahead in their awareness of their privileged position and refused to subject themselves to God's calling in their prophetic activities. The sin of spiritualism is always like that; it shakes itself free from the Word of calling, seeking an honor to which it has no legitimate claim.

Miriam's punishment was related to her sin: the one who had boasted of an ordination, an anointing by the Holy Spirit, was profaned and disgraced in Israel. The wrath God directed against that unholy spiritualism was dreadful. It was as though Miriam's heavenly Father had spit in her face.

Miriam was punished—but not Aaron. The likely reason for this is that the pride began with Miriam. In her spiritualistic pride, she despised the Cushite woman whom Moses had married. It is not known whether Zipporah had already died. Nor is it recorded how Moses met his Cushite wife. She may have belonged to the Hamitic tribes that lived a nomadic life in the wilderness of Sinai or to the mixed folk that had left Egypt along with the Israelites. In any case, she was beneath the spiritual level of Miriam and Aaron. Apparently such pride was foreign to Moses, for he entered into a marriage with a non-Israelite woman—a union that was not forbidden by law.

Main thought: *The one called by God is faithful.*

Unspiritual pride. From Kibroth-hattaavah the Israelites traveled to Hazeroth, a new stopover in the wilderness of Paran. Here a quarrel broke out between Miriam and Aaron on the one hand and Moses on the other—a breach in Israel's leading family. On the one side stood the mediator and on the other side the high priest and the prophetess.

Apparently Miriam's dissatisfaction had been building up for a long time. Wasn't she a prophetess? Hadn't she led the women of Israel in praising the Lord on the shore of the Red Sea? And hadn't the Lord spoken through her as well as Moses? But she was never given proper recognition; she was always subordinate to Moses. A prophet or prophetess should rank above everyone and everything else!

How foolish of Miriam! A prophet must never brag about what he has received from the Lord. And he is only a prophet by virtue of his calling by the Lord. A prophet must of necessity be completely subject to the Word of God's calling. Moses desired to say only what the Lord called him to say, but Miriam wanted to go far beyond such limits.

What was brewing within her came to the surface when Moses took a Cushite woman as his wife—a woman not of Israel but of the line of Ham. This was allowed by law; only marriage with a Canaanite was forbidden. Moses, the mediator, did not despise the heathens and saw no disgrace in such an alliance if the heathen became a believer in the Lord. In such a case, the person would be taken into Israel by his or her faith and because of the alliance. Our Mediator Jesus Christ does not despise the heathens either. Instead He sanctifies them by having them acknowledge the Lord's covenant with His people. But Miriam, who was proud of her gift, thought this marriage far beneath the spiritual position of her family. Thus she despised that heathen woman.

She expressed her dissatisfaction to her brother Aaron, a weakling who listened to what she had to say, just as he had heeded the voice of the people during Moses' absence. When Aaron hesitated, arguing that Moses was the mediator and as such was called by the Lord, she replied: "But don't you wear the chest-

piece with the Urim and the Thummim in it, by which the Lord
speaks? And am I not a prophetess? Moses is not the only one
through whom the Lord speaks." In this way she overcame
Aaron's resistance and turned him against his brother.

Together they went to Moses and reproached him for his
marriage. When Moses tried to justify what he had done by saying
that it was not contrary to the Word of the Lord, they rebelled
openly. Didn't *they* also have the Spirit of the Lord? Didn't *they*
know the mind of the Lord—perhaps even better than Moses at
times?

There you have the difference: Miriam and Aaron divined from
their own hearts, from their own proud thoughts, what the mind
of the Lord might be, while Moses simply asked what the Lord had
said. Moses' whole life of service was controlled by the Word of
the Lord. It's so easy to become proud once we think we know
something. Then we cast aside the law of the Lord and despise
anyone who does not know what we think we know.

Faithful in the whole house of the Lord. Again we read that
the Lord took note of what was going on. He saw the pride of
Miriam and Aaron and cursed it. Few things are so abominable to
the Lord as people priding themselves on the gifts of the Holy
Spirit and misusing them. That's why the Lord suddenly intervened.
He summoned Moses, Aaron and Miriam to the entrance of the
outer court and appeared to them there. Aaron and Miriam were
told to step forward. Then He said to them: "A prophet is never to
prophesy out of his own heart or his own thoughts. A prophet
never has anything to say other than what I reveal to him. Indeed,
a prophet is entirely dependent on My Word: what he is to say will
be made known to him in a dream or a vision. Moses lives only by
My Word, which possesses and guides him. Therefore he is faithful in My whole house, in My service in the midst of all My people.
And because of this faithfulness, I speak to him face to face; he
sees the likeness of the Lord, a form of My glory. He hears and
sees what no man has ever yet heard or seen. Why, then, have you
risen up against him?"

What great honor the Lord bestowed on Moses! He received
this honor solely because he subjected himself to the Word of the

Lord. Because of his submission, he was faithful in everything. He was a faithful servant in the house of his Lord, that is, in Israel, in the midst of the Lord's people.

Moses is surpassed by our Lord Jesus Christ, who did only what God commanded Him. He was not a servant in the house of His Lord; He was a Son set over the house of His Father—which is also His house, for the people of God are also His people (compare Heb. 3:1-6 with Num. 12:6-7).

How often do we think of our faithful Mediator? In contrast to the wrongs we do and all our pride, He never goes against the will of His Father. The Mediator vouches for us before His Father.

Shamed for her sin. In anger the Lord turned away and left, and the cloud lifted from above the tent. Thus God made it known that the worldly pride of Miriam and Aaron was an abomination to Him. When Aaron looked at Miriam, he saw that she was leprous, white as snow.

What a disgrace! The prophetess who was consecrated to the Lord was now desecrated, unclean. She would have to be banned from the community. Aaron was deeply shaken and said to Moses, "We have acted foolishly, but please do not permit our sin to be visited on her with such severe punishment."

How meekly Moses had endured their initial rebellion! Although he had not been personally offended, he had seen clearly that Miriam and Aaron were rebelling against the Lord. It was a question of their life in relation to the Lord. Thus Moses was now able to pray to the Lord on behalf of his sister: "Heal her, O God, I beseech thee."

Our Mediator also prays for us, even after our most hideous sins. He sees that we are sinning against God. Moses had to base his plea on the blood that would one day be shed, but our Mediator can point to His own blood, which has already been shed for us.

The Lord did indeed hear the mediator Moses, but Miriam was to endure her punishment for seven days. If her father had spit in her face because she had behaved badly toward him, she would have had to bear her shame for seven days. Now that God had let it be known that her pride was an abomination to Him, she would have to live outside the camp for seven days as a leper.

For seven days the people of Israel remained at Hazeroth, waiting for Miriam to be healed and accepted again. Fortunately, the shame of our infidelity and the curse of our pride has been removed by the faithfulness of our Mediator. That's why Miriam could be healed and accepted again, and that's why sinners are accepted now.

48: Light Shining in the Darkness

Numbers 13-14

In John 1 we read: "In him was life." The One referred to, of course, is the Word that was from eternity, the Angel of the Lord, the One who brings to fulfillment the communion of God's covenant. The life of fellowship with God was in Him. And that life was the light of men. This light, then, is the light of God's grace in His fellowship (before the fall, the light of God's favor). This light shines in the darkness. In Israel, too, there was darkness, and the darkness did not comprehend it. Yet the light is not overcome by the darkness.

What John says is illustrated in this story. There were only a few in Israel who understood the light of God's covenant fellowship. That light must have made them aware of the light shining on the land of Canaan, which was open to them. But if Canaan was nothing more to them than a land flowing with milk and honey, it would be closed to them. When it came to the question of Canaan, the hearts of the Israelites were not prepared for a bold advance in faith, for they did not perceive the fellowship of God. In that fellowship, nothing is impossible.

This difference is also at the root of the difference of opinion between the spies. Most of them saw Canaan as a land that devoured its inhabitants. Because it was unusually fertile, the groups of inhabitants were continually battling one another for possession of it. And time and again they were attacked by foreign conquerors. Possessing that land was just too dangerous.

Without God's fellowship, living in such a land is indeed a dangerous matter. Therefore the unbelieving Israelites wanted to go back to Egypt. Joshua and Caleb, however, knew that God would give them the land, and that His communion would protect their lives there.

At this point one thinks naturally of the Church's fear of conquering the world for Christ's sake and of already inheriting the Kingdom in principle. For the Church, culture has often been a land that devours its inhabitants. Yet it is open to those who see the light of God's communion. In our time, too, whole generations die in the desert because of their fear.

343

Because He was angry, God told Moses that He would destroy the people. Behind that anger, however, lay His everlasting favor, for Christ's sake and for the sake of His covenant. Moses appealed to the covenant, and then God again showed His goodwill, which was hidden at first by His wrath. His wrath was completely real and was directed against all thoughts of the flesh. Those thoughts of the flesh will be erased, but the people will be saved.

Still, this generation would die in the wilderness. Within the context of this judgment, God declared that the whole earth would be filled with the glory of the Lord. In the destruction of the present generation, all peoples would be made aware that flesh deserves death, and that the salvation of mankind is the fruit of God's free mercy.

Main thought: *The light shines in the darkness, and the darkness has not comprehended it.*

Two viewpoints. The people of Israel had crossed the great Wilderness of Paran. Once they reached Kadesh, they were close to the borders of Canaan. Therefore the people asked Moses to send some men ahead to spy out the land, and the Lord ordered him to comply. Each tribe sent one of its leading men, which made a total of twelve spies.

At Moses' command, they went through the whole land from the south to the north and back again. They found that Canaan was an extremely fertile land with heavily fortified cities. In one area there were giants.

Once the spies were back at the camp, they reported to Moses and the people gathered around them. They spoke of the land's fertility. As proof they brought with them some pomegranates and a cluster of grapes, which two men carried on a pole on their shoulders. But they also spoke of the fortified cities and of the giants, who were sons of Anak.

This report scared the people—which was what most of the spies had intended, for they were afraid themselves. They had not looked at the land with an eye to God's granting them His fellowship there. Instead they had disregarded God's promise as they surveyed the land. Hence they came to the conclusion that the land could not be conquered, and the majority of the people saw it their way. Many of them were concerned not with communion with

God but with the fertitily of the soil. As they saw it, Canaan was a
land they could not enter.

Two of the spies, Caleb and Moses' helper Joshua, had looked
at the land from a different point of view, that is, in the light of
God's promise. They had wandered through it as its future posses-
sors in God's name. For them the land lay wide open, and they
believed that God would indeed bring them into it. What we see
depends on how we look at things. If we look with the eyes of
faith, nothing is impossible for us, but without faith nothing is
truly possible.

Caleb tried to calm the mounting storm, speaking out of
faith, but some other spies interrupted him: "We will not be able
to conquer Canaan. And even if we did conquer it, we would not
be able to maintain ourselves there, for many people want to
conquer and possess that land because of its extreme fertility.
That's why the people there live in such strongly fortified cities.
Only giants like the sons of Anak, in whose eyes we are like grass-
hoppers, can maintain themselves there."

Because of such reasoning, fear got the upper hand among the
people. Fear is always the opposite of faith. Faith had not put
the people's hearts in Canaan, and therefore they could not enter it.

Tumult. The report brought back by the spies caused a great
uproar among the people. They accused God of bringing them into
the wilderness with their wives and children to perish. They even
wanted to replace Moses, who took the Lord's side, with another
leader who would take them back to Egypt.

Moses and Aaron were horrified. Fearing the Lord's anger,
they fell on their faces before the assembly of the people. What
was to come of this? Wouldn't the Lord destroy all the people
gathered there in a single moment of fury? Joshua and Caleb tore
their clothes and urged the people to believe the Word of the Lord.
In place of fear they proposed faith: "Those peoples in Canaan
are like a meal for us. We will devour them! Their shadow, their
protection, the shield of safety above their heads will be taken
away from them, for the Lord has delivered them into our hands."
That's how faith sees things.

But the spell of fear kept a tight rein on the people, who wanted to stone Joshua and Caleb. At this point the glory of the Lord appeared in His dwelling place. There was the God of the covenant, who terrified His people. He had not appeared for nothing. If we are in communion with the Lord, we must not fear, for fear becomes an abomination.

The name of the Lord. The Lord revealed His anger to Moses. If it were not for the Lord's plans, He would have had no choice but to destroy this people. He said to Moses: "They refuse to believe My Word, in spite of many signs. I will strike them with disease and cast them out. Then I will make a great nation of you instead."

But Israel had a mediator, in whom was the Spirit of the Lord Jesus Christ, our Mediator. This mediator, Moses, interceded on Israel's behalf. After all, there was still the covenant and God's promise to consider. But if no one grasped the promise in faith, it could not be fulfilled. Moses was the one who reached for the promise at this critical juncture.

How do God's promises fare now, when we so often forget them in our lack of faith? Our Mediator in heaven clings to those promises, and that's why they are fulfilled.

Moses pleaded: "The Egyptians and all the nations know what You have done for us. They have also heard that You dwell among this people and are seen face to face, that you give Yourself here to us, and that we enjoy wonderful fellowship with You. If this people were to perish now, everyone would say that even this fellowship could not bring us into Canaan. Surely the communion of God's grace is able to accomplish anything! It is even able to overcome unbelief. Moreover, at Sinai You proclaimed Your name in my ears, saying that You would certainly not clear the guilty. But before that, You said that You are patient and abounding in steadfast love, forgiving iniquity and sin. Are You not the God of the covenant, the One who always takes the initiative? Your punishment cannot be retribution or revenge. Instead it must be a disciplining of Your people."

In response to this intercessory prayer, the Lord revealed that in His anger He would be merciful for the sake of His Word and thus would forgive the people again. His people would enter

Canaan, but not that particular group of adults. All who were 20 years of age or older He would discipline by letting them die in the wilderness. The next generation would inherit Canaan. For 40 years the Israelites would wander in the wilderness, just as the spies had spent 40 days wandering through the land. Those who were over 20 would live out their lives, but they would not see Canaan. Their children, whom they had feared would be taken away from them by the Canaanites, would enter the land.

God would use this judgment to glorify His name over the whole earth, for it would show all peoples that no one is worthy of entering the land of God's communion. Only the grace of God, which overcomes every obstacle, brings us there. Because those Israelites perished in the wilderness, God's name has been glorified for us as well. We, too, weary the Lord with our unbelief. If we would only see the power of God's free compassion and entrust ourselves to it! Only that surrender can give us the courage to do battle with the enemy. The land is a gift of God, but so is the courage to enter it. If only we would see that everything springs from Him!

The land closed to the Israelites. Moses had to take this message to the people. Only for Joshua and Caleb had the Lord made exceptions. When the people heard what the Lord had decreed, they mourned greatly.

That night they thought of something. They were not yet ready to submit to the Word of the Lord. Who knows what the Lord would have done to help them if they had obeyed and had borne their crosses in faith? But they had been held back by their own fears. Therefore a plan took shape during the night. Instead of turning back into the wilderness the next morning, as the Lord had told them to do, they prepared for battle, intending to conquer the heights on which the Amalekites and Canaanites lived. Once more they were going their own way.

Moses tried to warn them, asking what they would accomplish against their enemies without the Word of the Lord, without His communion, without faith. They insisted on going ahead anyway, even though Moses and the ark did not go with them.

What a daring bunch they were! There they went, in their own strength. But they were attacked and defeated by the Amalekites and Canaanites, who pursued them far to the south. Thus the land remained closed to them. It is only opened up by the Word of the Lord and our faith in it.

49: The Head of the People Upheld

Numbers 16:1-40

The rebellion of Korah, Dathan and Abiram is one of the few bits of history relating to the 40 years that Israel wandered around in the wilderness. Apparently its purpose is to tell us how the older generation of Israelites died there.

The sin of the three conspirators was their rejection of Moses as head of the people. By rejecting Moses as mediator and head, they were also rejecting God's covenant. The consequence of such a rejection would be the breakdown of Israel as the people of God. This rejection of Moses is comparable to the rejection of the Christ, which is even now causing breakdown in human life. The life of men and nations can flourish only when Christ is recognized as the Head.

Moses was struggling for his position among the people, for a recognition of his legitimacy and calling as the one appointed by God. But his struggle was also a fight for the preservation of the covenant and thereby the salvation of Israel. By rejecting Korah and his fellow conspirators, God upheld Israel's head and thus preserved the covenant bond with the people.

Apparently the rebellion began with Korah. As a member of the tribe of Levi, he was out to get the priesthood for himself. However, he convinced the Reubenites Dathan and Abiram to join him. As Reubenites, these two men were jealous of the tribe of Levi, which, through Moses and Aaron, provided the leadership of the nation. But they were prepared to join with the Levite Korah against Moses, through whom the Lord spoke, requiring covenant obedience. The rebellion was definitely against the head whom God had appointed—and thereby against the Lord Himself. Pilate and Herod became friends in their rejection of Jesus.

349

The punishment was according to the sin. A hole opened in the earth, and the three men went down into Sheol alive (to use the words of Scripture), together with their households and all their fellow conspirators. This was a vivid illustration that there was no place for them among the people of the covenant. With their households, they were rooted out. Their name would pass away with them, and their grave would not be marked.

Main thought: *The Lord preserves the nation's head.*

The rejection of the head. Following the Lord's command, the Israelites had turned back into the wilderness. For 40 years they were to wander about, and all who were 20 years of age or older would die there. Perhaps because of this punishment, some of them returned to the Lord and were saved for eternity. But there must have been others who hardened their hearts.

Now that there was no Canaan in sight, only death in the wilderness awaited them. Hope no longer urged them on or even held them together. The bonds between the Israelites must have become looser and looser. Likewise, the bonds uniting them with Moses, their head, by whom the Lord led them, must have weakened. Their personal lives were full of hardships, their family life was being corrupted, and their national life threatened to fall apart. Finally they rejected their head. With all their complaining and plotting, they finally reached the point of no return.

Korah was a Levite (a member of the same tribe as Moses and Aaron) who grew jealous of their positions as leaders of the people. If only he himself could be high priest someday! Then life would hold some joy for him, even though he had to wander around in the wilderness. At least he could enjoy some outward glitter and honor. He was in no position to challenge Moses and Aaron on his own, so he stirred up some mischief. He thought of the tribe of Reuben, Jacob's oldest son, a tribe that envied the leadership role entrusted to the tribe of Levi. He plotted with two Reubenites, Dathan and Abiram. Korah would be the high priest, and the 250 men who joined him in the rebellion would be priests. Dathan and Abiram would be entrusted with the leadership in non-spiritual affairs.

With more than 250 men, they went to Moses and Aaron, arguing that *all* the men in Israel were holy to the Lord and could carry out the special service of the Lord. Moses and Aaron were accused of being interested only in furthering their own careers.

How could such a thing happen after all the signs the Lord had given the people through Moses? These men did not know or honor the Lord. Right away they forgot the Lord's mighty deeds. Unless our faith enables us to see God's grace in His mighty deeds, we will not be aware of the wonder of those deeds, and they will make no lasting impression on us. To accept the Lord is also to receive the one whom the Lord has appointed as mediator and head. The rebels said that they wanted to serve the Lord, but by rejecting the Lord's appointed, they were rejecting the Lord Himself.

Even today, many people insist that they want to serve and honor God, but they reject Christ, the Mediator and Head. If the Christ is not King over our whole life, God is not really God for us.

Thus Korah and his fellow conspirators rejected the Lord and the covenant He had made with Israel. Among God's people, no one can lead except those whom the Lord has called to positions of leadership. If the rebels had succeeded in putting themselves in positions of leadership, the covenant would have been broken and Israel would have been destroyed as a covenant people. What was the Lord going to do?

The mediator's struggle. When Moses heard what the rebels had to say, he fell on his face. How could they reject the calling of the Lord and thus the Lord Himself? What would happen to Israel now? The Lord would vent His anger. Otherwise all Israel would be destroyed.

Moses tested the rebels. The next morning those 250 men were to come with censers, put fire in them, and sprinkle incense on them. Then the Lord would reveal His chosen priest. It was as though Moses was reminding them of the death of Nadab and Abihu, who had also wanted to offer sacrifices in their own way but had been struck by the fire of God's presence.

Moses warned them: "You Levites are the tribe chosen to serve in the sanctuary, although you cannot all be priests. Why don't you show your gratitude for that privilege instead of wanting more than the Lord has given you? You are rebelling not against Aaron but against the Lord." But Moses' warning did not register. The rebels did not take the Lord into account or recognize His right to call anyone He chose.

Dathan and Abiram were not at this meeting, but Moses had been told of their involvement. He summoned them, but they refused to come, saying: " With a false promise you got us out of Egypt, and now you let us die here in the wilderness. You have not kept your promise. You did all that just to establish yourself as leader over us. Your only concern is yourself."

Their answer stirred up Moses' anger. He prayed to the Lord not to respect the incense offering of those rebels, arguing that he had never been self-seeking and had never sought to harm the people. Moses knew that the Lord would not respect their offering, but now he prayed that the Lord would reject them, showing His anger toward them.

Moses prayed to keep his position as head of the nation, but it was not his personal interest that concerned him. The preservation of the covenant and of the nation was dependent on his being retained as mediator. The rejection of the 250 rebels would have to show that Moses was to remain the mediator. Therefore he again insisted that the malcontents appear the next morning with their answers.

It's a good thing that Moses kept his place as mediator and head, for Israel's salvation was at stake. It's also a good thing that the Lord Jesus Christ remains Mediator and Head, even though many reject Him. He also prays against those who oppose Him, so that His people may be saved. He intends to secure God's covenant with His people.

An answer to the mediator's prayer. The next morning, Korah and his followers brought their censers to the entrance of the meeting tent. How did they dare? Didn't they remember what God had done to Nadab and Abihu? In their unbelief, they were blind not only to the Lord's grace but also to His judgments.

Korah had called the whole congregation of Israel together. Once they were all gathered, the glory of the Lord appeared to the entire assembly. The Lord ordered Moses and Aaron to move away from the others, for He intended to destroy the whole assembly. But the two leaders prostrated themselves and prayed: "Some have sinned—especially one man, Korah. The whole nation has not broken with You, for we, the representatives of Israel, are steadfast on behalf of the whole nation. You cannot, then, reject them all."

Evidently all the people had withdrawn to their tents at the sight of the Lord's glory. At the Lord's command, Moses told them all to move away from the tents of Korah, Dathan and Abiram. When the rebels died an unusual death by entering Sheol alive, the people would see that the Lord had appointed Moses as their head, and that Moses had not elevated himself to that office.

Scarcely had he spoken when the earth opened up. The rebels, together with their households and everything that belonged to them, were swallowed alive. All Israel fled from their screams. Moreover, the Lord's fire struck and consumed the 250 men who had wanted to make an incense offering on their own. Thus, for Israel's good, the Lord upheld Moses as head of the nation, but those rebels were forever removed from fellowship with that head and with the nation.

God also retains Jesus Christ as our Head, with whom we will be joined eternally in a glorious union. Breaking with Him means destruction and death. How many will be destroyed because they have chosen to break with Him?

A reminder. At the Lord's command, Aaron's son Eleazar scattered the fire and incense from those 250 censers far and wide. But the censers themselves had been brought before the Lord; they were holy, even though the men who had carried them had been singled out for divine punishment. The censers were now to be made into hammered plates as a covering for the altar of burnt offering.

The bronze plates would be a constant reminder to Israel that the Lord had kept Moses as head, that no one serving the Lord may take any honor upon himself, and that all God's people flourish only in fellowship with their Head. Let us not desire to create our own place in the Kingdom of God. Instead we should serve gratefully in the position to which God has called us in communion with the Lord Jesus Christ.

50: A Thriving Priesthood

Numbers 16:41—17:13

When murmuring broke out again, Moses sent Aaron among the people with his censer. That was the only means left of dealing with the situation. This time Moses could no longer say that if God would not forgive the people's sin, he as their head should be blotted out of God's book since he shared in their guilt. The people had broken off all communion with him and no longer regarded him as their head. Nor could Moses make any further appeal to God's honor among the heathens, for God had said that it was through the death of that generation that He would fill the earth with His glory. Even less could he argue that God could not destroy the whole nation since there were only a few who had sinned. The fact of the matter was that all the people had rebelled. The intercession of the high priest, symbolized by the incense, was the last resort.

The real intercession was not by Aaron but by the One of whom Aaron was but a shadow. Only by His sacrifice and His intercession would He gather His people. Even if His people want to break with Him, their communion with Him is assured. The significance of the work of the future High Priest had to be revealed to Israel.

The blossoming of Aaron's rod did not only mark Aaron as the man God had chosen but also foretold that the office of high priest, if executed according to God's instructions, would thrive and bear fruit. He who has been ordained of God the Father is also anointed with the Holy Spirit.

Twelve rods were brought into the tabernacle, with Aaron's rod representing the tribe of Levi. At this point, Manasseh and Ephraim must have been considered as one tribe, i.e. Joseph.

Main thought: *The One ordained of God is also anointed with the Holy Spirit.*

354

Spiritual blindness. The judgment on Korah, Dathan, Abiram, and the 250 men who brought incense into God's presence on their own authority terrified the people, but it did not turn them to God again. Their hearts didn't even tremble before the majesty of God. They simply blamed Moses and Aaron for the destruction, as if Moses and Aaron exercised a kind of magical power.

The men who were slain were leaders among the people. The very next morning, the people rose up against Moses and Aaron, accusing them of killing the Lord's people and sinning against the Lord.

How could they be so blind? But if we do not see the grace of the Lord and thus do not believe in Him, we cannot see His majesty in His judgments either. We always have other explanations ready.

Incense for atonement. When the people who joined in opposition to Moses and Aaron came to the meeting tent, the cloud hovered over it in a peculiar way, just as on the day when the tabernacle was first set up. The glory of the Lord shone again through the cloud.

The Lord told Moses and Aaron to move away from the people because the Lord was going to consume them. Instantly the punishment descended. Man for man, the people suddenly began to fall down dead.

In horror Moses and Aaron fell on their faces, but Moses understood that there was no basis left for him to plead for the people. The only thing to turn to now was the high priest's office, which the Lord Himself had instituted. He Himself desired the intercession of the high priest with the rising incense, promising that such prayer had power.

Our human prayers have no power in themselves, for no one can intercede with God on behalf of another person. Christ's prayer, though, would have all power because He would give Himself for the people. His work as High Priest was symbolized by Aaron's work, which had its own power because of what Christ had done.

Therefore Moses sent Aaron among the people with his censer containing incense and fire from the altar. Wherever he went, the plague was halted. There he stood between the dead and the living, making a gulf between the people and the judgment. The plague came to an end, although some 14,700 people had died.

A thriving office of high priest. The people had already received a sign that the Lord had placed Aaron in the office of high priest. To strengthen the people's belief that Aaron was called by God, the Lord provided another sign.

Moses was to take the rod of the head of each tribe and write the tribe's name on it. He was to write Aaron's name on the rod belonging to the tribe of Levi. The tribe of Levi was not chosen because of Levi's merits. In His sovereign good pleasure, God had given this tribe the privilege of serving in the sanctuary, but it continued in that service because of the calling of Aaron, whom God had chosen.

A man's rod was a sign of his power, and the rod of the head of a tribe was a sign of his authority. But a rod is just a branch that has been cut off. Because it is dead, it cannot sprout anymore.

All power and authority among men has been cut off from communion with God and has become a withered branch. By His gracious fellowship, however, God can bring to life what has died and make it sprout; He can make authority a blessing. No one *deserves* to be a priest and thus a blessing to others. Only someone called by God will receive the Spirit of communion from God and will thereby be made a blessing.

Accordingly, God promised that the rod of His chosen one would sprout. Moses was to lay the twelve rods in the sanctuary. The next day he brought them out. Lo and behold, Aaron's rod had blossomed and even bore almonds! A miracle! Dead wood had been stirred to life. In a single night it had borne fruit.

Human life that had died spiritually and could no longer serve the Lord was stirred to life in the Lord Jesus, and He again stirs new life in those who belong to Him. But He does this in those who acknowledge Him as the High Priest chosen by God. He is an everlasting blessing to the people. All who do not acknowledge Him will perish. Thus Israel had to acknowledge Aaron as the high priest called by God, for Aaron was a type of the Christ.

Humbling themselves. The Israelites finally acknowledged the sign. In that rod's renewal of life, the people saw something of the glory of the Lord. Very much afraid, they said to Moses: "Behold, we perish, we are undone, we are all undone."

Whether this was an expression of genuine humility is not clear. In any case, the people bowed before God, which is always the first step in faith.

At the Lord's command, Moses laid the rod which had blossomed in the sanctuary before the ark, to be a witness to the people. Those who acknowledged the sovereign election of God would live, but those who rejected the chosen one would die.

51: The Living God

Numbers 20:1-13

Moses' sin at Meribah was not his striking the rock: he became unfaithful to his calling as mediator. Up to that point, he had always been able to pass on the complaint to the Lord whenever the people murmured. The people were not in the right relation to God, but they would come to Moses, and Moses would pass the problem on. To that extent he was a true mediator, for he did not take the Lord's place but showed that there is indeed a living God.

The Lord could not become a mere symbol, an idol in a niche, while Moses and his rod took over. Yet, because Moses was deeply discouraged at Meribah, he took the complaint personally. As if he had to do it all himself, he asked: "Shall we bring forth water for you out of this rock?" The Lord was eclipsed by Moses and Aaron. Now even Moses and Aaron did not see the Lord as the living God, the God of all grace, the God who supports His people in their plight in the wilderness.

For this reason, the Lord reproached them: "You did not believe in Me and sanctify Me in the eyes of the children of Israel." Because Moses and Aaron exceeded their authority and acted as God before the people, they were to be removed from their positions between God and the people. That's how jealous God is of His honor and His covenant relationship with His people. No matter how much the people may have forfeited their claim by sin, they remain *His* people.

Main thought: *The Lord sanctifies Himself as the God of His people.*

The name of the Lord profaned by the people. The period of

358

wandering through the wilderness was finally coming to an end. In the first month of the fortieth year, the people were in the Wilderness of Zin, and they camped at Kadesh. Miriam, the prophetess, died and was buried there. She was not permitted to enter Canaan either. Earlier she had broken away from Moses and sought what she did not deserve. Only those who are obedient can serve God.

At Kadesh the people all gathered together. No bands of men went out to find water and pasture for the herds. Everything had to be prepared for the final journey. The time had finally come. On to Canaan!

Because there were so many people packed into a limited space, water became a problem. Once more, after 40 years, the people quarreled with Moses. Their thirst threatened them with death, and the herds were dying off, but what could Moses do? Still, they did not cry out to the Lord.

When we go to men with our complaints, we are going to the wrong place for help. If we complain to men, our complaints always come back to us. Our suffering becomes more intense, and we are even more inclined to revolt.

The people complained to Moses and rebelled against him. They even said that they would rather have died with the previous generation in the wilderness than waste away at Kadesh without water. They emphasized the drawbacks of the place: no grain, not a fig, no vines, no pomegranates, and, of course, no water to drink. We do the same thing in our rebellious complaining.

By complaining to Moses, the people were profaning the name of the Lord; they were acting as though Moses was the God of the people—and not the Lord. The Lord did not even exist as far as they were concerned. The real and vital covenant relationship, in which they were the Lord's and the Lord was their God, had no meaning for them. To them the Lord was not the living God; He was more like a dead idol. Moses was everything for them. The only way to meet the Lord and live in communion with Him is by faith.

The name of the Lord profaned by Moses and Aaron. Moses had always been able to divert these charges from himself and pass on the people's complaint to the Lord. He had always been a true

mediator, not standing in the Lord's way. He had always known
how to handle the complaints, bearing in mind that they were not
his concern but the Lord's. But now he could take it no longer.
He became bitter.

With Aaron, he turned to the meeting tent. Together they fell
on their faces, and the glory of the Lord appeared to them again.
The Lord told Moses to speak to the rock before the assembled
people, and it would then give water. He was to call upon the name
of the Lord by the rock, appealing to God's mercy in His covenant.
In that way the Lord would be revealed. The rod, the sign that
God was with him, was to be in his hand while he made this appeal.

But Moses was discouraged and embittered. He still had the
feeling that he had to help the people personally. He and Aaron
did not look on the Lord as the God to whom alone this people
belonged. Standing in front of the rock, Moses shouted to the
people: "Hear now, you rebels; shall we bring forth water for you
out of this rock?" In his utter exasperation, he did not have proper
regard for the Lord's command to call on the name of the Lord.
Instead he struck the rock twice with his rod, as though his strength
and the rod were supposed to save the day.

The Lord's response to Moses and Aaron. To the shame of
Moses and Aaron, water immediately came out of the rock, and
the people were able to drink. But the Lord told the two leaders
that they would not bring Israel into Canaan, for they had stood in
the Lord's way. They had not directed the people to the Lord but
had behaved as though they themselves had to handle the matter
for the people, as though they could perform miracles with that
rod. This hid the Lord from Israel's eyes.

There is nothing the Lord desires so much as to be revealed to
His people. Israel was actually His people, for He belonged to
them and they to Him. He alone was to be honored by that people
as the living God. No one is allowed to eclipse His name, which
was why Moses and Aaron were punished so severely.

Moses and Aaron had failed as mediators. There is only one
Mediator who has never failed, who has never caused the glory of
the Lord to be obscured. When He was on earth, He was able to
say: "I have manifested Your name to the men You gave Me out of

the world" (John 17:6). Through Him we see the glory of the father.

Christ also atoned for the sin of Moses in his mediatorial work. The Lord turned the dishonor Moses had done His name into honor again. The Lord was also sanctified in Moses. As a result of this judgment upon Moses, the people saw even more clearly what the Lord wanted to be to the people of His covenant.

Still, Moses received grace. Through Christ's atonement, all that was sinful in Moses' service has been erased; all that remained was that in which he had been faithful. Hence the final conclusion drawn about him in Scripture is that he was faithful in all God's house.

But this grace is not only for Moses. In the life of all believers, everything that was sinful will be wiped away. Only their service to the Lord will abide forever.

The Lord's response to the people. The people must have been surprised that water flowed from the rock despite their rebellion. No doubt they also felt ashamed. Where did that water come from? If we have a proper understanding of such matters, we will say that it came from the grace and mercy (steadfast love) of God. The Christ would one day atone for the sin of the people. Therefore there was mercy and forgiveness again and again.

When the people looked at that rock from which the water flowed so abundantly, the believers among them must have thought of the Redeemer, the Angel of the covenant, from whom God's goodness streamed to them time and again. Thus that rock, too, must have symbolized the Christ. By this searching of their hearts, the Lord was sanctified in them. Once more the Lord alone was great among them.

However, the judgment on Moses and Aaron was also a judgment on the people. How heavily they were all punished! By their rebellion, they had driven Moses and Aaron to the point where they forgot the Lord. The people had trapped their leaders, which has happened so often in history. Many of them probably came to their senses through this judgment. In their confession of guilt, the Lord was glorified among them, for the Lord is truly great for us when we humble ourselves before Him because of our sins.

52: Humiliation

Numbers 20:14—21:9

Edom refused Israel passage through its territory. Edom regarded itself as self-sufficient, but it was also influenced by its hatred of Jacob as heir to the promise. Therefore the Lord commanded the Israelites to go around Edom's territory rather than force their way through it. This was humiliating for Israel.

We should bear in mind that on the journey through Edom, the Angel of the Lord went ahead of the Israelites. He was considerate of Edom and humbled Himself. This Angel was the Christ, who came not to be served but to serve. He also washed the disciples' feet and ordered them to wash each other's feet. Here is the breach in the self-sufficiency of men and nations. The people of God must learn to humble themselves.

Even before the messengers had returned, Israel began its journey toward Mount Hor. There Aaron died. In the sin at Meribah, Aaron had carried out his high priestly duties in a way that seemed to proclaim his self-sufficiency. Moses and Aaron had not passed along the people's complaint to the Lord. When Aaron was stripped of his garments, it was clear that the priesthood had been tarnished. But when Eleazar was clothed in those same garments, Israel was to understand that the priesthood was based solidly on God's grace.

In the battle with the king of Arad, the people vowed to annihilate the cities of those Canaanites completely. They certainly could have used the spoils from those cities during their journey through the wilderness! Yet, those cities had been devoted entirely to the Lord. Therefore the spoils from Arad were also devoted to the Lord: they were put under the ban.

The bronze serpent on the pole is a sign of corruption overcome. Thus it symbolizes the Christ. The One who was made sin for us was lifted up on the cross, where the sin upon Him was rejected and overcome.

That the Israelites asked for Moses' intercession when they were bitten by the snakes showed that there was a different spirit within them than they had manifested earlier. We now see them looking to the Lord in faith, out of the depths of humiliation. This they learned to do from having to look to the bronze serpent.

Main thought: *In their humiliation, the people learn to look to the Lord.*

Humbled in the sight of Edom. At Kadesh in the Wilderness of Zin, the people prepared for the journey to Canaan. They were camped south of Canaan, but they did not want to enter the land from the south. Because of the steep hills, the land there would be most difficult to conquer. Moses wanted to circle around the land to the east, but that would mean passing through the territory of Edom.

The Edomites were descendants of Esau and in that sense were brothers to the descendants of Israel (Jacob). Esau and Edom had broken away from the promise of God's covenant; the Edomites regarded themselves as self-sufficient and felt no need of the Lord. But in the depths of their hearts, they hated the Israelites because of the blessing of the promise.

When Moses sent messengers to ask permission to pass through Edom, with the repeated promise that Israel would not take anything or do any damage, the Edomites refused because of their self-sufficiency and their hatred of this brother nation. The Edomites even sent out their armies to defend their borders against Israel.

How irritating this must have been for Israel! Were they now going to force their way through? No, for the Lord commanded them to circle around Edom by the long and difficult road to the south, through the wilderness.

How this humiliated Israel in the sight of Edom! But the humiliation was not Israel's alone. Ahead of Israel, in the sign of the cloud, went the Angel of the Lord, that is, the Christ. *He,* too, journeyed around Edom, humbling Himself before Edom. In fact, He would come later not to rule or remove by force whatever stood in His way but to serve. He was able to surrender His own rights so that God's rights could prevail. That's just what happened on this occasion. One day God would judge Edom, but the Christ, who would come to reveal the love of God that seeks out the lost, journeyed around Edom.

How He humbled Himself on earth! He alone was able to give up His rights for God's sake. He did that for our sake as well, to atone for our sinful pursuit of our own interest. By His Spirit, He wishes to instil in us the desire to humble ourselves for God's sake. That's what He did in Israel, for the people followed Him willingly on their circuitous route around Edom.

Priest by grace. Even before the messengers had returned from Edom, that is, before the people knew they would have to take the long, roundabout route, they made a trip to Mount Hor. There God revealed that Aaron's time had come. God ordered Moses to climb up the mountain with Aaron and Aaron's son Eleazar. There he was to strip Aaron of his high priestly garments and put them on Eleazar. Then Aaron would die.

Up the mountain they went, the three of them. It was a difficult trip, especially for Aaron. Up on the mountain he was stripped of his high priestly garments, for by his misuse of the priesthood at Meribah he had forfeited his claim to them. At Meribah he had not acted as the servant of God; he had wanted to be something in his own right instead. This self-sufficient priesthood was now condemned. He was not to be Israel's high priest when the people entered Canaan.

In Aaron's punishment, the whole people was being condemned and humbled. The rebelliousness of the people had led to the sin of Moses and Aaron. Now the people were being punished through the death of this leader. But the office of high priest would be perpetuated in the person of Eleazar. This would make it clear to the people that it was by pure grace that the priestly office remained among them.

For Aaron it was definitely a humiliation. Yet, even in his death he could return his priestly office to the hands of the Christ, from whom he had received it. The Christ would atone for his sin too. One day Aaron, along with all believers, would be God's priest forever in the name of the Christ.

The land of Arad devoted to God's judgment. On the way to Mount Hor, the Israelites were attacked by the king of Arad, who lived in the south of Canaan (the Negeb). This king even captured some of the Israelites.

The people of Arad were Canaanites and therefore had to be destroyed—and not spared, as Edom was. The Israelites vowed that if the Lord would be with them in the battle, they would completely destroy the cities of Arad and all that was in them. They would dedicate them to the Lord and to His judgment.* The Lord was indeed on their side, and the southernmost cities were taken and given to Him as promised. The remainder of the land of Arad was destroyed only later, after the Israelites had occupied Canaan.

The Israelites could have made good use of the spoils of Arad on their journey through the wilderness. But they had promised to devote them all to the Lord, and that's just what they did. Now they showed a different spirit than they had manifested earlier. All they wanted was to be instruments in the Lord's hand. This setting apart of the cities of Arad for destruction was a prophecy about the wiping out of all the Canaanites. It was also a prophecy pointing ahead to the day when all God's enemies will perish. Then the Christ will be victorious, and His people will judge the world.

Looking to the bronze serpent. After the battle against the king of Arad, Israel proceeded under the guidance of the Angel of the Lord toward the south, around the land of Edom. Now they were treading the path of humility willingly. On the way, the Lord would surely provide them with everything they needed.

But on this journey, too, they didn't have enough water. At once the people's faith became weak again, and they rose up against Moses. They gave no more thought to God's mercies, not even to the manna.

Again the Lord confronted them in His anger. He sent poisonous snakes among the people, and many died. Then they confessed that they had sinned against the Lord and against Moses, and asked Moses to pray for them. They certainly demonstrated a different spirit than they had before. There they lay, humiliated in their misery and guilt, while proud Edom triumphed on its heights. Yet that miserable people of Israel was much greater than self-assured Edom, for God would reveal Himself to Israel in His grace. Our lives are rich only because of what we see of God's grace and receive of it.

---

*They would "put them under the ban." Here again we find this use of *ban* in the Old Testament, as we noted earlier (p. 272).—TRANS.

At the Lord's command, Moses made a bronze serpent and lifted it up on a pole. Anyone who was bitten by a snake would be healed if he looked to this bronze serpent. Of course there was no healing power in the bronze serpent itself; it was only a sign that the decay of sin was conquered by God's grace.

The display of this bronze serpent was a prophecy of the display of the Christ as the One accursed for our sake on the cross. Whoever looks to Him in faith will be saved.

The people of faith are still humiliated in the world, but in their midst is the revelation of God's grace in the cross of the Christ. God's people are not self-sufficient. Yet they are rich in this grace of God.

53: Blessed by the Lord

Numbers 21:10—24:25

After the Israelites journeyed around Edom, they conquered the land of Sihon, king of the Amorites, and of Og, king of Bashan. Evidently the Amorites had pushed eastward out of Canaan, across the Jordan, and had conquered the northern portion of the territory of the Moabites. Originally this area of Transjordan, which was once in the hands of the Moabites, did not belong to the land God had promised Israel. But now that the Amorites had taken possession of it, it became part of Israel's heritage.

As long as Israel journeyed along Moab's eastern border, Moab treated Israel kindly. Perhaps the Moabites were hoping at the time that Israel would lose the battle with Sihon. But after Israel conquered Sihon and Og, the Moabites grew fearful at the prospect of having Israel as a neighbor, although Israel did not plan to attack Moab.

Balaam apparently came from a line of fortune-tellers and magicians, but he had heard of God's mighty deeds on Israel's behalf. Rumors about the Israelites had spread as far as Mesopotamia. Balaam's words also remind us of prophecies from the time of the patriarchs. Had those words come down to Balaam, or did the Spirit of the Lord suggest them to him, without Balaam knowing that they had been spoken in prophecy in former days?

In any case, Balaam had some knowledge of the living God. This knowledge must not be thought of as mere rumors about God's deeds for Israel's sake; it was rooted in a more general knowledge of God that had been preserved from former times.

It is curious that the Angel of the Lord appeared to Balaam and was not unknown to him. Evidently the Angel of the covenant did not appear first to Abraham; this manifestation was already known to the peoples before Abraham's time. Thus Elihu could also speak of this Angel (Job 33:23). Hence we must bear in mind that the Lord had revealed Himself earlier to Balaam, perhaps through the Angel of the covenant.

We see Balaam hesitating between two opinions. On the one hand he practices fortune-telling and witchcraft, but on the other hand he receives revelations from the Lord. Apparently the Lord had not yet cut Himself off entirely from the nations. Here we have the last signs of the struggle between the revelation of God's grace in the covenant and the darkness of heathendom. Nor should we forget that God granted this revelation to Balaam because He was going to bless Israel.

Balaam, however, did not submit to the revelation of God. On the contrary, he tried to manipulate even this revelation, falling into the usual trap of those who practice magic. The real intent of magic is to gain mastery over the divine powers and thereby over the deity, in order to harness the deity for one's own purposes. Like Balak, Balaam still thought he had both blessing and curse in his own hands. But on his way to meet Balak, the appearance of the Angel of the Lord taught him that he was subject to the Word of the Lord and could only say what God told him to say.

Three times Balaam blessed Israel. Numbers 23:23 is probably to be read: "For there is no witchcraft in Jacob or fortune-telling in Israel. At the proper time it is said to Jacob and to Israel what God does." Balaam, then, was prophesying about the revelation of God in Israel, in contrast to the fortune-telling and magic and witchcraft found among the heathens.

When Balaam prophesied the fourth time, he spoke of "what this people [Israel] will do to your people in the latter days." In the light of the prophetic perspective, we must understand the phrase *the latter days* as referring to both the first and second coming of Christ. Balaam said: "I see him, but not now; I behold him, but not nigh" (Num. 24:17). Here he was prophesying about the latter days, when a star would come forth out of Jacob.

Main thought: *The Lord reveals that Israel is the one blessed forever.*

Plotting a curse. After the Israelites had journeyed around Edom, they proceeded along the eastern border of Moab. The Moabites, too, were related to Israel, through Lot (Gen. 19:30-7). Israel had not been promised possession of this land. Therefore the Israelites did not invade the territory of the Moabites.

The northernmost part of the kingdom of Moab, however, had been conquered by a Canaanite, Sihon, the king of the Amorites. The Amorites did attack the Israelites, but God delivered mighty Sihon into their hands. The Israelites also conquered the territory to the north, the land of Og, king of Bashan. Thus, with God's help, a large area in Transjordan came into their possession. This, too, the Lord promised them as an inheritance.

It must have been an amazing feeling for the Israelites to be walking on land that would be theirs, even though they were not yet in Canaan itself. The Lord literally delivered their enemies into their hands. The power of even the strongest of them was broken.

At first Moab had allowed Israel to pass quietly along its borders. But now Israel camped just to the north of Moab's territory, right by the Jordan. Because of those amazing victories over Sihon and Og, Balak, the king of Moab, began to fear Israel. There was a power in Israel that could not be conquered by force of arms. Balak consulted with the elders of the Midianites, who lived in his vicinity: "Israel will now lick up everything around us, as the ox licks up the grass of the field."

They discussed the prospect of bringing in another power that could break the power in Israel. Their thoughts turned to Balaam, a prophet and fortune-teller in Mesopotamia. In this man there was a strange combination of the fortune-telling to be found in heathen circles and the revelation of the living God. Apparently the Lord revealed Himself to Balaam and allowed him to go on with his fortune-telling at the same time.

The Lord had some surprising plans for Balaam. Through him, the Lord's blessing on Israel was to be revealed to all peoples. But this prophet hoped he could use the revelation of the Lord to his own advantage, just as he used his magic and fortune-telling. The Lord had other plans: the roles would be reversed. The Lord would use Balaam instead.

The Word of the Lord is not for us to use to advance our own interests. Instead it is there to possess us. Balaam could not and would not surrender to the Word of the Lord. He continued to cling to his fortune-telling, with which he would have to perish.

This was the man they decided to call in. Israel was blessed by the Lord, which was Israel's strength. Balaam, they thought, had power over blessing and curse; his curse could break the power of the blessing.

When the messengers from Balak came to Balaam with magnificent gifts, he made them wait, telling them that he would ask the Lord during the night. That's where Balaam began to go wrong. Didn't he know that he was being petitioned by the enemies of the Lord's people, who were also the Lord's enemies? He was not allowed to be of service to them. But Balaam was not out to serve the Lord. He served only himself.

Still, he did not dare go along with their plan right away. He sensed that he would be clashing with the Lord's people, about whom he had heard a great deal. Could it be that this people had sinned against the Lord? Could he somehow compel the Lord to curse them? How far he was from being prompted by love for the Lord and His covenant and covenant people! He sacrificed everything else to further his own ends. He speculated on the possible unfaithfulness of the covenant people—as though the Lord did not remain faithful to His people forever!

In the night, God came to Balaam and asked who these men spending the night with him were. With this question God was trying to show Balaam their intent in relation to the favor He was showing Israel, so that Balaam would realize his own unrighteousness. In answer to Balaam's response, God said that he was not to go with the messengers to curse Israel, for Israel was blessed.

But Balak would not give up so easily. A second and larger group of even more powerful delegates came to Balaam. He was promised still greater rewards. Balak assumed that Balaam's refusal was only a way of bargaining for more. Balaam denied this explicitly, saying that he could not go against the Lord's will even if Balak were to give him a house full of silver and gold. Still, he had the messengers stay overnight again. He would ask what the Lord wanted—as if the Lord had not already answered once and for all! Within Balaam lived the devilish hope that a breach could be found in the wall of God's faithfulness surrounding Israel.

That night God told Balaam to go with the messengers, but he would only be allowed to say what God told him to say. The Lord had not changed toward Israel. In the initial refusal, Balaam and Moab had been spared. Now the glory of the Lord's faithfulness toward His people was going to be revealed to His enemies. In contrast with their persistent godlessness, God's faithfulness would appear all the more glorious.

All the plotting of God's enemies promotes the greater honor of His grace and faithfulness. (Think of Psalm 2.) Israel was in fact hated and persecuted because she had the promise of the

Redeemer and therefore was safe.

Bound by God's will. Because of the Lord's Words during the night, Balaam had been tied down to a certain extent. He had understood that Israel was blessed, and that he would not be able to accomplish anything against the Word of grace that rested upon Israel. Yet, while he traveled on, the desire for honor and reward again raised in him the hope that for one reason or another he would be able to curse Israel.

Because of this evil hope, the Lord's anger was kindled against him. The Lord sent His Angel to meet Balaam. This was the Angel of the Lord, the Angel who had appeared so often to Balaam, the Angel who led Israel in the wilderness. This Angel was the Lord Himself, our Lord Jesus Christ. He met Balaam to tell him that this people, for whom He led the way and in whose midst He lived, was blessed.

When the Angel of the Lord appeared before Balaam on the road, Balaam didn't see Him. Because of his sin of greed, his eyes had been blinded. Although the Lord no longer appears to us today as He did to Balaam, our sin makes us blind to the glory of the grace of the Lord which has appeared to us in Jesus Christ.

The donkey on which Balaam was riding saw the Angel of the Lord and turned off the road. Because of us, the whole creation is alienated from God, but God is going to reveal Himself again to the entire creation for Christ's sake. And that's why God could show His glory here to a donkey.

Three times the Angel of the Lord appeared, but Balaam did not see Him. Three times Balaam beat his donkey, which finally spoke up and reproached him for the ill treatment. That his donkey spoke at all was a miracle, but it is also a sign that the whole lower creation is against those who misuse it. God has appointed us kings over the creation, to use it in His service, but we misuse the creation in the service of our own passions. The Lord Jesus Christ said that the stones would willingly shout for joy to His honor, but the stones could also speak of our shame.

As a result of his donkey speaking, Balaam was ashamed of the passion and greed that had aroused him. This shame was the means by which God opened his eyes to the Angel of the Lord.

God reproached Balaam for not having seen Him, for being blinded by passion. Hence the Angel of the Lord confronted him as an enemy and would have killed him if his donkey had not shied away. It was merciful of the Angel of the covenant to reveal Himself as an enemy to Balaam, so that Balaam could bow before Him with his whole heart. It is likewise merciful of the Lord Jesus Christ to come and meet us when we are on the wrong track.

Balaam was terrified. He said he was willing to go back, but in the depths of his heart he did not submit to the Word of the Lord. He did not stand on Israel's side but remained his own man. The Angel of the Lord did not demand that he return; He demanded only that Balaam say what he was told to say. Thus Balaam would not pronounce a curse on Israel—only a blessing. If only Balaam would learn to pronounce that blessing with his whole heart!

Blessed three times. Balak received Balaam with great honor. He went to the borders of his land to meet him and reproached him for having hesitated so long. Did Balaam fear that the king wasn't able to give him whatever he desired? Remembering the lesson he had been taught on the way, Balaam warned the king that he would only be able to say what the Lord told him to say.

Balak offered a sacrifice for the success of the venture. This was probably a sacrifice to the Lord, whom Balaam professed to serve. What an abomination! In conjunction with the sacrifice, Balak had a sacrificial meal served.

The following morning, Balak brought Balaam to the heights of Baal. From that point, one could look out over a fourth of the Israelite camp. Balaam asked Balak to sacrifice seven bulls and seven rams on seven altars as a burnt offering to the Lord. Then Balaam withdrew to find out from the omens what the Lord's will was. Thus he was still resorting to heathen ways. But the Lord met him and spoke to him. Balaam called His attention to the sacrifices, as a heathen would do in speaking to his gods. But those sacrifices would hardly please the Lord! The Lord then put in Balaam's mouth the words he was to speak.

Balaam prophesied: "I have been summoned to curse Israel, but how can I curse the one whom the Lord has not cursed? As prophet I see that people before me. They will live alone among all the nations. While all the nations perish, this people shall be preserved. Who will be able to count this people? Who will be able to count even this fourth part that I now see? And who, in the future, will be able to count all who by faith will belong to the people of the Lord? It is a people that the Lord makes righteous before Him in the covenant. I would wish to belong to this people on my death."

Balak raged at Balaam because he had blessed the people of Israel. Still, he hoped that there might yet be a chance to draw down a curse upon them. Therefore he took Balaam to another place from where he could look out over the people, namely, the heights of Pisgah. After the same preparations had been made, the Lord met Balaam again and put in his mouth the words he was to speak.

Balaam prophesied the second time: "The Lord is no man that He should change his mind and curse what He has once blessed. In His covenant, He is faithful to His promise. He has no reason to curse Israel, for although the people are sinful, He forgives their sins and heals the miseries into which they have fallen as a result of those sins. The Lord Himself dwells in their midst. Shouts of exultation ring out at the name of God their King. He brought them up out of Egypt, and they are invincible. There is no magic or fortune-telling among them, for the Lord lives in communion with them, revealing Himself to them and speaking to them."

Beside himself with rage, Balak forbade Balaam to say any more. Yet he wanted to try it once more, for the power of that people could only be broken by a curse. He now brought Balaam closer to them, so that he could distinguish the order of the tribes in the encampment. The same preparations were made again, but this time Balaam did not withdraw as before to look for omens. He knew that the Lord would reveal to him what he had to say; he knew that he was in the power of the Lord. The Spirit of the Lord even came upon him, so that he could see Israel's future with ecstatic eyes.

For the third time Balaam broke out in prophecy: "In the spirit I see Israel's destiny and future. How fair are your dwellings, O Israel! How richly blessed by the Lord! You are unconquerable. You will overcome all your enemies. You are the blessing of the earth. Blessed will be everyone who blesses you, and cursed everyone who curses you."

In desperation Balak sent Balaam away. He provoked him by saying that he would have made him rich if he had cursed Israel. The Lord, whom Balaam professed to obey, had kept the prophet from this honor. In response Balaam pointed out that he had warned the king in advance. Israel had now been blessed three times by the Lord, and it had been publicly delared to the heathen nations what God in His grace desired for His people. In the Christ, His people is indestructible. This is the honor of the grace of the Lord.

The latter days. Before he departed, Balaam said to Balak that he still wanted to tell him what God would do in the latter days. In a state of ecstasy again, Balaam saw things that others could not see. Now he saw far into the future.

He prophesied first about Israel's relation to Moab and Edom, the two countries that acted with hostility toward Israel: "Not in the near future but in the distant future I see a star, a scepter rising out of Israel, that is, a king who will destroy Moab and Edom." This was how Balaam prophesied about David—and especially David's great Son, the Messiah, the One who would conquer all the enemies of God's people, the One who would be an eternal King for His people.

After that he spoke of the Amalekites, the first nation that had attacked Israel on its journey through the wilderness. This nation would be destroyed; it would be made an example to all who hate God's people.

He also spoke of the Kenites, the descendants of Moses' brother-in-law Hobab. They had joined the Israelites and secured for themselves a safe dwelling place in the shadow of God's covenant. Thus they would not be destroyed until a world empire subjected the whole world.

At the very end he spoke about the final judgment, by which even the world empires would perish. Who could survive when God came in judgment? Only God's people would live forever, and everyone who belonged to that people.

After saying all this, Balaam went his way. Because of the Lord's blessing, the people of the Lord were forever safe.

54: The Sovereignty of God's Justice

Numbers 25-36

At Shittim the Lord's justice prevailed as a result of the action taken by Phinehas, but the people apparently hesitated to submit to this justice, which demanded the death of sinners. Only the step taken by Phinehas brought the people to complete submission. We realize this when we compare the announcement that 24,000 men fell as a result of the plague with what Paul says about this matter, namely, that 23,000 died (I Cor. 10:8). Those 23,000 died as a result of the plague, while another 1,000 had to be hanged. The people hesitated to carry out the required execution, and the plague continued. The action of Phinehas finally made the people submissive.

God's justice was victorious also in the extermination of the Midianites and the death of Balaam. Evidently Balaam had sought protection from the Midianites. It's possible that when he fell into the hands of the Israelites, he told them how he had blessed them, in hopes of escaping death. It must have made an impression on the Israelites that they themselves had to carry out the judgment on the Midianites, the nation with which they had previously sought a union.

The justice of the Lord would continue to hold sway over Israel in Canaan. The inheritance would be distributed according to lot, that is, as God directed. Moreover, God would give instructions about rights of succession, so that each tribe would keep its inherited possession. Finally, the blood shed in the land of the inheritance would have to be avenged. In the case of unintentional manslaughter, the cities of refuge would provide an escape, although the guilt would not be lifted for those seeking refuge there. This unintentional manslaughter, too, is one of the miseries resulting from sin in general. Only the death of the high priest would provide complete deliverance from the guilt. As a symbol of the Christ, the high priest would take the guilt with him into his grave.

All these things were to impress it upon the people of Israel that they lived under the sovereignty of divine justice. This justice would not only be restored by the death of the Christ: as a result of His death, it would come to full, gracious dominion. Christ's death does not release us from the claims made by this justice; this justice controls us, guarantees our place among the saints, and makes our life secure.

Main thought: *The people of the covenant live under the sovereignty of the Lord's justice.*

The victory of the Lord's justice in Israel. The attempt to curse Israel had failed. Nevertheless, the Moabites and the Midianites and even Balaam remained Israel's enemies. After Balaam had blessed Israel three times, he found protection among the Midianites. Now that the curse of God could not touch Israel, he advised the Midianites to tempt the people. The Midianite and Moabite women were to invite the Israelites to their sacrificial meals. The people of Israel would certainly succumb to this temptation, and thereby they would break their covenant with the Lord.

Balaam's advice was followed. The prophet appears to have had a good grasp of the people's weakness, for they fell right into the trap set for them. This happened while they were camped at Shittim, just to the east of the Jordan River, ready to enter Canaan as soon as the Lord gave the word. How little the favor of the Lord meant to the people!

The anger of the Lord was kindled, and hundreds died. The Lord ordered Moses to have the chiefs and judges killed. All who were guilty of this sin, which was a violation of the Lord's rights over all of life and over the service of His people, were to be hanged. This infringement of His rights had to be atoned for by death and a curse on the sinners.

Evidently the people hesitated to carry out the Lord's command. They did not submit to God's justice; His honor was not the most important thing for them. They stood weeping in front of the door of the meeting tent. Would the people put themselves and their personal ties before the rights of God?

The matter suddenly came to a head. One of the Israelites

brought a Midianite woman into the camp to commit sin with her. This was a dramatic illustration of how the sin was now penetrating the Israelites camp: the sin would be committed while the people stood weeping before the meeting tent, unwilling to avenge the Lord's rights by killing the sinners.

Then the Spirit of the Lord entered Phinehas, son of the high priest Eleazar. Rising and leaving the congregation, he killed the Israelite man and the Midianite woman with his spear. This bold deed finally got through to the people, who then submitted to the rights of the Lord by slaying the ones who had sinned. Thus the plague, which had killed thousands of Israelites as a punishment for sin, was halted at last.

Since Phinehas had stood up for the Lord's rights and had put those rights above everything else, the Lord promised that the office of high priest would be kept in his line. Because of what Phinehas did, the people were converted to recognizing the Lord's justice and honoring it. In this regard Phinehas was a forerunner of the Lord Jesus Christ, who loved divine justice so much that He gave His own life to reconcile it.

The plague was halted after one Israelite was killed by Phinehas and others guilty of the same sin were hanged. But this does not mean that the death of any man could appease God's wrath on all of Israel. In this death of the guilty, God was looking ahead to the death of the Christ, through whom sin would be atoned for and divine justice restored. Do we ourselves see that the first thing in the world and in our own lives is the victorious rule of the Lord's justice?

Israel's inheritance. Only when God's justice had again won the victory in Israel could the Lord arrange for Israel to take possession of the land. He commanded Moses to have a census taken according to the tribes and families. The people were in the presence of the Lord, and it was a new generation. All those who had sinned at the border of Canaan the first time had died in the wilderness. Only Joshua and Caleb would cross the Jordan with the others. This new generation would receive the promised land.

Once Canaan was conquered, the land would have to be distributed by lot among the various tribes. The designation of each

tribe's inheritance would not be by any man but by the Lord
Himself: the tribes would draw lots. Each tribe could then say that
it had been granted its portion by the Lord. Therefore they would
have to serve Him in their land.

No part of any tribe was to go over to another. If a man died
without sons, his daughters would inherit his possessions, but they
were not allowed to marry outside their own tribe.

The tribe of Levi was appointed for the special service of the
Lord in the sanctuary. Each tribe was to give a few cities and the
pasture lands around them to the Levites. Thus the Levites would
live scattered among all the tribes. Since the tribe of priests would
be in regular contact with all the people, the tribes would be more
likely to remember that all of life had to be consecrated to the Lord.

Because of his sin, Moses was not permitted to lead the people
into Canaan. On one of the high peaks in the area where Israel was
now camped, he would die. Therefore the Lord ordered him to lay
his hand on Joshua in the presence of the high priest Eleazar and
all the congregation, thereby commissioning Joshua as his successor and investing him with some of his authority. Moses did so. He
himself had asked the Lord to designate a successor, so that the
people would not be like sheep without a shepherd. In making this
request, the mediator Moses was asking for just what God intended
to give His people. God will always appoint a leader for His
people. He has done that for us by giving us the Lord Jesus Christ,
whom He Himself has appointed for us.

The tribes of Reuben and Gad and the half tribe of Manasseh
asked Moses for permission to take possession of the land that had
already been conquered on the eastern side of the Jordan, for they
had many cattle and the land east of the Jordan was excellent for
pasturing the flocks and herds. The Lord told Moses to give these
tribes what they asked for, on the condition that their forces would
help in the conquest of Canaan. This they promised to do.

Thus the Lord made all the arrangements for Israel to take
possession of its inheritance. Israel received this inheritance from
His hand and was to serve Him in it. The Lord's faithfulness
would keep it for Israel and would see to it that each one could
hold on to the place assigned to him. Joshua would bring them
into their inheritance. The Lord Jesus Christ likewise brings the
people of God into the life of His Kingdom. Each of the saints has

his place secured for him by God's faithfulness.

Vengeance upon the Midianites. At the express command of the Lord, Israel made war against the Midianites to pay them back for the crime they had committed when they seduced the Israelites. This vengeance would be a public display of the honor of the Lord's justice. A thousand men from each tribe were sent off to fight. They were accompanied by the ark and by Phinehas, the son of the high priest Eleazar. Phinehas bore silver trumpets in his hand to sound the signal in the battle that would let the Israelites know that the Lord was with them.

The Israelites defeated the Midianites and killed all the males among them, including their kings. Balaam was also killed. They burned all the cities in which the Midianites had lived and took with them the women and children and all the spoils.

When they got back from their expedition and wanted to bring their booty into the camp, Moses and Eleazar went to meet them outside the camp. They were angry that the women and children had been spared. Weren't the women the ones who had tempted Israel? In any case, the people of Midian were to be wiped out. Therefore all the boys and all the married women would have to be killed. Only the girls and the unmarried women they were allowed to take as servants.

Here the Israelites themselves had to execute judgment on the people with whom they had joined in sin. This must have shamed them greatly. Did they themselves deserve a better fate? That Israel was not wiped out was only due to the tender mercy and faithfulness of God; it was only because of the covenant in which He wished to live with His people. Atonement for that people was made through the blood of the Christ, but the Midianites, who were outside the covenant, perished.

The Lord Himself made the arrangements for dividing up the booty. The men who had fought received half of it; the rest of the people received the other half. However, all of them had to dedicate a certain portion of what was theirs to the Lord, by giving it to the Levites. The booty had been received from the Lord's hand; it was also to be consecrated to the Lord. The Lord's rights held sovereign sway, even over the spoils of war.

Blood vengeance. Under the rule of the Lord's justice, life had to be protected. The life created by the Lord, the life with which He wishes to live in communion, is holy to Him. Therefore any blood shed on the sacred inherited possession would have to be avenged. If someone was killed, his nearest blood relative would have to see to it that vengeance was carried out. The Lord's justice had been violated by the act of manslaughter and would therefore have to be restored by the death of the murderer. God can never condone sin.

Yet, no injustice may be committed in the process. It could also happen that someone unintentionally hit another person hard enough to kill him. Should the nearest blood relative take action in such a case? To be sure, blood had been shed on the sacred inherited possession, but God in His covenant is a righteous and gracious God. When someone killed another person unintentionally, he was allowed to flee to one of the designated cities of refuge, which were scattered throughout the land. There he would be safe until the judges in Israel had made a decision in his case. If it was proved that he had indeed acted unintentionally, the one seeking vengeance was not allowed to kill him as long as he remained in the city of refuge. The blood that had been shed cried out from the ground, and therefore he was not allowed to move around freely in the land.

This unintentional manslaughter again showed very clearly how sin had brought the destruction of life in its wake. The blood continued to cry out for revenge, but at the same time there was merciful escape possible in the cities of refuge. The grace of the Lord was then a protective shield.

Only after the high priest died was the one who had killed again permitted to move around freely in the land. It was as though the high priest, who, during his lifetime, always atoned for the sins of the people in the sanctuary, took all that had happened up to his death into the grave with him—as though his death signaled the dawning of a new age.

Of course the death of the high priest did not atone for the sin. But through this practice, Israel would learn to hope for the Christ, who would indeed take all the sins of His people with Him into the grave. When He arose, it would be without our sins. Then a new life in freedom could begin.

55: The Word Is Very Near You

Deuteronomy 29-34

On the one hand Moses said to the people: "But to this day the LORD has not given you a mind to understand, or eyes to see, or ears to hear" (Deut. 29:4). On the other hand he said: "But the word is very near you; it is in your mouth and in your heart, so that you can do it" (Deut. 30:14). The latter verse is quoted by Paul in Romans 10:8. It means that grace is not earned by us in any way but is granted by God alone. As long as we do not see that, as long as we are not conquered by the Word of grace, we cannot understand the meaning of the Word of the Lord or His mighty deeds, and the covenant is difficult for us. The idea of the Word being very near governs this whole section, in which Israel is told once more what the covenant involves.

The song of Moses was meant as the song of the future. Therefore the Israelites were to learn it. In the future it would witness against Israel. Yet the end of the song prophesied about the vengeance of the Lord upon Israel's enemies and thus the triumph of God's grace in His covenant. Here we have the same idea, that is, that grace will have the last word in the covenant, which is guaranteed by the Lord's faithfulness. Of course this does not rule out the use of the means of grace. The designation of Joshua as Moses' successor, the command that the law be read every seven years, the Lord's own prediction of apostasy, and the song of Moses are all means of grace.

When Moses blessed the tribes of Israel, he saw them in the light of God's coming at Sinai. There God had met His people in the covenant. Because Moses proceeded from the establishment of the covenant when he blessed the Israelites, he was able to see a great deal of light in the future history of the tribes. God's faithfulness would allow them to live.

Moses' death must be seen in its significance not only for Israel but also for Moses himself. Even in his death, the surety of the Word that is very near to Israel is revealed.

When we read here of "the word," we should think also of the
eternal Word (John 1), that is, the One who maintains the covenant
fellowship between God and His people, the One who led Israel into the
wilderness as the Angel of the Lord. Because it is *His* Word, it has the
power to subdue Israel and can be in the mouth and in the heart of His
people, sometimes before they are even conscious of it.

Main thought: *In God's covenant, the Word is very near His
people.*

The renewal of the covenant. Before he took leave of the
people, Moses repeated the law of the Lord to them and spoke of
the Lord's blessing and curse. When he had finished, he summoned
all the Israelites encamped in the fields of Moab to renew their
covenant with the Lord.

Moses began to speak to the people: "You saw all the great
miracles which the Lord performed before your eyes in Egypt and
afterward. Yet, to this day, you have not understood them. You
have not yet understood that the Lord wants to be everything for
you, that you may surrender completely to Him, and that you are
not to trust in your own strength at all. Let us now renew our
covenant with the Lord, the covenant He made with us at Sinai.
See what the Lord has been for us and intends to be—and accept
His grace. We renew this covenant not only for ourselves but also
for the foreigners who dwell among us and for the generations that
will come after us.

"If you do not keep the covenant, the Lord will overthrow the
place where you dwell, just as He overthrew Sodom and Gomorrah,
and He will scatter you among the nations. All who see it will talk
about it, for it will be a witness to them, and they will say: 'The
secret things, that is, what He intends to do with His people Israel
in the future, belong to the Lord our God, but the revealed things,
that is, this destruction of Israel, are a witness to us and to our
children, so that we will keep the covenant with the Lord.' "

Evidently Moses foresaw that other nations would be taken
up into God's covenant. That's the situation now. To us the
destruction of Israel is a testimony. Our life will also perish if we
do not keep God's covenant. What God intends to do with Israel

in the future we do not know. Despite all their sins. He has not broken His covenant with that people; persons who fear the Lord are still coming forth from among them constantly. This is a testimony to us of God's faithfulness.

Moses also promised: "You will experience a turning to the Lord again, and He will gather you—no matter how scattered you may be—to the fellowship of the true people of the covenant. Therefore, do not say that God's covenant is too hard for you. You do not have to climb up to heaven or go across the sea to fetch it. God will give you everything, and in His covenant He has brought it very near to you: He has put the Word of His grace in your mouth and in your heart. Why not, in faith, accept His favor in your heart? Then you will be righteous—free from sin before Him. And why not confess with your mouth that God is your God? Then you will be blessed in your whole life, and you will be privileged to serve Him in freedom."

It is as though Moses spoke these words to the people of our time as well. He even alluded to all who would live in the covenant after his own time. It has been revealed to us especially that we do not have to look for grace anywhere, for it has come very near to us in the Lord Jesus Christ. In His covenant and through Christ's cross, the Lord has put grace in our mouth and in our heart.

The Word's struggle for victory. At the end of his address on this occasion when the covenant was renewed, Moses called on heaven and earth to be witnesses against Israel. That's how mightily the Spirit of the Lord struggled in Moses to get the people to understand the Lord's faithfulness in the covenant, so that they themselves would remain faithful. Moses would do anything to bring that about. Hence he introduced Joshua to the people as leader in his place. The Lord would be with Joshua and would continue to lead the people as before. The Angel of the Lord would go before them, and Joshua, the leader appointed by God, would act in conjunction with Him. In this situation, neither Joshua nor Israel needed to fear the nations they would meet on the way. This Angel of the Lord is our Lord Jesus Christ, who has become man and leads His people in the world.

After repeating the entire law to the people, Moses wrote it in a book. This book the Levites were to keep in the sanctuary. Every seventh year it was to be read to Israel, so that all generations yet to come would know the Lord's covenant. We can never know enough about the covenant.

After this the Lord Himself appeared to the people in the pillar of cloud. He predicted that Israel would forsake Him and that He would therefore have to hide His face from the people. The Lord said this not to make the people despair but to make them understand that in themselves they had no strength and were not faithful—so that all their expectations would be realized by the Lord's faithfulness.

Moses also had to compose a song and write it down. The Spirit of the Lord inspired this song. It was to be sung in Israel through all ages, for it would be a witness against Israel if Israel should be unfaithful. It would then be clear to what lengths the Lord had gone to warn His people. In this song, the Spirit of the Lord in Moses called heaven and earth as witnesses against Israel.

The name of the Lord be praised, for His work is always glorious. He is a refuge for His people. When He scattered the peoples at Babel and directed the nations, He was thinking of the people of His covenant. These people are the hub of all the nations; they are the blessing of the whole earth, for God takes pleasure in them. That's why He blessed them so much. But when God has made them rich, they will go and serve other gods, and then God will scatter them. He will never abandon them completely, however, for then their enemies could boast that they were mightier than the people in whom God, for Christ's sake, is well pleased. One day God will defeat Israel's enemies, for they are *His* enemies, and on that day He will exalt His people.

This is what Moses said in His song, and the Israelites sang it after him. They can still sing it. They live with the promise that God's grace will have the final say. We may sing this song too, for it is the song of God's people of all ages. This song witnesses against us, and heaven and earth witness against us as well when we reject the Lord. Yet, the final word will be His Word of grace to His people when He passes judgment upon the unbelieving. The Word of grace will be the last thing heard, for it is not spoken in vain. This Word is the life of His people.

The prophetic blessing. The last thing Moses did as mediator before he died was to bless the tribes of Israel in the name of the Lord, just as Jacob had blessed his sons. He laid the blessing upon the people in the name of the Lord, and it remained in effect throughout Israel's history. No man can bestow such a blessing—only the Christ. The Spirit of the Christ, however, was now working in Moses, just as this Spirit had once worked in Jacob.

He prophesied much good for the tribes. Yet, how could he do this, for the history of those tribes would be a history of sin and misery? He could do it because he saw this history in the light of the covenant that had been established at Sinai. Because of the Lord's faithfulness, grace would defeat the sin of the people time after time, and the tribes would belong to the Kingdom of God forever, no matter how many of them would fall away.

"The Lord came to you at Mount Sinai," Moses declared. "His glory illumined the whole area at the time. He was surrounded by many thousands of angels. Indeed, everything we saw was majesty.

The One at whose command the angels go and serve loves the nations. That's why He appeared to you and gave you His covenant and law through me. By this covenant and law, you are to become a blessing for all nations. In His grace He sought you out and—through you—all the nations. He is the One who blessed us at Sinai. That blessing I now pass on to each tribe."

Moses then proceeded to bless the tribe of Reuben, Jacob's oldest son. In that tribe there was a good deal of sin and little to be seen of the influence of God's Spirit. Still, Reuben's tribe would live before the Lord and would hear and pursue His calling, even though its members were few in number. Through punishment God would sanctify life in that tribe.

After that Moses went directly to Judah, the royal tribe. Out of Judah, Israel's true King would be born one day. Judah would lead Israel. Levi was the priestly tribe and would teach Israel God's covenant. Benjamin was God's beloved, borne by the Lord upon His shoulders. Joseph was blessed with great prosperity. And so Moses continued, predicting the future of the tribes in the light of God's covenant. He concluded by declaring that Israel was blessed because her King and abiding protection was the Lord.

This blessing is not significant only for the people of Israel;

it applies also to the present covenant people, which is one with that people of old. If we belong to this people, it is as though we were present for this blessing, as though Moses raised his hands in blessing over us too. He did it in the name of the Lord Jesus Christ, who is the true Mediator of His people. Because of this, his blessing has power. The Lord's blessing continues to be effective and is not far from us if we belong to this people; it is in our mouth and in our heart. Let us rely upon it and tell others about it!

The enduring Word of the Lord. Now the time had come for Moses to die. The Lord ordered him to go up Mount Nebo, a peak of the Pisgah range, which was part of the Abarim range.

Moses went up the mountain before the eyes of all Israel. The distance between Moses and the people became greater and greater. They must have stared after him as long as they could see anything at all. Finally he disappeared from view. They would never see him again—not even his dead body, for the Lord Himself would bury him.

Israel's mediator and shepherd had been taken away from the people for good. All flesh is as grass—even Moses, although he had lived to the age of 120 without his eyes becoming dim or his natural strength weakening. God had blessed him with a long life and with strength. Yet he, too, was as grass. Death is our lot because of sin.

The Israelites had to understand that since even Moses passed away, they would have to build not on Moses but on the Word of the Lord, which had been spoken by Moses. Indeed, all flesh is as grass, but the Word of the Lord abides forever. It is this Word that is very near to the Lord's people in the covenant.

We can only build upon the Mediator Jesus Christ, who is Himself the Word of God, who Himself puts the bond of communion between God and His people into effect. He, too, died for our sake, but He was victorious over death.

Perhaps Moses was raised from the dead, which could be why God Himself buried him. It may be that Moses did not see corruption in the grave. If so, it was for Christ's sake, who alone by His obedience was able to gain the victory over death. One day all who are His will be raised to eternal life and be glorified, just as He and Moses were.

Before Moses died, the Lord made something special happen to him. From the mountain on which he stood, the Lord allowed him to look out over the whole land of Canaan. The Lord strengthened his eyes to let him see all over the land. This was a miracle—a miracle of God's favor. Moses was not allowed to lead Israel into Canaan, but he was allowed to see the land.

Was that an extreme torment for Moses, a bitter reminder of his failure as leader of the people? No doubt Moses looked at Canaan with great longing, but now he must have understood that only in the name of the Christ, the Angel of the Lord, should he have led the people to that land. This Angel was going to do it Himself—through Joshua.

Moses must have been glad to surrender his calling into the hands of this Angel from whom he had also received it at the burning bush. He was now entering a higher calling in which he would be permitted to see the glory of the Angel of the Lord, the glory of His Kingdom, and his own service in that Kingdom. Thus all Moses' desires were fulfilled in a higher sense. One surprise for him would have been his resurrection. One day, much later, when the Angel had become flesh and was on earth as our Lord Jesus Christ, Moses was privileged to appear to his Lord and say to Him at the beginning of His suffering that he, Moses, had been able to lead the people of Israel only by the strength of the Christ.

Moses died, and the people mourned him for 30 days. After that they followed Joshua, the leader who possessed the Spirit of wisdom, the leader upon whom Moses had laid his hands.

In Canaan

56: Brought into Canaan

Joshua 1—5:12

We speak of Israel not as entering Canaan but as being *brought into* Canaan. The Lord brought Israel into Canaan by His strong arm. This event is a revelation of the Lord Jesus Christ, especially when Israel is led through the Jordan. This can be seen particularly in the ark of the covenant, the sign of the Lord's presence in Israel's midst. The sign of the ark was fulfilled in the Christ, who cut off the waters of the Jordan (Josh. 3:14-17). Thus we cannot ignore the symbolic significance of this event. Yet we must present it in such a way that the children understand it.

The crossing of the Jordan is not to be regarded as an isolated event. We are spiritually one with the Lord's people of that time, and their experience is also ours. The experience of that people is to be seen first of all as the experience of the One who is their Head—Jesus Christ. He passed through the waters of God's wrath in order to enjoy a life of eternal fellowship with God.

We, too, pass through the waters. But we must be careful not to identify the waters with death and Canaan with heaven! Canaan is the land of communion with God; it is the Kingdom of God, of which we must be citizens in this life.

Passing through the waters is dying with Christ, in order to live with Him eternally. We move down a trail that we did not encounter yesterday or the day before—the strange, previously hidden trail along which God's grace leads us. Thus we, too, are led through the Jordan: the Christ was in the midst of that people, and we were in Him. For Israel and for us, the path through the Jordan is the way of faith in the Christ, who goes before us and prepares the way.

In Joshua 5 we are told of the circumcision of the entire nation. Evidently circumcision had been neglected in the wilderness after the people's disobedience (see vs. 5-6). The few Israelites who were 40 years of age or older had been circumcised, but not the younger generation.

391

The Lord had not broken His covenant after Israel's sin, then. He still led the people in the pillar of cloud and of fire, and He still sent them manna. Yet, the full covenant fellowship enjoyed in the covenant signs was suspended for a time. After He brought the people into Canaan, God once again bestowed His full communion upon them, and the reproach of the Egyptians was refuted.

Gilgal means *turning* or *circle*. This name reflects the taunt that although God had let His people out of Egypt, He could not bring them into Canaan and was going to let them die in the wilderness. Moreover, at Gilgal the Passover was kept again for the first time. Thus both sacraments took on their significance again for Israel.

Main thought: *The Lord leads Israel by faith into the land of Canaan.*

The calling of Joshua. Moses was gone. Because of his disobedience, he had not been allowed to lead the people into Canaan. However, the Lord had chosen a successor to Moses, namely, Joshua, who had long assisted him. Therefore, when the days of mourning for Moses were over, the Lord spoke to Joshua's heart, telling him that he was to lead the people into Canaan. The Lord would now give the entire land to the people, and He would be with Joshua as the leader of the nation.

It certainly was a difficult task that the Lord gave Joshua. If Moses had groaned under that load, how would Joshua ever be able to carry it? Accordingly, the Lord charged him repeatedly to be strong and of good courage, for none of his enemies would be able to withstand him. However, he was not to be rash and daring, as unbelievers can be. All his courage was to be drawn from his faith that the Lord would be with him. Then he would be strong-hearted not only before Israel's enemies but also when confronted with Israel's own evil desires. If the people wanted to follow paths of their own choosing, he was to stick to the Word of the Lord as the Lord had made it known, especially through Moses. He was to meditate on that Word every day, so that it would dwell in his heart and give him the courage of faith.

Joshua immediately entered upon the calling God had given him, for he believed the Word of the Lord. He had the officers of the people, whose duty it was to keep the genealogical and birth records of the tribes, tell the people to prepare provisions for several days, for the Lord was now going to bring them into Canaan. Also, he addressed the tribes that were to continue living on the other (eastern) side of the Jordan,* telling them that they were to keep their promise to help the other tribes in the battle for Canaan. The reply was that they would do as Joshua commanded them, just as they had formerly obeyed Moses. Furthermore, they said that anyone who disobeyed Joshua would be put to death.

In answering Joshua they used the very same words the Lord had used: "Be strong and of good courage." How wonderful this must have been for Joshua! He had accepted the calling of the Lord in faith, and now the Lord had caused the people to accept Joshua as their leader. Joshua's calling struck a responsive chord in the hearts of the people, and they all said amen to that calling.

Happy the people who have received a leader from the Lord, who are bound to their leader by the Lord! Such a people is secure. God has given us an even more wonderful Leader, namely, the Lord Jesus Christ. And God wants His Spirit to make a place for this Leader in the hearts of all who believe. We follow Him through life, and therefore we are safe.

Preceded by the Spirit of the Lord. The Lord had promised to give the land of Canaan to His people, but that did not mean that Joshua and the people did not have to fight for it. Hence Joshua sent out two spies to inspect the land, especially the city of Jericho, which lay directly in their path. The spies crossed the Jordan, entered Jericho, and found lodging in the house of a prostitute, thinking they would remain undiscovered there. But the arrival of the two strangers did not go unnoticed in the city; they were immediately suspected of being Israelite spies.

The king of Jericho sent some men to the house of Rahab, the woman who had taken them in, to capture the suspected spies. But the two Israelites had an amazing experience. Rahab feared she would be discovered and hid them on the roof under some stalks

---

On the other side of Jordan or *beyond Jordan* are terms reflecting the later condition of the majority of the people's dwelling west of the Jordan.—TRANS.

of flax. She outwitted the king's messengers by saying that the spies had gone out the gate toward evening. Surely they could still catch up with them if they hurried!

Rahab had told a white lie to save the spies. Like any other lie, it was a sin. But there was something else to be considered. This woman deserted her own people and king, choosing to protect the Israelite spies. That would seem to be treason. Apparently she feared that the Canaanites would be conquered and hoped to save her own life by helping the spies.

Still, that wasn't all that was going on in her heart. Once she had gotten rid of the king's messengers, she talked with the spies up on the roof, telling them how she felt. She informed them that the Canaanites were afraid; all their courage had abandoned them now that Israel was there to conquer Canaan. They were well aware of what the Lord had done on Israel's behalf, how He had opened the waters of the Red Sea and made a path for His people through it. They knew how Israel had defeated the two powerful Amorite kings. "The hearts of all the Canaanites are melted," she said. For herself she confessed: "The Lord your God is God in heaven above and on earth beneath. Compared to Him, our idols are nothing."

In her heart she chose the true God, who was able to save His people. She chose for the honor of the God of Israel and the rights of His people as opposed to her own people, in whose sin she had been living. Thus she was not just trying to save her own neck through treason; she was seeking the protection of the God of Israel when she asked that her life and the life of her family be spared on the day Jericho was captured. Although she herself still lived in sin, she was freed from the sinful paganism around her in the depths of her heart. She must have been thinking these matters over for a long time. Moreover, she must have seen it as a special providence that the spies had sought refuge in her house. No doubt she later gained an even better understanding of God's wonderful way of grace in such matters.

How marvelous this whole affair must have seemed to the spies! Not only did they hear that the Canaanites had lost courage and the strength to resist, they also encountered a confession of the God of Israel while they were in enemy territory. Evidently the Spirit of the Lord had preceded them. The Spirit of the Lord Jesus

Christ, who lived in the midst of Israel, had not only stripped the Canaanites of their power but had established bonds between Israel and Rahab that they knew nothing about. He terrified their enemies and led a sinful Canaanite woman to confess the God of Israel. How amazing this divine revelation was to those spies! God was already at work in the midst of that heathen land!

The two spies promised the woman that her confident request would be granted: she and her family would be spared. Rahab had specifically asked that her father, mother, brothers, and sisters be saved too. How different she was in spirit from the other Canaanites! When the spies swore that she and her family would be spared, they laid down three conditions: that she would not betray the spies, that all the members of her family would be in her house when the time came, and that she would make it possible for them to identify her house, which was located on the city wall, by hanging a scarlet cord from the window.

Rahab then let the spies down from her house by a rope. On her advice, they remained hidden for three days in the hilly country around Jericho. When the king's messengers gave up the search, the spies came out of the hills and passed over the Jordan to return to Joshua and tell him all that they had seen and heard. Joshua learned that the Spirit of the Lord was in the midst of Israel's enemies, who already considered Israel's victory a certainty. Thus, all Joshua and Israel had to do was follow the Lord and receive what He had made ready for them.

This is always how the people of the Lord proceed. He leads the way in difficulties and has overcome them before we get there. He lays claim to the entire world, blessing and cursing as He wishes. If only we would believe as Joshua and the people of Israel then believed!

The amazing way to Canaan. Then Joshua and Israel set out from Shittim, where they had been camped, and came to the Jordan, where the Lord made them stay for three days. All this time they were looking out over the Jordan, which was full of water. It was harvest time. Up in the mountains, where the Jordan had its source, the snows had long since melted. Then the rainy season came, when the Jordan became a deep river with a current so rapid that people could not swim in it without risking their lives. The Lord had the Israelites camp before the river for three days, so that they could all see how impossible it was for an army to enter Canaan accompanied by wives and children.

At last the Lord revealed Himself to Joshua and told him that He would bring the people into Canaan by an unknown way, a new way they had not passed through yesterday or the day before. By leading Israel in this amazing way, God would begin to promote Joshua before the people as Moses' successor.

Joshua told the people to sanctify themselves, that is, to wash and put on clean clothes. However, this exterior cleansing was only a symbol of the cleansing of their hearts, which meant that they confessed their sins before God and once again broke with those sins. If they did not do this, they would not be able to meet the Lord, who would appear in their midst as their God. Receiving deliverance from the Lord was not enough. In that deliverance they had to know the Lord and worship Him, coming closer to Him.

The Israelites did sanctify themselves. The next day, at the Lord's command, Joshua told the priests that they were to take up the ark of the covenant and carry it in front of the people. The ark of the covenant was a sign to believers of God's presence among them. God is also among His people in the Lord Jesus Christ, who came down to us. Thus, in the ark the Lord Jesus Christ was actually going before them. Between the ark and the people there was to be a space of one kilometer. That way not only those at the front but all the people following in the broad column could keep the ark in view. All eyes were to be on the ark, which was a prophecy of the coming of the Lord Jesus Christ.

The moment the priests stepped into the Jordan, the waters flowing from the north were cut off, just as the Lord had promised. Those waters rose up in a wall, while the water that had already passed that point streamed on, creating an ever wider dry path across the Jordan. The Lord Jesus Christ was the One who was making this dry path for Israel. The priests with the ark moved to the middle of the riverbed and remained standing there. All the Israelites filed past the ark as they crossed the Jordan, so that all of them could see who had prepared the way into Canaan for them.

Through a miracle, then, the people of Israel entered Canaan.

This was only possible because they believed in the Lord, who was close to them in the Lord Jesus Christ. That's how they came into the land in which the Lord intended to dwell with them always.

We should all take the time to think carefully about that amazing crossing of the Jordan, for all believers actually follow the very same route that the Israelites took. Even the Lord Jesus Christ entered into eternal communion with God by way of that amazing route—through His death on the cross and His resurrection. And all believers know that if they are privileged to live with the Lord, the old life dies in them and a new life is born.

I am not speaking here of death, for we do not have to wait for our death in order to live with the Lord and have eternal life. This eternal life in fellowship with God can be ours in the here and now. If we have come to this eternal life, then we have taken this amazing route, for it is impossible for us, as sinful human beings, to come directly to God. Our sins and God's wrath lay between Him and us. But the Lord Jesus Christ has prepared a way for us through that barrier—if only we believe in Him! Just think of the Israelites, who all walked past the ark and looked at it as they entered Canaan! We are likewise to look to the Lord Jesus Christ and achieve eternal peace with God.

At the Lord's bidding, Joshua ordered that one representative of each tribe take up a stone from the dry riverbed of the Jordan. The twelve stones were set up at the Israelites' first campsite after the crossing and stood there for a long time as a reminder of that amazing event. Joshua even had stones set up at the spot where the priests had stood in the middle of the riverbed. Those stones would be visible when the water in the river was low. There they stood, a memorial to remind Israel of the Lord's mighty acts.

Another renewal of the covenant. The first place they stopped overnight after the crossing was Gilgal. Here they remained for several days in peace, and here the Lord gave them His special blessing. They were undisturbed because the miraculous crossing of the Jordan had struck terror into the hearts of the Canaanites, all of whom were now afraid to attack Israel.

In the wilderness, the Israelites had sinned grievously against the Lord by their unbelief. The Lord had not abandoned them; He was their God and kept His covenant with them, but He had not granted them complete covenant fellowship. The sacraments of circumcision and the Passover, which were signs of the covenant, had not been used during the years the Israelites spent wandering in the wilderness. This was a tremendous loss.

In our time, too, it can be so wonderful when there is communion or baptism in the church. Then the Lord is very close to His people, and His love delights them. This is what the Israelites in the wilderness missed. But here, at their first campsite in the land of Canaan, the sign of circumcision was given to all who had not received it. Then all the people celebrated the Passover as God gave them His full communion again.

How close the Lord was to them now! By speaking to them, the Lord made those days a feast. He told Joshua that he was to name that place *Gilgal,* which means *turning,* for there the Lord had turned away from the people the reproach of the Egyptians. While the Israelites wandered for 40 years in the wilderness, the Egyptians said that the Lord had indeed led them out of Egypt but added that they would all die in the wilderness because the Lord could not bring them into Canaan.

At this point the daily manna stopped falling, for the people could now eat the grain of the new land. Thus the Lord had fulfilled all His promises in a wonderful way, just as He always keeps His promises.

57: Set Apart to the Lord by the Ban*

Joshua 5:13—8:35

All of Jericho with its inhabitants and treasures was to be devoted to the Lord for destruction. All the people were to be killed; everything that could be burned was to be burned. The metal was to pass through the fire and then be set aside for use in the sanctuary.

Anything that had not given itself of its own free will to the Lord was to be put under the ban; that is to say, it was to be set apart for divine judgment. Within the covenant people, this meant anyone who broke the covenant. Among the nations it meant any nation that had fallen away into complete godlessness.

Jericho was to be utterly destroyed so that Israel would see from this example that the Canaanites, with everything they owned, had fallen under the ban of the Lord's judgment. The Commander of the army of the Lord declared: "I have now come" (Josh. 5:14). What He meant was that He had come to strike the Canaanites with judgment.

Still, since the metal was to be donated to the sanctuary, it is apparent that what had been judged could still be sanctified to the Lord. This is also clear from the fact that the Israelites were allowed to take for themselves the treasures of the other cities in Canaan, on the condition that those treasures be dedicated to the Lord in how they were used.

How was it possible to devote to the Lord something that had been judged? Only in virtue of Christ's undergoing judgment and devoting Himself to God blameless once He had passed through death. For this reason, the earth, too, can pass through the fire some day and then be devoted to God in its renewed form and be given to believers for their use. Even now, the earth is temporarily sanctified for Christ's sake and has been given to believers for their use. For the time being, the earth is

---

*See the note on ban in the Old Testament (p. 272).—TRANS.

already sanctified in the Kingdom of God. The fact that Israel may make use of the treasures of Canaan is a prophecy pointing to the sanctification of the earth for Christ's sake.

The Commander of the army of the Lord, that is, the Angel of the covenant, certainly did come to bring Canaan to judgment, but He also came to give Canaan's treasures to Israel. Thus His coming is actually a blessing for the people of the covenant. We are to look at the blowing of the trumpets around Jericho in the same light. The sound of the trumpets always signifies the Lord's coming, more specifically, the coming of the covenant God to His people. When God came to Jericho to destroy His enemies, He saved and blessed His people and opened Canaan up for them.

Jericho fell into Israel's hands without a fight. This would teach the Israelites that God gave their enemies into their hands and that Canaan was a gift from the Lord, even though they would have to go on fighting for it.

There is a discrepancy, however, in that 30,000 men are first mentioned in connection with the ambush behind Ai (Josh. 8:3) and later 5,000 (vs. 12). It may be that some copyist made a mistake in the case of the first number.

The final section of these chapters of Joshua records the setting up of the tables of the law. The account is kept short because Deuteronomy 27 had already described in detail how this was to be done. As soon as the Israelites captured Ai, Joshua and all the people marched to Mount Ebal and Mount Gerizim. From the very beginning, the use of the conquered land was to be placed under the sovereign rule of the law of the Lord.

Main thought: *For Christ's sake, Canaan is devoted to the Lord.*

The Commander of the army of the Lord. After the people had crossed the Jordan, Joshua knew that the conquest of Canaan must begin. Before them lay the strong fortress of Jericho, and Joshua's thoughts turned quickly to that city. Thinking about how best to take it, he withdrew to an isolated spot in the field where the army was camped. Suddenly he saw someone standing before him with a drawn sword in His hand, ready to strike. Joshua went up to Him and asked: "Are you for us or for our enemies?" The reply he received was: "I have come as the Commander of the army of the Lord."

Who was this Commander? He was the Angel of the Lord, who had led Israel through the wilderness and had appeared to

Abraham long before, the Mediator who already appeared in human form at that time. Now He appeared with a drawn sword in His hand, for He was about to strike the Canaanites with all their treasures and put them under a solemn ban; that is to say, He would give them over (devote them) to the judgment of God. The godlessness of the Canaanites had reached its peak. He called Himself the Commander of the army of the Lord, that is, of the armed forces of angels. With His angels, He was going to fight for Israel. Joshua and the Israelites were to do battle with the Canaanites, but He was the One who would annihilate them with His armed forces.

Perhaps Joshua did not understand immediately that the figure before him was the Lord Himself, the Angel of the Lord, who had appeared so often to Moses. But he did realize that he was dealing with a messenger from God. Therefore he prostrated Himself and asked: "What does my lord bid his servant?" He was told to take off his shoes, for the place where he stood was holy. Then Joshua understood that he was confronting the Mediator Himself. The Lord Jesus Christ is Himself the holy God.

The Lord had come to strike Canaan with judgment. He would show that He Himself—not Joshua and Israel—was punishing Canaan. How? By delivering Jericho, which of course had closed its gates, into the hands of the Israelites without a battle. All the Israelites had to do was walk around the city once a day for six days and then seven times on the seventh day. The Lord alone conquers His enemies and the enemies of His people.

That all of Canaan had fallen under the judgment of God was to be shown by Jericho's fate: all its inhabitants and treasures were placed under the ban. In other words, they were to be devoted to the Lord. The inhabitants were to be put to death—all of them. The city and all that was in it would then be consumed by fire. Only the metals were to be saved. Once they were melted down and sanctified by fire, they could be used for the sanctuary.

Because of sin, the whole earth fell under the judgment of God and therefore had to be put under the ban. We were not to use anything of the earth. Indeed, we ourselves were delivered up to judgment. However, the Lord Jesus Christ submitted to that judgment on our behalf. In His death on the cross, he was delivered up to the judgment of God, but He arose from the dead and lives to devote Himself and His own and the earth to the Lord. Because of His sacrifice, we may already become God's children and again use the earth in the Lord's service. One day the whole earth will be renewed and sanctified to the Lord.

That it was possible for something to be delivered up to judgment and again be sanctified to the Lord is clear from the fact that the metals could be offered for service in the sanctuary. The Israelites did not have to burn the treasures of the other cities in Canaan. They were commanded to put the inhabitants to death, but they were allowed to take the cattle and the other possessions for their own use, in order to serve the Lord with them.

Do we ever ponder the fact that we ourselves and the whole earth have fallen under divine judgment because of sin, and that it is only because of the Lord Jesus Christ that we may live and enjoy the treasures of the earth? Once we realize this, we must see to it that we make use of all those treasures to serve the Lord.

Judgment upon Jericho. Joshua passed the order of the Commander of the army of the Lord on to the people, and all the armed men marched around Jericho the first day. The ark of the Lord was carried in the middle of the procession, as a sign that the Lord was in their midst. In front of the ark walked seven priests, carrying their trumpets and blowing them. The blowing of the trumpets was a sign that the Lord was about to show His grace to His people and His wrath to His enemies.

Six days they walked once around the city, and on the seventh day they did it seven times. There stood Jericho, still strong with its ramparts and its mighty men of valor. At the same time, it was surrounded by the people of the Lord, with the Lord Himself in their midst. And it was indeed delivered into the hands of the people—or rather, the judgment of God, which would redeem His people. Likewise, the whole world, which is at odds with God, still appears to be strong, but it is delivered up to the judgment of God and is given into the hands of the people of God, who will triumph over it.

The Israelites had to walk around Jericho for seven days. During those marches, they had to keep silent. For seven days Israel had to wait faithfully upon the acts of the Lord. He might not be coming today or even tomorrow, but He certainly was coming! The people awaited Him in faith. Let us, too, await His coming in faith, for He will judge everything that is sinful in this world and bless His people.

At the end of the seventh march on the seventh day, Joshua cried: "Shout; for the LORD has given you the city." Then the power of the grace of the Lord upon His people became evident: at that very moment, the walls of Jericho collapsed. The Israelites pressed into the city from all sides. The inhabitants of Jericho were put to death, and all their possessions were devoted to the Lord.

Only Rahab and all who were in her house were spared. She and all who belonged with her escaped the judgment, for she had believed in the God of Israel and in faith had harbored the spies. Her escape shows us how we may escape the judgment by faith in the God of the covenant.

After the city was destroyed, Joshua swore an oath to the people that whoever undertook to rebuild the walled city of Jericho would be cursed before the Lord: all his sons would perish during the reconstruction. Jericho was always to remain an open city, as a sign that the Lord had given the land and its cities into the hands of His people, and that the Lord protects His people like a wall of fire surrounding them.

Judgment in the army. Next Israel turned to Ai. On the advice of the spies whom Joshua had sent out ahead, only 3,000 men marched against this small city. But they were defeated and 36 of them were killed. At this the hearts of the people melted, and Joshua tore his clothes—not just because of this minor defeat but because it turned out that Israel was *not* invincible. As a result, the Canaanites would regain their courage, surround the camp of the Israelites, and destroy them. How, then, would God win glory for His great name? Such was Joshua's complaint to the Lord.

The Lord answered that all the people were to blame since one of them had disobeyed the covenant and taken some of the booty of Jericho for himself. Apparently the Lord and His rights in judgment meant nothing to that man. In his greed he had despised the Word of the Lord. That's why the Lord could not accompany the people into battle. Until the people had pronounced judgment on that covenant breaker, the wrath of God would settle on the whole nation, and the nation itself would come under judgment.

At the Lord's command, lots were cast. Achan, of the tribe of Judah, was shown to be the transgressor. He confessed that he had buried in his tent an elegant Babylonian robe, 200 shekels of silver, and a bar of gold. Therefore all Israel stoned Achan and his entire household in the valley of Achor. Stones were raised up over their corpses, and all their possessions were burned.

Achan's entire family shared in his punishment, for every family shares the guilt of its members. It is true that God decreed that children are not to be punished for the sins of their parents, but Achan's crime was certainly not committed without the knowledge of his family. Therefore they all came under this divine judgment.

We would do well to pay attention to this sin of Achan. Don't we possess a great deal too, and don't we use much of what we have in this world without confessing that it has been given to us to use because of Christ's suffering, and that it is therefore sanctified to God? Don't we withhold much of what the Lord has entrusted to us?

After this purification of the army, Joshua followed the Lord's command by marching against Ai once more. This time the Lord told him to use a trick—by preparing an ambush on the western side of the city. The Lord gave the city into the hands of the Israelites. Its inhabitants were put to death, and the king of Ai was hanged on a tree until evening. The city was burned. The Israelites kept only the cattle and the spoils of the city for themselves. The Lord had given them those spoils. Through the Lord Jesus Christ, the treasures of Canaan would be sanctified and given to Israel. We, too, receive the earth's treasures for Christ's sake.

The tables of the law. The Israelites had already conquered the first section of Canaan and taken possession of it. In this land of Canaan, they were to serve the Lord and live in covenant with Him according to the law which the Lord had given them through Moses. Therefore Joshua could no longer postpone carrying out an order that Moses had given when he repeated the law before the people.

He headed north with all the people. He did not have to fear that the Canaanites would attack them, for the terror of the Lord filled them all. Their destination was a pair of mountains—Ebal and Gerizim. He built an altar on Mount Ebal, where the people dedicated themselves to the Lord through burnt offerings. They also offered some thank offerings. Next he wrote the law of the Lord on two stones, which he set up on Mount Ebal. He then had six tribes stand on Mount Ebal and six on Mount Gerizim, opposite each other. The priests stood in between the two peaks and read the law of the Lord to the people.

When they read the curse with which God threatened the people in case they should be unfaithful, all the people on Mount Ebal shouted, "Amen," and when they read the blessing promised by the Lord, the people on Mount Gerizim cried, "Amen." Thus they called down the curse of the Lord upon themselves in the event that they should depart from the law of the covenant. In faith they could expect His blessing if they walked in the ways of His covenant.

Joshua, following the command of Moses, saw to it that this ceremony took place very soon after the invasion of Canaan had begun. The Israelites' whole life in Canaan was to be subject to the law of the covenant from the very outset. Today we have a somewhat different relation to the law of the Lord than Israel had. Nevertheless, our entire life must be lived in accordance with the law of the Lord. From the very beginning, our life in this world is to be holy to the Lord.

58: The Righteousness of God

Joshua 9-12

Apparently Canaan was conquered in accordance with a divine plan. The Israelites burst into the very middle of Canaan—Jericho, Ai, the cities of the Gibeonites. After this Joshua defeated the kings of the south, led by Adoni-zedek, at Gibeon and on the slope of Beth-horon. Finally, he dealt with the kings of the north, led by Jabin of Hazor, in the battle of the waters of Merom.

The Gilgal mentioned here is probably not the place where the Israelites first camped after crossing the Jordan. It must be another Gilgal, between Shechem and Jerusalem. The Israelites arrived at this Gilgal when they went south from Mount Ebal.

There can be no doubt that the Israelites had to keep their oath to the Gibeonites. Saul later tried to exterminate these people, but that was a crime that had to be avenged with blood. It's true that the oath was based on the deception of the Gibeonites, but the Israelites were also to blame for not asking about the will of the Lord.

The unwilling Israelites now had to include the Gibeonites in their life as a nation. That this happened in such a way was due to God's leading. Israel had to learn that the Canaanites were people too, people who found protection in the oath within the sphere of God's justice. Israel did not have the right to deal with the Canaanites arbitrarily. If the other Canaanites were to be wiped out, it was only to avenge the righteousness of God. Mere passion was not to be allowed the upper hand in the battle against the Canaanites. When the five kings in the cave of Makkedah were to be slain, Joshua said: "Be strong and of good courage." That was just what the leaders and, indeed, all Israel needed in order to carry out God's judgment upon the Canaanites.

It is in this spirit that we must tell the children the story of the destruction of the Canaanites. God's righteousness must be brought home to them. Someone who places human life above the rights of God can never tell this story properly, for such a person will allow himself to be guided by a sentiment for which Christ had to atone on the cross. Our human life finds true protection only in submission to the righteousness of God, that is, the divine righteousness that has been restored by Christ and demands our recognition.

Main thought: *God's righteousness is maintained in the extermination of His enemies.*

The intruders. After the events at Mount Ebal and Mount Gerizim, the Israelites camped at Gilgal, a place in the heart of the country a little to the south of these mountains (not the same Gilgal where they first camped after crossing the Jordan). There a strange delegation came to Joshua—men who apparently had traveled far, for the holes in their wineskins were crudely patched up, their sandals were worn out, and their bread was moldy. They said they lived far away and thus did not belong to the Canaanites. In the distant land where they lived, they had heard of the Lord's mighty deeds on Israel's behalf. Their people now wanted to make a covenant with Israel.

At first Joshua was suspicious. He said: "Perhaps, in spite of what you say, you live among us." But a glance at their footwear and their bread was so convincing that he did not bother to ask the will of the Lord through the high priest. Joshua and the elders made a covenant with the visitors and swore to it in the Lord's name.

By the time the Israelites reached the cities of the Gibeonites, three days later, they realized that they had been deceived. When Joshua rebuked the Gibeonites, they replied that they had heard that Moses had ordered the extermination of all the Canaanites.

Now, Israel was not permitted to break an oath. It was the fault of Joshua and the elders that they had entered into the covenant lightly. If the oath were ever broken, the name of the Lord, by which it was sworn, would be disgraced.

The Israelites grumbled to Joshua and the elders that the Gibeonites would now have to continue living among them. The only thing Joshua could do was curse the Gibeonites and condemn them forever to menial service in connection with the sanctuary. Thus Noah's curse upon Canaan (Gen. 9:25) was finally fulfilled in this sentence upon the Gibeonites: Canaan became a slave of slaves for Israel.

We should not try to excuse Joshua by arguing that the Gibeonites acknowledged and worshiped the God of Israel, for their attitude was completely different from Rahab's. God can never be honored through deceit. In the case of the Gibeonites, there was no looking to the Spirit of the Lord, who worked in Israel. Because Joshua did not ask the will of the Lord, the Spirit of the Lord was grieved in Israel's midst and the Lord's name was dishonored. Since Joshua did not inquire in faith about the Lord's will, God's wisdom was withheld from him in this case.

Yet, all this happened under God's guidance. Against its will, Israel now had to absorb the Gibeonites into its national life. Through this experience, the Israelites had to humble themselves and learn that of themselves they were no better than the Canaanites. They owed all their privileges solely to the gracious covenant of God. The Gibeonites, too, were people who could seek protection within the sphere of God's justice, to which the Israelites had sworn the oath. If the other Canaanites were to be wiped out, it was only for the sake of the righteousness of God, against which they had committed the most extreme offenses.

The kings of the south. When the kings of the south heard what had happened, they made a covenant among themselves at the suggestion of Adoni-zedek, king of Jerusalem. Together they attacked the Gibeonites, who had bound themselves to Israel. In their distress, the Gibeonites sent a message to Joshua.

After a fast night march, Joshua and his army attacked the allied kings, who thought that the Israelites were still far away. The Spirit of the Lord filled them with the fear of Israel, and they fled. Their flight was to the northwest, their aim being to get through the mountain pass at Beth-horon and reach the plain in which their fortified cities lay. At the hills of Beth-horon, the Lord caused large hailstones to fall on them. More of them died under the hailstones than by the swords of the Israelites.

While the Israelites pursued their enemies, Joshua cried out to the Lord. In the name of the Lord, he commanded the sun and the moon to stand still. At his word, that day lasted almost twice as long as an ordinary day. That was a divine miracle. God has the passage of time in His hand, and He made both the hail and the passage of time serve the cause of His people. At that point Joshua exercised authority over the natural course of things as a type of the Christ, who exercises authority over all creation. In that sovereign rule, Christ sees to it that the cause of His people is victorious and executes judgment upon His enemies.

During the pursuit, someone brought a message to Joshua that the five kings had hidden in a cave at Makkedah. Joshua ordered that the entrance of the cave be closed off with stones. That way the Israelites would not be held up from further pursuit.

The whole army later assembled at Makkedah. There was no longer an enemy of Israel left that dared to start anything. Joshua then had the five kings brought out of the cave. He commanded the chiefs of Israel's men of war to put their feet on the kings' necks. Then he told them to summon their courage and put the kings to death. They did not need any courage to put defenseless enemies to death, but they did need it if they were to put them to death in the name of the Lord. They were to execute the judgment of God's righteousness upon these kings. Thus their death was to be a sign to the Israelites that God would also execute judgment upon their other enemies. In this act of judgment, they had to acknowledge themselves as exclusively the Lord's.

One day God will judge all who are His. In ourselves we are no better than those kings and the rest of the Canaanites. If there is to be salvation for us, it is because the Lord Jesus Christ reconciled God and restored justice for us. Under the justice of God, He suffered death that we might live by justice.

The execution of those kings must have made quite an impression upon the Israelites. Through this experience, they were to learn that they were privileged to live solely in virtue of the gracious justice of their God.

After these events, Joshua captured many cities in the south. The Israelites wiped out all the people but kept the cattle and the spoils for themselves, according to the gracious providence of God on behalf of His people.

The kings of the north. When the report of Israel's victory reached them, the kings of the north formed an alliance under the leadership of Jabin, king of Hazor. They joined their forces to form a very large army. This army, which included many horses and chariots, assembled in a camp in the north, by the waters of Merom.

The Lord told Joshua not to be afraid, for He had given this army into his hand. In all haste, Joshua marched his army to the north, attacked the army of the kings, and destroyed it. Just as the Lord had commanded him, Joshua had the chariots burned and the horses hamstrung: he had his men cut through the tendons of the horses' hind legs and then kill them. This act was to be a sign to Israel that anything outside of God that man relies on is rejected by God and will cease to be. In God's sight, the strongest power amounts to nothing.

The first city Joshua captured was Hazor. He burned it down because Jabin of Hazor had led the resistance. After this he took the other cities. He also defeated the sons of Anak, the giants of whom the Israelites had previously been so afraid.

Now all of Canaan was in his power. To be sure, not all the cities had been conquered yet, nor were all the Canaanites wiped out. But the mopping up could take place later, for the Canaanites no longer had any strength to resist.

By the hand of Israel, God had executed His righteousness upon the Canaanites. Do we all realize that He will execute His righteousness upon us as well unless we find reconciliation through the blood of the Lord Jesus Christ and protection in His covenant?

59: The Heritage of the Saints

Joshua 13-22

The second big task for Joshua was the division of Canaan among the twelve tribes. It's likely that the following procedure was used: first lots would be drawn to see which tribe was to take its turn, and then another lot would be cast to determine what portion of the land fell to that tribe.

Because Canaan was divided by lot, it was the Lord Himself who allotted each tribe its inheritance. It's remarkable how the lot went. Only Caleb (of the tribe of Judah) was allowed to choose for himself the portion that the Lord had promised him for his faithfulness. It happened that the tribe of Judah was the first to be designated by the lot: it received a portion of land in the south. Thus Caleb's inheritance fell within Judah's territory.

The next to be designated were Ephraim and Manasseh. Thus Joseph followed upon Judah, in accordance with the significance for Israel of these two sons of Jacob. Ephraim and the half tribe of Manasseh received an inheritance in the central and northern part of the country.

The remainder of the land was then divided among seven tribes. (You will recall that Reuben and Gad and the other half of the tribe of Manasseh had received an inheritance on the eastern side of the Jordan.) Joshua had the rest of the land surveyed and divided into seven parts.

The lot fell first to Benjamin, and that small tribe received the territory between Judah and Ephraim for its inheritance—just a small area. After Benjamin came Simeon, also a small tribe, which received a territory south of Judah's, an area that was still counted as belonging to Judah. Thus the prophecy of Jacob was fulfilled: Simeon and Levi would be scattered through Israel. The rest of the land was then given to the five other tribes.

The Levites received cities to dwell in among the other tribes. We are not to assume that only Levites would live in those cities. But adequate

411

room had to be made for them in those cities and the land around them.
The cities of refuge were also Levite cities.

The Levites did not receive an inheritance of their own, for the
Lord, the God of Israel, was Himself their inheritance. At that time,
service in the sanctuary was still separate from service of the Lord in
one's own inheritance. When heaven and earth are renewed, these two
groups of people will be one. The dwelling of the Levites in the midst of
the other tribes was to be a constant reminder that all Israel was set apart
for the service of the Lord.

After Joshua had received his inheritance, he modestly withdrew.
After all, the Lord was Israel's King. By faith Israel was to obey the Lord
and seek His guidance. Here Joshua is a type of the Christ: when all
things are subjected to Him, He will Himself be subjected to the One
who put all things under Him (I Cor. 15:28). This distribution of Israel's
inheritance by the Lord Himself, through Joshua, is a sign to the faithful
that their inheritance is secure. All believers will receive their inheritance
from the Mediator.

Main thought: *In the name of God, the inheritance is
distributed to the saints by the Mediator.*

The inheritance of Judah and Joseph. After the victory over
the kings of the north, the Lord commanded Joshua to proceed
with the division of the land among the tribes. As a matter of fact,
Joshua had become old and would not live to see the day when all
the Canaanites were wiped out. But the division of the land could
not wait. Joshua was responsible for carrying it out, as a continuation of the work of Moses, who had already assigned the territory
east of the Jordan to the tribes of Reuben and Gad and the half
tribe of Manasseh. Thus Joshua, like Moses, was to play the role
of mediator in this work.

Caleb, the son of Jephunneh, came to ask Joshua for the
portion of the land that the Lord had promised him for remaining
faithful to Him after he had spied out the land of Canaan many
years before. At the time, the Israelites were especially afraid of
the sons of Anak. Hence the Lord had promised their hill country
to Caleb. His request was supported by the tribe of Judah, to
which he belonged.

These giants, these sons of Anak, had already been conquered by Joshua, but they were not yet entirely wiped out. That would have to be taken care of by the one to whom their land was allotted. The same condition went with all the land parceled out to the tribes: each tribe would have to wipe out the Canaanites that remained in its assigned territory.

Apparently the Israelites dreaded this task. They would have preferred to remain at Gilgal as one army. But Caleb, in an act of faith, dared to take on his inheritance. He pointed out to Joshua that although he was 85 years old if he was a day, he was nevertheless just as strong as when he had spied out the land of Canaan at the age of 40. Through his faith, the whole tribe of Judah was challenged to take possession of its inheritance.

At his own request, then, Caleb received Hebron and some land around it. When the drawing of lots began, the tribe of Judah received an inheritance in the south, the land surrounding Hebron.

Caleb quickly went to work to conquer his allotted territory. The Lord gave the sons of Anak into his hand, but how would he take the fortified city of Debir? Caleb promised to give his daughter Achsah as wife to the man who took Debir. His nephew Othniel succeeded in capturing this city. The Lord continued to instil faith in His people, and their faith gave them courage and strength. At Achsah's request, Othniel received a more fertile piece of land near Debir.

The other members of the tribe of Judah also began to wipe out the Canaanites. But they were unable to drive the Jebusites out of the stronghold of Jerusalem. They lacked the faith to tackle that fortified position with courage. Its conquest was reserved for David, who became Israel's king much later.

The tribes received their territories by lot, that is, from the Lord Himself. Thus they received their portion of the land from His own hand. But they themselves had to wipe out the Canaanites that remained in their territory. God likewise gives us our place and inheritance in His Kingdom now and forevermore. But we have to struggle to possess what He has given us. If, in faith, we see that our place has been allotted to us by the Lord and is forever certain, we will have the courage to struggle on.

After Judah was taken care of, the inheritance of the tribes of Ephraim and Manasseh was allotted. Jacob had promised Joseph that he would receive a double portion, and therefore his sons

Ephraim and Manasseh were counted as sons of Jacob. Since the tribe of Levi did not receive a separate inheritance, the land was indeed divided among twelve tribes.

Ephraim and Manasseh received the central part of the country and all that lay to the north. They, too, began with the work of wiping out the Canaanites. They were not always successful, for although they could defeat them in battle, they did not manage to kill all of them.

These two tribes then came to Joshua to complain that they had received too small an inheritance. It was as though they had received a single portion together. Joshua pointed out that they had indeed received a large territory, an inheritance for two tribes. All they had to do was clear the forest up in the mountains and wipe out the Canaanites. But they complained that they couldn't drive the Canaanites out: the Canaanites with their iron chariots were too strong. Joshua reprimanded them and demanded that they continue to fight the Canaanites in faith. If they had the faith, they would be able to conquer them, no matter how strong their enemies were. Therefore they did not receive any more land. We, too, can often be dissatisfied with what God has assigned us in life, with the place He has appointed for us in His Kingdom, for we are not willing to possess what He gave us in faith.

The inheritance of the other tribes. The distribution of the land was proceeding too slowly; the tribes were reluctant to take possession of the land and start the warfare. What a lack of faith Israel displayed at this point! Still, the Lord remained faithful to His Word: He would give His people what He had planned for them.

Because of this reluctance, Joshua had all Israel assemble at Shiloh and set up the meeting tent. Israel would have to acknowledge once and for all that the Lord lived in Canaan. And if He lived there, He would see to it that His people had a safe dwelling place there. They would be privileged to live under His shadow.

Shiloh means *rest*. The Lord came to His rest there after the journey through the wilderness. He would also provide rest for His people. The Angel of the Lord was at Shiloh—the Lord Jesus Christ, who was to be born of the tribe of Judah. Jacob had already called Him *Shiloh,* that is, *bringer of rest.* Even more than before, Israel could expect that He would one day appear in the flesh.

Joshua rebuked the remaining tribes for hesitating. Each of the tribes was to appoint three men, who together would go up and down the land and suggest a division of the land into seven portions. This was done. Then the rest of the land was distributed among the remaining seven tribes. Benjamin received the territory between Judah and Ephraim. And Simeon came to dwell to the south of Judah, under the shadow of Judah, as it were. Simeon lost any independent significance among the tribes later, just as Jacob had foretold. The five other tribes received the rest of the land.

At the end of this process, the Israelites pressed Joshua to choose a piece of land for himself. He chose a portion within the territory of Ephraim, for he belonged to that tribe. Once he had completed the work of the Lord, he withdrew to this piece of land. Joshua did not wish to be Israel's king, for the Lord Himself would be the leader of His people.

The inheritance of Levi. At the Lord's bidding, the tribe of Levi was the only one that had not received an inheritance. This tribe had been set aside for special service of the Lord in the sanctuary. The oldest son in the house of Aaron would always be high priest. All the sons in that line were to be priests, and all the Levites were to assist in the tabernacle. They lived in large part from the gifts and offerings of the whole nation.

All the tribes were to serve the Lord in their newly assigned territories. But at this time, the special service in the sanctuary was still marked off from this general service of the Lord. One day this distinction would fall away. When the Kingdom of God has come, all will serve the Lord at the same time in His rule over the whole earth and worship Him with adoration and praise.

The Levites were to live in the cities of refuge and also in various other cities in the territories of the other tribes. The presence of the Levites was to be a constant reminder to all the tribes that they possessed their inheritance in order to serve the Lord in it. Through the mediation of the priests, they were to bring the Lord praise and adoration for the majesty which He displayed in His grace toward Israel.

The unity preserved. The time had now come for the fighting men of the tribes of Reuben and Gad and the half tribe of Manasseh to return to their own territory on the other side of the Jordan. They had faithfully kept the promise to help the other tribes in the conquest of Canaan. With their share of the spoils, they returned home after Joshua thanked them for their help and admonished them to remain faithful to the Word and covenant of the Lord.

Once they came to the Jordan, they erected a large altar on the western side of the river. As soon as the other tribes heard about this, they assembled at Shiloh and formed an army to make war against their brothers, for they assumed that the tribes across the river had set up the altar to offer sacrifices to the Lord upon it. Then there would be two places where the Lord was served with sacrifices. But there was only one place where the Lord wished to dwell in the midst of His people, and only one altar. If this sin was to be tolerated, the wrath of God would be felt by all Israel. The people would be divided in two, and the covenant, in which the people were one, would be broken.

Before they went into battle, however, the Israelites west of the Jordan sent a delegation headed by Phinehas, the son of the high priest Eleazar. When this group reached the other side of the Jordan, Phinehas solemnly rebuked the tribes there because of the sin they had committed, reminding them how the Israelites had sinned earlier and how the Lord had been against the whole people.

Phinehas was told in response that the tribes east of the Jordan had not intended to offer sacrifices to the Lord on this altar. Instead the altar would be a sign for all of Israel that the tribes on the eastern side of the Jordan also had the right to participate in the service on the one altar at Shiloh. They had been afraid that the two communities, separated by the Jordan, might become estranged from each other, and that the tribes to the west of the river might someday refuse to allow the eastern tribes to participate in the service of the Lord at Shiloh.

The tribes that had gathered to do battle heaved a great sigh of relief and thankfulness when they heard this answer brought back by the delegation. Now it was clear that the large altar had been erected only to preserve the unity of Israel's public worship. Thus there was great enthusiasm in all the tribes to keep the covenant with the Lord and to live in obedience.

The Spirit of the Lord had not departed from Israel, no matter how grievously and how often Israel had sinned against its God. This same Spirit will never depart from His people. Because of Christ's obedience, He will always see to it that His people live in His fellowship.

60: Confirmed in the Inheritance

Joshua 23-24

Many of us like to tell the story of Joshua's farewell to Israel. Our thoughts go roughly as follows: Joshua, an old man, admonishes the people once more before his death to remain faithful to the Lord and His calling. Then we add that this final exhortation was not really effective, for the people of Israel did in fact forsake the Lord later.

The history now before us must not be told in this way. Such an approach must be ruled out completely, for if we were to use it, we would not be telling the gospel of the Lord Jesus Christ. In this story particularly, we are to see Joshua as a type of the Christ; as the mediator between God and men, he renews God's covenant with the people and thereby confirms the people in their inheritance. This perspective comes through especially in Joshua 24.

The people presented themselves before God, and Joshua spoke to them as though he were in God's very presence. We are not to say that Joshua's efforts were in vain, for this renewal of the covenant was instrumental in ensuring that there was an elect remnant, that is, a group of faithful believers left. After the exile, God brought these people back to their inheritance to await the Messiah in the promised land. By means of this renewal of the covenant, God left Himself a way to fulfill His promises.

There is another danger to be avoided here: we must not allow ourselves to be led by the thought that the believers in Israel comforted themselves at Joshua's grave with the hope that their leader's soul was now in heaven. The emphasis in Scripture lies elsewhere. When we are told about the burial of Joshua, we are told about the place where he was laid to rest in the earth. Scripture focuses on the burial itself. The same applies to the burial of the bones of Joseph and the burial of Eleazar. Joshua and the others were buried in their inheritance as a sign that they would have a part in the resurrection of the dead, and that in their sacred inheritance they would possess their portion among the saints, that is, those who have been sanctified. By means of those burials in the promised land, the bond between the people and the land was strengthened.

Scripture is the book for the earth. The Bible views the earth in the light of heaven, of course, but it remains the book for the earth. Our portion on this earth, in the here and now, is a guarantee of our portion on the earth when it is renewed one day. We should also view burials of our time in this light. One day we will possess our portion among the saints on the earth. Thus, our entire position on the earth in the present is secured in the covenant.

Main thought: *Joshua, as a type of the Mediator between God and men, confirms Israel's possession of the inheritance.*

Joshua's exhortation. Joshua had been Israel's leader in the conquest of Canaan and had distributed the land among the tribes. Now he was an old man. He felt that his end could not be far off, but his work was not yet finished. He still had a message for the people. Therefore he gathered all the representatives of the people: their elders, the heads, the judges, and the officers, who kept the records. We are not told where they met. Although Scripture does not name the site, it was probably Shiloh, where the tabernacle had been erected and the ark of the covenant, the sign of God's presence, stood.

What was Joshua going to say to those representatives of the people and, through them, to all the people? Was he going to admonish them to remain faithful to the Lord? No, that was not the first thing he had to say. First he told them that the Lord had given them this land. He was the One who conquered all the peoples they had met on their way. To be sure, there were still some Canaanite peoples that had not yet been wiped out, but the Lord would also deliver them into the hands of the Israelites. If God's people would only believe, they would know no fear and no one would be able to withstand them. Therefore Joshua first gave them God's promise. They were to accept this promise in faith and cleave to the Lord. Then they could go on to wipe out the remaining peoples and would have no desire to mingle with those Canaanites who had cursed the Lord.

There was some danger, of course, for the Canaanites were highly developed and were more familiar with agriculture than the Israelites. Would the Israelites come to admire them for their abilities and accept their leadership? If they would only dare be themselves for the Lord's sake!

The Lord had chosen the Israelites and wanted to be their God. Therefore they should not allow themselves to be taken in tow by the Canaanites and should be sure not to mingle with them. Then the Lord would lend them His support so magnificently that a single Israelite could put a thousand Canaanites to flight. But if they did not incline their hearts to the Lord and instead mixed with the Canaanites, the Lord would allow the Canaanites to become strong again. The Canaanites would tempt the Israelites, trap them, and gain power over them.

The people saw how the Lord had fulfilled all His promises. He would be just as sure to carry out His threats, if the occasion arose. He would cause the Israelites to perish in this land if need be. After speaking these words, Joshua let the people go home.

The covenant renewed once more. Joshua knew that what he had done was not enough. He would have to present the people to God and renew the covenant between God and Israel. In this ceremony, he would be a mediator between God and the people. Joshua could do that only as a type of the true Mediator, Jesus Christ, who stands between God and us, providing a guarantee that God and His people will remain united forever. This Mediator was going to atone for the people's sin and thus heal the breach between God and the people. Only in the power of this Mediator would Joshua be able to mediate between God and the people.

Joshua called the representatives of the people together again. This time he summoned even more representatives than the time before—as many of the people as were able to come. They were to meet him at Shechem, a historic place. Shechem was where the Lord first appeared to Abraham when he entered the land of Canaan. Abraham had built an altar to the Lord there. The people must have been thinking of these things when they were called together by Joshua.

At Shechem Joshua now prayed with the people. Thereby

they presented themselves before the Lord. It was as though the heavens above them had opened. Then Joshua addressed the people in the name of the Lord. It was as though they were in the presence of God.

He spoke to the people for a long time, unfolding their history since the calling of Abraham. But in this long address he said essentially one thing, namely, that it had been the Lord's initiative to show concern for Abraham when his fathers were still serving idols. The Lord had brought Abraham out of those surroundings so that he could serve Him. Time and time again, it had been the Lord who had taken the initiative in saving the people and averting disaster. It had also been the Lord who had caused them to inherit Canaan. They had not conquered the land; the Lord had put their enemies to flight before them. The spoils had fallen into their hands. They lived in houses that they had not built and ate the fruit of vineyards and oliveyards that they had not planted. The Lord had chosen to be their God and had given them all these things.

Now the Lord demanded a response. The Israelites would have to decide whether they chose for the Lord and His favor or for the idols instead. "Choose this day whom you will serve," Joshua said to them in the name of the Lord. The Lord Himself was giving them this choice. "As for me and my house," said Joshua, the mediator, "we will serve the LORD." The Spirit of the Lord enabled him to speak out in this way. The Spirit of the Christ was speaking in him. This was the determining factor in Israel. Thus the Christ declared on behalf of all His people that He would serve the Lord. And we may live lives of service in His power, by faith in Him.

All the people answered: "We will serve the Lord." But did they know what they were saying? Joshua said to them: "You cannot serve the Lord, for He is a holy God. He is a jealous God and will not forgive your transgressions or your sins. The Lord wants to be everything to you. If He is not everything to you, if you do not depend wholly on Him and serve Him alone, He cannot be anything to you. Then He will consume you."

But is it really possible to serve the Lord, then? Isn't a life of service an oppressive and cramped existence? No. If we surrender entirely to Him, it's very easy. Then we live a full and rich life, for

He keeps us and guides us in all of life.

The people repeated that they wished to serve the Lord. Then Joshua said to them: "You have now heard it from one another, and you will be witnesses against each other if you abandon the Lord to place your trust in someone or something else." He also recorded in a book all that had happened at Shechem, so that it could be read to the people often. Furthermore, he set up a stone as witness to them.

At Shechem the covenant between the Lord and His people was renewed. But would Israel keep this covenant? Many Israelites did wander away from the Lord later. But there were always some who lived out of faith. This faith has been preserved through all ages. And when the Redeemer came, there were believers awaiting Him. The renewing of the covenant at Shechem helped make this possible.

To us, too, the Lord says: "Choose whom you will serve." He wants to bestow His favor upon us as well. If only we would choose for Him! If your response is that you do want to choose for Him, remember that it's possible only if you surrender completely to Him. The Lord is either everything to you or nothing. There have been many who said that they wanted to serve the Lord but later turned away from Him. They had not surrendered to Him with their whole heart.

The burial of Joshua, Eleazar, and the bones of Joseph. With that Joshua's work on earth was finished. He sent the people away from Shechem. Not long afterward he died, at the age of 110. He was buried on the land given to his family as an inheritance.

There the people stood around his grave, undoubtedly in deep mourning. What a loss they suffered in the passing of Joshua! Yet, they lived in the faith that Joshua would be resurrected one day at the appearing of the Redeemer to enjoy his inheritance forever among God's children. In that same spirit, they also buried the bones of Joseph, which they had brought with them from Egypt. Joseph himself had asked to be buried in the land that was their sacred inheritance, as a sign of the link between the people and that land.

Another important Israelite died—the high priest Eleazar, the son of Aaron, who had been Joshua's right hand, just as Aaron had been Moses' right hand. And all the elders were buried. Thus Israel's link with its land was continually being strengthened.

Has this expectation of Israel's been fulfilled? The Redeemer appeared, but the resurrection of the dead has not yet taken place. When He returns one day, all will rise from their graves. Then believers will possess the earth forever. The burial of believers is also a sign of their link with this earth. The believers will one day be glorified along with the earth.

When the Lord Jesus returns, all the expectations of believing Israelites and our expectations as well will be realized—if we have lived by faith. This the Lord Jesus Christ earned for us. He gives us our eternal inheritance among the saints. The place He now gives us on earth is also a sign and guarantee of this inheritance.

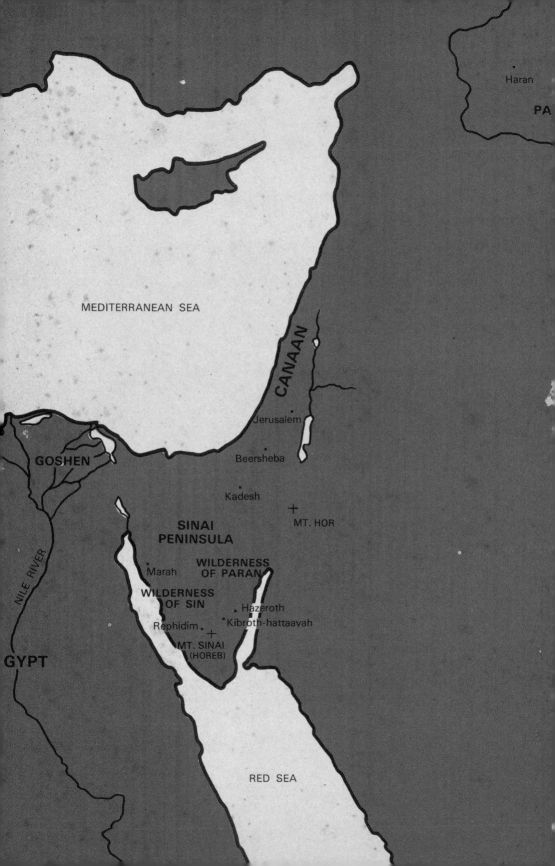

Haran

PA

MEDITERRANEAN SEA

CANAAN

Jerusalem

Beersheba

GOSHEN

Kadesh

MT. HOR

SINAI
PENINSULA

WILDERNESS
OF PARAN

Marah

WILDERNESS
OF SIN

Hazeroth

NILE RIVER

Rephidim

Kibroth-hattaavah

MT. SINAI
(HOREB)

GYPT

RED SEA